DAILY LIFE IN

EARLY MODERN JAPAN

The Greenwood Press "Daily Life Through History" Series

DAILY LIFE IN

EARLY MODERN JAPAN

LOUIS G. PEREZ

The Greenwood Press "Daily Life Through History" Series

GREENWOOD PRESS
Westport, Connecticut • London

Library of Congress Cataloging-in-Publication Data

Perez, Louis G.
    Daily life in early modern Japan / Louis G. Perez.
        p.   cm.—(The Greenwood Press "Daily life through history" series, ISSN 1080–4749)
    Includes bibliographical references and index.
    ISBN 0–313–31201–X (alk. paper)
    1. Japan—Social life and customs—1600–1868.   I. Title.   II. Series.
    DS822.2.P47   2002
    952'.025—dc21   2001023336

British Library Cataloguing in Publication Data is available.

Library of Congress Catalog Card Number: 2001023336
ISBN: 0–313–31201–X
ISSN: 1080–4749

First published in 2002

Greenwood Press, 88 Post Road West, Westport, CT 06881
An imprint of Greenwood Publishing Group, Inc.
www.greenwood.com

Printed in the United States of America

The paper used in this book complies with the
Permanent Paper Standard issued by the National
Information Standards Organization (Z39.48–1984).

10 9 8 7 6 5 4 3 2 1

Contents

Preface

All scholarship is collaborative. The written word is but a culmination of recursive thinking. It is a product of years of education, of seemingly aimless thinking, of heated arguments in stifling seminar rooms, of endless poring over cranky and fusty tomes, of shuffling through reams of dusty documents written on crumbling paper, of wastebaskets filled with crumpled false starts, of friends poring over one's drafts in search of elusive solecisms, of editors' blue penciling, of smudged galley proofs, of excretal index cards, and of silly, pretentious prefaces. No wonder that some author, perhaps Oscar Wilde (when in doubt, cite Wilde or Ambrose Bierce), said that he "loved everything about writing, except the paper work."

Many good friends helped me wrestle with this new project. A diplomatic historian by training (and of the nineteenth century to boot), the idea of examining daily life in the eighteenth century was not my own, but I have grown to love it. It has been a very pleasant task, rather like a mid-life retooling (but not a crisis!). I have read with great interest the works of the principal specialists in material culture history and often wondered what internal logic helped them to create a sense of discipline. I now know.

Emily Michie Birch, editor at Greenwood Press, approached me to see if I was interested in the project, probably as a result of a textbook I had recently published with Greenwood. I was dubious from the start, but since I had been similarly unsure when I began the textbook manuscript, I promised to consider it. I soon convinced myself that it was something worth considering. I read three examples of this series and found myself utterly fascinated.[1] Perhaps that was the trap that Ms. Birch had cunningly laid for me. Within a week I was collecting information, even before I realized that I had a new research project.

From that point I once again became the Relentless Library Fiend, devouring every seemingly interesting title that might contain any information worth noting. A number of books became models and founts of information.[2] Serendipitously, my good friend Roger Purdy of John Carroll University overheard me talking about the project and asked me to present a preliminary paper to the Midwest Japan Seminar, of which he was then chair. I prepared a small, provocative essay titled cheekily, "Kuso Happens: Nightsoil as Life in 18th Century Japan,"[3] which I presented to the shocked members of the seminar gathered at Wittenberg University, the home of another good friend, James Huffman.

As is usually the case with my teaching, I learned far more from the participants of the seminar than they could have possibly gained from me. I single out in particular Phillip Brown of Ohio State University, who gave me his copiously annotated copy of my paper, much to my benefit. He and others at the seminar raised many substantive issues and pointed out conundrums, anachronisms, and solecisms. I am indebted to all of them because that essay has become part of this book. I hasten to say, however, if they had been more diligent in discovering my errors, this would be a far better product.

A number of exceptional students in my History of Japanese Civilization course in the autumn of 1999 at Illinois State University provided bibliographic groundwork as we collectively examined "Material Culture of Japan's Eighteenth Century" that semester. Many were called, but few were chosen. The best of them were Kelly Rushing, James Pala, and Charles Ian Chun. I am indebted to them for their fine work. Ms. Rushing was further rewarded for her exemplary work by having her essay published in *Recounting the Past*, the student journal in the Department of History.

A year into the project, my long-suffering friends at Illinois State University, Roger Thomas and Jim Stanlaw read the manuscript. Roger suffered through my pompous pronouncements on topics about which he knows far more than I: poetry, the Japanese language, and music. His wife Michiko served us a magnificent meal while Roger slipped into his self-described "schoolmarm" persona, politely pointing out my errors. Roger's wife Michiko and Nobuko Adachi (both professors in their own right) also helped mark up the manuscript until it looked like it had bled to death. Jim deserves special thanks since this is the second manuscript that he has read for me. Perhaps the fact that I solemnly promised to stop foisting these manuscripts upon him for as long as I am in my current position as an administrator was sufficient incentive for him to render that service the second time.

I wish to thank Kenji Miki, Director of the Asia Library at the University of Michigan who spent an afternoon (and bought me lunch!) poring through the library's extensive collection of ukiyo-e. He generously arranged for publication rights to several prints and sent his folks in the photo duplication office off to do the voodoo that they do so well. I owe Roy Hanashiro of the University of Michigan-Flint (and another Midwest Japan Seminar stalwart) a debt of gratitude for bringing me to Ann Arbor (another lunch!) and introducing me to Kenji-sensei.

The collective efforts of Bernd Jesse, Assistant Curator, Mary Ruth Albert, Asian Art Technician, and Nicole G. Finzer, Photo Rights Assistant, all at the Art Institute of Chicago, are appreciated. They helped arrange for me to use three ukiyo-e as illustrations. I also wish to acknowledge the generosity of the Currency Museum at the Bank of Japan in Tokyo for allowing me to use their electronic copy of the "Appearance of Paper Money."[4] Finally, I acknowledge the budding artistic talents of several students who suffered through my East Asian Civilization course (4,000 years in three weeks! A dynasty a day!) in the summer of 2000. Their line drawings are individually credited in the captions of the relevant illustrations. That, and the paltry points of extra credit, are the only rewards they will receive for their work.

My wife Karla deserves much gratitude for all the hours of companionship and household chores that she has had pilfered away by five book manuscripts and a score of articles. She is long-suffering and deserves much more than a mere dedication of a book. Nevertheless, I dedicate this one solely to her. My son Mark has been deprived of countless hours of Web surfing and Tomb Raider because his old man was constantly hogging the computer. Perhaps one day he will thank me for it.

The two best secretaries at Illinois State University, Cherie Valentine and Sharon Foiles, have once again facilitated the printing (and reprinting) of the manuscript. Emily Birch, series editor at Greenwood Press, deserves thanks for her initial offer and for her continued patience. Of course the production team (especially Leanne Small, who authorized the reimbursement check for the illustrations, copy editor Barbara Goodhouse, and Rebecca Ardwin, who served as production editor at Greenwood) merit praise for their fine work. I am tempted to blame the lot of them for any mistakes that have slipped through, but alas, any errors are solely my responsibility.

A brief note about Japanese words and names as they appear here: Macrons are short horizontal lines over some vowels (chiefly "o" and "u") and indicate that the vowel is to be "doubled," that is, to be pronounced twice. Proper nouns that should contain macroned vowels but have appeared without them in common English-language publication (Kyōtō, sumō, and Tōkyō, for instance) are written here without macrons. Japanese surnames appear first, except in bibliographic citations. For instance, Chie Nakane will appear as Nakane, Chie in references to her many publications.

NOTES

1. Robert Garland, *Daily Life of the Ancient Greeks* (Westport, CT: Greenwood Press, 1998); Karen Rhea Nemet-Nejat, *Daily Life in Ancient Mesopotamia* (Westport, CT: Greenwood Press, 1998); and David Carrasco (with Scott Sessions), *Daily Life of the Aztecs: People of the Sun and Earth* (Westport, CT: Greenwood Press, 1998).

2. Engelbert Kaempfer, *The History of Japan: Together with a Description of the Kingdom of Siam*, 3 vols., trans. J. G. Scheuchzer (Glasgow: James McLehose and Sons, 1906). The reports of Carl Peter Thunberg are published, along with those of other travelers, in Richard Hildreth, *Japan: As It Was and Is* (Wilmington, DE: Scholarly Resources, 1973); Basil Hall Chamberlain, *Japanese Things* (Rutland, VT: Tuttle, 1971; the first edition was *Things Japanese*, London: Kumpf, 1890), Michael Cooper, ed., *They Came to Japan: An Anthology of European Reports on Japan, 1543–1640* (Berkeley: University of California Press, 1965).

3. Kuso is the most common epithet used in Japan for excrement.

4. http://www.imes.boj.or.jp/cm/english_htmls/history_09.htm.

Introduction: Japan in the Eighteenth Century

This study has two primary purposes. The first is to examine the neglected "everyday Japan" of its common people. The idea is to capture a flavor of "nonelite" people and attempt to recapture what the ordinary life of everyday Japanese was like. In so doing, I wish to examine what the common people did in their normal lives. What were their lives like? How did they live? What did they eat? What tools did they use? What was "normal" and "natural" for them? We have a better (though still imperfect) idea of what the social, political, and economic elite did in their lives through governmental documents and through their diaries and letters. The lower classes, as defined by the Neo-Confucian ethos employed by the government, constituted perhaps 95 percent of the population, yet we know very little of the lives of peasants, artisans, and petty merchants except what the elites tell us about them. The primary goal here, then, is to give voice to the common man and woman in eighteenth-century Japan.

My second goal is to capture Japan in its most natural and normal state—that is to say, to study Japan before it became "modern," or, more properly, "Western." The question of when Japan became a distinct and unique society has long been debated. Many have argued that Japan absorbed a Chinese cultural paradigm in the sixth century and then spent the next millennium adapting it to its own reality. Then, in the mid-nineteenth century, Japan sloughed off that Chinese influence, as if it were merely an outer garment, to be replaced by a new Western paradigm. When, then, was Japan most "Japanese"? Perhaps before the Chinese cultural package arrived in the sixth century (though some would argue that Japan was under the cultural influence of its neighbor Korea before that). But one would struggle to describe that period since it was fundamentally preliterate. Archeological evidence, oral traditional histories, and a very limited artisanal and artistic body of documentation are, even in the aggregate, insufficient to recreate any sense of everyday life. I believe that the best way to see Japan at the height of its uniqueness is to examine the eighteenth century.

By 1700 the Tokugawa regime called *bakufu* (literally "tent government") had been in power for nearly a century and had nearly another century and a half left to reign over Japan. So the "middle years" of the late feudal era correspond almost exactly to the eighteenth century. The Tokugawa had been at pains to create a new Japanese social and political framework in the first decades of the seventeenth century. By 1700, the system was an orthodoxy. Over a half-century had passed since Westerners had rambled around the country nearly untrammeled. Western Christians had been banished from Japan and their religious philosophy had been nearly completely extirpated (though not forgotten). The country had been almost totally isolated from the rest of the world since 1640. Only a few tightly regulated Chinese, Korean, and Dutch merchants were allowed to come to Japan, and Japanese had been forbidden to travel abroad.

By the end of the century, Japan was beset by a new round of foreign encroachment. By turns, Russia, Great Britain, and the United States assailed Japanese shores. Arguably, Japan had to adjust to this new economic imperialism by becoming more "modern" (at least technologically) in order to avoid the fate of Asian neighbors like India and China. By the middle of the nineteenth century Japan had begun to employ Western ideas in science and technology, and by the end of the century it was as Western as any Asian nation ever would be. One can argue, then, that the eighteenth century was probably the most consciously Japanese period in the country's history.

The so-called *baku-han* (combination of bakufu and *han* or domain governments) governmental system had been established in 1603 when Tokugawa Ieyasu had accepted the title of *Seii-tai-shōgun* ("Barbarian-Subduing Generalissimo") as military deputy of the emperor. The system had its origins in the last decade of Toyotomi Hideyoshi's rule when he had gathered around him his liege warlords (*daimyō*). He had tried to reestablish the idea of centralized bureaucratic rule after more than a century of almost constant civil warfare. The premise of this idea was to "centralize" feudalism—seemingly a contradiction in terms. Each daimyo was required by Hideyoshi, and later by Ieyasu, to swear loyalty to the emperor's military deputy, but was allowed to maintain almost complete regional autonomy of his own han domain.

By 1700 the country had experienced nearly 500 years of feudal rule by warlords, and therefore the idea that the emperor reigned, but did not rule, was natural and normal. The Neo-Confucian ideology of the twelfth-century Chinese philosopher Chu Hsi had been adapted to Japan's social and political ethos by Hideyoshi and perfected by his successor, Ieyasu. The basic premise was that human society reflected the natural cosmic laws and that people were separated into four social classes according to hereditary occupations. By 1700, the *samurai,* or warriors, had become civil bureaucrats and administrators. They had laid down the engines of war and taken up the tools of the educated literati. They therefore remained at the top of the social scale by virtue of their administrative contributions to society. Before 1550 or so, the samurai had been part farmer, part warrior. Now they were urban administrators.

The farmers ranked next because they contributed food, the staff of life. They lived in small peasant villages close to their ancestral farms. By 1700 they had been left to their own devices and administration. Samurai and their merchant agents still collected taxes in the countryside, but by and large the peasants took care of their own lives. Beneath them were the craftspeople who produced utilitarian items for all of society. Some of these artisans had been farmers a century before, but now they had inherited the artisan skills of their ancestors and did no farming. Most in fact were now city folk who produced their crafts to be sold elsewhere by other people. The final stratum was that of the merchants, who were considered to be a parasitic class that served society only by moving goods from place of production to areas of consumption. A century before they had been largely itinerant movers of goods; now most were sedentary city folk. Far beneath these four classes were people considered to be nonessential (often called *hinin* or "nonhuman")—beggars, thieves, musicians, actors, prostitutes, and, surprisingly, priests and other religious persons.

Yet, as far as the daimyō and their samurai were concerned, the lower classes existed only in the abstract, in much the same manner that present-day politicians think of the masses. The people in eighteenth-century Japan were nameless, faceless, and unfamiliar to the samurai. A century before, many of the samurai were part of the people. They arose from their ranks, fought with and against them, shared their food and their lives. But now the samurai lived in castle towns and in large commercial and administrative urban centers, while the people slogged through their anonymous lives out in the periphery. Nearly 90 percent of the population lived in the rural countryside and therefore rarely if ever encountered the samurai who wrote the histories and literature of the period. Another 5 percent of the people lived cheek-by-jowl with the samurai, and yet the latter scarcely deigned to acknowledge their existence. The *chōnin*, or city folk, merely served the samurai as merchants, artisans, servants, and purveyors of every sort.

It is not surprising, then, that we know very little about the everyday lives of the people. We know only what the literate guardians of politics and morality have chosen to tell us about them. If we wish to know them and give voice and agency to their history, we must employ unusual and novel forms of documentation.

We here attempt to gain access to their lives through other avenues of investigation. We can find out something about the people through their folktales, theater, songs, and popular and commercial art (of which Japan has one of the earliest and most extensively developed systems in the world). We must search through didactic and religious stories, agricultural manuals, temple and village registers (which include records of birth, death, marriage, adoption, and divorce), tax records, lawsuits, petitions, and land deeds. Recently, archeologists have expanded their studies from the distant to the more recent past. They have given us much information on the material culture of the eighteenth century that we can add to this eclectic melange of documentary evidence.

If the picture presented here is a messy and imprecise one, it is because their lives were similarly so. It is one composed from obstructed glimpses and snatches of overheard conversations, from incomplete and smudged copybooks, from discarded and broken tools and utensils.

Obviously, because the vast majority of Japanese common people were illiterate in the eighteenth century, they did not leave written records to tell us what their lives were really like. Without their letters, diaries, petitions, or journals, we must extrapolate from the written word of their social, economic, and political "betters" tell us about the commoners. We may also glean information from the remnants of the commoner material culture. It is the sad truth that the millions of people who lived and died before us will remain mute if we don't find some way to find out what their lives were really like. It is sobering to think that the bowls and cups that they ate and drank from, the candlesticks that gave dim light to their gloaming, the crude boxes that held their meager material possessions, and the crudely-fashioned tools and implements must give voice to these otherwise forgotten people.

Unfortunately, some critics of material culture historians have suggested that we have somehow become inured to the pain and suffering of medieval Japanese. To me, the idea that we feel less empathy and outrage at oppression when we discover that the extent of misery was a little less than previously imagined is ludicrous. Is a famine less devastating if we discover that a thousand people rather than ten thousand people died? Is an 1,800-calorie-per-day diet that much less wasting and debilitating to one's health than, say, a 1,600 calorie one? Just how many angels must dance on the head of a pin?

Is our image of the extent of human brutality and depravation materially or significantly changed to discover that the peasants occasionally ate their fill or occasionally drank enough sake to become inebriated? Does it somehow lessen our outrage to find that some peasants killed their infants in hopes of a better economic life rather than because of the grinding poverty imposed upon them by a rapaciously oppressive government? Does the fact that some urban women wielded considerable power over their families than we previously imagined ameliorate the misogyny of the society as a whole? Is our historical image of the era endangered by any of this? Obviously, I do not think so.

Many scholars have made tremendous strides in recapturing the past of ordinary Japanese people, including Susan Hanley, Anne Walthall, Anne Jannatta, Thomas C. Smith, and others who have studied the feudal period, as well as Basil Hall Chamberlain, Lafcadio Hearn, George Sansom, Mikiso Hane, Kozo Yamamura, Robert Smith, Michael Lewis, Gary Leupp, and many others who have examined the more recent past. I will steal shamelessly from them all, but in a righteous cause: to recover the everyday life of eighteenth-century Japan.

Chronology

1724	Playwright Chikamatsu Monzaemon dies
1732	Famine
1736–41	Gembun Era (Nengō System)
1741–44	Kampo Era (Nengō System)
1744–48	Enkyo Era (Nengō System)
1745	Ninth Shōgun, Ieshige
1748–51	Kan'en Era (Nengō System)
1751–64	Horeki Era (Nengō System)
1758	Aoki Konyo publishes first Dutch-Japanese dictionary
1760	Tenth Shōgun, Ieharu
1764–72	Meiwa Era (Nengō System)
1769	Nativist scholar Kamo Mabuchi dies
1772–81	An'ei Era (Nengō System)
1781–89	Tenmei Era (Nengō System)
1783–86	Tenmei famine, series of peasant uprisings (ikki)
1786	Eleventh Shōgun, Ienari; famines and epidemics continue
1787	New economic reforms (Kansei)
1789–1801	Kansei Era (Nengō System)
1793	Russians visit Hokkaidō
1793	American ship *Eliza* calls at Nagasaki; allowed to trade
1798	Motoori Norinaga completes commentary on *Kojiki*

I

Early History

Using archeological evidence, it is apparent that the many islands of Japan have supported life for perhaps three millennia or more. Scholars suggest that the archipelago's first distinct culture was that of the Jōmon people, who probably came from northeast Asia via Korea.[1] These people lived in nomadic hunting and gathering groups concentrated in the valleys along Japan's eastern shoreline. Their Neolithic culture was perhaps not very different from the cultures of Pacific Oceanic, littoral Southeast Asia, or the Maritimes of northeast Asia from whence the Jōmon people came. They are named after a distinct decoration on their pottery made by pressing ropes into the still-wet clay. They shared the Japanese islands with another culturally distinct people. The Ainu, who are more similar culturally to the peoples of southern Siberia, were (and continue to be) linguistically and culturally distinct from the Japanese.

The Jōmon practiced an animistic religion and probably lived in small tribal groups in round dugout enclosures. They were omnivorous and used few sophisticated tools of any kind. Yet they managed to feed themselves amply if the shell mounds around their habitations are any indication. They lived rather peacefully along the riverbanks and seashore, but also ventured into the nearby hills in search of nuts, berries, roots, and slower animals. Recent evidence suggests that they practiced a rudimentary form of agriculture.

About three centuries before the Common Era, the Jōmon technological and social paradigm was gradually superseded by that of a new people, called Yayoi by archeologists. Evidence suggests that the Yayoi

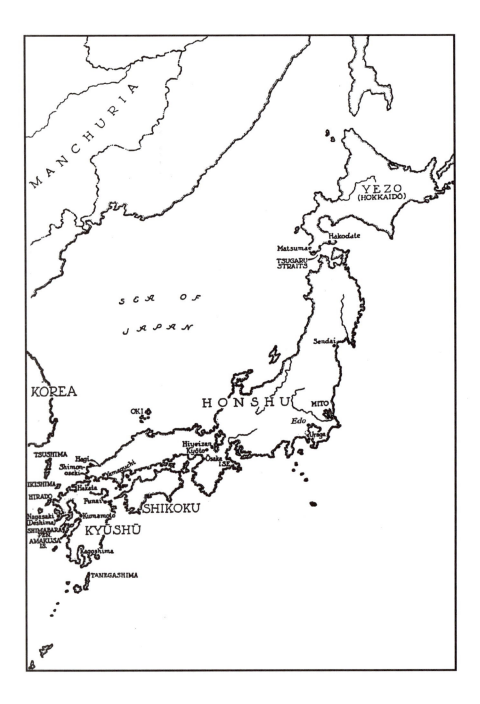

were probably ousted from their Asian homelands in Korea and northeast Asia, settling in what is now known as the Kinai in Japan, namely the area along the Inland Sea. This society brought, among other innovations, metal tools, wheel-thrown fired pottery, and wet-rice cultivation to the archipelago. Their religious system resembled the animistic beliefs that still exist in southern Siberia and along the Maritimes. Genetically, they seemed to be distantly related to the Jomon people already in Japan, so we may say that the Yayoi were merely another immigrant wave that overlay previous settlements.

Archeological excavations suggest that the Yayoi were in turn superseded by a new wave of immigration five centuries later. This new group, called Kofun, or Tomb people, after the distinctive keyhole-shaped tombs they employed, are probably the immediate ancestors of the Japanese people. Whether this new wave of immigrants was really a conquering "horse-rider" invasion is open to debate,[2] but by the time that Japan appears in the first Chinese dynastic histories, we have evidence of a new society, clearly distinct from that of the Yayoi peoples. They apparently came with horses and other accoutrements of continental warfare. The distinctive clay figurines (*haniwa*) that were ensconced around the tombs tell us much about the technology and lifestyle of the Kofun people. They show sophisticated freestanding pottery kilns, elaborate armor for the warriors as well as for their horses, and colorful religious rituals.

Whether they conquered the Yayoi or merely predominated by virtue of their superior technology, a half-century later the Kofun had established a very different form of government. In fact, the Chinese histories suggest that Japan might have been a matriarchal admixture of shamanic and warrior systems of government at this time.

Stories of a Japanese embassy sent by a Queen Himiko provide ample evidence that families lived in matrilocal (uxorial) unions, where inheritance descended through the maternal line. Female religious fetishes as well as Japan's chief deity, the Sun Goddess, suggest a shamanic system where females predominated in religion, and perhaps in government as well. Himiko was said to have pacified the country after extensive warfare; when she died a man tried to succeed her through force. The tribal leaders apparently preferred another female shamanic leader to rule in peace, so he was replaced by a thirteen-year-old queen called Iyo.

By the late fifth century c.e. the society predominant in Japan had evolved into a confederation of fictive kin- **Imperial Japan** ship units (*uji*), each with its own tutelary (often ancient ancestor) spirit-gods (*kami*). There is ample evidence that there had been a long period when the uji had struggled to gain dominance over each other. By the fifth century, they had formed a peaceful confederation dominated by the imperial house called Yamato, which ruled as the first among equals. The apparently loose confederation of semi-autonomous regional states coagulated into something like a centralized bureaucratic state, borrowing a Confucian statecraft and a Buddhist religious paradigm from Tang China in the late seventh and early eighth centuries. Japanese religious and political leaders self-consciously emulated and adapted this Chinese cultural worldview into their own reality. The new Japanese religious and political systems became an amalgam of Chinese models and Japanese pragmatic adaptation, chiefly interpreted by emigrant Korean intellectuals who intermingled with the Japanese elite.

By the time that Japanese began to write their own histories (the *Kojiki* [Record of Ancient Matters] and *Nihon Shoki* [Chronicles of Japan]), using the Chinese orthography (see Chapter 5) in the eighth century, the leadership of the country had codified their own domestic historical and religious orthodoxies. The Japanese emperors, it would seem, were direct descendents of the divine creators as well as of the chief deity, Amaterasu-omi-kami, the Sun Goddess. They derived their imperial charisma and legitimacy from her and from their shamanic and priestly functions. That is to say, Yamato emperors were simultaneously semidivine secular leaders and chief priests in the religious cult later known as Shintō ("The Way of the Gods"). The uji tribal leaders acknowledged the religious and political sovereignty of the emperor and were in turn invested with some of the imperial charisma by virtue of being appointed imperial governors over their own regional areas. Each area worshipped its own tutelary spirits (kami), who were often deified ancestors, but who were just as commonly thought to be the animist forces in nature.

The new official Confucian and Buddhist imperial system was incorporated by Japan's first Buddhist "saint" (*boddhisatva*), Imperial Prince and Regent Shotoku Taishi, who drew up the celebrated new Seventeen Article Constitution. This document was more exhortatory and instructional than it was political, let alone juridical. It encouraged the people to be respectful and honorable and to behave in a filial manner to the emperor, their symbolic "father." The imperial family officially adopted Buddhism as the state religion, building sumptuous temples throughout the land in order to establish its legitimacy among the people. It sought to incorporate the Confucian social philosophy of benevolent and moral rule into its governance. Over the centuries the imperial state fused these borrowed social and religious ideas together with native folk and Shinto beliefs, creating a distinctively Japanese amalgam.

This central bureaucratic state built around itself an impressive capital situated first in Nara, then Nagaoka, and eventually in Kyoto in the late eighth century. Soaring pagodas and gorgeous Chinese-style temple complexes surrounded the imperial palace compound. The ornate and majestic Buddhist architecture reinforced the legitimacy of the imperial house and gave focus to the entire society. The uji chieftains-cum-imperial governors abandoned their rustic capitals in favor of the new capital, becoming its new nobility. Their native uji were required to send portions of the agricultural produce to the capital to maintain the new governors. This agricultural subsidy became, in effect, a kind of institutionalized national tax. For at least four centuries the imperial house administered the land through its governors and military deputies.

In theory, the emperor owned all land. A periodic census helped to distribute the land to local farmers, who paid a portion of their harvest as symbolic as well as real tribute for the emperor's magnanimity. The emperor appointed moral and benevolent ministers to govern the people. For a time a corvée system was employed as a means of taxation. The common people were required to supply free labor for public works projects as well as to staff a national army. Priests served society as well as the imperial house by ministering to the religious and psychological needs of all. They also kept the kami and Buddhas happy and content through various propitiatory ceremonies. The system seemed to meet all social needs and cover all cosmic bets.

By the late twelfth century, however, the imperial house's magnanimity proved to be its undoing. Over the years the government had encouraged wealthy magnates to undertake expensive public works and social programs in return for tax shelters. Imperial and other powerful regional lords mounted and maintained militias in defense of the national periphery. Their chief adversaries were still the Ainu who preyed on Japanese villages in the northern portion of the island of Honshu. Imperial military leaders were allowed to keep tax-free estates (*shoen*) in order to support these militias. Similarly, wealthy families were allowed to develop shoen from land reclaimed from forest, swamp, and tidal basins. Buddhist temples were given shoen to subsidize their charitable and religious works. Before long, however, the tax-free land outstripped the imperial revenue land, and the government began to delegate more and more authority to shoen managers.

In the middle of the twelfth century two shoen houses, the Taira and the Minamoto, both related to the imperial house itself, began to confederate smaller landholders into larger, more powerful military factions. Eventually the Taira defeated the Minamoto in a gigantic struggle of alliances. But because the Taira had spared the young sons of the defeated Minamoto chieftain, the Minamoto eventually triumphed in the 1180s. The charismatic victor, Minamoto Yoritomo, established a military bastion in Kamakura, the homeland of his former captor, now his father-in-law. Yoritomo accepted the title of *Seii-tai-shōgun* ("Barbarian-Subduing Generalissimo"), once reserved for the leader of imperial forces against the Ainu. Shōgun Yoritomo created a crude but effective

Early Feudalism

military bureaucracy, which he called *bakufu* (literally, "tent govern-ment"), where he governed his vassals. This field headquarters admin-istered rough martial law over most of the land through his chief vassals (*gokenin*) and through an administrative liaison with former imperial governors. Within a decade the shogunal authorities controlled most of the country, creating an amalgam of civil and military administration while maintaining the fiction that the imperial house in Kyoto continued to rule through its military deputy in Kamakura 300 miles to the east.

The Minamoto house died out, but the bakufu was perpetuated through the efforts of Yoritomo's strong-willed and efficient widow, Hōjō Masako. The bakufu continued to rule well into the fourteenth cen-tury despite a number of destabilizing economic, social, and political elements. As the bakufu slid into corruption and inefficiency at the end of the thirteenth century, the successors to Yoritomo's gokenin vassals vied with each other for larger shares of the Kamakura patrimony. This domestic unrest was exacerbated by two unsuccessful invasion attempts by Kublai Khan's Mongols.

These Mongols, having swept throughout most of Asia and even into eastern Europe, tried to extend their ruthless administration into Japan in 1274. The invasion came south through Korea and landed in northeast Kyushu, where it was met with fierce and stubborn resistance by the local warlords (*daimyō*) at the head of mounted warriors (*samurai*). The amphibious Mongol assault was stymied for several weeks while the bakufu marshaled the eastern daimyō, and Japanese Buddhist and Shintō religious leaders prayed ceaselessly for divine deliverance. The religious incantations seemed to be more effective, because a typhoon foundered the Mongol ships and forced the invaders back to Korea. Parenthetically, this typhoon, called "divine winds" (*kamikaze*), seemed to reinforce the idea that Japan was the "Land of the Gods."

Kublai was not so easily deterred, and seven years later another, even larger invasion force assaulted the Kyushu coast. Once again the Japa-nese put up a doggedly efficient defense behind a long seawall built during the interim. The battle raged until yet another kamikaze typhoon drove the Mongols into the sea. Because the bakufu did not collect taxes from the individual daimyō, it had nothing with which to reward the valorous Kyushu defenders, let alone anything with which to pay the eastern and northern daimyō who had led their forces across Honshu to Kyushu. There being little in way of spoils of war, the daimyō vassals of the bakufu were understandably frustrated. In their minds, the bakufu had broken the feudal contract between lord and vassal: they had pro-vided service, but he had not duly rewarded them.

Coupled with the already high state of dissatisfaction with the bakufu, various powerful daimyō continued to search for an alternative confed-eration to better suit their individual needs. The imperial house sensed this discontent and attempted to fish in troubled waters by mounting a campaign to restore power to the Emperor Go-Daigo in the early part of the fourteenth century. The bakufu managed to suppress this uprising for a time, but many of the disgruntled daimyo saw an opportunity for change.

Eventually Ashikaga Takauji, a relative of the Hōjō bakufu regents, sent to suppress a new outbreak of rebellion, broke ranks with his allies and joined the "loyalist" forces. Ashikaga briefly allowed the imperial restoration but soon grew tired of Go-Daigo's studied nepotism and apparent incompetence. He cobbled together a new military coalition, placed Go-Daigo under house arrest, and "accepted" the title of shōgun from his powerless captive. He seized lands previously controlled by the bakufu and the allies of the emperor, which he parceled out to his own confederates. He established a bakufu of his own in the Muromachi ward of Kyoto.

The new bakufu was subtly different from the previous Kamakura bakufu in terms of organizational and administrative structure, but basically also operated on the basis of feudal contractual obligations between the shōgun and his vassal daimyō. The latter continued to administer their own semi-autonomous lands but came to the aid of the bakufu when called upon. In return, the bakufu served as a kind of a national arbiter between these powerful military men, administering what passed for social justice during the era. Despite the fact that Go-Daigo escaped his captors and established a competing imperial government in Yoshino to the south,[3] the Ashikaga shoguns kept the imperial institution under tight rein, and continued to derive their civil legitimacy from the imperial charisma.

This authority sufficed to run the country for over a century, but the shōgunal government itself soon lost all but **Civil War** titular power to its vassals. By the late fourteenth century the daimyō had begun to build castles to defend their own lands. Samurai, who had previously functioned as a rural elite, living in manor-like enclaves within their feudal patrimonies, were now increasingly required to live within the new castles. Castle towns (*jokamachi*) sprang up to service the samurai, and before long these jokamachi became almost autonomous economic and political units. Many of the daimyō now began to prey upon weaker lords, and before long the bakufu was shown to be too weak to serve as a central political deterrent to out-and-out civil war.

In the mid-fifteenth century a series of regional squabbles decimated the capital itself, and the country descended into a period of civil war (*Sengoku*). This century of almost constant warfare drained the society of much of its social energy, as competing daimyō fought each other in hopes of creating their own hegemony. Estimates vary, but demographers tell us that perhaps one-tenth of the male population was constantly involved in warfare, with the attendant destruction of life and property. It was not until a series of three almost larger-than-life military leaders reconsolidated the country in the late sixteenth century that peaceful civil government reigned once again in Japan.

The first of these overlords was Oda Nobunaga, who rose rapidly to power due to his use of strategic terror, administrative acumen, and a new military technology, the gun. Portuguese adventurers brought the gun to Japan. Although the arquebus was clumsy, expensive, and wildly inaccurate, it had devastating killing power. It was available to most daimyō who could afford it, but most found it inferior to the traditional Japanese weapons of sword, spear, and arrow when wielded by the ferocious samurai. Nobunaga, however, solved the problems of its use by employing ingenious Japanese metal artisans to replicate and even improve the gun. Since it was now domestically produced, it was cheaper and therefore more plentiful. Nobunaga solved the inaccuracy problem by employing phalanxes of gunmen in murderous efficiency.

He brutally forced his enemies to accept his suzerainty. By the early 1580s he had defeated most of his rivals, including the Buddhist temple complexes, which maintained huge armies themselves. Perhaps two-thirds of the country was under his bloody thumb before he was forced to commit suicide by a disgruntled vassal general. Nobunaga's chief vassals fought briefly for control, which ended in a compromise whereby one, Tokugawa Ieyasu, accepted the overlordship of another, Toyotomi Hideyoshi. Hideyoshi rewarded Ieyasu for his perspicacity (discretion being the better part of valor) with the grant of the enormous Kanto Plain in the east. Ieyasu had to defeat Hideyoshi's enemies there, but once he did, he actually directly controlled more land than did Hideyoshi.

Nevertheless, Hideyoshi managed to wield tremendous power throughout the country. He used that power to slowly consolidate authority and control over most of the country. In a series of brilliant tactical moves he began to isolate and control the various economic and political forces that had kept the country divided for over a century. He subdued his rivals into vassalage, forcing them to yield to his almost complete civil and military authority. He disarmed the inessential foot soldier–arquebusers (*ashigaru*), forcing many into "super-peasantry" positions as hereditary rural administrators (*gono*). Other samurai he spurred into a costly invasion of Korea, which kept them away and occupied for nearly a decade. Intricate systems of economic and social controls were imposed on the leaders of the country, and he created ingenious and elaborate methods to keep others in check.

Concomitantly, he imported a sociopolitical philosophical system known as Neo-Confucianism in order to control society. Explained elsewhere (see Chapter 4), the system seemed almost tailor-made for sixteenth-century Japan. With a little adaptation, it served Hideyoshi and his Tokugawa political successors very well.

By the time Hideyoshi died in 1598 he had established the framework of a social, economic, and political system that predominated in Japan for nearly three centuries.[4] Tokugawa Ieyasu, who succeeded Hideyoshi, inherited the system. Ieyasu saw the benefits of the philosophy and therefore adapted it in order to perpetuate his familial control over the archipelago.

Because his adolescent son Hideyori succeeded Hideyoshi, the country soon once again fell into warfare. Ieyasu gathered many of the eastern daimyō and won a decisive battle against the western coalition in 1600 at the battle of Sekigahara, mostly through subterfuge and bribery. Ieyasu accepted the title of shōgun in 1603 but quickly passed it on to his son in order to legitimize the familial succession. This new bakufu was established in the jokamachi Edo (which would eventually become Tokyo).

Ieyasu and his two successors cobbled together an ingenious and complex checks-and-balances system (see Chapter 3) to rein in the economic, social, and political powers within the country. This system was called *baku-han* because it combined two interrelated government boards, one to manage the bakufu, another to administer the 270 semi-autonomous feudal domains (*han*).

Being technically in control of the entire country, the bakufu spent the first two decades actually managing the fractious daimyō, who chafed under Tokugawa control. In 1614 many of the disgruntled daimyō flocked to the standard of Hideyoshi's son, Hideyori, now an adult. Ieyasu came out of "retirement" to personally lead the bakufu coalition. Through guile and subterfuge Ieyasu first lured the "rebels" into Ōsaka castle and then destroyed them there.

The only (though perhaps largely imaginary) independent political force left was the Christians in the country. Brought to Japan by European Jesuits in the sixteenth century, Christianity had flourished in the southwest island of Kyushu around the Christian-administered port city of Nagasaki. Estimates of the number of converts run as high as 300,000, which might have been as high as 4 percent of the population of the country. Many samurai and not a few daimyō had converted, which worried the aging Ieyasu. Hideyoshi had passed anti-Christian edicts in 1587 and 1597, but had never rigorously enforced them. Part of the problem was that Nobunaga, then Hideyoshi, and finally Ieyasu had all benefited from the burgeoning trade dominated by the Portuguese. In addition to the arquebus, the traders had brought Chinese products, primarily silk, purchased at their continental entrepot, Macao.

Just when Ieyasu was dealing with the rebellion at Ōsaka castle, he decided that Japan could do without the latent domestic power of the

Portuguese and their European Roman Catholic brethren, the Spanish. He banished foreign priests and began the long, inexorable persecution of native Christians. Two decades after Ieyasu's death, a tax rebellion broke out in Shimabara, close by Nagasaki in Kyushu. The uprising was led in part by some dispossessed samurai who employed Christian battle flags and shouted out Christian slogans as battle cries. The bakufu imagined that Japanese converts were about to try to Christianize the country by force in concert with their European brethren. The fact that this very thing had been done in the Philippines by Spaniards in 1598 made the Tokugawa justifiably paranoid.

The Shimabara Rebellion was extinguished quite easily, and with the help of Protestant Dutch ships, which bombarded Shimabara castle from the sea. In very quick order the bakufu set up a draconian eradication campaign to rid the country of all Christians, foreign and domestic. In 1640 the country was closed (*sakoku*) to all foreigners except a few Chinese and Korean ships and even fewer Dutch ships, which were allowed to ply their trade at Nagasaki. Foreign priests were ferreted out and tortured to death, and native Christians were persecuted until they renounced their faith. Those that would not were tortured and executed. Except for a few hundred "hidden Christians" (*kakure kurishitan*) who remained faithful on the southern islands off Kyushu, the country was bereft of Christians for the next two centuries.

For the next two centuries Japan would be relatively isolated from the rest of the world. Few foreigners came to Japan, and even fewer Japanese left. This put an end to the period when Japan was nearly the center of world trade in Asia. Thousands of Europeans had come to Japan, some of whom had stayed for decades. Tens and perhaps hundreds of thousands of Japanese had sailed all around Asia, trading with China, Korea, and much of coastal Southeast Asia. Now, except for perhaps a hundred Dutchmen annually, for no European women were allowed, no Europeans came and went.

The Tokugawa regime refined its other social, economic, and political methods of control. An indication of how successful this governance system really was is the fact that, except for a few sporadic peasant uprisings, the country was free of warfare for two centuries, which is why this period has been called the Pax Tokugawa.

The eighteenth century was almost exactly in the very middle of this period. By 1700 the Tokugawa bakufu had controlled the closed country for sixty years. In 1800 it still had some six decades left before it was replaced by an imperial restoration.

A Brief Social Commentary   Chinese social and religious antecedents had overwhelmingly influenced the millennium preceding the eighteenth century. When Japan had begun to import the social and political Confucian ideology in the seventh and eighth centuries, it had done so in search of a more sophisticated and more rational system by which to rule the country. The Chinese model certainly served those purposes and goals. But because the Japanese did not fully understand that Confucianism and Buddhism were separate philosophies within the Chinese body politic, they had some initial difficulties in adapting Buddhism to Japanese folk beliefs. Yet Buddhism would permeate the Japanese paradigm to such an extent that after a couple of centuries the Japanese themselves had great difficulty (should they have wanted to) in separating what was Buddhism from what was native Shintō.

Many religious historians in fact argue that Shintōism probably did not exist in the essentialist form prior to the late Tokugawa period. As such, Shintō was more properly a formalist conglomeration of numerous local indigenous religious cults. Each region worshiped its own local kami and probably very rarely even thought of its belief system as part of a larger religion. Without an elaborate ethical or even religious philosophical system, Shintō could not hope to directly compete with Buddhism. In addition, Buddhism had acquired an elaborate priestly tradition in China as well as a sumptuous aesthetic iconography, and a technologically superior architectural expression of spirituality and community.

When Buddhism was inculcated into Japanese culture, mostly through the efforts of charismatic shamanic Buddhist missionaries (*ubasoku*) from Korea, it became intricately intertwined with local Shintōist beliefs. Since Buddhism had an elaborate cosmic rationale, Shintō was grafted into it at the peripheries. Kami were judged to be local manifestations of Buddhas; Shintō superstitious and purification rituals were subsumed into Buddhist religious practices; even the religious architecture was conflated.

Because much of the Chinese written literature was similarly an amalgamation of Confucian and Buddhist philosophies, it was not surprising that all of these philosophies became symbiotically intermingled in Japan. Japanese literature, which developed first as a self-conscious mimicry of the Tang Chinese style, evinced all of those intellectual influences. The first histories conflated the religious myths of the native animism with the verities of Confucian social morality. The poetry and prose writing similarly influenced the conventions of both societies. Art was similarly influenced, as was architecture. In all cases, however, the Chinese influences predominated, if for no other reason than because the Chinese technologies and cosmologies were far superior to those of the Japanese.

It was not until the latter part of the tenth century that Japanese aesthetic sensibilities began to predominate. In literature this was accomplished primarily by court women who refined the Japanese aesthetic to high culture. The beauty of such classics as *The Tale of Genji* and *The*

Pillow Book by two court ladies (Murasaki Shikibu and Sei Shonagon, respectively) became a model for romantic literature for the next millennium. A profusion of poets, artists, calligraphers, and artisans refined and distilled a distinctively Japanese aesthetic taste at the same time. Most of the art was produced and appreciated primarily by the social, economic, and political elite of the country, but it was later emulated and appreciated by the more plebeian folk.

In terms of religion, various Chinese schools of Buddhist interpretation spread to Japan, each seemingly to fill particular religious and social needs. Pureland sects flourished during Japan's descent into feudal warfare, as did Zen; both had briefly flourished in China during similar bouts of civil war. Japanese priests seemed to be continually on pilgrimages to China and even India in search of truth. When they returned to Japan they brought back with them a host of religious ideas as well as many and sundry technological innovations. Koreans also wafted into Japan in flight from political or religious persecution, and they too became purveyors of new ideas and products. For their part, Japanese priests, artists, and artisans creatively adapted these new imports and, over a generation or two, created their own expressions of art, craft, or religion.

Lest one think that the Japanese were imitators and adapters only, we should hasten to say that native Japanese products had their own innovators and inventors. The primary examples are in military and artisanal technologies. The Japanese sword was without doubt the most technologically sophisticated steel weapon in the world at the time, and Japanese armor had concomitantly evolved as well. Japanese longbows were distinctively different from most Asian types. They were as powerful and as accurate as any in Asia.

Fans, umbrellas, and various other wooden, paper, and straw crafts were superior to virtually any other similar products in the world. Japanese lacquered goods became wildly popular throughout the world, as did miniature curios like pocket fobs (*netsuke*), decorative sword guards (*tsuba*), needle cases (*etui*), and pillboxes (*inro*). Japanese pottery was virtually unrivaled in the world except for Chinese and Korean goods. Japanese woodblock prints (*ukiyo-e*), miniature horticulture (*bonsai*), and the Zen arts of tea (*chanoyu*), flower arrangement (*ikebana*), and garden landscaping (to mention but a few) would captivate the aesthetic appreciation of people the world over in the late nineteenth century.

The century of endemic warfare between 1467 and 1570 had stifled and weakened much of Japan's social and cultural development. To be sure the military technological sector flourished, regrettably so. Religious expression flourished in the mountain retreats of the Zen monasteries, as did certain forms of artistic expression. But the almost constant and continual warfare channeled the energies of most people away from cultural pursuits. The brutish samurai raped, pillaged, burned, and murdered their way across the countryside; scarcely anything or anyone was safe from their rampages. Not until the triumvirate of military consolidators, Nobunaga, Hideyoshi, and Ieyasu, managed to quell the fighting was Japanese society able to return to peaceful cultural life.

By the eighteenth century Japan had had nearly a century of peace. The people that lived then had no personal memory of the brutality of endemic civil war. For as long as they could remember they had been able to live their everyday lives in relative peace and tranquility. Even the poorest peasants lived infinitely better than virtually anyone had done during the Sengoku era.

That is not to suggest that the everyday lives of the common folk, the focus of this study, were idyllic ones. They were not; they were quite the opposite. Yet as we shall see, their lives were not as horrible as some would have us believe. Even in remote rural villages the peasants had substantial autonomy over their lives. They worked hard to pay high taxes and just to survive in a harsh environment. Yet most were fairly well nourished and comfortable in their meager circumstances, at least when compared with their distant cousins in China, Southeast Asia, Africa, North and South America, and even Europe. Ample evidence suggests that their life expectancy rates were probably about the same as those in northern Europe and vastly better than those in the rest of the world.

The city commoners were even better situated in their lives than their peasant brethren. Most lived in cities that were infinitely cleaner and safer than anywhere else in the world. They enjoyed a diet that was both more varied and more nutritious than any commoners had elsewhere. They had clean water, safe streets, sewage and trash removal, and even efficient local government. Their justice was harsh, but generally relatively fair. Their material culture and lifestyle were the equal of those of common city dwellers the world over. They enjoyed a high degree of literacy (in a very difficult orthography), access to cheap entertainment and to peaceful religious expression (except for Christianity), as well as relatively good and cheap medical care. Arguably, except for women, Japanese commoners in the eighteenth century enjoyed an excellent everyday life equal to that lived in most parts of the world. There are some scholars who would not except women from this characterization, particularly when compared to Chinese women, for example.

The exception for women was tied to patriarchal ideas of female inferiority, but also to the fact that neither Japanese religion gave much thought to either the souls or the lives of women. Prostitution and concubinage were not only tolerated, they were encouraged. Many women lived bleak and degrading lives within the society. Even free women were routinely degraded in their marriages and other relationships with men. Perhaps some Christian societies at the same time had begun to treat their women somewhat better. If that can be proven, then Japanese women perhaps fared worse than their Christian sisters. But Japanese women's lives, brutish and degrading though they indisputably were, probably were no worse than those of most women of the world at that time. That in and of itself is a sad commentary on the eighteenth century.

In the search for that everyday life, we will examine various aspects of eighteenth-century Japanese life. It will be remembered that this is not an examination of the high culture of the elite. There are sufficient sources for that. In the following chapters we will examine the quotidian material culture of the common people in Japan.

NOTES

1. For a more complete treatment of Japan's history, see my work, *The History of Japan* (Westport, CT: Greenwood Press, 1998).

2. Compare Gari Ledyard, "Galloping Along with the Horseriders: Looking for the Founders of Japan" (*Journal of Japanese Studies*, 1:2 [Spring 1975], 217–54) and Walter Edwards, "Event and Process in the Founding of Japan: The Horserider Theory in Archeological Perspective" (*Journal of Japanese Studies*, 9:2 [Summer 1983], 265–95).

3. A compromise was reached a decade later that specified that the Northern (Kyoto) and Southern (Yoshino) lines would alternate in succession, but after the lines were reunited, the Ashikaga never honored their promises.

4. And some would argue that it continues, only slightly altered, into twenty-first-century Japan.

2

Population

The population of Japan in the eighteenth century is something of a demographic wonder. Not surprisingly, after a century of civil war (with its attendant high death rate from killing, famine, and the lack of an adequate agricultural work force), the population exploded in the next century. It is estimated that the population in 1600 stood at about 17 million. By 1721 it had increased to about 30 million. But then it remained basically static for the next century. Demographers were at a loss to explain this anomaly.

Many Marxist critics argued that that the class struggle brought on by burgeoning capitalism caused tremendous famine and epidemic diseases among the poor peasantry. To be sure there were some famines at the end of the eighteenth century and the beginning of the nineteenth century, but they alone cannot account fully for the population stagnation. Absent war, in the classic Malthusian ideology of "natural checks" on population growth, that left epidemic diseases. The historian Ann Jannatta has effectively destroyed that myth. It has been known for a long time that peasants practiced infanticide. It was argued that they did so because of the grinding poverty. After all, female infanticide in China was widespread during economic crises.

Demographers recently have argued convincingly that the population stagnated in the countryside because of a conscious attempt by peasants to improve their own standard of living. It would seem that eighteenth-century Japanese peasants became aware of the inexorable link between

population growth and poverty and therefore decided to limit their population growth.

When Hideyoshi had linked population, land, and tax rates, it might
have created the germ of an idea in the minds of the peasantry. He, and
then Ieyasu after him, limited the size of villages to 400 people, farming
roughly 400 *cho* (a total of about 1,000 acres) of land, in order to produce
400 *koku* (each equivalent to about five bushels) of tax rice. This was for
administrative purposes, but it was also social engineering. Perhaps the
linkage of the allotment of land and assessment of taxes convinced peasants that in order to increase their standard of living they had but two
choices.

First, since they could not appreciably increase the size of the land
assigned to them, they would have to increase the productivity of the
land one way or another. Land reclamation by means of swamp drainage, hillside terracing, and inlet landfills was very labor-intensive, expensive, and time-consuming. But the land was finite. And what was to
stop the government from subdividing the newly made land into another
400-cho village staffed by 400 people paying 400 koku of rice? Experience
taught the peasants that hybrid seeds and better agricultural techniques
and tools led to slow increases in productivity.

Second, they could decrease their own numbers. However it was that
they became convinced that the second alternative was an easier and
more reliable way to improve their lot than the first, our evidence proves
that is precisely what they did.

Birth Control   The three most commonly used methods of population control are contraception and prenatal and post-
parturition actions. The most effective means of contraception in eighteenth-century Japan was to limit the number of people
who were allowed to reproduce. This was not done by any government
fiat, however, but by the peasants themselves. Only one son per peasant
household was allowed to take a wife. Any others were forbidden to
marry unless they could provide their own land. Some did this by marrying women whose parents did not have sons. The young man would
be adopted into his in-laws' household and bear their name. A few other
peasant boys might be fortunate enough to inherit reclaimed land or land
made fallow by some calamity (an epidemic, typhoon, earthquake, or
some other catastrophe that destroyed the owners of land), but most had
to remain unmarried. Young women who were not married to inheriting
sons would be forced into celibacy, and not a few became concubines or
prostitutes.

Village societies mocked families with more than three children, and
there were strong social taboos against older women giving birth. There
is evidence that methods of birth control other than socially enforced

sexual abstinence were common. The so-called rhythm method was not unknown, but coitus interruptus was more common.

Folk medicine, which was primarily Chinese in origin, had a long history of using herbal concoctions for contraception. Chinese medical books are full of vile-tasting brews that were usually ingested (almost always by women, of course), but occasionally were applied vaginally as spermcides. As in most professions, the secrets of these concoctions were passed on from father to son (in the case of physicians) or from mother to daughter-in-law. Recent studies have discovered that many such concoctions actually had some medicinal worth. We can see from the graphic depictions of sexual activity in the *shunga* or "spring pictures" genre of woodblock ukiyo-e that various mechanical contraceptive techniques were used as well.

Along with coitus interruptus, it appears that the Japanese experimented with various forms of condoms. Marriage manuals suggest that the intestines of various animals and fish were used. Some scholars credit the Japanese with the invention of condoms made from fish intestines, which were popularized among Portuguese sailors during Japan's "Christian Century."[1]

Chemical compounds to induce abortion were popular and fairly inexpensive, and we know from bakufu edicts attempting to stop mechanical abortions that they were prevalent as well. Pictures indicate that the chosen instrument of externally induced abortion was an evil-looking metal tool resembling a curved knitting needle. But by far the most common means of population control was infanticide. Infanticide, as noted earlier, was well known in China. But what is interesting in Japan's case was that it was used rather differently, that is, not as a response to abject poverty, but as a means of social engineering.

> Among the apparent objectives of infanticide . . . were: overall family limitations; an equilibrium of some sort between family size and farm size; an advantageous distribution of the sexes of the children; possibly the spacing of the children in a way convenient to the mother; and the avoidance of a particular sex in the next child.[2]

Peasant families needed at least one son to perpetuate the household, of course, but more than one son often caused more difficulties than having girls. Because of high infant mortality due to disease and malnutrition, many families wanted to have two sons as a kind of social security. But more commonly, after being assured of one son, girls were preferable. Girls could be hired out, married out, or even sold. But one must remember that adoption of sons-in-law was common in Japan, so in effect girls could inherit too. Given the fact that some farm tasks were by tradition gender specific, girls were needed as farm workers. Various scholars have pointed out that daughters could be used as social "glue" to bind two families together. Advantageous social, political, and economic relationships could be created by giving one's daughter in marriage or concubinage.

Neither Buddhism nor Shintō considered infanticide a "sin." Since Buddhism taught that life is an illusion and that a person's goal was to return to the great whole, then infanticide was just an acceleration of the process of reincarnation. In fact, one of the telling euphemisms used for infanticide was "sending back"; the implication was that the baby was sent back to Buddha. Another euphemism, more familiar (and rational) to the farmers, was "thinning out" (*mabiki*), which connoted removing excess seedlings to let the remaining ones thrive. Shintō was quiet on the subject, and since its priesthood did not lecture on morality (until the late nineteenth century anyway), there were no problems from that corner of society.

In terms of spacing children, a woman who was pregnant was effectively sterile until she delivered her child, so that was a crude means of birth control; especially so if the child was going to be disposed of at birth anyway. Folktales tell of the midwives who attended at births coming prepared with a bowl of water. If the "correct" gender was born, then the baby was washed in the bowl. If the "wrong" gender appeared, the baby was immersed and drowned in the water. The bowl was called the "sending-back bowl."

Since there were no real legal penalties or moral injunctions against infanticide then, for the peasant it was considered to be the single most reliable and technically least complex (as well as medically less dangerous for the mother than abortion) method of population control.

> [T]he practice does not appear to have been primarily a response to poverty; large landholders practiced it as well as small, and registered births were as numerous in bad as in good growing years. Also infanticide seems to have been used to control the sex sequence and spacing of births and the sexual composition and final size of families. In short, it gives the impression of a kind of family planning.[3]

Population Trends   As noted above, the population stabilized at about 30 million for the entire eighteenth century. According to some estimates, as much as 10 percent of the population lived in cities. Japan was arguably the most urbanized country in the world at the time (see Chapter 11).

Demographers tell us that life expectancy in eighteenth-century Japan was not substantially different than in Britain and France and considerably longer than in the rest of Europe and all of the rest of the world.

As best as can be determined from village and family registers (*koseki*), the average life expectancy was around forty years. Susan Hanley attributes this to a relatively healthy diet, good personal hygiene, excellent sewage disposal (see Chapter 15), the lack of many disease epidemics, and also to the salubrious climate. Thomas C. Smith suggests that infanticide may have had some positive effects as well, including

> the selective elimination of visibly weak or deformed infants; the restriction of population to numbers generally within the capacity of the village to support; some matching of family size to family resource[s]; the particularly severe restraint of fertility in bad times; less wear and tear on mothers; and less infection because of smaller families.[4]

NOTES

1. I am indebted to Charles Boxer for bringing this to my attention in personal correspondence.

2. Thomas C. Smith, *Nakahara: Family Farming and Population in a Japanese Village, 1717–1830* (Stanford: Stanford University Press, 1977), 83.

3. Ibid., 147.

4. Ibid., 58.

3

Governance

[E]ven though the Tokugawa bakufu was constructed around a system of status differentiation, it involved a shōgun's authority, as necessary, and adapted to the movement of history by boldly employing
men of talent regardless of their social status. This . . . enabled the
Tokugawa system to survive for 265 years [amid] violent shifts in
the historical current as the mode of production was changing from
feudalistic to capitalistic.[1]

The Tokugawa regime has often been called a political anomaly in that
it claimed to rule from a national center, forcing the feudal warlords
who ruled in decentralized nearly autonomous domains (han) to swear
allegiance and pay obeisance in the bakufu's capital, Edo. This oxymoron
of "centralized feudalism" was based on a governance system called
baku-han. Each feudal lord governed his own han in semi-autonomy in
terms of administration, taxation, and justice, and even maintained a
military force that did not obey the commands of the bakufu. The bakufu
demanded complete loyalty from the daimyō and forced them to reside
in the national capital for half of their lives, and to maintain their relatives in Edo as hostages.

In other times and in other places, the baku-han system might be called
a confederacy or a proto-federalism. In eighteenth-century Japan it was
a continuation of the pragmatic political compromise reached in 1600
after Tokugawa Ieyasu had won a decisive battle at Sekigahara. It re-

flected the military and political reality of 1600 but also characterized the Rube Goldberg–like device that was established by accretion in order to keep the various powers in check. The compromise had been working for a century by 1700, and the Tokugawa shōgunal administrators must have reasoned, "If it ain't broke, don't fix it."

Ieyasu had "frozen" society, the economy, politics, and military power in 1603 when he had accepted the title of Seii-tai-shōgun ("Barbarian-Subduing Generalissimo") from the emperor. He had quickly passed the title over to his son in 1605 in order to establish the sense of dynastic legitimacy that had eluded Nobunaga and Hideyoshi before him. He rewarded his longtime loyal allies with land confiscated from his enemies and had incorporated these *Fudai* ("hereditary") daimyō into his administration and had ensconced them at strategic bottlenecks throughout the Japanese archipelago. His former enemies, men who had only recently sworn loyalty to him, he classified as *Tōzama* ("Outsiders") and surrounded them with their own ancient enemies as well as Fudai and Tokugawa stalwarts.

By the time of the third shōgun, Iemitsu, who as Ieyasu's grandson, the baku-han system was in fairly good working order and most of the major aspects of governance were in place. Able men selected from among the Tokugawa entourage (*hatamoto*) administered the bakufu. Although the administrative pool was considerably circumscribed, the bakufu made a point of selecting the most able men despite their relative social ranks. A board of senior councilors (*rōjū*) handled foreign, religious, imperial, financial, and daimyō affairs. In short, they handled all of the issues regarding the management of the country as a whole.

Another board, staffed by Fudai daimyō, called "junior councilors" (*wakadoshiyori*), handled the affairs of the Tokugawa family. These tasks included managing the judicial, political, social, and financial affairs of the extensive private Tokugawa estates, which amounted to nearly one-third of all the arable land in the country. In addition, they oversaw the administration of all the gold, silver, copper, coal, and iron mines in the country. The board appointed ministers (*bugyō*) to administer the five large cities in the country: Edo itself, Kyoto, Ōsaka, Nagasaki, and Sendai. Parenthetically, by 1700 this board had created a mutually paranoid check over the bugyō by appointing at least two men to each position to watch over each other while they administered the cities. In Nagasaki, three bugyō spent four months each in Edo in rotation, two of them always being in residence in Nagasaki. The bugyō in turn appointed intendants (*daikan*) to administer smaller areas of control. The wakadoshiyori also appointed bugyō to watch over the affairs of the temples and shrines and others to manage the considerable financial interests of the Tokugawa family.

All of these Fudai daimyō did these tasks in addition to managing

Principal Officials of the Tokugawa Bakufu

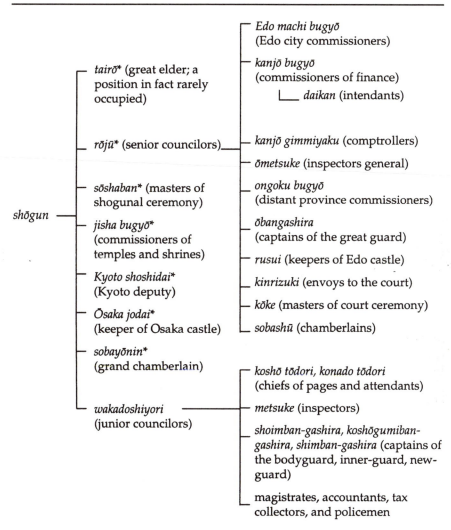

*Positions held by fudai (hereditary vassal daimyo). All other positions were held by hatamoto and gokenin (liege vassals).

Source: Adapted from *The Kodansha Encyclopedia of Japan* (Tokyo: Kodansha, 1989), 9:54.

their own domains. They met in Edo twice a month, corresponding with their time in the capital as part of the "alternate attendance" (*sankin-kotai*) system.

The rōjū who required that the daimyō administer their own han with justice and efficiency controlled the daimyō. A daimyō could be removed from office if his han was mismanaged. Prime evidence of mismanagement was if the peasants of his han were in rebellion. As noted earlier, each daimyō was required to maintain a separate residence in his han and another in Edo, where he spent at least half of his life. Sankin-kotai required that his family remain as hostages in Edo, and that the daimyō maintain a samurai entourage appropriate to the productivity (*kokudaka*) of his han. This was designed to sap the daimyō's finances, but also to create an aura of pomp and circumstance in Edo. Daimyō had to designate their choice as heir early in their own careers in order to ensure that the heir remained in Edo as a hostage. Daimyō could not adopt, marry, or make other social alliances without the shōgun's permission. They were required to engage in costly national public works at the behest of the shōgun and were instructed to tear down all "superfluous" castles; most daimyō were entitled to only one per han.

An elaborate system of spies (*metsuke*) was established, often incorporating the younger siblings or jealous concubines of the daimyō as well as wandering monks, minstrels, nuns, blind masseurs, and anyone else who could insinuate themselves into the daimyō courts.

Another important aspect of the baku-han system was the seclusion of the country after 1640. The official reason for the "closed country" (sakoku) had been a Christian-led rebellion in 1637–38 in the Shimabara Peninsula in the southwest. But there were other reasons why the seclusion made good political sense. It kept foreigners at bay and under tight control. Chinese, Korean, and Dutch traders were restricted in Nagasaki, and that helped control the importation of guns from abroad. This redounded to the benefit since it meant that of the bakufu the lion's share of profits from other foreign trade ended up in the coffers of the bakufu itself.

Since Japanese were forbidden to leave the country, it made the control of daimyō as well as pirates on the periphery very much easier. Ocean-going ships were tightly restricted, which made any planned marine invasion of Edo extremely unlikely. Of course the bakufu rounded up as many guns and cannon as it could and padlocked them tightly in government armories.

Perhaps all of these irregular and overlapping systems of governance were necessary because the Tokugawa did not, in fact, actually govern the entire country. By no stretch of the imagination can the bakufu be said to have been a national government. The baku-han system integrated the various governance devices, but at the end of the day, the daimyō were almost autonomous within their 270 individual domains. Perhaps if Ieyasu had managed in 1600 to conquer the some one hundred enemies designated as Tōzama, he might have truly centralized and nationalized his government. But even that was extremely unlikely since in addition to the 98 Tozama, who controlled nearly 40 percent of the

land, there were over 170 *other* daimyō. The baku-han reflected that reality. Given that the system endured in relative peace for more than two
and a half centuries, one must concede that it worked tolerably well.

An important part of the bakufu governance system
was the Neo-Confucian social philosophy, which was at   **Social Control**
the heart of the political and economic gestalt. The separation of socioeconomic (and therefore political) classes (*heino-bunri*) allowed the bakufu to rule by division of power. As explained in Chapter
4, the dominant political philosophy posited that society was naturally
divided by function. The samurai ruled, peasants produced food, artisans manufactured, and merchants moved materials from places of production and surplus to areas of consumption and demand. The social
standing of each class was determined by the relative morality of its
function. Moral, benevolent, and wise samurai administrators governed
the upright but naïve, childlike farmers; the yeoman artisans produced
other social necessities; and the greedy merchants benefited from the
endeavors of those above them.

In addition, Hideyoshi and later Ieyasu had separated the warriors
from their natural allies and vassals, the peasants. Samurai had been
forced to live within castles by virtue of military expediency. Hideyoshi,
who had himself risen from peasant ranks, decided that, in order to
pacify the country, peasants should plant and harvest rice and should
be removed from the battlefield. Ieyasu had seen the wisdom of this
social control and had forbidden samurai to return to the countryside.
This physical separation of warrior from the land was integrated with
the social and moral distance between samurai and merchant in order
to provide checks and balances necessary for social peace.

The bakufu went to almost irrational lengths to create and preserve
social, economic, and therefore political distance between the classes.
Sumptuary decrees were issued regularly and routinely in order to ex-
acerbate the existing social distances between classes. Even rich merchants and peasants were forbidden to wear clothes, eat food, build
residences, entertain, or even speak in a manner inappropriate to their
social station. Miscreants were rounded up and publicly shamed and
punished harshly for such behavior. Such public displays went a long
way in creating a sense of antagonism between the classes. The people
were reminded that such social distance was natural and normal and
perhaps even predetermined by fate and karma.

> It was the government's belief that to maintain the proper relation-
> ship between the bushi [samurai] and the other classes, there
> should be hierarchical distinctions, not only in their functions, but
> also in the quality of their dress, food, and housing, in behavior
> and speech, and in intellectual and cultural activities.[2]

Local Governance As in the case of the daimyō, the bakufu administrators delegated most of the actual governance to local bureaucrats. In the some 63,000 rural villages (*mura*), the bakufu simply had neither the manpower nor the interest to actually govern such obnoxious bumpkins. Daikan regional administrators occasionally ventured out into the provinces to "inspect," particularly at harvest times, in hopes of garnering a few bribes to turn a blind eye to tax-collection irregularities. Otherwise, the villages were left to hereditary headmen (*gonō*) who actually administered village affairs. The particulars of that administration are covered in Chapter 10. Suffice it to say that as long as the mura paid the assessed taxes and were not in open rebellion, the bakufu and the daimyō left them to their own devices.

That is not to say that the samurai did not interfere in the lives of the peasants. They did plenty of that. But essentially the ubiquitous sumptuary laws and the plethora of other picayune laws and official notices that were circulated to every village were all done in the abstract and not the particular. That is to say, the samurai treated all villages, and therefore all peasants, as nameless, formless, interchangeable parts of the body politic. God forbid that the samurai ever had to actually encounter one of the smelly, uncouth, dirty little rotters. It was much preferable to issue orders and depend on the headmen to actually enforce the strictures. A century before, rough, rustic samurai ancestors had conducted censuses; it was now left to their effete urban bureaucratic descendents to issue orders and assess taxes.

It has been estimated that the actual paddy land doubled over the years by means of land reclamation projects and improved irrigation techniques. Certainly actual grain production had nearly doubled,[3] yet except in a few cases, the bakufu administrators did not even bother to take new land surveys. This is true partially because surveys were costly and time-consuming, but the major reason for not doing them was that they were trouble and because there was simply no incentive for bureaucrats to do so.

When it was tried by a few financially strapped daimyō, the peasants immediately went into a uproar. Uprisings followed petitions, and no daimyō could afford to have the bakufu think that he was not in full control of his domain. Even if a bureaucrat discovered hidden fields or ferreted out secreted yields, who profited from it? Certainly not the bureaucrat. Most likely the extra tax went into the daimyō's bottomless pockets or, worse, went to pay some fat merchant moneylender.

There was much swaggering contempt for the peasants in general during the period. Despite the Neo-Confucian strictures of "benevolent rule," many daimyō and samurai ascribed to the popular notion that "with peasants and sesame seeds, the more you squeeze them, the more you get from them."[4] Official tax rates increased beyond the semi-official "five for the lord—five for the farmer" during financial hardships, but it is difficult to believe that the peasantry could have survived for very long on such short rations.

Abundant evience suggests that the farmers were often hard strapped, particularly in times of drought. Famine was not unknown in many parts of the country, in fact. But again, demographers and economic historians have recently almost uniformly agreed that the peasants' lives were not as horrible as had been previously thought. No doubt most villages hid rice and lied about actual yields. Cottage industries, by-employment, and "cash" crops proliferated during the century. None of those items ever appeared on the tax records. Wills, bequests, charity records, and other material culture documents attest that most farmers were relatively more comfortable than we have been led to believe. At least they seemed to be better off than their Chinese cousins were at the same time. Evidence suggests that the simple fact that the samurai had been removed from the land allowed Japanese farmers to fare better than peasants in other societies.

If that was true of the peasants, we must conclude that the *chōnin* (city dweller) were even better situated **City Governance** than their bucolic brethren were. Bakufu governance in the cities, despite the fact that the samurai lived cheek-by-jowl with the chōnin, was just as abstract and disinterested. This is partially due to the nature of the origins of cities in Japan.

Most large cities were the result of castle construction during the sixteenth century (see Chapter 9). Defensive emplacements concentrated military power within the stone and earthen ramparts of the castle. Samurai came to reside around the very walls of the castles, within the protective moats. Outer walls were then constructed to protect these warrior residences. Merchants, artisans, and peasant construction workers were lured to areas outside these walls, and before long, another concentric ring of earthen walls was built to protect these essential servants and workers. The chōnin (literally, "ward people") therefore lived in their own enclaves. The samurai neither cared nor wished to know what went on there, as long as the workers completed their tasks.

The samurai treated the chōnin like all camp followers, that is, they insisted that they obey orders and remain peaceful. Samurai administrators merely deputized "substantial citizens" within the chōnin community to enforce the peace. Often the samurai tried to organize the neighborhoods into five-man mutual-responsibility groups (*gonin-gumi*), much as peasants were organized in their villages. In some cases that seemed to work, except often the groups came in conflict with other domestic administrative units. Some occupations formed their own guild-like groups (*za*) for purposes of governing the profession in terms of quality, price, and supply of manufactured goods. The za often took

on rudimentary administrative tasks as well. Often the za merely rear-
ranged the gonin-gumi, sometimes by changes in residence, occasionally
by simply changing the names of the people to align with the artificially
created gonin-gumi!

As the cities grew into full-fledged castle towns (jokamachi) the bugyō
appointed chōnin as ward elders (*machi-doshiyori*). Very often, the za or
the gonin-gumi elected these men themselves and merely presented the
machi-bugyō with lists of their choices. Usually, as long as these leaders
kept the peace, the samurai left them alone and thanked their lucky stars
that they never actually had to deal directly with these ruffians.

All of the chōnin neighborhoods mounted their own fire-watch and
safety patrols. These were made up of chōnin citizens, but the more
dangerous jobs, such as fireman, were contracted out to professionals.
Very often the firemen were *hinin-eta* (outcastes), who were paid in a
kind of insurance scheme. Chōnin paid a flat fee for the protection, but
were expected to "tip" and reward actual service. The firemen would
expect to be paid for saving one's house from the encroaching holocaust.
If they were not paid, one could not expect to get much service the next
time around. The firemen's main job was to quickly disassemble the
houses that were in the path of the fire. These "hookers" and "pullers"
could very rapidly take a house apart (see Chapter 9) and cart it out of
harm's way. Others would help the residents quickly take out any heirlooms and deposit them in safety.

Eta-hinin also performed other essential services in chōnin neighborhoods. They collected and removed human waste (see Chapter 15) and
removed garbage from collection points. They removed the bodies of
dead animals from the streets as well.

There was no regular tax on merchant activity (see Chapter 16), but
there were many license fees, ground rents, and other economic imposts
(known collectively as "appreciation money" or *reikin*) to be collected.
The machi-doshiyori collected these sums and turned them over in a
lump sum to the samurai administrators. The samurai could not have
cared less how the money was allocated, assessed, collected, or extorted.

The same was true of the Licensed Quarters, the entertainment districts
of large cities. In Edo, the Yoshiwara had a seven-foot-tall wall surrounding it; the bakufu did not particularly want to keep the denizens in, but
rather to keep samurai out. The inmates kept their own peace, collected
fees, and generally administered their own area. The bakufu took the
money and did not ask questions. The many samurai that sneaked into
the area disguised at night were not there to investigate. They were there
to have fun.

The only times that the samurai became involved in the administration
of the chōnin districts was when they were searching for criminals, absconders, or profligate samurai. In general, they usually depended on

the machi-doshiyori to ferret out these people, since the chōnin had infinitely better information anyway.

The samurai had their own administration systems within their own residential areas. The system was **Samurai Control** much more elaborate and official than was that of the chōnin. By and large, the samurai ruled by status, so the system was infinitely more complicated. Lower-ranking samurai, no matter how able and charismatic, could simply not tell upper-ranking samurai, no matter how inept and stupid, what to do. There were therefore several layers of administrators within the residential areas. The daimyō delegated authority to his immediate subordinates, and they commanded the vassal samurai in most things. But what about fire marshals, or neighborhood patrols, or dogcatchers? Imagine some middle-ranking fire marshal trying to force the children of his superior to stop playing with fire. Much formal negotiation and arbitration clogged the administrative machinery of every samurai residential neighborhood.[5]

In the smaller cities and towns there was always some kind of samurai control. In the jokamachi, the daimyō developed their own administrative units, very often constituted on bakufu models. There is a great deal of internal logic here of course. Why reinvent the wheel? Since the bakufu commonly issued laws and urged the daimyō to develop similar ones for their administration, the daimyō usually went along. If any question arose regarding administration of their han, it would be simpler to defend if their own independent systems were similar to those of the bakufu.

As in the chōnin neighborhoods, the eta-hinin often performed necessary services for the samurai for pay. The samurai wanted even less to do with these poor souls than with the chōnin, so they acknowledged their elected leaders as well.

Most samurai-controlled cities maintained separate judicial courts for samurai and chōnin. Unless a chōnin **Legal Controls** had committed a very serious crime, however, the samurai did not usually become involved in their punishment, preferring to let the chōnin handle their own justice. In the case of samurai, however, there were commonly formal courts for their adjudication. Most daimyō had their own "house codes," which were copied from bakufu codes.

These house codes were more like exhortations meant to remind everyone about the Neo-Confucian ideology of benevolent moral behavior than they were actual legal codes. Not surprisingly, the laws were enforced by situational ethics. Samurai were expected to behave wisely, and often their punishments were harsher than for chōnin since the former *should* have known better. Higher-ranking samurai administered all law enforcement. They took into account known legal precedent as well as any mitigating circumstances.

Legal historians suggest that the system was much better than one would ordinarily imagine considering that none of the samurai judges had any real legal training. Punishment was usually quite harsh, but judgments were rendered fairly equitably. In most cases, dissatisfied litigants could appeal to higher authorities, but usually did not because often the punishment rendered there was even harsher than in the lower jurisdiction.

The general rule of thumb in legal cases was to keep and to restore the peace. Anything that disturbed the peace of the group was punished with an eye to restoring harmony. Often both sides of a dispute were punished equally—not because the judges did not wish to render justice, but because they were primarily concerned with restoring harmony as well as deterring new litigation. Public flogging and exposure to the taunts of the crowd usually sufficed to create a sense of real dread in most miscreants. In some areas trial by ordeal continued well into the eighteenth century. Litigants were required to pick up red-hot metal and then examined to determine who had been injured and who had been protected by the kami or Buddhas.

Horrible death sentences for more serious crimes also went a long way toward keeping the peace. Death came slowly as miscreants were executed by roasting, burning, crucifying, being drawn apart by oxen, or the dreaded "death of a thousand cuts." The latter death took days as prisoners were stripped naked and then wrapped tightly in fishnets. Executioners would by turns slice off bits of skin that protruded through the net, and then cauterize the wound with sake or with hot metal, only to repeat the process endlessly until the person died of shock.[6]

Compared to these punishments meted out for murder, stealing from taxes, counterfeiting currency, rape, or arson, minor crimes such as gossiping, brawling, theft, gambling, and petty violence were punished less severely. The idea was to make the punishment distasteful enough to give anyone pause before engaging in rowdy behavior. Lest one think that Japanese justice was particularly barbaric compared to Western societies at this time, Kaempfer noted:

> Hence it is, that in this heathen country fewer capital crimes are tried before the courts of justice, and less criminal blood shed by the hands of publick executioners, than perhaps in any part of Christianity. So powerfully works the fear of an inevitable shameful death, upon the minds of a nation, otherwise so stubborn as the Japanese, and so regardless of their lives, that nothing else, but such an unbounded strictness, would be able to keep them within due bounds of continence and virtue.[7]

The mutual-responsibility system of gonin-gumi kept most people in line because one's compatriots preferred not to share one's punishment.

Often when gonin-gumi members saw the beginnings of a problem, they rushed to arbitrate and smooth things over lest the quarrel lead to a public scene that could not be ignored by the higher authorities. The guild-like za also often became involved in disputes involving their members. Obviously, few people wished to involve outsiders and bureaucrats in otherwise internal affairs. As in most societies, the adage was "only a fool goes to court willingly."

The first of the official law codes was issued in 1615. The *Buke shohatto* (Regulations for Military Houses) dealt mostly with rules for marriage, adoption, succession, and "proper behavior." Two decades later, regulations regarding sankin-kotai and anti-Christian controls were added. Separate laws were issued regarding the administration and control of religious institutions. The *Shoshū jiin-hatto* (Regulations for Shrines and Temples) limited the amount of land and power that could accrue to the religious establishments.[8]

Virtually every daimyō copied the bakufu laws, but administered them independently. Bakufu and domainal edicts were posted on village and machi notice boards together. They were often nearly identical. Only in the very most abstract sense, then, could it be said that there was anything like a national legal system. Every city, machi, and han, and virtually every village administered its own individual system of justice. Each was jealously intent on keeping these matters internal and free of outside interference. For its part, the bakufu preferred it that way as well. The adage was not "the squeaky hinge gets the oil," it was "the nail that sticks out gets hammered down." Words of wisdom.

Perhaps this is as good a place as any to consider peasant uprisings, since they involved so many issues of governance and jus-   *Ikki* tice.

> Tokugawa warriors did not govern in a vacuum, and they did not rule over passive and supine subjects. Instead they had to respond to unrest by vigorous attempts at political reform. Warriors and leading intellectuals agonized over the problem of social disorder beginning in the mid-eighteenth century. For some, the inability of the bakufu to keep the peace meant that it should be replaced with a new principle of order.[9]

The some 63,000 individual villages of Japan sometimes responded to perceived injustice from their samurai overlords with collective violence aimed at redress. These uprisings, called *ikki*, which means something like "united action," varied in size, scope, and ultimate goal, but all were carefully considered responses to injustice. Since the punishment for the leaders of such violent uprisings was certain death, villagers did not enter into them rashly. Ikki were uniformly considered to be a desperate last resort, entered into only when all other means of amelioration had been exhausted. As Anne Walthall eloquently has written:

> In the ideal harmonious village, everyone agreed on what was to be done, and all cooperated in maintaining the subsistence level of the village as a whole and in performing its obligations to their warrior ruler. But the system of collective responsibility also meant that problems over the land tax or over commercial regulations [affected] everyone and provided a basis for organized uprisings.[10]

When all manner of normal negotiations and appeal had been exhausted, the whole village rose as one and marched off in search of justice. Usually the causes of these uprisings (for they were not revolts or rebellions) were to be found in increased taxes, refusals of tax deferments after a drought or similar natural calamity, or new regulations judged to be discriminatory or potentially ruinous to the village. Since the villages had no real representative voice in the samurai administration, village leaders were often coerced into writing letters of protest or sending petitions (*shūso*) to whichever government ruled over them. These letters were dangerous. "Ringleaders" (i.e., people who signed their names) were often punished for their temerity, so village headmen were understandably reluctant to take such steps. Only when village collective social and moral pressures had been brought to bear was a headman willing to do so. Often this required outside discussion as well since han-wide petitions (*kokuso*) were deemed to be more powerful. They were usually more successful as well. And fewer village leaders were punished; so, there being strength and anonymity in numbers, these petitions were often quite attractive strategically.

But since the samurai harshly and haughtily refused many petitions, the next step often seemed more palatable to the village leaders. If one was to be executed for writing a letter or petition, why not risk the same punishment for leading an ikki? After all, in for a penny, in for a pound. Secret meetings were held where all the heads of households would discuss possibilities. "Appeals by force" (*gōso*), whereby the village marched en masse to present a petition to the government, were one alternative. Since gōso were specifically illegal and punishable by death for the leaders, another alternative might be a mass absconding. Peasants would simply disappear into the mountains and refuse to plant or harvest their crops.

More often, when the sources of the injustice were local greedy absentee landlords or usurious moneylenders, the village might choose a simple "bash-up" (*uchi-kowashi*) of the homes or shops of these villains. An anonymous attack on a rice warehouse or a well-planned raid to destroy all financial documents might actually solve the problem. Often, to be sure that all records were destroyed, the homes and businesses of these local villains were smashed up and burned to the ground. Rarely was there any lethal violence against the people themselves, but it was not unknown.

But if the target of the uprising was the daimyō or the bakufu itself, careful planning was in order. Various subterfuges were tried to convince the samurai that there were no real leaders, that the ikki were spontaneous common responses to moral injustice. Religious symbols were employed to suggest that villagers were merely following the will of the kami and the Buddhas—in other words, that this was a religious crusade. In many accounts, villagers told uniform stories of how local Buddhist statues came to life or superhuman figures compelled them to follow them in search of cosmic justice. Strange lights, comets, lightning, and other cosmic phenomena were said to lead the ikki as well.

More often, minor ikki were aimed at rich gonō or other village authorities themselves. In many mura, the headship was hereditary. These men all too often took advantage of their position to enrich and empower themselves. Since most villagers were illiterate, the gonō handled all correspondence and interpreted government edicts at will. Village taxes were assessed and paid collectively, so a corrupt gonō could cheat and embezzle almost at will. When the villagers tired of this, a *murakata ikki* (uprising against village leaders) might ensue. Usually the samurai treated these ikki most leniently, since the return to village harmony was more important than punishing the leaders. Often the result was a collective village board made up of men elected from among the heads of all the households, not just from among the gonō.

In all of these uprisings, the peasants firmly believed that morality and justice were on their side. They appealed to the Neo-Confucian (and even Buddhist) philosophy of wise, benevolent, and moral administration that was the raison d'être of the samurai. They coerced local teachers, priests, or other intellectuals to couch all petitions in the accepted language of the Neo-Confucian classics. Many samurai were sympathetic. Occasionally these latter men ameliorated punishments, singling out only a few of the most aged leaders for execution, and sometimes they even admonished or replaced local administrators.

After all, the entire society operated under nearly identical ideas about social propriety. The wealthy were to behave benevolently toward the less fortunate. The discontented participants in ikki therefore were very careful to issue manifestoes and petitions beforehand explaining their actions in Neo-Confucian social terms. Confessions, stories and chronicles written afterward almost uniformly suggested that the protestors and rioters had ample moral reasons for their actions.

Finally, we should consider why ikki became so common during the eighteenth century. Marxist historians have long pointed to the increased incidence of ikki as proof that the rising capitalist oppression forced the peasants to rebel in a classic class warfare. The idea is that the rising class consciousness was the upheaval that forced the Tokugawa out and ushered in an imperialist restoration. They ignore the fact that ikki actually increased in the next Meiji era.

Anne Walthall and other historians have suggested other reasons and causes.[11] For instance, it should be noted that although most ikki leaders were punished harshly, many peasants considered the outcome to be positive. Samurai administrators, as noted, sometimes were sympathetic. They tended to accept the righteousness of murakata-ikki more often than not. Distant administrators sometimes wearied of continual ikki incidents in particular areas and solved the problem by sending out an inspector and even by replacing local administrators deemed to be corrupt or inefficient. Ikki aimed at tax recision or at least deferment after natural disasters were often successful in part. Uchi-kowashi aimed at local financial bullies often went virtually unpunished. All of these results seemed to have accomplished the original goals of the participants in the ikki.

Second, if every daimyō and every bakufu intendant had responded to every ikki by destroying the entire village, not just a few wizened leaders, I would argue that ikki would have ceased almost immediately and forever. Truth be told, the samurai administrators often became convinced that the poor peasants probably had good and moral reasons for what they did. Just as a samurai could sometimes explode in anger and violence in the face of injustice, perhaps peasants could too. They still had to be punished for having disturbed the harmony of society, of course. But many samurai at least sympathized more with the peasants than with their corrupt administrators, even if they were samurai.

Third, there was the inherent criticism of the ikki itself in terms of baku-han administrations. Scarcely any daimyō could afford to appear to be incompetent in the eyes of the bakufu. Positive proof of corruption or incompetence was to have one's peasants in rebellion. In the seventeenth century, at least, several daimyō had been relieved of their positions, and not a few lost their entire domains because they had not governed their lands and people with benevolence and wisdom. Virtually every ikki came to the attention of the bakufu, and often daimyō were at least questioned about such disturbances when they annually attended the shōgun in sankin-kotai. Without question, this served as an impetus for peasants and as a deterrent to harsh punishment by the daimyō.

Fourth, several sociologists have suggested that peasant rebellions actually increase as their expectations for a better lifestyle rise. That is to say, when peasants fare better economically, they are more likely to rebel in order to maintain that better life. They perceive new imposts and taxes to be attempts to rob them of the little that they have gained and therefore as extortion. Mikiso Hane has eloquently observed that when real famine struck in Japan the peasants "starved to death in silence."[12] When new taxes were imposed on a village or when traditional exactions were not postponed or forgiven for a village that had recently suffered a temporary setback caused by a natural disaster, they rebelled. Acts of the kami and nature the farmers understood. Extortion, moral corruption, and incompetence were different.

Finally, and this is perhaps most difficult to prove, the posthumous fame and praise accorded to the ikki leaders might have contributed to the whole problem. Songs and fireside sagas abounded in praise of these courageous men in virtually every mura in Japan. The name of Sakura Sogoro is familiar to virtually every peasant in the land. Most could not accurately name the current daimyō of their han, much less the incumbent shōgun or emperor, but they all knew Sakura's story. In the mid-seventeenth century he had selflessly sacrificed himself and his entire family by quelling a potential ikki. He had fearlessly infiltrated the shōgun's apartment to deliver a petition personally. For his boldness, his whole family was executed, but the shōgun saw to it that the local samurai administrators were sacked and that taxes were reduced for Sakura's region of Chiba.[13] Folklorists have identified no less than a dozen songs and a score of embellished stories about Sakura in virtually the whole country. Such legends undoubtedly contributed to the actions of individual village headmen. It was as powerful as the admonition to young Christian boys to "dare to be a Daniel." Virtually everyone knows the name of Robin Hood, but the Sheriff of Nottingham is remembered only by his title.

NOTES

1. Shinzaburō Oishi, "The Bakuhan System" (Mikiso Hane, trans.), in Chie Nakane and Shinzaburō Oishi, eds., *Tokugawa Japan: The Social and Economic Antecedents of Modern Japan* (Tokyo: University of Tokyo Press, 1990), 35.

2. Donald H. Shivley, "Popular Culture," in John W. Hall and James L. McClain, eds., *Early Modern Japan*, volume 4 in *The Cambridge History of Japan* (Cambridge: Cambridge University Press, 1991), 711.

3. From 18 million koku (90 million bushels) in 1597 to 26 million koku (130 bushels) in 1700 alone. Anne Walthall, *Social Protest and Popular Culture in Eighteenth Century Japan* (Tucson: University of Arizona Press, 1986), 5.

4. Gary P. Leupp, *Servant Shophands, and Laborers in the Cities of Tokugawa Japan* (Princeton: Princeton University Press, 1992), 7.

5. For good discussions about urban control systems, see Nobuhiko Nakai, "Commercial Change and Urban Growth in Early Modern Japan" (James L. McClain, trans.), and Chie Nakane, "Tokugawa Society" (Susan Murata, trans.), both in Hall and McClain, *Early Modern Japan*, 519–95 and 213–31, respectively.

6. Michael Cooper, ed., *They Came to Japan: An Anthology of European Reports on Japan, 1543–1640* (Berkeley: University of California Press, 1965), 151–53.

7. Engelbert Kaempfer, *The History of Japan: Together with a Description of the Kingdom of Siam*, 3 vols., trans. J. G. Scheuchzer (Glasgow: James MacLehose and Sons, 1906), 2:310.

8. See James Wigmore's study, *Law and Justice in Tokugawa Japan* (Tokyo: Kokusai Bunka Shinkokai, 1969). A shorter version is available in the *Kodansha Encyclopedia of Japan*.

9. Walthall, *Social Protest*, 225.

10. Ibid., 2.

11. Ibid., 18; Nakai, *"Commercial Change"*; Sato Tsuneo, "Tokugawa Villages and Agriculture" (Mikiso Hane, trans.), in Nakane and Oishi, *Tokugawa Japan*, 37–80; and others.

12. Mikiso Hane, *Premodern Japan: A Historical Survey* (Boulder, CO: Westview Press, 1991).

13. See account in Lewis Bush, *Japanalia: A Concise Cyclopaedia* (Tokyo: Tokyo News Service, 1965), 312.

4

Religion

The religious life of eighteenth-century Japan was very complex. It was an amalgam of many rich traditions, the primary one being the nativist conglomeration of folk beliefs generally called Shintō ("the way of the gods"). After the sixth century or so, a series of Asian continental religious influences were imported, adapted, and fused with the native beliefs and with each other. The result was a rich, varied, and quite sophisticated philosophical and religious amalgam that seemed to thrive very nicely in Japanese society.

> The peculiar nature of Japanese religion has brought forth two conspicuous cultural features. One is a distinct separation in the sphere of activities between the religious system and the ethical system. The other is the close relation between religious value and aesthetic value.[1]

Within the religious system, Buddhism predominated, particularly since the bakufu treated it very much as an extension of its own social-political control. Shintō remained very much alive and at the core of rural village life within the circle of agrarian-centered rituals and festivals. Both Buddhism and Taoism heavily influenced it, but it still retained its native soul. Christianity had been banned through a series of government edicts at the beginning of the seventeenth century, and continued to be anathema to the state until 1873. Except for a few crypto-Christians (*kakure kurishitan*) who hid out in remote southern islands, native converts had been stamped out or tortured into apostasy in a firestorm of religious persecution after the mid-seventeenth century.

The ethical system remained fundamentally the purview of Neo-Confucianism. Buddhism had acquired a patina of secular morality during its millennium in China and had continued to advocate loyalty to the emperor through his military deputy, the Tokugawa shogun. But for all intents and purposes, except for an obligatory threat to the karma of miscreants, the bakufu appealed to Neo-Confucian morality in its laws and edicts.

As suggested above, the Japanese aesthetic was very much a function of its religious base. The two predominant influences during the period were Zen Buddhism and the rustic simplicity of Shintō. In the urban environment, the riotous and sumptuous aesthetic taste of the chōnin was the result of an unconscious reaction to the austerity of Zen. But one might argue that the formation of Shingaku, its own secular civil religious system, also contributed heavily to the chōnin artistic taste.

This chapter examines the state of religion in eighteenth-century Japan by taking each religious system in turn. Neo-Confucianism is included here, though one could argue that it belongs more properly in Chapter 3. Because the Japanese treated it very much like a secularized religious ethos, we will place it here.

Shintō   Some scholars claim that Shintō, at least as it is currently understood, probably did not exist prior to around the late sixteenth century. When Oda Nobunaga adopted it as the native creed in the 1570s, he did so in a conscious attempt to create an alternate set of ideas to counter and undermine his military enemies, the large Buddhist secular establishments. Parenthetically, he also tried to employ Christianity as another such ally against Buddhism.

Prior to that time, Shintō was very much a chaotic set of regional and localized belief systems that coexisted almost independently of each other. Without belaboring the issue, each extended fictive kinship group (*uji*) in the prehistorical past created and adopted local tutelary spirits as their spiritual ancestors. These amorphous spirits (kami) seemed to coexist with humans, animals, and other life forms, sometimes influencing them, at other times being influenced by everything else. This animist (and perhaps pantheist) amalgam was like a rich stew of beliefs.

The preeminent uji, the Yamato family, chose for its tutelary kami the paragon of fertility and life: the sun. Other lesser uji chose appropriately subservient kami, and a new philosophical system was created, one which coincided with economic, political, and even geographic realities of the time. When the time came for Japan to write its history, using borrowed Tang Chinese ideographs, the imperial Yamato house incorporated its kami, the sun goddess Amaterasu-omi-kami, as chief deity and progenitor of all Japan. A creation story fused separate tribal histories into the official history of the Japanese people within the *Record of Ancient Matters* (*Kojiki*) and the *Chronicles of Japan* (*Nihon Shoki*, sometimes abbreviated as *Nihongi*).

The written histories gave the imperial house a charismatic legitimacy, but the religious explanation left much to be desired as a complete religion, let alone a moral system. This is partially because the Shintō amalgam lacked a divinely inspired canon of religious ideology, but it also lacked a hierarchy of knowledge, morality, organization, or priesthood. It was rather a hodge-podge of taboos, ritual pollution, ablution schemes, folklore, divination, magic, and superstitions. Until the seventeenth century or so, no attempts were made at systemization, rationalization, or organization, perhaps because after the sixth century there was no real need to do any of those things. The Chinese cultural package (a term I have used elsewhere)[2] provided everything that the imperial house in particular, and the Japanese in general, could ever need or use. As we shall see shortly, Buddhism, Taoism, and Confucianism provided for virtually every eventuality except for the unique native cultural affinity that Shintō alone could provide. Hence its survival in the face of the infinitely more sophisticated Chinese systems.

Shintō did provide the Japanese with an intense connection to their environment. Every aspect of their cosmic flora, fauna, and geologic surroundings was linked inextricably to their very being. Everything shared the same life force; everything could be, and perhaps latently was, kami. Everything influenced and was influenced by everything else. Humanity was intrinsically part of its environment. The following quotation by the eminent scholar Motoori Norinaga (1730–1801) succinctly expresses how the Japanese in the eighteenth century considered the kami.

> In ancient usage, anything which was outside the ordinary, which possessed superior power or which was awe-inspiring was called kami. Eminence here does not refer merely to the superiority of nobility, goodness or meritorious deeds. Evil and mysterious things, if they are extraordinary and dreadful, are called kami. . . . There are again numerous places in which seas and mountains are called kami. This does not have reference to the spirit of the mountain or the sea, but kami is here directly of the particular mountain or sea. This is because they were exceedingly awe-inspiring.[3]

I would argue that because Shintō seemed to incorporate the agrarian rhythms into its very being, and because it remained overwhelmingly rural because of Japan's topography, it remained an integral part of Japanese society. The farmers were constantly reminded of its imperfectly understood verities and mysteries imbedded deeply within the agricultural rhythms of life. Shintō was incorporated into every ritual, ceremony, and festival. Every dreaded superstition, taboo, and psychic phobia cried out for Shintō ablution and purification. In short, Shintō served.

Many of the oral folk traditions of ancient Japan seemed to be inextricably submerged in the idea of random luck. Why did good things happen to bad people? Why did good people suffer? Why me? The answers were as complex as the questions, but fundamentally were tied to the fact that the spirits were as flawed as was humanity. Good spirits and bad spirits alike were capricious, hungry, suspicious, jealous, and greedy; in short, they were as perverse as humans were. One needed to cajole, flatter, propitiate, dupe, and bribe the kami in order to avert catastrophe. And even then, if one did everything one humanly could, perhaps the kami were hung over that day. But one had to cover all bets, and Shintō had as many (more!) possible remedies as there were problems.

The local shrines, of which there were found to be 110,967 in a government survey a century later,[4] shared some commonalties. The "holy," or, to use Motoori's words, "awe-inspiring" area around the shrine was commonly set apart by a crude lattice fence, or sometimes was designated by paper or straw ropes. The traditional *torii* gate of a single crossbeam mounted on two uprights led directly to a fount of water where worshippers were to ritually cleanse themselves before approaching the worship area. The rinsing of the mouth and hands usually sufficed. Then, one approached the "worship sanctuary" (*haiden*).

This might be an actual thatched building with distinctive exposed crossed roof beams, or more commonly merely a rustic shed. If it were the latter, worshippers would approach the haiden and clap their hands to catch the attention of the kami housed therein. If the haiden was more elaborate, a bell or gong might be attached to the front, with a straw rope with which to sound the device. In either case, the front of the haiden was "sealed" by stringing across the entrance the traditional *shi-menawa*, a double-stranded straw rope. This was to represent the rope used by primordial spirits to keep the Sun Goddess from retreating to her cave (the "do not retreat rope," *Shiri-kume-na-nawa*), and therefore taking sunlight with her.

Within the more elaborate haiden might be another structure called "chief sanctuary" (*honden*), which might be compared to the "holy of holies" apartment in other religions. In the simple shedlike haiden, the honden would have to be imagined as a separate space. In whatever circumstance, some symbolic object housed therein represented the kami. This was not the kami, of course, only a representation, but it was considered to be the place where the kami visited or lived when in residence. This was most commonly a mirror (which was the symbol of Amaterasu, the sun), but it might be paper, rock (especially those with holes worn

The Inner Shrine at Ise, Torii in foreground. (Photo by Louis G. Perez)

through by water), a relic of an ancestor (who had become kami), a crystal, or virtually anything "awe-inspiring."

Sometimes, of course, there was no haiden. That was because a mountain, a craggy boulder, a strangely shaped tree, or a river was the kami. Then, only the torii, and perhaps a shimenawa, designated that the area was sacred. Whatever the designation, worshippers approached individually, or sometimes in a small group. There were no prescribed prayers, no accepted rituals, and no mandatory ceremonies. Very often there were no priests or caretakers about. The worshipper was alone with the kami and could approach, entreat, cajole, dance, or do virtually anything that seemed to be appropriate.

At the larger and more elaborate shrines, particularly those staffed by attendant priests, there was much more to "do." Tiny wooden placards called *ema* (literally, "horse pictures") were sold for a few coppers, particularly for the illiterate. Apparently the ema harkened back to an earlier age when horses were actually sacrificed to the kami. It was later reasoned that the kami could just as well do with pictures of the horses. It was believed that the ema "carried" the prayers to the spirits. People who could not write their prayers on small pieces of paper (and then tie them to the lattice fence) could buy an ema that some artisan or priest had drawn crude pictures upon to represent in rebus form what one needed from the kami. These could be tied to the lattice or any convenient tree to remind any forgetful kami what one had asked for. Also, one could purchase small inexpensive talismans, which one would then affix to the lintel of one's home to ward off evil.

Some of the larger shrines (such as Atsuta, Izumo, Ise, or Kitano), had *miko* ("spiritual children") attendants, commonly young virgin girls, who danced in short ceremonial rituals. The shrines dedicated to Hachiman, the kami of war, staged other rituals, such as the wildly popular Yabu-same mounted archery tournaments. Other shrines staged *Noh* performances or *sumo* wrestling (see Chapter 21). The variety was astounding and often seemed chaotic, but no one seemed to mind in the slightest.

At the smaller local shrines, children learned from their parents to offer gifts to the kami, commonly fruits of their agrarian labors. They were conditioned from experience that the most common gifts were two pounded rice cakes (*mochi*), one stacked on another to represent a mirrored image of the other. But one could bring virtually anything. Balls of cooked sticky rice, daikon radish, chestnuts, red beans, small cruets of sake, straw sandals (*waraji*)—in short, something of importance to the worshipper. But there were no rules, regulations, or levels of instruction in this worship. It was to be earnest and from the heart.

To be sure, Shintō priests and shamans had their mystical chants (*nor-ito*), and had a fair number of symbolic accoutrements, including wands, branches of evergreen *sakaki* twigs, and sheaves of rice, all of which they used to some symbolic effect. Priests who presided at weddings or other social ceremonies seemed to know what they were doing, but Zoroastrian acolytes might as well have done it in Persian.

Most peasant families kept a crude "god-shelf" (*kamidana*) in their homes where they could commune with ancestors and kami. The first portion of a meal might be placed there to symbolically feed the kami. Many people confused the rituals with those performed in front of the analogue home Buddhist altar (*Butsudan*), but probably felt that it was important to propitiate the kami even if the ritual was done clumsily and improperly.

As we shall see in the discussion on religious calendar (see Chapter 6), the Japanese tried to cover as many bets as they could think of. There were many generic ceremonies and rituals within the year whereby one could propitiate unknown forces, and have a ripping good time in the process. It certainly helped that the rice wine (sake) was simultaneously an elixir, a sacrament, a symbol of life and fertility, and an intoxicant to boot. Shintō, then, was chiefly practiced in the festivals (*matsuri*) and in the observance of shamanic taboos, divinations, and superstitious rote behavior.

Buddhism Buddhism was as philosophically sophisticated as Shintō was simplistic. It abounded in written canons in several languages (notably Sanskrit and Chinese). During its millennium of experience in China it had acquired a complex moral system

Butsudan: lacquered wood "Buddha shelf" with
folding cabinet doors. Note Buddha statue in the
back, ancestral tablets on the left, hanging oil
lamp and scroll on the right, flower, food, incense
and bird statue offerings in front. (Drawing by
Meggan M. Beyers)

and an elaborate priestly hierarchy. It came to Japan with a rich artistic
tradition as well as music, architecture, and medical technology, to mention only the obvious attractions.

The basic truths seemed to be simple enough for any layman to com-
prehend: life is painful illusion. Humans are doomed to an endless cycle
of painful incarnations until they are rid of attachment and desire (which
cause the pain). The path to release is through realization of the preceding truths. Know and you will be released. But therein lies a cosmos of
interpretation and contention. What is truth and how shall we know it?

In eighteenth-century Japan there were scores, perhaps hundreds, of
schools of truth within Buddhism. The schools that had enjoyed earlier
popularity, such as Kegon, Shingon, and Tendai, had been superseded

Matsuri Koshi. (Photo by Louis G. Perez)

by Zen and the various so-called Amida Pureland sects (*Jōdo, Jōdo-shinshū, Nichiren*) that held that single invocations of religious formulaic chants were sufficient for salvation. Perhaps 70–80 percent of those who professed to be Buddhists at the time were adherents of some manner of Pureland Buddhism. Virtually all of the peasants were, but their religiosity needs some qualification.

Every person in Japan after 1640 was required to register with the local Buddhist temple, of whatever sect, to prove his or her contempt for Christianity by performing *fumi-e* ("treading in icons"). The system of "temple surety" (*terauke seido*) ensured that Japan was free from the seditious Christian religion. Most people therefore "belonged" to whatever temple was established in the mura or machi in which they lived. But most, it can be argued, probably ascribed to the teachings of one of the Pureland schools, and of course one's religion was as much inherited as was one's status, profession, and property.

There were some Pureland believers among the samurai and chōnin as well, but the former were more often believers (if not practitioners) of Zen. It is said that among the chōnin, they could more properly be described as cultural Buddhists, but concentrated their spiritual energies more toward a secular philosophy known as *Shingaku* (Heart Knowledge) that was heavily influenced by Neo-Confucianism.[5]

The large temple complexes were mere shells of their former pomp and power. They had been stripped of their extensive tax land during

Daibutsu Statue in Kamakura. (Photo by Louis G. Perez)

the sixteenth century and now existed, or rather eked out an existence, by offering service and solace to the populace. Their chief sources of income were to chant sutras at funerals and commemorations, and at particular matsuri (see Chapter 6). Weddings had ceased to be a Buddhist rite and were now really secular in form, if still Shinto in spirit. The other social rites of passage (adulthood, adoption, inheritance, retirement, etc.) were similarly secular. As one Buddhologist has observed:

[A]s it [Buddhism] became firmly established among the Japanese populace, its practices became closely associated with ceremonies in honor of the dead and of ancestors. Ancestors are not necessarily one's own biological forbears, but predecessors in the household line. Ceremonies in honor of deceased family members and ancestors are an essential obligation of descendents, a means to secure ancestral assurance for household prosperity and good fortune.[6]

During the eighteenth century, funerals could only be conducted at Buddhist temples. This was partially to ferret out crypto-Christians who might wish to bury their dead in their own religious ceremonies. It was also a method of keeping track of changes in village population. Temples were required to keep careful registers of all funerals conducted.

The corpse was ritually bathed, the head shaved, and then the body was wrapped in a plain cotton kimono. It would then be cremated (and soon, considering that bodies were not embalmed or kept refrigerated, except naturally, of course, during the winter). After a short family vigil (*otsuya*), when friends and neighbors brought condolence gifts for the family, the ashes were interred in a designated cemetery. The priest would chant special funerary sutras, and then often a symbolic vegetarian meal was shared. The deceased would receive a posthumous Buddhist name (*kaimyō*), which would be written by the priest on two commemorative tablets (*ihai*). One tablet would be tamped into the earth where the ashes were buried, and the other was given to the family to ensconce in their home altar (Butsudan). These ancestral tablets were usually rough, crudely planed laths of wood, but wealthier patrons could buy stone or lacquered wood tablets.

There were carefully prescribed mourning conventions. There were two types: the actual mourning period (*imi*) and the period during which relatives were not to engage in certain acts (*buku*), such as entering Shintō shrines, wearing brightly colored clothing, eating meat, drinking sake, or, in some areas, trimming one's fingernails or shaving one's head. The length was strictly prescribed for each period, appropriate to one's relation to the deceased. For example, a son was required to keep forty-nine days of imi and thirteen months of buku for his parents. For cousins one observed three days of imi and a week of buku. In-laws merited ten days of imi and one month of buku. Perhaps not too surprisingly, women were to observe thirty days of imi and thirteen months of buku for their husbands, but men only twenty days of imi and three months of buku for their wives.[7]

There were also prescribed visits to the grave (*haka mairi*) at seven, fourteen, twenty-one, thirty-five, forty-nine, and one hundred days after the funeral, then on the first, third, seventh, thirteenth, seventeenth, twenty-third, twenty-seventh, thirty-third, thirty-seventh, fiftieth, and one-hundredth anniversaries. Obviously, grandchildren and great-grandchildren usually had to assume the burden after a while. In practice, the forty-nine and one hundred day visits were the most important since a meal was served at that time. The local priest was usually summoned, or the whole family might pay for a commemorative meal at the temple.[8]

More informal rituals, usually consisting of burning incense or offering food, were relegated to the Butsudan. For most peasants who might forget some of these anniversary ceremonies, they could "catch up" at matsuri or some other visit to the temple by paying a few coppers to have a priest include the neglected dearly departed in his sutra chant. As noted in Chapter 6, there were many opportunities (or obligations) to attend to the graves, tablets, or actual ghosts of one's ancestors.

Parenthetically, several of Japan's most persistent taboos and superstitions resulted from funerals. For instance, it was thought unlucky to wrap one's kimono right over left, or to tie one's kimono sash (*obi*) with two knots instead of one, since that is how the corpse is dressed. Handing objects from one set of chopsticks to another recalled the way that bones are picked from cremated ashes. Chopsticks left standing in a bowl of rice are unlucky since that is a dead man's meal. Also, pouring hot water into a cold bath (instead of the reverse) brings bad fortune since that is the manner corpses are bathed. Sleeping with one's head pointing north tempts fate since that is the position of the corpse at the vigil.

Buddhist priests also played the important role in society of being cultural custodian of the past. Literature, both religious and secular, reposed in temple storehouses, as did most of Japan's art treasures over the centuries. Indeed, had it not been for the temples, much of Japanese cultural tradition would have gone up in flames during the ubiquitous and almost constant warfare of the previous three centuries. Countless treasures incorporated into the decor and wealth of many daimyō castles were lost to history.

One might be tempted to conclude that Buddhism was spiritually effete and served no religious purpose in the lives of eighteenth-century Japanese. But this was no more the case than with Christianity in Europe and the Americas at the same time. As such, the temple was still at the heart of Japan's spiritual life, whether it was for spiritual solace or moral education. Rural education took place in temples, and the institutions were called "parish schools" (*terakoya*) if only because frequently the temple was the only public building in the environs. Also, in rural Japan at least, the monks were virtually the only literate persons, except for a few village headmen. They often served as scribes and teachers for the villages. They maintained and nurtured cultural literacy for the community. Many of the priests (particularly Zen monks) were Neo-Confucian scholars, and not a few had read the few Shintō writings as well.

The temple was intimately and organically integrated into the life of the people. It was the center of not only religious but communal life as well. Small Shintō shrines shared space with every temple. Virtually every temple in Japan is "guarded" by the kami. The distinctive religious crossbeam spanning two upright stele (torrii) portals leads the worshipper toward a washing font where one rinses one's hands and mouth. These ablutions are Shinto in origin, but seem altogether appropriate to cleansing oneself before ascending onto a temple veranda.

Bell pulls and small lattices serve Shintō and Buddhist roles alike. The sound of the bells or gongs catches the attention of the Buddha as well as the resident kami, and adherents affix pieces of paper or small votive placards (ema) on which prayers are written to fences and lattices. The use of salt as a purifying agent is more Shintō, but most temples are protected by small piles of the stuff in the corners of a room. Incense serves both religions as well. The smoke of incense is more Buddhist,

Matsuri Koshi. (Photo by Louis G. Perez)

but Shintō also uses it as part of its symbolic ablutions. In some shrines the kami are anthropomorphized into figurines that contain some of the basic Buddhist iconography. In eighteenth-century Japan, one should not be overly surprised to find that the kami and Buddhas themselves had been conflated in the minds of the peasantry. The Sun Buddha Vairokana was often confused with Amaterasu herself, and the small protectors of children (*Jizo*) can be of either faith. Amida and Kannon (the Buddha of Mercy) were commonly thought to be kami by most peasants, who no doubt were covering all religious bets.

As indicated previously, the temple served secular needs as well. To crosscheck family and village population registers, government bureaucrats used the obligatory anti-Christian *terauke seido* (village registers). Because virtually all samurai were literate as a matter of course, there was not the need for ecclesiastics to serve as bureaucrats as in Europe and Latin America. But some samurai and most peasants became literate at the feet of priests, though usually using secular Neo-Confucian texts.

Finally, many of the matsuri took on Buddhist iconography. Many astute priests seized the opportunities to teach or preach their own truths, and I would wager that they all used the festivals to enhance their meager coffers. We know of many temples that would bring out their artistic treasures, not just to air them out, but to raise a few coppers paid by curious revelers. We also know of many priests who doubled in duty, dabbling in shamanic activities as well as serving as custodians for the neighboring Shintō shrines.

For the eighteenth-century peasant at least, religion was therefore a conflation and amalgam of beliefs and rituals. Probably few cared about the intricacies of religious doctrine. What most concerned them was efficacy. If Shintō talismans were sold along with Buddhist amulets, and if Shintō shrine lattices held Buddhist prayers, who cared? As long as the typhoon kami spared the village, the locusts stayed away during Buddha's birthday, the rains came at appropriate times, and the evil wormlike kami beneath the earth stayed content and did not cause earthquakes—well, who could say what had been effective religiously?

Confucianism is properly considered a secular social and political philosophy rather than a religion. **Neo-Confucianism** However, it was treated very much like a religion in eighteenth-century Japan, particularly in its Neo-Confucian incarnation. It was essentially the chief moral system for the society and formed the very raison d'être of the samurai class. Although it never assumed the independent semi-religious charisma in Japan that it did in China, it became virtually inextricable from Buddhism in the period. Apart from the samurai themselves, the chief adherents and scholars of Neo-Confucianism were Zen monks. Not surprisingly, then, it became virtually indistinguishable from the religious ethos of the period.

The basic tenets of classical Confucianism were elaborated by the Chinese philosopher K'ung Fu-tzu in the fifth century B.C.E. He taught that society properly reflects the harmonious cosmos. Social hierarchy is natural and proper and best expressed in the normal human family relationships best characterized by the filial piety that governs relations between father and son. Wisdom is a consequence of experiential learning as well as a product of formal moral education. Nature determines these hierarchies, and humans are best served when moral men rule by example and maintain the natural cosmic harmony in society. Women, being naturally more emotional than men, are to be protected in benevolence, and children are to be nurtured and educated in the proper moral conduct.

The Confucian system prevailed in China for nearly two millennia. But by the twelfth century that society had perhaps outgrown the old formal system if for no other reason that the technologies and population made it unwieldy and cumbersome, given to corruption and formalism. The twelfth-century philosopher Chu Hsi had posited a system of reforms that became known as Neo-Confucianism, called *Shushi* in Japan. Neo-Confucianism was not regarded as religious philosophy. Rather,

the discourse of the Tokugawa was concerned more with the achievement and maintenance of a stable and harmonious society, placing the responsibility for maintaining that delicate equilibrium at the heart of both man and the cosmos squarely on the shoulders of man.[9]

As practiced in eighteenth-century Japan, Shushi maintained that society was properly divided by profession into four main hierarchical and hereditary social classes. At the top were the intellectual-warrior samurai who governed morally because of their superior education. Below them were the peasant farmers who contributed agricultural products to the whole society. Beneath the peasant was the artisan-craftsman who processed agricultural products into manufactured goods for the benefit of everyone. It was right and proper that merchants should be relegated to the bottom of society since they contributed little to the society except the movement of goods from areas of surplus to areas of demand. Merchants were little more than parasites that fed off the lifeblood of the productive classes. Their venality damned them to social opprobrium.

Tokugawa Ieyasu and his military predecessors Oda Nobunaga and Toyotomi Hideyoshi had attempted to extend governance beyond rule by fear and military power to civil legitimacy. Japanese Shushi scholars were employed to write apologia, which were widely disseminated at all levels of society. Within a few generations Shushi had become so thoroughly entrenched as social and political orthodoxy that it took on the trappings of natural law. The bakufu philosopher Hayashi Razan wrote:

> [W]e cannot allow disorder in the relations between the ruler and the subject, and between those who are above and those who are below. The separation into four classes of samurai, farmers, artisans and Merchants . . . is part of the principles of heaven and is the Way which Was taught by the Sage.[10]

In terms of the samurai ruling class, the warriors were coerced and cajoled into a life of bureaucracy. They were told that the moral sage (which apparently they were to become magically) was to value the literary (*bun*) as well as the military (*bu*) arts. Aphorisms abounded to reinforce that henceforth they were to wield the writing brush as adroitly as the sword. They were to become the Elder Brother that nurtured their younger siblings in the absence of the father. They were to be the wise and loyal ministers defending their daimyō, shōgun, and emperor like the Chinese retainers of the fabled dukes of Zhou and Xun. They were to be the arms of their daimyō, the feet of the shōgun, the loyal swords of their emperor. The role of the samurai is covered elsewhere (see Chapter 2). Suffice it to say here that the samurai accepted their new role with alacrity and good grace because they believed that it was central and essential for a harmonious society.

Of course for all society Neo-Confucianism provided a legitimizing cosmic raison d'être. Every loyal subject was to fulfill his cosmic fate by epitomizing his social and political roles. Each class was hereditary, complementary, and mutually exclusive. Everyone was to be content in the honest and sincere pursuit of a life appropriate and proper to one's role in society. The greatest crime was to assume airs beyond one's station in life. The catch phrase was *taigi-mibun*: behavior according to status.

Peasants were constantly reminded how important their contribution was for social harmony. Virtually every government edict reinforced the verities of Shushi morality. Peasant fathers were to rule their households and nurture their children in the moral ways of the ancestors. Children were to be dutiful to their parents; wives were to obey their husbands. Village headmen were reminded that they were the elder brothers, and, if the local priests were not shepherds to their flocks (sheep being practically unknown in Japan), they were certainly to act as moral models and advisors.

As such, Buddhism played an integral role in reinforcing and spreading the Neo-Confucian truths. Zen monks had returned from their religious sojourns in China bearing the Shushi canons. They studied them to find ways that they could contribute to society. They became the local teachers in parish (terakoya) schools. They instructed samurai and even daimyō and bakufu ministers. The semi-official orthodoxy of virtually every Buddhist priest and monk was that one's karma determined one's social station. Proper behavior meant to live a righteous life, according to one's cosmic incarnation. One would be rewarded in the next life. Proper behavior helped work off one's karma. In the next life, good souls were incarnated as samurai; immoral people were reborn merchants, eta, or even animals. Obviously this was a powerful religious and philosophical reinforcement for social control.

For the common chōnin Shushi was a less palatable philosophy if only because it heaped calumny and opprobrium on the heads of hapless merchants. It was limited and cold comfort to be promised karmic rewards in the next life if one had to suffer the slings and arrows of the current one. Nevertheless, not a few wealthy merchants commissioned (or wrote themselves) House Laws to legitimize their own moral taigi-mibun. They enjoined their successors to rise early, work hard, live frugally, trade honestly, and live exemplary moral lives. They hired Shushi masters to instruct their children and tried hard to live honestly and honorably.

Those chōnin who blanched at the thought of the immoral profligacy of their peers in the Licensed Quarters flocked to the teachings of Ishida Baigan (1685–1744), who wrote simplistic moral treatises that argued that sincerity and honesty should be the core of chōnin life. A proto-religion called Heart Learning (Shingaku) resulted from his ideas. Essentially Neo-Confucian in philosophy, it also borrowed heavily from Buddhism and even cited ancient Shintō fables in its moral instruction.

Shamanism Finally, we must also consider the importance of magic, geomancy, divination, and other shamanistic practices and beliefs in the country. This is obviously as amorphous and as chaotic as can be imagined by the term folk belief. If anything, Shintō is systematic by comparison. There is only the plethora of regional and local practices employed by charismatic practitioners. Most of these men and women knew a smattering of the major religious teachings, but used them eclectically and probably haphazardly.

The Taoist geomancy of "Wind and Water" (*feng shui*) had entered Japan throughout the millennium before at the hands of thousands of Chinese and Koreans who had fled to Japan. A number of these political refugees became itinerant Buddhist missionaries (*ubasoku*), who practiced their own brand of religion, much of it liberally laced with Taoism. The primary principle of Taoism is that the earth reflects the greater cosmic balance of energies. The Way (Tao) is best maintained when cosmic complementary opposite elements are balanced in nature. The cosmic binaries of light-dark, dry-moist, male-female, high-low, ethereal-earthy, and so on, affect everything and are, of course, affected by everything else. When the elements are in balance, then the cosmos is in harmony. The essential goal of humanity is to discover how best to maintain that harmony. Hence the need for diviners and geomancers.

One can see how these ideas would meld wonderfully and almost effortlessly with essential Shintō. Over the years, the two amorphous conventions meshed together rather like two banks of fog, and before long the Taoist feng shui geomancers were also simultaneously Shintō shamans. Not that there were schools, curricula, diplomas, or license requirements in this profession. Charismatic practitioners made their own livelihood, based on success and perceived efficacy.

In the countryside shamans probably lived on the cusp of social respectability. We are told that many were principally agrarians who supplemented their incomes by doing a few spiritual tasks throughout the year. They were consulted at lifecourse junctures and crises. Obviously one could not tempt the fates by locating new fields, ditches, roads, houses, and other buildings without resorting to someone who knew about these things. We are told that no Buddhist temple was even contemplated before a shaman could examine the feng shui of the ground. People who had experienced a run of extraordinary bad fortune would consult a shaman for a remedy. Often, all that was needed to "channel" the energy was to "unblock" the natural flow, using mirrors, new ponds, or relocated fences.

Shamans could also divine the future and determine auspicious times for virtually any change in life, such as travel, marriage, adoption, purchase of significant property, and so on. They could consult with the spirits, talk to one's ancestors, and sometimes sit in judgment as disinterested arbiters. Their power was limited only by their reputation, their fees only by the ability to pay and the need to believe.

There is little evidence that shamans behaved in antisocial "black magic" ways. Spells and hexes were usually things to be removed by shamans, not to be induced by them. But shamans being human, it is not unthinkable that greed might lead some of them to behave in this negative way. If it had been common we would expect to find bakufu and daimyō injunctions and laws against it. In general, however, shamans were sought to cure bad fortune, not to cause it.

NOTES

1. Kishimoto Hideo, quoted in H. Byron Earhart, *Religion in the Japanese Experience: Sources and Interpretations*, 2nd ed. (London: Wadsworth Publishing, 1997), 3.

2. Louis G. Perez, *The History of Japan* (Westport, CT: Greenwood Press, 1998).

3. See Earhart, *Religion: Sources*, 10.

4. Cited in ibid., 22.

5. See Tetsuo Najita, *Visions of Virtue in Tokugawa Japan: The Kaitokudo, Merchant Academy of Osaka* (Chicago: University of Chicago Press, 1987).

6. Morioka Kiyomori, quoted in Earhart, *Religion: Sources*, 74.

7. See the convenient chart in Richard Hildreth, *Japan: As It Was and Is*, 2nd ed. (Wilmington, DE: Scholarly Resources, 1973), 441. Compare with Basil Hall Chamberlain, *Japanese Things* (Rutland, VT: Tuttle, 1971), 337.

8. See chart in Chamberlain, *Japanese Things*, 337–38.

9. Earhart, *Religion: Sources*, 106–7.

10. See ibid., 114–15.

5

Language

The Japanese spoken language is a very rich and complex one. It is richly laced with words of the natural environment, particularly of the forests and ocean. Although there is considerable controversy as to the origins of Japanese, most linguists would agree that its syntax and structure are related to the Altaic language groupings of Central Asia, which include Mongolian, Manchu, and Korean as well. There are also many words borrowed from Polynesia and the other South Pacific archipelagoes. So, like Japan's ethnic-genetic origins, the spoken language is apparently primarily from continental Asia, with a significant contribution from littoral Southeast Asia.

Sentence structure typically contains nouns that have no inflections for gender or plurality, but context and word "markers" can connote those meanings. Verbs and adjectives can conjugate for tense, and the "stem-forms" of these words can acquire conditional and negative fragments that create seemingly long and complex "agglutination" compounds. For instance, the verb *kanjiru* (to feel) can agglutinate the word particles *saserare* (caused to), *nak* (is not), *katta* (was), and *raba* (if), to form the perfectly normal, though somewhat cumbersome, verb compound *kanjisaserarenakattaraba* (if I had not been caused to feel). There are particles that indicate direction (to and from), possession, and location. Adjectives and adverbs are somewhat different than in English, but nevertheless generally modify and precede nouns and verbs.

Animate subjects are differentiated from inanimate, and human from nonhuman, and different verbs are used for each. Numbering usually requires "counting markers" to differentiate whether one is counting people, animals, flat objects, long thin ones, or round objects and the like. This is similar to using the English "pair" to indicate objects (pants, scissors, jeans, and eyeglasses) that do not seem to be plural, or a "cup of" for liquids (tea, coffee, cocoa).

The language does not have stress accents as in most European languages, and each syllable is given almost equal stress, cadence, and meter. Unlike Chinese, which is tonal, Japanese is rapid-fire, with each syllable and word pronounced in a rather metronomic manner. Nonspeakers have suggested that Japanese sounds like "pebbles tumbling downstream." The five vowels (a, e, i, o, u), which are pronounced as in Italian or Spanish, can also form two-vowel diphthongs (ai, ei, au, etc.). They can stand alone to form one syllable or combine with consonants (ka, ni, so, mu, etc.). Platal consonant combinations can occur (kyu, byo, ryu, etc.), and double consonants indicate a kind of glottal pause accent (kok-kai, shup-pan). Verbs come at the end of sentences, but sometimes question markers (*ka? no? wa?*) or conjunctions like "so," "therefore," and "however" (*wake, desu ga, soro soro*) appear. Case markers following nouns such as *wa, ga,* and *no* can help differentiate between subjects and objects.

The language is very status-conscious, there being separate nouns, verbs, and even sentence structures that change according to whom one is speaking. A distinct style known as "honorific speech" (*keigo*) indicates that the person to whom one is speaking is a social superior. A separate set of words indicates that one is condescending to a social inferior as well.

Japanese acquired a number of loan words primarily from Chinese in the millennium (sixth–seventeenth centuries) of Japanese cultural, religious, and philosophical borrowing. Since the mid-nineteenth century Japan has borrowed thousands more loan words from the West, particularly from English. In the eighteenth century, however, with the exception of a few leftover Portuguese words (pan—bread; tempura—fritter; jabon—soap), and some garnered from the Dutch in Nagasaki, the Japanese language owed much more to spoken Chinese.

The eighteenth century was a time of tremendous reform and standardization of the Japanese language. A number of "nativist" (*Kokugaku*) scholars, notably Motoori Norinaga (1730–1801) and Fujitani Nariakira (1738–79), undertook a serious examination of the language, building on the work of Kamo Mabuchi.[1] Because they sought to examine the native roots of Japanese society, they delved deeply into the foundations of the spoken traditions in search of "authentic Japan." They sought to differentiate between what was native and what was alien, with the idea that that which was Japanese was inherently superior to all that was foreign.

Accordingly, they examined the early writings of the Japanese, going back to the first written records. In so doing, their philological studies helped to standardize written as well as spoken conventions.

Prior to that time, there were apparently significant regional differences in the oral traditions. It is suggested that the denizens of the far northern reaches of Honshu had considerable difficulty understanding the residents of Shikoku; and the people of the "back of Japan," the area around Kanazawa, did not speak the same dialect as the Kyoto folk or the people of Edo. The forced travels of samurai from all over the country in their annual sojourns (*sankin-kotai*) in Edo most likely helped to smooth out some of the differences between regional dialects. But most people did not travel very far from home, so undoubtedly they continued to communicate in distinctive ways within their native regions. It has also been suggested by at least one historian that girls who had been servants in Edo samurai families brought both manners and a standardized language home to their own natal households.[2]

The work of Motoori and Fujitani as well as that of Kamo before them helped to resolve these differences somewhat, at least among intellectuals. Their philological studies had even greater influence, as they set national standards for writing and pronunciation of the written orthography. By the end of the century it may be said that most Japanese wrote and spoke a common language.

Written Language

Japan did not have an orthography prior to the seventh century, when it began to import the Chinese cultural paradigm. At first, Japanese learned to write Chinese from their continental brethren, but gradually adapted the orthography to the native spoken language. This in itself was a tremendous accomplishment, since the spoken Chinese in its hundreds of dialects and Japanese are about as different from each other as Navaho is from Italian.

Although there are some controversies regarding the nature of the Chinese written characters (*kanji*) in China, perhaps the most succinct explanation remains that of George Sansom. He argues that each kanji is

> [a] symbol which, through a curious but pardonable confusion of thought, is usually styled an ideograph, but is much more accurately described as a logograph. It is a symbol which represents a word. As contrasted with symbols which, like the letters of an alphabet or syllabary, [represent] sounds or combinations of sounds.[3]

When the Japanese began to adapt kanji for their own use, they had both semantic and oral components and were based on Chinese pronunciation. Japanese, therefore, had to adapt the kanji to native usage employing characters sometimes to stand for ideas and sometimes to represent sounds. A kind of shorthand syllabary (*kana*) was invented by the Japanese to write verb and adjective suffixes, as well as to write particles to indicate possession, and to differentiate subject from object (in Chinese these things are indicated by placement in a sentence). There were actually two related kana syllabaries: the round or cursive (*hiragana*) were used to accomplish the tasks cited above, and an angular (*katakana*) set was used in the same general way that italics are used in English, that is, to indicate special words or to indicate stress. Katakana was also used extensively by Buddhist monks to make Japanese-language notations within Asian sutra texts.

Because there are only about fifty kana in each set, these syllabaries were quite simple to memorize and could easily be used to phonetically write native Japanese words. Women in particular employed the kana system for personal correspondence, for poetry, and even for prose writing. This "woman's hand" (*onnade*) produced a rich panoply of literature which flourished in the tenth–eleventh centuries in courtly Kyoto (see Chapter 22).

The orthography is considerably complicated by the pronunciation of the kanji. One system of pronunciation (*on-yomi*) mimics the way that the kanji were pronounced in Chinese when they were borrowed. As many words or characters were borrowed at different times or from different sources, there are numerous on-yomi pronunciations for each character today. One, *to-on-yomi*, mimics the sounds of Tang Dynasty pronunciations; another, *so-on-yomi*, uses Sung Dynasty sounds brought by Zen monks to Japan during the Muromachi era.

Another pronunciation system (*kun-yomi*) takes the sounds of the Japanese native word. This system also has alternate pronunciations for even native words, so that some kanji have up to six alternate readings!

Because Chinese was the language of Confucian (and later Neo-Confucian) political and social writings—as well as that of religion (Buddhism and Taoism)—many kanji took on special pronunciations from those systems. Chinese poetic allusions complicated the orthography as well. It was not really until the eighteenth century that philologists began to standardize the written language throughout the country.

The political pretensions of the Tokugawa bakufu also helped to standardize both spoken and written language systems. The bakufu issued a plethora of edicts, admonishments, and commentaries to the various feudal warlords (daimyō), who after a time learned to mimic the bakufu style of writing. Similarly, the thousands of samurai who accompanied their daimyō to Edo as part of sankin-kotai gradually mimicked the spoken dialects of the capital, if for no other reason than not to appear to be rustic rubes.

The Edo chōnin also developed their own rough patois, which became the language of the licensed entertainment quarters. No doubt traveling merchants took the language back to Ōsaka, Kyoto, and other cities as well. As noted, perhaps servant girls helped to "civilize" their own speech and that of their families after a season in service to samurai households. To be sure, regional dialects continued to flourish in remote areas, particularly in the small offshore islands or deep in the mountains. But by the end of the century scholars agree that the standard Edo dialect had become the common language of the nation.

Because the orthography borrows from the various political, social, and religious written traditions of China, the Japanese language has become a rich amalgam of historical and poetic allusion. The vocabulary of the learned elite is enormous because it borrows from so many discourse conventions. Sanskrit Buddhist terms flavor even ordinary speech and writing. When other foreign loan words flooded into the language in the mid-nineteenth century and beyond, Japan acquired thousands more words and the *roma-ji* (Roman letters) as well. Little wonder that written Japanese has been characterized as "without question the most complicated and involved system of script employed today by any nation on earth; it is also one of the most complex orthographies ever employed by any culture anywhere at any time in human history."[4]

This is undoubtedly so in the case of non-natives attempting to master the language. It is to the credit of the Japanese educational system that 125 million Japanese citizens do so.

NOTES

1. An excellent concise exposition of the Japanese language is Willem A. Grootaers' article "Language" in the *Kodansha Encyclopedia of Japan* (Tokyo: Kodansha, 1989). Much of the following material is taken from that article, as well as George Bedell's piece, "Japanese Language Reforms," in the same volume.

2. Notably Gary P. Leupp, *Servants, Shophands, and Laborers in the Cities of Tokugawa Japan* (Princeton: Princeton University Press, 1992).

3. George B. Sansom, *An Historical Grammar of Japanese* (Tokyo: Tuttle, 1928), 2.

4. Roy Andrew Miller, *Nihongo: In Defense of Japanese* (London: Athlone Press, 1986), 1.

6

Time

It always seems to astound Westerners that other societies have a totally different sense of time than does Christendom. As in most cultures, it is always assumed that one's own cosmology is based on unchanging natural laws, and therefore other systems are by definition wrong. In Japan, time was based upon ancient Chinese ideas regarding celestial and cosmic influences on humanity. One must remember that Chinese astronomy was superior to that of the West until after the fourteenth century or so, when Western scientists surpassed the Chinese. So, by the eighteenth century Japan was scientifically behind the times, if one can forgive the pun.

In fact, the Japanese never really developed the preoccupation with astronomy that characterized other cultures such as the Aztec, Egyptian, Indian, or Persian. The reason that the Japanese depended so much on the Chinese calendar was that they scarcely understood the celestial reasoning behind it. Whenever Japan was isolated from Chinese influence the Japanese calendar went astray until a Buddhist monk returning from China would correct it.[1]

The Japanese calendar was based on the lunar cycle as well as on the Chinese astrological sense of time. The lunar calendar contained twelve months of thirty days each, which of course trailed the solar calendar by five days per year. The Chinese were not particularly abashed by this temporal anomaly, and simply added a full thirteenth (intercalary) month every six years. This presumably made as much sense to them as the European solution—adding an extra day to five months, and having a twenty-eight-day February to which one day is added on leap years—makes to us.

Taoists in China maintained that there were five elements (earth, wood, fire, water, and metal), five directions (center added to the traditional ones), and twelve zodiacal seasons. As in the Western zodiac, each lunar season corresponded to an animal (rat, bull, tiger, hare, dragon, snake, horse, goat, monkey, cock, dog, and boar) as a mnemonic device. In addition, the days were divided into twelve segments (which we call hours) that were not of identical lengths. They could be adjusted to accommodate the varying amount of daylight during the seasons so that both sunrise and sunset were always at six o'clock.

There being no six-day creation story in China, there was therefore no common sense of a week. But, in addition to the four regular seasons, the Chinese further divided time into twenty-four minor seasons (*setsu*) of fifteen days each. Therefore, one can say that setsu were something akin to the British fortnight in the Chinese sense of time. The days of a month were numbered consecutively and had no proper names (Monday, Tuesday, etc.). In fact, neither did the months. One spoke of "the fourth day of the sixth month" rather than "Tuesday, June fourth."

Indeed, the fifteen-day setsu and the thirty-day months were both less important than the sixty-day cycle. The five directions multiplied by twelve zodiac animals completed a "perfect" sixty-day cycle. Six such cycles made 360 days. Taoists believed that the world was in balance and harmony when the full cycles were allowed free rein. Not surprisingly, the "age of man" corresponded to sixty years.

It was believed that human personality (and even fate) was determined by the various time integers. Astrologists could predict personality based upon the time of day, month, and year in a sixty-year cycle when one was born. One should hasten to add that it was as accurate (and self-fulfilling) as any Western astrological computation. Indeed, the guide to this system, *The Book of Changes* (*I Ching*), has achieved some renown in the West recently.

Added to this conundrum are a number of Japanese native ideas about time that complicate the matter even further. It was believed that the kami, particularly the ancestors, approached humanity in certain rhythms. The equinox and solstice changes in the sun were only the most obvious. New moons, eclipses, and other celestial changes also indicated specially auspicious or dangerous days and times for humans. The "shining" (*harebi*) auspicious days were celebrated as holidays when the kami were to be propitiated.

To complicate matters even further, there were Buddhist anniversary dates that were thought to be lucky or taboo for certain events, tasks, and rituals (marriage, harvest, planting, travel, etc.). This is all said to make the reader aware that Japanese dates in the eighteenth century

were somewhat more malleable than those one is accustomed to en-
countering in most historical documents. For most farmers, the calendar
was a complexity that could only be mastered and maintained by the
learned Buddhist monks. For their part, the priests did nothing to make
the people less reliant on their knowledge. They kept watch over time,
tolling bells at the changing of the hours and reminding the peasants
when a certain harebi was approaching. As we have seen, the temple
priests not only dominated the world of humanity, they also kept track
of the rhythms of the dead as well. Observing death anniversaries kept
the village safe from offending dead ancestors, and kept the temple in
livelihood.

In terms of numbering years, the Japanese followed the Chinese system, which enumerated not consecutively from some fixed point, but
according to reign periods (*nengō*). This is not so alien when one thinks
of societies numbering "the fifth year in the reign of Henry VIII" or "the
third year in the second Roosevelt Administration." Actually, had the
nengo always been coterminous with the reign of emperors, the system
would have been easier to fathom. Japanese instead tended to change
the nengo to change the fortune of society. When a particularly inaus-
picious catastrophe (earthquake, eruption of a volcano) hit the country,
the nengo was often changed to give symbolic meaning to an "end of
fortune." It was expected that the kami would be fooled into thinking
that a new era had dawned and that whatever had caused them to wreak
havoc upon Japan had been settled. Since one could not wait until New
Year's to change one's fortunes, nengo sometimes changed in the middle
of the year. Any given year could be the last in the previous nengo and
the first of the new one. For instance, the fifth year of Gembun (1741)
was not only the first year of Kampo, but also the fifth of the twelve-
year reign of the Emperor Sakuramichi. It was not unusual, then, for a
single emperor's reign to encompass one, two, and even three nengo.

According to Japanese cosmology written in the *Kojiki*, time had begun
with the ascension of the first emperor, Jimmu, to the imperial throne in
660 B.C.E. If they had been counting from that fanciful date, then the first
year of Kyowa (1801) might have been listed as 2461. Scarcely anyone
except a few imperial court astrologers had any such idea. Certainly no
one within the bakufu knew or cared much. The people in the countryside cared more about how many days it was until harvest or until the
ancestors returned (*Obon*) to the village.

The calendar was governed by the phases of the moon but
punctuated by religious observances that were a mixture of   **Calendar**
nativist Shintō and imported Chinese Buddhism and Taoism.
Each local shrine and temple had its own particular and unique days of
observance, but some holidays were honored throughout the country.
These latter were primarily agrarian in nature. Planting, transplanting,

and harvesting rhythms were incorporated into this religious calendar, which resembled a farmer's almanac.

The calendar was also heavily influenced by a separate overlay of taboos and superstitions. There were unlucky as well as propitious days, directions, and times of day. Every farmer seemed to know these instinctively, but calendars were published to remind them as well. Shamans abounded throughout the country to foretell and interpret the signs, omens, and astrological events.

It was believed that evil spirits predominated and would approach humans from the northeast. Talismans and amulets were hung in that quarter of residences, and no home had an entrance that faced that direction. On certain days it was considered unlucky to make any journey; on others people refrained from specific tasks involving the preparation of certain foods. Marriages, matsuri, and even funerals were planned around this calendar, and virtually everything was done communally on auspicious "lucky" days appropriate to the season. Certain religious rituals were performed on specific days in order to rid the village or machi of seasonal or occupational pollution.

Indeed, the village communal matsuri were in fact times of celebration and conviviality, but the original intentions were to propitiate the kami and placate the evil spirits. The kami were paraded around the village on portable shrine palanquins (*mikoshi*) to ensure good luck and to drive away evil forces. As we examine the list of matsuri, it would be good to remember the words of the sixteenth-century Jesuit friar Alejandro Valignano, who observed in some exasperation:

> They also have rites and ceremonies so different from those of all the other nations that it seems they deliberately try to be unlike any other people. The things which they do in this respect are beyond imagining and it may truly be said that Japan is a world the reverse of Europe; everything is so different and opposite that they are like us in practically nothing.[2]

The year was a highly structured round of observances (*nenju gyoji*) that began with New Year's (*oshogatsu*).[3] In the lunar calendar used in the eighteenth century, shogatsu began (around the middle of January) with bonfires at the entrances of the village or machi to light the way for the tutelary kami. Everyone was required to clean one's house thoroughly to drive out ritual as well as real dirt and pollution. The now cleansed home was then protected by the Shintō holy rope called *shimenawa*. This double-braided straw rope represented the one used by the kami to keep Amaterasu from returning to her cave (symbolic night) after having been lured back to light the world by dancers in primordial

Shimogamo Procession. (Photo by Louis G. Perez)

time. The shimenawa was also common in every shrine and represented the threshold between the sacred and the profane.

Pounded-rice cakes (mochi) were added to the special vegetable stews (*zoni*) that were cooked during the season. Ritual decorations were made of special branches combined with bamboo; they were believed to ensure fertility in the coming year. Also, two plump mochi cakes were stacked with the smaller at the top. This was called variously *osonae* ("honorable offering") or *kagami* (mirror) mochi, which simulated the mirror central in all shrines. Gifts were bestowed on children by their parents, and the whole family made a round of visits to honor teachers, patrons, and supervisors.

Traditionally, it was the time to settle all debts from the previous year, to start the year with a clean financial slate. In some areas, particularly among the samurai, people would visit the nearby shrine devoted to the kami of war, Hachiman. There, they would buy a ritual white-fletched arrow to ensure good luck for the year. It was believed that all of the year's bad fortune would be attached to the arrow, which would then be burned when one bought a new one the following oshogatsu. In all other areas, families made their first visit to local shrines and temples. Parenthetically, the bakufu used oshogatsu as an anti-Christian day of reckoning. Since most sojourners returned to their native homes (*furusato*), they would be required to tread (*fumi-e*) on Christian images to symbolically demonstrate their contempt for that religion.

Seven days after oshogatsu the kami were thanked for the gift of the seven herbs (*nanakusa*). Traditionally, a few days later everyone opened up the earthen storehouses (*kura biraki*) and the contents were set out to air. Often there would be an impromptu tour of the area to appreciate the neighbors' heirlooms. This was more common in the city than in the villages. On the fifteenth day of the first month the whole country paused to commemorate the anniversary of Buddha's death. Sutras were read around the clock, and for a small gift priests could be persuaded to think of a person's ancestors during the chanting.

Two weeks later the first day of spring (*setsubun*) was observed (corresponding to February 3). Another ritual cleansing took care of any pesky evil spirits. Toasted soya beans were hurled into the corners of the house while one shouted, "Out with the devils!" (*oni wa soto*), and then one went out into the garden and coaxed the good fortune to come inside by shouting, "In with good luck!" (*fuku wa uchi*). Undoubtedly some children used the opportunities to accidentally pelt younger siblings, and visiting in-laws were said to be very circumspect at setsubun. Traditionally one counts the beans that one eats that day, adding one to the sum of one's age for good luck.

First Horse (*Hatsu uma*) festival was celebrated in many parts of rural Japan in the early part of the second month. This was celebrated at the shrines dedicated to the fox kami (*inari*). It was thought to be the appropriate time to fertilize mulberry trees and to plant barley. In many regions, special festivals and rituals (*hari-kuyo*) were performed for "broken things." This was to praise the kami of objects that had served humanity. Broken or worn needles in particular were brought to Awashima shrines throughout the country, where they were stuck into a block of tofu, the idea being that this was their "soft" place of repose after having being stuck into "hard" things during their service.

At the same time, Buddhist sutras were chanted in honor of elephants that died to provide man with ivory and for cats who gave their skins for samisens.[4] This was followed by a celebration of the day traditionally given for the foundation of Japan (February 11), the accession of the first emperor, Jimmu. A week later (the twenty-first day) was celebrated as a commemorative for the death of the Buddhist priest Kobo Daishi.

Young girls looked forward to the Doll Festival (*Hina Matsuri*) on March 3, when ornate dolls were displayed in tiers in the main room of the home. In the eighteenth century in many areas of rural Japan, the dolls still represented the evils of the year, and so they were tossed ceremoniously to be carried away by swift-running rivers. In most areas, however, the dolls were elaborately costumed, since they represented the noble courtiers at the emperor's palace. They also represented the growth and maturity of any girls in the household, who were toasted with a round of *mirin*, a sweetened cooking sake.

In some areas, the week before the vernal equinox was celebrated as a day to honor and to propitiate the tutelary kami (*haru no shanichi*). Special rituals were performed and offerings of spring fruits were laid at the local shrines. Together with the autumnal harvest matsuri, this celebration was the most joyous time of the year for rural Japan. Lots of drunkenness and frivolity characterized the celebration, and it was commonly agreed that anything said on that day would be taken in jest (a kind of April Fools). In modern terms, it was a day to let off steam and to clear the air of any long pent-up animosities.

At the ides of March, Japan celebrated the vernal equinox (*haru no higan*). Another round of offerings was made to the kami, but also the Buddhas. It was a time to visit and clean the ancestral graves. Traditionally, water was poured over the grave markers to ritually cleanse away all pollution. Mochi were offered to the ancestors, and also to all the children. Since most people returned to their native furusato, village headmen often took this opportunity to spruce up village registers.

In most areas of Japan this was the traditional rice planting season, so a festival to "go up into the fields" (*ta ue*) brought the peasants for the collective work. Other festivals were called to transplant on auspicious days, and others to drive insects away (*mushi okuri*). These days were never set precisely, however, being set by local shamans and geomancers according to complex numerological and astrological computations.

Among the most colorful of the celebrations was the Flower Festival (*hana matsuri*), which came in the first week of the fourth month. At this time villagers trudged up into the nearby hills to picnic and gather wildflowers. This symbolically represented recruiting the mountain kami to come down to be domesticated into paddy-rice kami. Since the matsuri coincidentally was held during the time generally celebrated as the birthday of the Buddha (April 8), temples held ceremonies when villagers could pour tea sweetened with licorice (*ama-cha*) over Buddhist statues. Parenthetically, ama-cha was supposed to ward off rats and other vermin, and was said to cure one of intestinal worms if drunk at this time.[5] This was also very often the opening of the spring sumo tournament (*Haru Basho*).

The first day of the next month was usually a good day to plant rice. Traditionally, the transplantation of the seedlings was done forty days later. The first week of the fifth month was Boy's Day (*tango no sekku*), when young boys were given gifts of bows and arrows and kites. Carp streamers were also flown to bring good fortune since it was believed that boys were like carp who prefer to swim upstream against the current.

The sixth month was the most dangerous cycle in Japan. Since it coincided with the start of typhoon season and also a period when many diseases circulated in the countryside, this is altogether understandable.

The month was chock-full of unlucky days, so, unlike in the West, very few marriages were celebrated at this time. The summer solstice (June 22) was said to be particularly precarious. A grand purification ceremony (*Oharai*) was celebrated at the end of the month throughout the country. Paper dolls became ritual scapegoats. They received all of the evils and then were burned at temples and shrines. Again, many amulets and talismans were sold.

The seventh month brought a sense of relief and regeneration. The poignant Star Festival (*Tanabata*) was celebrated to commemorate the annual conjoining of the star-crossed lovers (Vega and Altair), the herdsman and the weaver. The two had been sentenced to rendezvous in the heavens only once per year. The dexterous arts were celebrated in the festivals with displays of embroidery, calligraphy, weaving, and papermaking. Bamboos were decorated with colorful paper on which lovers had written wistful poems.

In the middle of the month, the ancestors were welcomed back into the home at the festival of the dead (*obon*). For two or three days the spirits were feted with gifts of food and sake and were entertained with dances by the whole village. Ancestral graves were refurbished and Buddhist priests were commissioned to chant sutras. Not surprisingly, priests made most of their income (along with fees for funerals) through the sale of amulets during this period. Finally, the now satiated and contented ancestors were sent on their way back to the netherworld. People gathered at the banks of the river to watch and to reminisce nostalgically as floating bright lanterns carried their ancestors away on the current. There was very little of the dread and foreboding of All Souls Day in the West. It was more similar to Halloween or Dia de los Muertos in Latin America.

The eighth month usually coincided with the first weeks of harvest. Depending on the area, various festivals were celebrated in this month. The most common to the country was Moon Viewing (*Tsukimi*), when the moon was brightest in the heavens. The First Fruits (*Niiname sai*) or Scything (*Kariage*) matsuri often were incorporated here, and then two weeks later the Harvest (*Shukaku*) Festival would be celebrated when the crop was in the storehouses. Without doubt this was the most joyous matsuri of the year, always celebrated before the tax collectors came to take away the samurai share. Often the last casks of the year's sake production were opened and consumed. Special rice dumplings (*tsukimi dango*) were made to represent the rice spears.

The autumnal equinox (*aki no higan*) in the ninth month corresponded to the end of the growing season. The rice-paddy kami were released to recreate back in the mountains and special gifts were given to the wind kami to ward off the end of the typhoon season. Often villages feted the tutelary kami (*aki no shanichi*) in the tenth month.

In the third week of the eleventh month the emperor was required to visit Ise Shrine to offer fruits of the harvest to Amaterasu and to his ancestors.

The twelfth month, like the sixth month, was a dangerous time. The country prayed to the water kami (*suijin*) to overpower evil and protect the villages from bad fortune. Preparations began for New Year's in the middle of the month called "the beginning of things" (*koto hajime*). Houses were repaired, evil spirits were exorcised, and the shimenawa were strung out at the entrance to protect the house. The winter solstice (December 22) accelerated preparations for the new year. On the last night of the year, visits were made to shrines in order to expel (*joya*) malignant spirits. And then the religious calendar started all over again with another oshogatsu matsuri.

NOTES

1. I am indebted to both Jim Stanlaw and Roger Thomas for pointing this out to me.

2. Michael Cooper, ed., *They Came to Japan: An Anthology of European Reports on Japan, 1543–1640* (Berkeley: University of California Press, 1965), 229.

3. I have consulted Miyake Histoshi's "The Yearly Round of Observances," reprinted in H. Byron Earhart, *Religion in the Japanese Experience: Sources and Interpretations*, 2nd ed. (London: Wadsworth Publishing, 1997), 207–12.

4. Frederic de Garis, *We Japanese: Being Description of Many of the Customs, Manners, Ceremonies, Festivals, Arts, and Crafts of the Japanese, Besides Numerous Other Subjects*, 3 vols. (Yokohama: Yamagata Press, 1949), 1:160.

5. Basil Hall Chamberlain, *Japanese Things* (Rutland, VT: Tuttle, 1971), 161.

7

Food

The peripatetic Kaempfer once again gives us pause as he describes the wonder of Japanese food in his quaint English:

> all sorts of plants, roots, and prigs, which the season affords, wash'd and clean'd, then boil'd in water with salt; innumerable other dishes peculiar to this country, made of seeds of plants, powder'd roots, and vegetable substances, boil'd or bak'd, dress'd in many different ways, of various shapes and colours, a still-subsisting proof of the indigent and necessitous way of life of their ancestors and the original barrenness of the country, before it was cultivated and improv'd to what it now is.[1]

Japan developed as distinctive a cuisine as can be found anywhere in the world. Highly influenced by Chinese and Korean (and even Portuguese) tastes in its earlier history, Japan developed a unique taste and diet during its two centuries of sakoku isolation. Tastes and culinary conventions would change rapidly after the mid-nineteenth century with the second coming of the West, so eighteenth-century tastes may arguably be said to be the most "natively" and distinctively Japanese.

Traditionally Japanese did not eat much meat. Most historians argue that the traditional Buddhist proscription against killing and eating animals is responsible for this lack of animal protein in the Japanese diet. However, as Susan Hanley notes:

Though meat from four-legged animals was proscribed by Buddhism, those who could afford to hunt ate wild birds, and outcast
classes are known to have eaten animal flesh. This would lend credence to the argument that people gave up meat eating more because commons, woods, and open fields gave way to cropland than
because Buddhism proscribed it.[2]

Simply put, the argument she refers to is that the population density
in Japan made cattle and pigs too expensive and difficult to raise even
for personal use. The postage stamp–sized paddy rice fields simply could
not produce enough silage to maintain such animals. There were no
"open" fields in which to graze them because every speck of land was
employed in growing food for the huge population. Villages might cooperatively maintain two or three water buffalo for communal plowing,
but then that made them too valuable to eat. Chickens were sometimes
kept, but they were groomed for their eggs, not their meat. The chickens
were allowed to roam and scavenge, often on the grounds of religious
complexes.[3] Perhaps their association with sacred places reinforced the
idea that they were not to be killed and eaten.

Curiously, Heian era (794–1185) Japanese apparently ate a type of
cheese, but it fell out of use by the early medieval period. By the fifteenth
century they had developed an aversion for milk or other dairy products.
The European Jesuit Francesco Carletti was surprised that Japanese did
not drink milk, "for which indeed they feel as much disgust as we should
for drinking blood."[4] We have substantial evidence that Japanese made
exceptions to the Buddhist meat-eating proscription, especially with fish.
Several extant feast menus list a profusion of meat dishes among the
wealthy. One 1760 account lists "boar, venison, fox, wolf, bear, badger,
beaver, cat and wild dog."[5] In short, anything that wasn't fast enough
to escape was fair game.

Some culinary historians (admittedly a very specialized discipline)
have argued that the eighteenth-century Japanese diet was really set in
the Muromachi era when the *shojin ryori* (vegetarian) meals served in
Zen Buddhist temples began to predominate.[6] It was during this period
that foodstuffs such as steamed buns (*manju*), bean paste jelly (*yokan*),
fermented bean paste (*miso*), soy sauce (*shoyu*), green horseradish (*wasabi*), and tofu were introduced and became popular.

In the eighteenth century the Japanese ate an astounding variety of
foods. Virtually every specimen of flora and fauna had been tried and
every method of preparation considered. Kaempfer opined, "[L]ittle can
be thought of, but what appears at the table in some dress or other. Many
things, despised by other nations, make up part of their dessert and most
delicate dishes."[7] No doubt he was thinking of the grasshoppers, crickets,
grubs, worms, and other insects that his Japanese hosts feted him with

at banquets. Needless to say, it was to the credit of the Japanese that they did not faint at the sight and smells of the puddings and concoctions that the Dutch routinely ate at Deshima. Many Japanese still do not eat cheese, because they say that it "smells like dirty socks." One man's meat: another man's poison.

Given Japan's obsession with rice, one might be surprised to find that in the eighteenth century it was not a food staple for more than half of the population. The many Shintō religious allusions to rice, and the fact that most peasants were taxed in kind with rice as the main tax staple, all suggest that it was part of everyone's diet. Yet most peasants could not afford to eat it, at least not in its most costly form, "polished" sticky white rice. The Tokugawa bakufu (and therefore most of the daimyō) enjoined peasants to eat the "lesser" grains of wheat, millet, and barley, saving the rice for their social betters. There is a delicious irony (at least for the liberal cynic) that those people wealthy enough to eat white rice suffered from a vitamin deficiency because of it. The polishing process (see Chapter 12) removed all the nutrient bran, and consumers suffered from the lack of vitamin K, developing beriberi. It was called the "Edo Malady" because it seemed to have greatest effect there.

The diet, then, for the peasantry was a very meager and poor one indeed. Yet, demographers tell us that their caloric intake was not appreciably different from that of eighteenth-century European peasants, superior to that of other Asians, Africans, Latin Americans, and certainly better than that of North American slaves and poor farmers. Their salt and nitrite intake was abnormally high from the number of pickled and salt-preserved foods that they ate, but their average life expectancy rates were almost as high as those of northern Europeans at the time.

Most peasants ate the "lesser" grains that they grew on uplands and in rotation with rice crops. They cooked wheat, barley, and millet in one-pot gruels and porridges, spicing them up with all manner of herbs, vegetables, dried fish, and whatever else was available and seemed tasty. Several varieties and hybrids of those grains were grown regionally. Many fruits, berries, nuts, beans, edible grasses (particularly *hie*, which is no longer commonly eaten in Japan), tubers, legumes, and the like were gathered, cultivated, and eaten. Western visitors were astounded to find that in addition to all of the "normal" foods that they recognized from their own diets, Japanese ate many more. Horse chestnuts, sesame, daikon radish, poppy seeds, burdock fronds, and the aforementioned crickets, grasshoppers, and other insects were commonly eaten. In 1775 Carl Peter Thunberg marveled at the variety of herbs and spices that grew in virtually every piece of earth.[8] He reported fennel, dill, anise, succory, parsley, cayenne pepper, ginger, leeks, marjoram, sage, and a score more in addition to many plants and vegetables that he did not recognize.[9]

Virtually every edible (and some that probably should not have been) nut, berry, root, bark, and seed was incorporated into the Japanese diet. Even bitter acorns were pulped, washed with lye, and then rinsed to remove the lye taste. Many of these foods were consumed only to thwart the ravages of famine, but nevertheless, they became more common with culinary experimentation.

Probably the most miraculous vegetable matter was the sweet potato. Virtually every part of the plant could be eaten. The tuber root was very high in carbohydrates and could be stored for very long periods without serious spoilage. Its introduction from abroad in the medieval period saved thousands, perhaps even millions, of lives during food shortages. Two very severe famines during the 1730s and 1780s threatened to kill millions from malnutrition. The judicious use of sweet potato gruels mixed with straw, grass, bark, roots, and virtually every vegetable matter kept peasants alive (though barely so) through the cruel famines. Squashes, melons, pumpkins, gourds, and other vine crops were consumed in total as well. Rinds and stems were pickled, and the seeds were roasted and salted.

Japanese did wonderful things with beans and other legumes. "Green" legumes such as peas, snap beans, sugar pods, snow peas, and the like were cooked and eaten right along with their pods and husks. Others were shucked, dried, and cooked later. Several jams, jellies, and pastes were rendered by various methods to add sweetness, color, and of course protein to a vegetarian diet. Tofu, natto, shoyu, and other soybean products are covered elsewhere (see Chapter 13).

Japanese extracted a number of vegetable oils that they used to good effect. Sesame, safflower, rapeseed, and various nuts produced an ample supply of cooking oil, and much of it could be used in lamps as well. Candles were made from several sources—beeswax, of course, but a number of vegetable oils could be used as well. Peasants did not use much oil to cook; most things were roasted or boiled. In the cities sautés and grilling employed considerably more oil. Vegetable oils were also used to waterproof paper and cloth.

Obviously, peasant fishers and coastal dwellers ate a lot more marine products than their paddy-rice cousins did. Mountain folk subsisted on more forest products. In fact, most of the meat-eating (other than fish) was done in mountain villages, where wild birds and small animals could be obtained.

As a rule, most peasants ate only two meals a day. Most chōnin, who presumably worked at home, could therefore eat lunch (*chujiki*). Samurai were said to eat two meals, like peasants, but from the evidence, they routinely ate three when traveling. The typical meal was said to be *ichiju-issai*—one soup, one vegetable—but what that meant was as side dishes to rice or the other main course. The soup was ordinarily clear broth or miso. A few flecks of dried bonito shavings, a piece of tofu, a shard of seaweed, a swirl of egg, or other flavoring might swim in the soup, but even then it was 99 percent water. The vegetable might very well be a freshly cooked beet, carrot, sweet potato, or one of the myriad "greens," but more likely it was a pickled vegetable (see discussion of preserves, below).

Peasants who could afford a bit of white rice (mixed with other grains) did not eat it in the steamed sticky rice dish that seems to be the ubiquitous repast in modern Japan. To properly steam rice requires washing and rinsing the polishing powder off the rice. Then a precise amount of water is added; it is brought to a rapid boil and tightly covered over a uniform low heat until the water is absorbed. On the traditional open-hearth *irori*, this is very tricky indeed. More often than not, the rice burns at the bottom or dries into a hard crust on the sides. More commonly, then, water is added to the rice, boiled, and then decanted, and the rice allowed to "dry." The rice water was saved, to be used in several recipes. Leftover rice can be rolled into balls, which can be stuffed with all sorts of bean paste, vegetables, and the like and then wrapped in a leaf to be eaten as a snack in the field or on the road.

Rice was also ground into flour, which could be used to make all manner of things including *senbei* (rice crackers), *yakimochi* (grilled hard bread), steamed or boiled dumplings (*suiton*), and noodles. Pounded rice cakes (mochi) were a great treat, particularly in soups and as a snack at matsuri. Buns, cakes, noodles, and crackers were made from wheat and barley flour too.

Food for the chōnin and lower samurai classes was not altogether different than for their peasant cousins, except that there was a great deal more available for the city folk. Because the bakufu and daimyō feared that their armed samurai might rise in rebellion if deprived of food, most cities fared rather better than the countryside in times of want and famine.

The pitiless samurai took what they needed and cared little for the peasants, whom they thought of as subhuman anyway. Before the sixteenth century samurai lived out in the countryside in something like individual fiefs. Because they lived among the peasants, they probably were loath to see the bloated stomachs of starving peasant children. But in the eighteenth century, most samurai and chōnin never even actually saw the peasantry.

Not surprisingly, then, city folk routinely saw better and more food. Demographers suggest that chōnin and samurai probably consumed half again as many daily calories as the peasants. City folk also ate dramatically more protein as well. Ann Jannatta suggests that urban dwellers probably did not live too much longer than rural peasants, perhaps because of a somewhat greater risk of communicable diseases. In any case, the average Japanese was better off than other Asians, Africans, Americans (of both continents), and southern Europeans. Perhaps this was because they experimented with many different food sources and because few people lived more than fifty miles from an ocean abundant with food.

Drink   The two most popular drinks at the time were hot water and tea. The poorer folk often could not afford tea (let alone sake), so it was common to drink hot water with their meals. Experience taught them that with the exception of the high mountain streams, cold water often made people sick due to pollutants from farming communities. There were several superstitions regarding drinking cold water as well. A popular variant was to drink the water used to wash and "start" the cooking of rice. When the rice water began to boil, some would be decanted to allow the rice to steam uncovered. The peasants were right that this water was healthy. The boiling killed most of the bacteria, and the powder rinsed off the rice retained some of the nutrients left from polishing off the bran. Soups were mostly hot water also, and the most common way to rinse one's bowl after a meal was to pour hot water into it and then drink it.

By this time poor quality tea was relatively inexpensive. Peasant tea was often stems and lower leaves and required a considerably longer time to steep than the premium teas. It was common to toss a pinch of tea into a pot of water and let it boil for several minutes. It was less bitter that way, and the principal properties of tea (caffeine and tannic acid) steeped into the water anyway. A cheap alternative was boiled wheat tea (*mugi-cha*), which was often drunk after cooling during the hot summer months. Herb, citrus peel, and various grasses could add flavor and zest to hot water as well. Many had medicinal qualities as an added bonus.

Those who could afford good quality tea rarely drank anything else. Introduced into Japan by Chinese Buddhist priests, it was chiefly the drink of drowsy monks who would quaff a bowl of the bitter liquid to ward off sleep during late-night meditations. The Zen tea ritual (*chanoyu*) had popularized the drink in the medieval period, and by the seventeenth century it had become popular with the common folk as well. Two quotations from Kaempfer suggest that he too became an aficionado during his sojourn in Japan.

I Believe, that there is no plant yet known in the world, whose infusion or decoction, taken so plentifully, as that of Tea is in Japan, sits so easy upon the stomach, passes quicker through the body, or so gently refreshes the drooping animal spirits, and recreates the mind.[10]

To sum up the virtues of this liquor in a few words, it opens the obstructions, cleanses the blood, and more particularly washes away that tartarous matter which is the efficient cause of calculous concretions, nephritick and gouty distempers.[11]

The other major drink in Japan was of course sake. Older than written history itself, it had attained a prime status in the society and in the Shintō religion. Its preparation (see Chapter 13) had been refined over perhaps two millennia. By the eighteenth century it was produced in huge quantities, primarily in the larger cities, where white rice accumulated through taxation. There were perhaps a score of grades and common rankings, depending on their intoxicating properties, taste, clearness, and even smell. It was used as a social lubricant, of course, but also in various Shintō rituals. It was always thought to be an excellent offering to the kami, and it always seemed to be so pleasant to share a drop or two with the ancestors as well.

The bakufu issued an almost annual proscription against its manufacture and consumption among the peasantry, and it often advised the chōnin to avoid it as well. The fact that the proscription had to be issued so often and so regularly suggests that someone was not taking the rules very much to heart. Village headmen, when called on the carpet (the tatami?) by their samurai betters for allowing it in their villages, always appealed to the fact that sake had sacramental uses that could not be ignored.

Virtually any peasant with enough common sense to follow a recipe could prepare a preliminary liquor called "cloudy sake" (*shochu*), and a few could make pretty good sake as well. Few peasants could afford to buy sake from a proper brewer, but sake production was an excellent way to hide surplus rice, and it could turn a tidy profit or garner social prestige if it was donated to the local matsuri.

The word connotes something entirely different in Japan than in the American farmhouse. Generally what is meant **Preserves** was to pickle, though that suggests something quite different in the rest of the world too. Pickling, salting, or desiccating in Japan preserved virtually every foodstuff. The intent was to save the food for a time when the product would be otherwise unavailable. Japanese aficionados also wax poetic about preserving the crispness and pleasure of mastication as much as they do about the subtle or pungent flavors that pique and sate the appetite. The cynic might note that one could flavor and maintain the mastication value of twigs and sticks too; the important element here remains the nutritive and caloric value.

All sorts of vegetable matter was chopped and sliced into bite-size pieces that were steeped in brine or vinegar for months. Various spices, herbs, and seasonings (according to closely guarded secret recipes) were added to enhance the flavor of the pickles (*tsukemono*), though dill was never used for cucumber pickles, and chili peppers were not added to fermented cabbage (Korean *kimchee*) until fairly late in the nineteenth century. Every eighteenth-century farmhouse contained a tsukemono barrel. The pickles were kept tightly packed and sealed by a curious method of weighting the wooden lid with a large stone. That way, the cook could always tell exactly how much liquid (as well as how it tasted) was in the crock without lifting the lid. A few pickles accompanied virtually every meal, and it was this that constituted the vegetable in the traditional ichiju-issai meal.

Many foods were preserved in salt also. Most of these were marine products, but there were nuts and vegetables as well. The favorite was *umeboshi* (dried plum). Japanese did not jerk meat, but fish were packed in salt or desiccated. The most common was bonito, which when dried would flake into bits to flavor soup and stews. Sardine, squid, sea urchin, anemone, octopus, abalone, and hundreds of other marine products were sun-dried, often in thin slices to facilitate the desiccation. Scores of seaweed, kelp (*konbu*), and other ocean "grasses" were dried as well. Virtually everyone is familiar with the sheets of seaweed (*nori*) used to wrap a type of *sushi* (*nori-maki*), but a more common use was to cut it into strips for soup flavoring. It could be diced up into tiny pieces and sprinkled over steamed rice to good effect. It was used to wrap rice balls (*onigiri*) as well.

Fish was also pulped and pressed for oil. The resulting dross was dried into fishmeal cakes to be used for fertilizer. An astounding number of other marine products were routinely harvested, including whale blubber, baleen, ambergris, shark fin, squid ink, dried shrimp, cuttlefish, clams, mollusks, mussels, and oysters. A profusion of other products (including their skins, shells, and exudations) was harvested and eaten as delicacies or used in other ways. It would seem positive proof that Japanese will eat virtually anything when one considers the consumption of the otherwise poisonous blowfish (*fugu*). Not many societies would continue to eat such a product given the evidence that some people do not survive the gastronomic experience.

A hundred varieties of mushrooms, morels, and other edible fungi were consumed fresh or were dried to be used later. The same is so with many grasses, leaves, and barks. One may very well wonder how many people sickened or died in culinary experimentation, but virtually everything that grows in Japan was eaten. Even the peels and rinds of fruits, melons, gourds, and squashes were routinely preserved. Citrus peels were glacéed in sugar and eaten like candy. As far as sugar was concerned, Japanese did not extract it from beets, but relied upon the Satsuma han in the far western part of the country to import cane sugar from the Ryukyus. It was therefore expensive, but since the average eighteenth-century Japanese never developed a sweet tooth, even peasants could purchase a handful for a few coppers.

More problematic was salt. Because it is essential for good health, and because the Japanese developed several preserving methods based on salt, there was a great demand for it. Virtually any seaside resident could produce it by simple evaporation. But in order to produce the large quantities demanded by the society, other methods had to be developed. The most obvious and therefore the most common method was to accelerate evaporation by boiling seawater. This required a great deal of fuel to keep the kettles boiling.

In search of cheap fuel, some anonymous person tried burning dried seaweed. It was discovered that the ashes were very high in precipitated sea salt. *Moshiogusa* seaweed soaked in heavy sea brine was therefore dried, then burned (killing two birds with one stone) to heat the kettles. The ashes were dumped into the brine, the salt sinking and the carbon floating away when decanted. A constant steeping, drying, and boiling produced much more salt, much more quickly, than any other method.[12]

Most Japanese ate their meals at home.[13] For centuries the only places where one could eat out were in Buddhist temples. Most temples provided simple vegetarian meals **Restaurants** for pilgrims and for funeral commemorative meals. Indeed, some have argued that the temples provided a kind of model template for meatless meals for the society.

With the advent of the Tokugawa bakufu's sankin-kotai regulations, however, there were obvious reasons why hostels, inns, and restaurants would spring up along the major highways to Edo. The legions of samurai traveling with their daimyō to and from Edo required sustenance. The inns licensed by the bakufu to provide shelter for these traveling hordes branched out to provide meals for other travelers as well. Merchants and transporters of rice needed food and shelter too.

The second reason why restaurants became popular was the creation of Licensed Quarters to contain brothels and theaters within tightly controlled districts. Once the Gay Quarters had been established, it was altogether natural to provide a bit of a nosh for the revelers that flocked there. Indeed, many theaters catered snacks and even complete meals for their patrons. Because the theater bill might run for eight to ten hours, it was reasonable to provide food and drink during the performance.

Sake, tea, noodles, grilled skewers of foods, hot rice crackers, steamed buns, grilled *gyoza* dumplings, and bowls of soup were sold within the theaters and also at nearby stalls. Some suggest that the theater produced the cold "box lunch" (*bento*) that pervades train and bus stations through the country today. Many of these stalls put down roots, so to speak. They bargained with the landowners for permanent shops where patrons could dependably buy a quick, cheap snack, meal, or cup to satisfy their gustatory needs, going to or from satisfying their carnal appetites.

By the eighteenth century there were literally hundreds of such small shops, and perhaps a score or more regular restaurants in the Yoshiwara district of Edo alone. Similar eating places sprang up in Ōsaka, Nagasaki, Kyoto, Sendai, Kanazawa, and the other dozen or so large cities in the country. By mid-century there were perhaps thousands of places that made their regular livelihood catering food. Every post station along the five major highways had scores of food or drink shops. And there were fifty-three such stations along the Tōkaidō alone.

By the end of the century it is estimated that one-quarter of the male population in Edo ate their daily lunch (*chujiki*) at noodle stands and shops, and many more dined out at least once a week on the way to the theater or brothel. One must remember that there were twice as many men in Edo as there were women at any given time because of sankin-kotai, so the need for female companionship of any meaning took those men to the Gay Quarters. Samurai ate their two meals per day in their barracks or at communal kitchens within their daimyō's compound. Chōnin ate breakfast and dinner at home, but often took their midday break in food shops.

Within the Licensed Quarters tea and sake shops sprang up as places of assignation. Freelance prostitutes met prospective patrons in these shops, often serving as waitresses and maids as they waited. Originally, not much in the way of food was purveyed there, but an enterprising shop owner could always find a willing stall keeper to take up residence in his shop to provide a few salty snacks to encourage patrons to drink more sake or tea. For that reason, Japan developed an inordinate number of steamed, grilled, salted, and pickled tidbits to whet one's thirst. Japan's touted late night bar culture probably originated in late eighteenth-century Edo Yoshiwara.

We find abundant evidence that many of these restaurants, in Edo and Ōsaka especially, developed extensive and sophisticated cuisines. They took advantage of the popularity of cookbooks at the time and published their own as advertisements. Most were printed on cheap paper but very often included vibrantly colored woodblock (*ukiyo-e*) prints to attract the attention of customers. Perhaps a score or more restaurants in Edo (and a lesser number in Ōsaka and Kyoto) became renowned around the whole country, and not a few continue to exist and prosper two centuries later. The same can be said about popular urban inns (*ryokan*). For all of these popular establishments, it helped that writers of cheap pulp fiction referred to fictional characters patronizing actual establishments by name. The readers of these stories flocked to these places to feel part of the gay life. Perhaps they too would encounter a rare beauty and fall passionately (if tragically) in love.

River ferry with a floating "restaurant" boat alongside. Note the straw roof with straw hats and packages hung on the ridgepole. Woodblock print by Ando Hiroshige. (Courtesy of Asia Library, University of Michigan)

Cooking Styles

There were a number of specific cooking styles (*ryori*) that took on almost philosophic pretentions. As noted previously, the Buddhist vegetarian *shojin ryori* style probably was the most important method used throughout the country. Because meats were restricted, the style became especially inventive in creating savory dishes that were nutritious as well. Shojin integrated many new ingredients brought back from China by monks and pilgrims. Tofu, shoyu, natto, and the other soybean extracts came to Japan in the baggage of wandering monks.

The specialized style used in making food for matsuri (*gyoji ryori*) gained wide acceptance, but only as an annual luxury. Most of these highly spiced foods were simply too expensive to be eaten regularly, though some restaurants in the large cities produced them all year round. Special delicacies like pounded rice cakes (mochi), rice cakes smothered with sweet bean paste (*botamochi*), raw fish with vinegared rice (*sushi* and *sashimi*), and the various stews, dumplings, flavored sake, and the like, all were specific to the annual matsuri celebrations. Most village women knew how to prepare these dishes, but cookbooks abounded to remind them as well.

Banquet-style cooking (*honzen ryori*) is named after the short tray table (*honzen*) on which the meal is traditionally served at weddings, funerals, and special commemorative meals. Traditionally, since these meals were usually served at temples, this style was mostly vegetarian in ingredients. After a time, however, the meal began to include fish as well. The one soup and three side dish style employed the usual steamed rice, pickles, and clear broth soup, but also included sushi, sashimi, and grilled fish. Ideally, each dish was to have a taste distinctive from, but complementary to, the dish served before and after. A little rice began the meal, followed by the soup, then the other dishes accompanied by more rice. The pickles (*tsukemono*) and the rest of the rice concluded the meal. At more elaborate banquets, several trays could be presented in turn. Obviously only tiny amounts of each dish were eaten, and the visual presentation was often as important as the food itself. Without doubt, this style influenced Japanese cooking as a whole. Like the shojin ryori temple style, honzen ryori became a nationwide standard style.

Chakaiseki ryori has a curious beginning and a charming, evocative name. It means something like "tea (served) with stones in one's pockets." It refers to the Zen monks who placed warm hearthstones in their sleeve pockets to keep themselves warm during their cold winter meditations. The meager food served to them with the bitter hot green tea became the hallmark of this style of cooking. It is similar to the honzen ryori in content, though not in the quantity of food. Seasonal foods are incorporated, as are many pickles (for the winter) and very watery soups. A particular soup eaten at the end of the meal is called "washing chopsticks" (*hashi-arai*) and is intended to wash one's bowl as well as to take advantage of every little scrap of food left.

Kaiseki ryori was originally intended as snacks served with sake. Most of the foods were therefore similar to appetizers, that is, foods designed to whet one's thirst for more sake. Particular attention was paid to tastes that complemented the taste of sake. Traditionally, rice and hot tea (often together in *chazuke*) were served last to help one sober up before leaving the restaurant or sake shop. Kaiseki also employed the grilled skewers of the *yakimono*.

Yakimono, which means "grilled things," used several methods of grilling. "Small fry" fish like herring, *ayu*, *tai*, and sardines were skewered on a length of split bamboo or placed in wire meshes to be grilled directly on the charcoals. A salt grilling was also employed, as was grilling on hibachi iron grates. The fish were carefully gutted and cleaned before grilling and often basted with savory sauces. Vegetables, shellfish, and, in some regions, even meat were also skewered and grilled. Sometimes the food was dipped in beaten eggyolk and rolled in flour or fish paste after an initial grilling, and then regrilled to add a distinctive taste. This became the ancestor of *teriyaki* and *yakitori* styles as well.

Nabe ryori is really a very old style of cooking when peasants dumped virtually everything edible into one stew pot suspended over the open-hearth *irori*. Nabe is cooked in one pot over a brazier. A soup stock is boiled and then various vegetables are introduced and eaten as they cook in much the same way that fondue is made. A dish of rice and dipping sauces complement the meal as several people sit around the nabe pot and cooperatively cook their own dinner. Obviously, the combination of foods cooked would change the flavor of the soup after everything had been scooped out. It was always a special treat to drop in some noodles at the end and then share them and the broth. At New Year's mochi would be dropped in instead, and the sticky, glutinous jelly would absorb as well as sweeten the soup. *Sukiyaki* was a variant of nabe, as was the protein-rich fish stew (*chanko-nabe*) eaten by sumo wrestlers.

Hundreds of specialized dishes became popular during the eighteenth century. Many of them can be sorted into groups according to the method of preparation, but most are added to the various kinds of ryori as side dishes or snacks. We will touch upon only the most common types of preparation rather than list an exhausting schedule of specific dishes. *Agemono* are foods which are deep-fried in vegetable oil. Perhaps the most familiar to Westerners are *tempura*. The name comes from the Portuguese *temporas* ("timely"), which were foods eaten during the meatless Lenten "times." Shrimp and various vegetables are dipped in a flour batter and then quick-fried in very hot oil. *Kara-age* are foods rolled in arrowroot starch before frying. This tends to sear in the flavor while giving the surface a crunchy quality. Clams, oysters, mussels, and other shellfish are favorites that were commonly cooked this way and served as snacks or incorporated into the kaiseki ryori. *Suage* are foods fried without batter.

There are a number of vinegared dishes besides pickled vegetables. *Sunomono* was principally fish and vegetables dressed with marinades made of rice vinegar (*komezu*), shoyu, sweetened sake (*mirin*), bean pastes, salt, ginger, sesame oil, or a profusion of other spices. Originally intended to hide the taste of "scrap" foods, sunomono became a favorite, and even bream, prawns, and crab were flavored with vinegar concoctions.

Nimono are various kinds of stews, some of which could fit under nabe ryori. *Mushimono* means to steam the food. Most ingredients were salted or marinated before steaming. *Nerimono* was to beat the food into a paste, which could be seasoned, rolled into balls with beaten eggs, floured, and then fried or grilled. *Menrui* is a generic name for noodle dishes, including *somen, soba,* and *udon.* These were served in a large bowl of broth, sprinkled with bits of vegetable, meat, or whatever was left over from other meals. Similarly, steamed rice served in a large ceramic bowl (*donburi*) with other foods heaped on top, and rice gruels (*zosui*) both came under the name of *gohan-mono.* The various soups were called *shirumono.* Several key ingredients were used to make distinctively flavored types of soup. *Kombu* (sea tangle or kelp), dried bonito flakes (*katsuobushi*), fermented soy paste (miso), and shoyu are only the most common. *Yosemono* is made by adding agar to make a kind of gelatin.

A profusion of seasonings was added to foods. The list is nearly endless since regional and seasonal variations make the combination of spices, herbs, sauces, and other ingredients almost infinite. As noted, salt, shoyu, miso, vinegar, sake, mirin (sweetened sake), and, more rarely, sugar, were all very common. But so were the various herbs, seeds, dried grasses, nuts, berries, roots, seaweed, dried fish and marine products, and even flower petals. A special mixture called seven-taste pepper was sprinkled on many soups as well as noodle, rice, and other dishes. This was probably one of the first national commercial foods and is deemed an ancestor to the *Ajinomoto* that Japanese sprinkle on virtually every food eaten in restaurants. It consisted of red and brown pepper, poppy, hemp and rapeseed, dried orange peel, and diced nori seaweed.

All in all, Japanese in the eighteenth century had an astonishing number of flavorful foods available to them that helped to brighten up their otherwise drab diets. Most peasants rarely tasted more than perhaps a hundred, and most of those were relegated to matsuri. Rich peasants, travelers, and people who lived in the larger cities had thousands to choose from. As in all other agrarian societies, the producers of food saw the least of it. Their better-situated cousins could revel in the plethora of distinct foods; the peasants eked out a poor existence with soup, gruel, and a few pickles.

Various culinary tools were essential for cooking even the simplest foods. The most basic dishes could be pro- **Culinary Tools** duced using only a few implements. Chopsticks (*hashi*) were very easy to make and to use. Japanese hashi were much shorter than ones used by the Chinese. Simple split bamboo or smoothed straight twigs could be fashioned in a few seconds. Most Japanese had a personal lacquered pair, which was kept separate with his/her own individual bowl and cup.

Tradition dictated that the length of the hashi correspond to the span from one's thumb to one's pinkie, and they were to be used in specific ways lest one offend the kami. One was never to leave them stuck into a bowl of rice, since that is how small bowls of rice were offered to the kami and dead ancestors. One was never to gesture with or point the chopsticks at other people, and one was never to pass bits of food to another by transferring them from one set of hashi to another. The latter is because that is how bones are culled from the ashes after cremation. Simple courtesy prevented people from dipping into a common dish without turning the hashi around to use the butt ends to fish out something.

Ceramic bowls called *chawan* were intended for personal servings of soup, rice, or noodles. Virtually everyone, even poor peasants, had their own personal chawan. Smaller bowls (*hachi*) with lids to keep the contents hot were used for soup, tea, and even sake. This was the extent of the eating implements of most peasants. Many managed their meals with only the chawan and hashi. They cooked in large metal pots (*nabe*) into which they put all the ingredients of a meal except the tsukemono pickles, which were set in the middle for everyone to share. Most peasants owned a few simple knives or choppers, and most fashioned crude spatulas, spoons, and ladles out of wood in order to stir the food while it cooked.

Wealthier people, of course, had a profusion of culinary tools, all specialized for separate tasks and uses. The large platter (*sara*) was either lacquered wood or ceramic and was used for large communal dishes such as whole fish, steamed vegetables, and the like. Steamed rice or noodles were taken directly from their cooking pots and ladled into the individual chawan.

A scored clay mortar (*suribachi*) used with wooden pestles (*surikogi*) was used to grind ingredients. *Zaru* (bamboo baskets) were used as colanders; metal graters (*oroshigane*) were used to grate white radishes (*daikon*), green horseradish (*wasabi*), and other tuber roots; teapots (*kyusu*) were used to boil water; steamers (*nagashikan*), rice pots (*kama*), and large soup bowls (*wan*) were employed for obvious uses. In addition there were scores of very specialized utensils for very specific purposes. *Makisu*, for example, were lengths of split bamboo tied together that were used to roll sushi wrapped in sheets of dried seaweed (*nori*).

Tokkuri are long cylindrical ceramic bottles within which to warm sake, which was poured into thimble-size *sakazuki* cups. Special boning and slicing knives (*sashimi-bocho*), vegetable choppers (*usuba-bocho*), and other knives were used on wooden chopping blocks and cutting boards (*man-aita*). As noted, meals were served in small dishes, plates, bowls, and baskets, neatly arranged on legged wooden tray tables (*zen*) for maximum aesthetic effect.

The principal hearths were the traditional open-hearth irori, the hibachi grill, and the earthen stove (*kamadō*). The kamado were made of adobe-like clay and had doors for feeding the fire on the sides and one or more holes in the top where one could place several pots at one time. They resembled squarish Ben Franklin stoves.

Tobacco   Though technically tobacco is neither food nor drink, the Japanese categorize it as such, since their verbs that indicate ingesting anything by mouth include smoking. Tobacco was not native to Asia, being a product from the Americas. The Portuguese brought it to Japan in the sixteenth century. Cigar, snuff, and cigarette smoking never became popular, but pipe smoking was very common. By the early seventeenth century tobacco was grown in several areas, chiefly in the southwestern part of the country. It was cultivated, dried, and cured in much the same manner that it is all over the world. It was cut very finely and smoked in tiny "one puff" clay pipes (*kiseru*). It was not a long, leisurely, ruminating activity as in most of the world, but it was very much a social activity.

Every guest could expect to receive at least two offers of hospitality: a cup of hot tea and a smoke. Special *tabako-bon* braziers were kept handy at most inns, restaurants, teashops, brothels, and substantial homes. The brazier was filled with fine sand mixed with charcoal ash but had a small drawer built into the side where tobacco was stored. The guest was invited to fill one of the long-stemmed miniature pipes and light it with a live charcoal shard fished from the warming hibachi with a special set of iron tongs or tweezers. One could expect three or four puffs of smoke from a pipeful before passing it on. Waitresses, geisha, and maids specialized in the preparation of a properly filled and tamped pipe and could be depended upon to fish out a live coal with which to light it.

Many people, women as well as men, carried their own pipes and tobacco in special pouches, but they usually had to wait for an inn or teashop where they could get a light. It is said that if one was on the road after dusk and stumbled upon a group of beggars and vagabonds huddling around a fire, one could not pass without stopping to share one's pipe (and get a light in the bargain).

What passed for physicians in Japan (indeed, the world) recommended tobacco to soothe the nerves and settle the stomach. Perhaps the leisure of drinking a cup of hot tea and relaxing in social conviviality with a few whiffs of tobacco did visibly improve the humor of most people. It was said that even condemned criminals could not be deprived of a last puff of tobacco before shuffling off their mortal coil.

NOTES

1. Engelbert Kaempfer, *The History of Japan: Together with a Description of the Kingdom of Siam*, 3 vols., trans. J. G. Scheuchzer (Glasgow: James MacLehose and Sons, 1906), 2:328.

2. Susan B. Hanley, *Everyday Things in Premodern Japan: The Hidden Legacy of Material Culture* (Berkeley: University of California Press, 1997), 65.

3. Shinzaburō Oishi, "The Bakuhan System" (Mikiso Hane, trans.), in Chie Nakane and Shinzaburō Oishi, eds., *Tokugawa Japan: The Social and Economic Antecedents of Modern Japan* (Tokyo: University of Tokyo Press, 1990), 236.

4. Cooper, Michael, ed., *They Came to Japan: An Anthology of European Reports on Japan, 1543–1640* (Berkeley: University of California Press, 1965), 7.

5. Hanley, *Everyday Things*, 66.

6. Notably Watanabe Minoru in his work *Nihon shoku seikatsu-shi* (Tokyo: Yoshikawa Kobunkan, 1964).

7. Kaempfer, *History of Japan*, 3:314.

8. Thunberg (1743–1828) was a Swedish physician and botanist employed by the Dutch who visited Japan in 1775 and collected over 800 flora specimens.

9. Richard Hildreth, *Japan: As It Was and Is*, 2nd ed. (Wilmington, DE: Scholarly Resources, 1973), 396.

10. Kaempfer, *History of Japan*, 3:241.

11. Ibid., 3:240.

12. Louis-Frédéric, *Daily Life in Japan at the Time of the Samurai, 1185–1603*, trans. Eileen M. Lowe (New York: Praeger Books, 1972), 136.

13. The remainder of this chapter is based loosely on the article on "Food" in the *Kodansha Encyclopedia of Japan* (Tokyo: Kodansha, 19).

8

Clothing

By the eighteenth century Japanese clothing was fairly well standardized, not only in general style, but in size as well. Since virtually everyone in the country was of same genetic stock, there was little need to make several different sizes to accommodate for body size. A standard adult size was made for each gender, and another for all children. Adjustments could be made with a few tucks here and a few basting stitches there. Even today, the kimono (which simply means "clothing"), or, more accurately, the *kosode* robe, is made in the same general way.

Prior to the early sixteenth century there were really very few choices for clothing materials. The wealthy wore silk, and the poor wore rough clothing made from hemp, ramie, mulberry, or wisteria vine fiber. The introduction of cotton to Japan revolutionized clothing so that virtually everyone wore cotton for "everyday," and silk was saved for special occasions. In some regions of the country a mulberry-like bark was beaten into submission and worn as very rough clothing. The Ainu in the far north wore animal skins, but basically everyone else wore cotton.[1]

As in the West, there was an incredible variety of specialized items of clothing, mostly to designate social status, but a few to facilitate certain professions. Fundamental to virtually every costume was the kosode. This loose robe was simplicity itself. It was cut from a single simple loomed piece of cloth twelve yards long by fourteen inches wide. It was sectioned into eight rectangular pieces (two back, two front, and one each for the collar, overcollar, and two sleeves), and could be sewn together in an hour or disassembled for laundering within a few minutes. The pattern and length of bolt cloth were identical for every adult male (another for females). The children's kosode was cut to about two-thirds size and could accommodate children from about age six to about age thirteen, when they would be presented symbolically with their first adult kosode.

The robe was worn somewhat loosely by males with the front left panel folding over the right (to do the opposite was to tempt fate, since only a corpse was dressed right over left) to a comfortable snugness. The robe traditionally was held together with a simple sash tied at the waist. In the late sixteenth century women began to emulate entertainers who wore wide sashes (obi) that often immobilized their complete torsos from the hips to under the breasts. More often, the obi was about a foot wide and several feet long and was wrapped around the body several times to snugly encase the ribcage. Wealthy women tended to wear the more ornate embroidered obi, and men and poorer women wore simple dyed cotton ones.

In ancient times the nobility wore several layers of kosode, partly to keep the body warm in the drafty buildings of the court during the winter, but also to display a dazzling array of color-coordinated silk ensembles. The inner gowns were ankle-length, but the sumptuous (sometimes padded) outer gowns trailed after the wearer like a bridal train. The poor wore knee-length kosode, which they tucked up into the sash whenever they were at work.

The bakufu, being anxious to create artificial social barriers between classes, mandated what types of clothing were appropriate to each class. Almost each year the bakufu would reissue sumptuary edicts that forbade chōnin to wear silk, carry swords, wear samurai hairstyles, or otherwise dress ostentatiously. There were occasional but rare public punishments for chōnin caught dressing above their station. More commonly, when the bakufu chose to make a special spectacle of merchant parasitic wealth, a hapless merchant was paraded around in public wearing inappropriate clothes that were then stripped off his body before he was flailed and even executed. More often than not, this poor fellow was someone who had flaunted his wealth by wearing silk kosode or by allowing his wife to wear costly clothes and tortoiseshell combs in her hair. This hapless family might also have foolishly refused to present the bakufu with a "gift" at some appropriate time.

Peasants were rarely the problem, but the bakufu made sure that they were aware of the sumptuary decrees as well. The universal message boards in each village always had decrees tacked to them warning against wearing fine clothing, eating rice, and drinking sake. Some of the *gonō* village headmen could probably afford costly clothes, but most were careful not to distinguish themselves in such a manner because there seemed to be spies and jealous villagers around every corner.

The samurai wore the most elaborate and specialized cos-
tumes, but by the eighteenth century they had simplified their   **Samurai**
dress unless they were formally attired in the presence of their
daimyō or other high officials. Males wore a loincloth (*shita-obi*, which
means undersash) which was a simple cotton rectangle about eight
inches wide and five feet long. It was wound twice around the waist
and once between the legs, which any male would recognize as a prim-
itive jockstrap. A short open kosode-like shirt (*juban*) covered the torso.
In cold weather a padded underjacket (*dogi*) which resembled a loose
Eton or Eisenhower jacket might top this. Next came the kosode kimono,
which was tied with a simple obi. A samurai would then be considered
to be fully dressed when he donned a pair of cotton split-toed socks
(*tabi*) under ordinary split-toed straw sandals (*zori*). If he had to be prepared to run (as in battle), he might wear *waraji*, straw sandals that were
like zori except that they fastened around the ankles with straw cords.

On formal occasions there were several other pieces of uniform. The
daimyō and other very high officers might wear padded robes (*uwagi*)
that were often made of silk and might be embroidered as well. They
might also wear silk *shitagi* underwear instead of the shita-obi. An outfit
of silk trousers (*hakama*) and coat (*haori*) was more common for ceremonial purposes. Hakama were curious garments that resembled cu-
lottes and had their own obi-like belt sewn into the waist piece. The
bottoms of the hakama often had their own ties or leggings to gather the
material at the calf for maximum mobility. The haori was a sleeveless
coat that tucked into the top of the hakama. It was made of a very stiff
material that extended the shoulders like epaulets. Sometimes split bamboo or whalebone was inserted to give the wearer the appearance of
very wide shoulders. All of the samurai of one troop wore the same
color haori and hakama as a uniform. Circular patches (*mon*) that were
something like coats of arms were sewn high over each breast and high
in the middle of the back of the haori to designate which daimyō the
samurai served. In war, mon might be attached to kimono sleeves and
painted or embroidered onto battle flags as well. A triangular stiff (sometimes lacquered) silk hat (*eboshi*) completed the ensemble.

In war, the samurai wore suits of armor (see the section on military
products in Chapter 13) that made them look like tall armadillos with
their folds of overlapping lacquered iron pieces sewn with silk cords.
The samurai also carried a roll of deerskin, in addition to his engines of
death: two swords, a bow, and quiver. The deerskin was to be his seat
or pillow cover, but was sometimes used by his foe to carry his head
when it was taken as a war prize. It would also serve as a ceremonial
seat if a samurai were ordered to commit hara-kiri. In war most samurai
wore leather boots.

Most samurai carried a tobacco pouch (*tabako-ire*) anchored by a silk cord and fob (*netsuke*) to the obi. Some carried their own pipes and a piece of flint with which to light a fire. Frequently they carried an *inro* case in which they might keep their personal seal (*hanko*), any medicine, and other small amulets, talismans, copper coins, and the like. More often than not, such small items could also be wrapped in a handkerchief and dropped into the pouchlike corners of the kosode sleeve.

Handkerchiefs were not used to blow one's nose. That was done by blowing directly onto the ground, or into one's hand (which presumably would be washed very soon). By the eighteenth century many shops sold disposable paper tissue for that purpose (as well as toilet tissue). Parenthetically and tangentially, Japanese thought foreigners to be despicable because they blew their noses into cloth handkerchiefs and then *kept* them in their pockets. Westerners thought the Japanese uncouth for blowing their noses into the very hands that the Westerner wanted to shake in greeting.

Commoners   Ordinary folk wore similar utilitarian clothes. Males wore *fundoshi*, which were similar to the samurai shita-obi jockstrap. In warm weather peasants and common workers in the city wore little else. Over this, they wore cotton kosode, often tied with a length of straw rope or a cheap cotton rag. Virtually everyone carried a two-foot-long rectangular towel/scarf (*tenugi*) that could be tied around the forehead as a sweatband (and then it might be called a *hachimaki*). It could also be worn around the neck like a scarf; at the belt to be used to wipe sweat from the brow or armpits; bunched on the head like a turban; or used as a washcloth. Few commoners wore tabi or geta (wooden rain clogs), but most wore zori or waraji. Construction workers wore special padded tabi that allowed them to scramble around on scaffolding, often anchoring themselves to a spot by wrapping their big and second toes around the bamboo poles that served as scaffolding.

A fortunate peasant or commoner might own a padded overcoat (*kappo*) to be worn over the kosode. In the countryside straw raincoats (*mino*) could serve as snowcoats as well. Rice straw was simply bunched and basted to a scrap of cloth that could be fastened around the neck. Together with a sedge hat, this outfit could keep someone remarkably dry and warm. One European visitor marveled about the sedge hat; observing that "it is transparent and exceedingly light, and yet, if once wet, will let no rain come through."[2]

Cotton or hemp mittens (*tekko*) were common in the frostier northern climes. In the cities, most chōnin could afford a sedge hat and a cheap oiled paper (*kasa*) umbrella. Zori, waraji, and geta were easy enough to make or cheap enough to buy. Many men also wore legging gaiters (*kyahan*) around their legs, particularly in winter.

Chōnin store clerks usually wore *happi*, short kosode-like livery coats that were worn open. When they sported a mon-like symbol or fancifully

Clothing (clockwise from top left): man's kimono with narrow obi sash; woman's kimono with high, wide obi; mino straw raincoat, ami-gasa sedge hat, and waraji straw sandals worn by peasants; white wedding kimono with headdress (to hide the "horns of jealousy"). (Drawings by Kyle Dyer)

drawn kanji on the back they were called *shirushi-banten* ("advertising cloaks"). The distinctive colors of these coats designated the rank of the wearer in the shop. Higher clerks also tied a portable ink and brush (*yatate*) set to their obi to take orders quickly.

A short kosode robe (*yutaka*) was commonly worn when one came out of the bath (see Chapter 9), and there were many nightclothes (*yogi*), including one type that was like a sleeping bag with sleeves and a neck.

Women
Like the samurai men, their women dressed most fancifully and elaborately. Wealthy women might wear silk panties (*patchi*) and several layers of colored silk kosode to emulate the heroines of *The Tale of Genji*, but most wore one simple kosode and obi over their silken drawers. There were hundreds of dyes and dying methods, so the samurai kosode were often very colorful and otherwise elaborately decorated. Prints, patterns, and even painting directly on the cloth were all very common.

Samurai women were more likely to wear jewelry than men were. Rings were practically unheard of, though we can sometimes see them on the fingers of famous prostitutes and geisha in the ukiyo-e prints. Earrings were also extremely rare—practically unknown, in fact. The chief adornment was worn in the hair. Tortoiseshell and lacquered wooden combs were common, and geisha sported elaborate jeweled hairdressings as well. Flowers were also sometimes worn in the hair, often as much for their olfactory contribution as for their decorative qualities.

Wealthy women often carried parasols in their rare ventures into the sun. Most carried a fair number of accoutrements in their sleeves, including fans, handkerchiefs, combs, tweezers, makeup *inro*, mirrors, amulets, and sometimes a diminutive tobacco set.

Commoner women usually wore some kind of undergarment, usually a short kosode (*koshi-maki*), or a hip sash (*shita-jime*). Over the kosode they wore hip aprons (*suso-yoke*), pinafores (*hara-gake*) which were like backwards shirts, open at the back. They often wore tight breeches (*momohiki*) or flared trousers (*mompe*) that gathered and tied at the calf when they worked in the fields, particularly when stooping to transplant rice seedlings.

Children
Children were dressed like diminutive copies of their elders except for some curious though charming accoutrements. Most carried a charm-bag (*kinchaku*), which was often sewn into the corner of a sleeve. The cloth bag contained a paper amulet (*mamori-fuda*) of the children's patron and protector, Buddha Jizo. Most children in cities also had small copper tags fixed to their kosode or obi. On one side of the *maigo-fuda* was an etched astrological symbol; on the other side was the child's name and address. The idea was that any little ones who strayed away could be taken to one of the ubiquitous neighborhood police boxes where someone could read. Such lost children

could forthwith be reunited with their parents (along with a stern admonition to better corral the little scamps). It is an apt commentary on a society that gave such considerable freedom for children to play.

As suggested above, when children reached some appropriate age (it varied greatly by class, profession, and region), they would receive a symbolic set of adult clothes. Among samurai boys, the age was approximately fifteen, at which time the boy would be allowed his first set of hakama trousers. At the coming-of-age ceremony (*genpuku*) his head would be shaved in the *chonmage* style and he would be called by his new adult name. Among samurai girls, the age was often younger, thirteen or so, when they experienced their first menses. The girl would have her eyebrows ceremoniously shaved (*mayuharai*) and the false ones drawn higher on the forehead.

The poorer classes usually could only afford one set of clothes per year. Servants were very often given a new set at New Year's. The old set might be kept for an emergency change of clothes, or they might be resold or taken apart and used for other needs. Very often children's clothes could be made out of worn adult clothes. There was a lively trade in used urban kosode that were sold out in the countryside.

Children who had not attained full growth but had already been accepted as adults routinely had their clothes adjusted. A few basting stitches could shorten sleeves and hems, and extraneous material could always be gathered and tucked into the obi.

Hairdressing Although technically not clothing, the subject will be briefly examined here since it seems best to discuss everything that was worn for protection and style in one place.

Commoners rarely spent much time, energy, or treasure in dressing their hair. Peasant men did not have what we would call "haircuts" except if we include shearing in that category. Once or twice during the warm months someone in the village would round up several males and trim their hair down to the scalp. This was cooler in the summer and also had the advantage of ridding them of any lice accumulated during the winter. Otherwise, men would simply gather up loose strands of hair during the winter and tie them together into something like a ponytail. Chōnin men were shorn more often during the year. Many wore caps during the winter to keep the frost off the pumpkin.

Peasant women often affected a decorative bun worn at the nape. Some wore a comb or ribbon at matsuri, but during the rest of the year they wore their hair plain or tied with a straw cord. When working out in the sun women wore sedge hats or fashioned their tenugi hand towels into a bandana or turban. Chōnin women were more apt to decorate and dress their hair, but many tied their hair up into their tenugi or similar cloth. Wealthy chōnin women emulated the hairstyles of samurai women.

Headwear (clockwise from top left): metal gunjin-gasa samurai helmet; ichimegasa "gabled" sedge sun and rain peasant hat; shimada single-comb with multiple lacquered "pins," traditionally a married woman's hairdo; tate eboshi, a lacquered silk (or paper) formal samurai court hat; chonmage, the traditional samurai shaved head with bundled "top-knot." (Drawings by Julie Eisenbraun)

Samurai women, except for Kabuki *onna gata*, geisha, and prostitutes, wore the most elaborate and decorative hairstyles. The basis of most styles was the chignon bun, but there were hundreds of variations. There were distinct styles for little girls and young virgins; for young wives; for various stages of early, middle, and late matronage; and of course a distinct style for "retired" (old) women. Very few women dyed their hair (and then only to cover approaching gray), so decorations worn in the hair were the only colorful variations. As in most societies, the brighter colors of ribbons, combs, or pins were appropriate only to the very young. Older women had to make do with more somber-patterned ribbons.

Female (or, as in the case of onna gata [female impersonators]) entertainers were expected to invent new fanciful and elaborate styles virtually every week. Most geisha and high-class prostitutes went regularly to professional hairdressers. Their hair was washed, combed, oiled, and then decorated with all manner of combs, mirrors, pins, jimcracks, and gewgaws. Cascades and sculptures of hair were fashioned into improbable shapes. Little wonder that some geisha turned to wearing wigs. The onna gata had several wigs to choose from, and hairdressers were kept busy inventing new ones. Samurai and wealthy chōnin women often bustled off to their hairdressers immediately after seeing a new style. Woodblock ukiyo-e prints were handy to take along to show the disbelieving harried hairdresser what was the new rage. Some accounts cite improbably high hairdressing expenses for popular geisha. Many geisha "stables" employed their own private stylists to decorate the hair of all the women in the house. The larger and more famous brothels did so as well.

Can we also consider eyebrows here? In ancient times noble women shaved their natural eyebrows (*mayuharai*) and drew in decorative black brows (*mayuzumi*) using lamp soot an inch higher on the forehead. This was probably an emulation of highly painted concubines and imperial courtesans at the Tang Chinese court. Not many Japanese women in the eighteenth century continued this curious decoration, but some did. Some also continued to blacken their teeth (*ohaguro*) with rust-iron dust mixed with gallnut and lacquer. The effect was quite shocking to most Westerners, but was supposed to ensure that women did not look like "grinning skeletons" when they smiled or laughed. Some women painted their lips and rouged their cheeks with *benihana* (safflower paste). Most at least dusted their faces and necks with a white powder mixture of white clay and rice flour (*oshiroi*). Early in the seventeenth century a white lead powder was used until it was clear that it was quite toxic. Parenthetically (and again tangentially), it was the nape of the woman's neck that was the object of sexual desire for most men. Geisha and prostitutes artfully exposed that area with back-scooped kimono and delicate

Youngster helps woman dress her hair. Tea ceremony table at right. Woodblock print by Suzuki Harunobu. (Courtesy of Asia Library, University of Michigan)

makeup. A few loose strands of nape hair sent some men into sexual brain cramps. Go figure.

Samurai men had hairdressers too. Upon coming of age, the forelock was shaved and the long back hair was gathered up with a plaited string (*motoyui*) into a cascading topknot (*chonmage*) that looked something like the traditional lacquered silk *eboshi* hat that they wore at rare ceremonial occasions only. The hair was gathered into the chonmage so that war helmets fit the head better and did not slip around, as would have been the case if the head was closely shorn. Obviously the hairstyle continued long beyond the time samurai actually had to wear helmets. The hair was washed about once a week, carefully combed, and set into the immobile chonmage. Disgraced samurai were shorn of their topknot, and the *rōnin* ("masterless" or literally "wave men") who had lost their positions as samurai showed their status by wearing the hair long and loose or in a ponytail.

NOTES

1. See Reiko Mochinaga Brandon, *Country Textiles of Japan: The Art of Tsutsugaki* (New York: Weatherhill, 1986), and Sunny Yang and Rochelle M. Narasin, *Textile Art of Japan* (New York: Kodansha International, 1989), for good sources on early Japanese textiles.

2. Richard Hildreth, *Japan: As It Was and Is*, 2nd ed. (Wilmington, DE: Scholarly Resources, 1973), 284.

9

Buildings

The origins of housing styles employed in Japan into the
eighteenth century are the subject of much controversy. **Farmhouses**
The general shape and building materials are very similar
to those employed in Korea and much of Northeast Asia, but also have
distinct similarities to methods used in littoral Southeast Asia as well.
Archeological fetishes of prehistoric houses show a remarkable consistency for over two millennia. Both regions use heavy ridgepoles supported by log uprights. In the northeast, floors are usually smoothed and
beaten earth, though portions of the house may have raised floors as
well. In Southeast Asia, the whole house is usually raised on stilts to
keep it dry from marshy land below. In both areas, smoke is vented
through gables in the thatched roof rather than through chimneys. By
and large, Japanese houses bear remarkable resemblance to houses in
other parts of Asia. The house construction described below is of the
traditional *minka*, which means something like "folk homes." Later sections briefly describe other types of elite housing.

One difference in housing construction in Japan is the method of foundation. Most buildings the world over employ some manner of sunken
posts as the most common method of providing stability for the frame.
The idea is to immobilize the load-bearing walls to give stability to the
roof and to the whole structure. The Japanese employ a method that
depends on the very weight of the roof to stabilize the rest of the house.
The upright log columns are mounted directly onto flat boulders, which

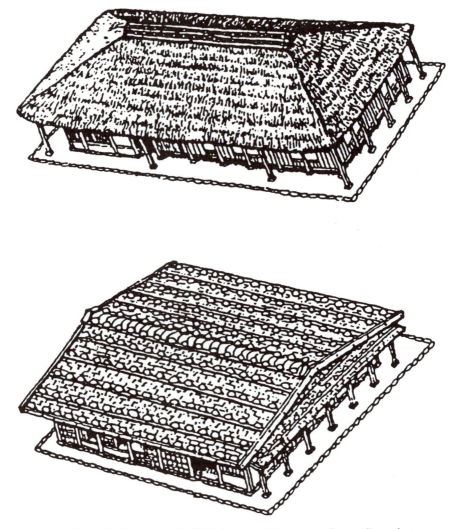

Types of thatched-roof minka (folk homes). Yosemune (hipped) roof at top;
kirizuma (gabled) roof at bottom. Rocks are placed below the eaves for
drainage. (Drawings by Jennifer Mool)

are imbedded into the earth. The heavy weight of the thatched roof is
transferred down the uprights.

There are commonly over a thousand earthquakes annually in Japan
(not all are felt throughout the entire country, of course). This type of
construction absorbs the movement of the earth with the least damage.
A house may be jarred completely off its rock foundations, but it is then
relatively easy to take it apart and reassemble it on its original boulders

Kirizuma (gabled sedge reed roof). Note the smoke trellis at the gable. Vertical poles descend from the roof onto foundation stones. (Drawing by Lacy Jones)

with minimal damage. If the house uprights had been rigidly immobilized in the earth, however, the house would vibrate itself to pieces. Similarly, the Japanese house can sway and adjust to the heavy monsoon and even typhoon winds that periodically hit the country.

Kaempfer acknowledged the difference in housing construction from his native Netherlands:

> I took notice, that the roof, which is cover'd with planks, or shingles of wood, rests upon thick, strong, heavy beams, as large as they can get them, and that the second story is generally built stronger and more substantial than the first. This they do by reason of frequent Earthquakes, which happen in this country, because they do serve, that in the case of violent shock, the pressure of the upper part of the house upon the lower, which is built much lighter, keeps the whole from being overthrown.[1]

Resting the upright poles on flat foundation stones also preserves the posts from rotting away from the ground moisture or being so easily eaten by subterranean termites and other insects.

Few wooden dowels (and virtually no iron nails) are used to fasten the house together. Uprights are often lashed to the roof joists, or, in the more sophisticated houses, an intricate post and lintel system joins the two with wooden locks. The roof frame consists of a single ridgepole that is held in place by simple triangular end frames. A few planks provide a frame for a thatched roof. An interweaving process that remains quite stable even in very high winds anchors layers of thick sedge.

In the countryside, the most common way of thatching is for gangs of young men to cut sedge reeds and then lay them out to season in the sun. The idea is to provide a uniform supply of thatch of equal age and consistency. The sedge is then hoisted up to the thatcher by strong young men. The thatcher expertly wedges and weaves the individual reeds into a thick mass, cutting the reed ends to create a uniform eave line for maximum drainage. As the thatch ages, the moisture solidifies the roof into a surprisingly solid and heavy mass that is nearly impenetrable. The smoke and heat from the fireplace within the house also help to "cook" and dry the inner portion of the thatch to keep the house remarkably dry. The best-made thatch roofs become a seedbed for wildflowers blown into them. The seeds are driven deep into the moist center and then sprout out to give the roofs a decorative fringe of flora in spring. Indeed, it became something of a tradition to insure good fortune for the residents by intentionally sowing wildflower seeds in the thatch.

The exterior walls were often formed by weaving split bamboo between the uprights or by fastening thick sedge mats in place. Sometimes a plaster of sticky mud was daubed over the mats, which dried into something like stucco. This provided additional protection from the elements. Most houses were relatively small, scarcely twenty feet on a side, without any dividing interior walls. As indicated, the floor was smoothed earth (*doma*), though in more prosperous families rough wooden planks could provide some dryness. Commonly, a wooden platform could raise the sleeping area off the ground, but many peasants merely covered an area with layers of straw topped with woven sedge mats.

Because most rural minka had only earthen floors, sometimes the inner area was raised above the surrounding area and shallow trenches were dug around the house to channel water from the roof away from the living quarters. Almost all homes had a large flat rock (*kutsunugi-ishi*— literally, "shoe removal stone") embedded into the entryway. People would remove and leave their sodden straw sandals or muddy *geta* (platform shoes) before entering the house. This entryway became the real as well as the symbolic locus of danger. Talismans and amulets were mounted above the lintel to ward off evil spirits. Because it was believed that these malevolent demons approached humans from the northeast, no farmhouse door was situated on that side. Most portals were little more than curtains, though some peasants fashioned reed mats fixed to bamboo frames to provide a more substantial door. There were no windows.

A bit of sunlight could waft into the dingy hut by way of split bamboo lattices that covered the ends of the triangular roofline. These were intended to waft away the smoke from the fireplace. Herbs and some vegetables were dried by hanging them up in the open roof frame. Some peasants created storage space by stretching a few planks to make an attic up in the rafters, but scarcely anyone ever created actual living space up there. Perhaps the thought of being shaken down out of a deep sleep in an earthquake was sufficient reason not to do so. But since there were no chimneys, one could be asphyxiated in one's sleep up there as well.

Most minka had "central heating," but only because the fireplace was sunken into the common floor of the one-room cottage. The open fireplace (*irori*) was sometimes surrounded with an adobe-like hearth. Most commonly a rope or chain was dangled from the rafters from which to suspend a cooking pot. Meals were one-pot affairs. Barley, millet, or, more rarely, rice-based gruels and porridges (see Chapter 7) with a few herbs or vegetables cut into the slurry sufficed to feed the entire family. Family members usually had their own wooden bowl and a set of chopsticks and spoon. A wooden ladle was used to stir the food while it cooked and then to scoop it out into individual bowls.

By the eighteenth century many minka had enclosed earthen stoves (*kamadō*) instead of fireplaces, but in most villages these were simply an expensive luxury. The major attraction of these stoves was that two or often even three or four different pots could be heated simultaneously. Also, it was somewhat easier to regulate the heat of the cooking pot; but most open hearths had a simple yet ingenious pulley device to vary the height of the pot from the flames below. Most were merely iron hooks on ropes or chains, which could be gathered up or released to raise and lower the pot. Others were thick wooden dowels into which notches had been cut at intervals. The cooking hook could be adjusted from one notch to another. Some of these were made of iron. Other contraptions were rigged by which two or more pots could dangle simultaneously. That way, water could be boiled at the same time that the stew was cooking so one could enjoy a bowl of tea (which also rinsed out the bowl) after a meal. Some cynics maintain that this is the origin of one of the country's favorite dishes, *ochazuke*. After a bout of drinking sake, one sobers up by pouring hot tea over a bowl of leftover rice.

As suggested above, the sleeping quarters were little more than a dry corner in the leeward side of the house. The whole family huddled together to share body warmth because virtually no family could afford to burn a fire through the entire night. Also, it was very dangerous to do so unless the fire was tended throughout the night. Few farmers had more than one set of clothes, let alone a separate ensemble for sleeping. People slept in their clothes and covered themselves with straw mats (*enza*), raincoats, and whatever else might provide warmth. By the eighteenth century most farmers could afford community cotton *futon* quilts stuffed with cheap batting. Many could also afford a thicker futon mattress as well.

The typical Japanese farmhouse was probably no cruder than most Asian, African, or European hovels were at the same time. And they were no more wretched than American sod huts, log cabins, or caves, for that matter. One nineteenth-century European visitor to Japan opined, "Though squalid and dirty as these places appear . . . they are immaculate in comparison with the unutterable filth and misery of similar quarters in nearly all . . . of Christendom."[2]

By the eighteenth century, we have good reason to believe that perhaps half of the peasants had graduated to more sophisticated housing, a type more familiar to those who imagine a "typical" Japanese house.

The Shoin Style   The open-sided house that became the standard during the seventeenth century is a modification of the post and lintel, foundation stones, and peaked thatched roof model described above. But this architecture owes much to the ubiquitous Buddhist temples built by Chinese artisans. This style raised the floor of the house two to three feet above the ground and employed an open-bay system that incorporated moveable and interchangeable sections of the walls and floor. The exterior walls were actually standard-sized screens mounted on rectangular wooden frames. These screens slid on recessed runners (*kamoi*) mounted in the floor and the overhead lintel between the upright house posts. The outer wall screens, called *amado* (rain doors), were usually thicker and more substantial than the inner screens (*shoji*). The amado were similar to the outer walls of the traditional farmhouses in materials. Thick sedge or woven split bamboo filled the area within the screen. The more expensive amado were sometimes covered with a thin veneer of wood. The amado could be slid on the runners to collect in a kind of closet (*tobukuro*) built into the corners of the house.

That left the inner shoji screens, which were made of translucent rice paper stretched over the wooden frames. Depending on the time of day and the weather, the amado could be scooted away to allow diffused sunlight through the shoji to flood the room. These shoji also slid on runners, so on hot summer days, or even on warm spring and autumn afternoons, they too could be whisked away to open the side of the house completely to the outside air. When the weather was nice, the entire house could become an open-air pavilion to enjoy the wafting breezes. Sliding screens (called *fusuma*) could form interior rooms on runners perpendicular to the outside walls. Fusuma were covered with heavy "China paper" (*kara kami*); during the summer reed screen fusuma (*yoshido*) could be mounted in the kamoi runners to allow air to circulate through the house. Fusuma would serve as doors between the rooms. Some fusuma were constructed with an open area at the top to allow for ventilation. The lintel area (*ramma*) above the sliding fusuma could also be fitted with smaller sliding screens, some of them opened or latticed to vent the air as well.

The amado, shoji, and fusuma were all of a standard size of approximately two meters high by one meter wide. This measurement, called *ken*, was also precisely the size of the tatami mat flooring. These rush woven mats were mounted on wooden frames and stuffed with tightly packed layers of straw. They were springy and plush enough to serve not only as carpeting, but also as mattresses. Edward Morse observes that "upon these mats the people eat, sleep, and die; they represent the bed, chair, lounge, and sometimes table, combined."[3]

Being tightly woven and seamed with strips of cloth, the tatami were easy to clean and stood long wear from bare or stocking feet. The tatami mats, being identical in size, could be lifted up and rotated around to even out the wear according to traffic patterns.

The entryway flat boulder where one removed one's shoes extended the life and preserved the cleanliness of the tatami for years. Most houses had an entry hallway (*genkan*) leading from the outside door and entry rock (which now served as a one-step stair to the higher area of the house) into the next room. Even in genkan with doma (earth floors), a wooden shelf (*shikaidai*) was usually built as a step into the house proper. This step would also serve as a shelf on which to store shoes. Cabinets and racks (*getabako*) were provided where one stored soft inside slippers and where one could leave one's wet, muddy, or dusty outer shoes and sandals. If asked, most peasants thought of this area as "outside" (*soto*). One was not really "inside" (*uchi*) until one passed into the tatami carpeted area.

In this style of housing, the living space within the amado and shoji was surrounded by a veranda-like space (*engawa*) under the eaves that was made of polished wooden planks. The engawa served as a four-to-five-foot recessed protector for the amado from the elements. When the amado and shoji were open, the living space was extended out into this area. Indeed, most Japanese considered the engawa merely as a threshold between the house and the garden. It also served as a convenient hallway around the house and out into the garden and to the privy so one did not have to traipse through the entire house. Hooks and locks were invented to keep outsiders from entering the house by merely sliding a few amado and shoji.

Ordinarily one room (the one closest to the garden) was designated as a formal reception area. In that room one exterior wall was made permanent instead of being formed by shoji and amado. Sets of recessed shelves (*chigaidana*, literally, "different shelf") were built into the wall,

Genkan (home entry). Shoes are left on the pebbled floor; a two-step shikaidai leads to a sliding-screen fusuma doorway. (Drawing by Elizabeth LeMaster)

and a recessed nook (*tokonoma*) was created to become the focus of the room. The shelves were also sometimes called "thin mist shelf" (*usu kasumi-dana*) because they resembled undulating swirls of clouds in early morning. The tokonoma (which means "sleeping place") was probably the remnants of the raised sleeping platforms in the minka. It was built up several inches above the surrounding tatami and separated from the chigaidana area by a decorative vertical post (*toko-bashira*) that was often chosen for its wizened or even grotesque shape. Commonly the post was not stripped of bark and was meant to convey the sense of the rustic outdoors. Some toko-bashira were decorated with brass, copper, or iron nails with large decorative heads (*kazari-kugi*) as ornaments.

Within the tokonoma artistic heirlooms or *objets d'art* were displayed. The convention was to hang paintings or calligraphy (often combined) mounted on vertical silk hanging scrolls. These *makimono* might be complemented by a flower arrangement (*ikebana*) in a prized vase or lac-

Tokonoma (decorative niche). At the left is a makimono (hanging scroll), to the right are the chigaidama shelves (also called usu kasumi-dana) with sliding drawer cabinet above. The tokonoma is divided by the rough-hewn toko-bashira. To the far left is the railing of the engawa (veranda). (Drawing by Meggan M. Beyers)

quered wooden bowl. Commonly, other heirlooms as well as the family register (*koseki*) were housed in cupboards integrated into the chigaidana. Paper, inkstones, writing brushes, and other writing materials were also usually stored in these sliding-door cupboards. Very often the Shinto (*kamidana*) and/or Buddhist (*Butsudan*) family altars were kept in this area as well. The seat on the tatami closest to the tokonoma was the seat of honor, followed by the one in front of the chigaidana.

Because Japanese did not use much furniture (see section on furniture below), the first impression of a Japanese house was therefore one of austere starkness. With the exception of the tokonoma area, no pictures or plaques were displayed on the walls. At second consideration, however, one could spot what one might consider to be decoration incorporated into the very construction of the interior space. Wealthy people could commission artists to paint pictures on the rice paper–covered fusuma. Whole murals could be drawn on a set of fusuma, or a single one could suffice for ornamentation. The open latticework in the ramma (lintel area) was often quite ornate, and in some holes were cut into solid wood blanks to form silhouette art or some fanciful pattern. The interior posts were sometimes wrought or carved into interesting shapes, and the tatami frames and seams were often of embroidered silk. The idea was to convey a Zen-like simplicity of the interior space with but a few subtle framing decorations.

Many of these pieces of furniture, and almost all heirlooms, were stored in small adjacent storehouses (*kura*). The kura were basically small adobe-like structures with thick rammed-earth walls and no windows. Stout wooden doors sealed the tiny structures almost hermetically. The kura, being nearly fireproof, served as sturdy storehouses for flammable items not currently in use. Often when fire approached, the inhabitants scurried around gathering up prized possessions, which were thrown into large trunks on wheels (*kuruma tansu*) to be conveyed out to the kura.

Which brings us to the garden. In Japan, unlike in most societies, the garden was seen as extended living space. Morse noted that "whatever is commonplace in the appearance of the house is towards the street, while the artistic and picturesque is turned towards the garden, which may be at one side [*sic*] or in the rear of the house—usually in the rear."[4]

The garden was carefully constructed (see the section on Zen arts in Chapter 22) to give the feeling of rustic countryside even if one lived in the center of bustling Edo. Special rocks, trees, flowers, hedges, mosses, and bushes were situated in precise patterns, as were stone lanterns, tiny "turtle" humped Chinese bridges, and other picturesque items, to construct an ideal landscape. Artfully laid flagstones were sunken to create footpaths that seemed to lead off into nearby forests, but usually only to the adjoining privy. Wells and cisterns were located to contribute to the impression of rusticity. As usual, people who lived in cities sought to recreate the rustic bucolic areas which they had fled with such alacrity for the benefits of urban areas.

The privy has a very special place in Japanese architecture. It was much more than a necessary but noxious area where one rid oneself of malodorous body wastes (see Chapter 15). Indeed, most Japanese incorporated the rustic style of their home into the privy building. Often a latticework enclosure overgrown with plants hid the doorway to the privy, and the stone path seemed just to disappear into a rustic hedge. As in the West, privies often took on various fanciful and euphemistic names. *Setsu-in* ("snow-hide"), *chozu-ba* ("washing place"), *benjo* and *yoben* (both mean "business place"), *koka* ("back frame"), *habakari* and *yen-riko* (both mean "reserve"), and *otearai* ("hand-washing") are but a few.

Many kitchens in Shoin style houses retained much of the squalor of the rural farmhouse. This area was never covered with tatami; often it was floored with duckboards that allowed water to fall beneath the house. Some even retained the packed earth doma of the farmhouse for kitchens, bath, and laundry rooms. Many houses retained open-hearth irori fireplaces for cooking, but most people could afford the adobe-like stoves (*kamado*). Water had to be hauled into these service areas. Many

Entrance to kura storehouse. Note the tile roof, stucco walls, and triple-thickness sealing door. (Drawing by Brian Larisey)

rural homes had their own wells, and the homes in the cities had common cisterns.

The Shoin style house was left unpainted on the outside, all the better to continue the rustic, austere effect. Bamboo lattices (*sodegaki*) often served as a surrounding fence, and these were planted with twining vines and plants to give privacy to the residents within. Again, to the untrained European eye the exterior of the house was very drab indeed. To quote Morse again:

The first sight, then, of a Japanese house is disappointing. It is unsubstantial in appearance, and there is a meagreness of color. Being unpainted, it suggests poverty; and this absence of paint, leads one to compare it with similarly unpainted buildings at home—and these are usually barns and sheds in the country, and the houses of the poorer people in the city.[5]

Traditional kitchen with a double-burner kamado stove in the center and two single-burner kamado to the right. Among the various other implements, note the ladle and dipper bamboo stacker. (Drawing by Lisa Slown)

Ironically, the Shoin style home was usually the residence of substantial people, that is, those who could afford the tatami, fusuma, shoji, amado, and engawa that were part of separate individual homes. The poorer peasants lived in the dank, cramped minka. Only the wealthy village headmen could afford the Shoin house. The ordinary chōnin could ill afford such luxury. Most of them lived in tenement-like communal buildings.

Blockhouses In most cities the majority of residents lived in long block-houses (*nagaya*). These were one-story tenements that were cut up into individual apartments. They shared a common

Benjo (traditional privy); straw zori sandals indicate direction of use. Note the louvered windows and wooden handle used to steady oneself. (Drawing by Becky Brtva)

roof, and apartments shared interior walls with their neighbors on either side. Each family had their own private doorways, but they frequently shared kitchens, and always shared wells, cisterns, and privies. Petty merchants and independent artisans usually incorporated a public space in the front part of the apartment and a private space in the back. They could set up stores, shops, storerooms, and workrooms in the front room and partition (often with only a curtain) that area from the living quarters behind.

The actual construction of the buildings was more like that of the rural minka than of the Shoin. Mud-wattled walls and thatched roofs were the norm in the beginning of the eighteenth century. By the end of the era, most chōnin blockhouses had substantial doors and walls as well as tiled roofs, and many even had a few tatami in the living quarters.

In most castle towns (*jokamachi*) most samurai families lived in chōnin-style blockhouses; a few high-ranking samurai could afford Shoin. In Edo, most of the common samurai were unaccompanied by their families, so they lived in barracks or occasionally in tiny cell-like apartments, if their rank warranted the privacy.

The very few wealthy among the chōnin and samurai lived in mansions that incorporated the finest of the Shoin amenities. These haughty

Top: wooden dovetailed hibachi brazier; irori (open hearth) suspended from ceiling with adjustment for height; two-burner kamadō adobe stove. Middle: ceramic hibachi; futon coverlet. Bottom: oshire (cupboard shelves) built beneath the stairs; decorative shelves; low writing table. (Top row drawings by Doug Adloff, middle row by Ryan Manshott, bottom row by Haley Schumaker)

folk could afford larger estates, gardens, several tatami rooms, and the servants to run the whole place. We need not concern ourselves here with the homes of the very top elite people, because castles and palaces have received perhaps enough attention recently. Those places, after all, were more like museums than homes. Most of their interiors were really formal public space to be used for business, reception, and ceremonial reasons.

As suggested, Japanese houses were remarkably free of fur- **Furniture** niture, at least in comparison to the chairs, stools, end tables, stands, racks, hassocks, lamps, and bric-a-brac that clutter up most Western residences. But behind sliding screens and beneath stair- cases, Japanese built handy cabinets or stored a number of pieces of furniture that could be trundled out when needed.

There were several types of chests. There were the large, deep wooden chests called *tansu*, in which clothes, blankets, and the like would be stored. Specialized chests took on the name of their contents. *Sho-tansu*, for instance, contained paper, inkstones, brushes, and other writing materials; *kusuri-dansu* contained medicines. There were chests for ac- counting books (*cho-dansu*), for storing futon and pillows in closets (*oshiire-isho-dansu*), for tea (*cha-dansu*), and for "things near at hand" (*temoto-dansu*)—scissors, a threaded needle, small coins, and the like. The latter were like the cluttered "junk drawers" found in most Western kitchens or bedside tables. Smaller chests, called *hitsu* (not to be confused with *hitsugi*—coffin), and the even smaller *inro*, which were carried in one's sleeve, were sometimes intended to be placed in the larger tansu, or to be slipped into drawers. Japanese made cunning use of every space by fashioning chests of drawers under staircases, in closets, and even below the floorboards and tatami. These cupboards were called *oshiire*, and were often shelves fitted with sliding doors. Such cabinets were usually built below or actually into the chigaidana shelves in the tokon- oma.

Another type of chest (*nagamochi-kuruma*, "car for durables") was kept handy for a quick retreat. The large trunks were mounted on wheels and were designed to whisk away one's valuables in times of fire. They were wheeled outside to the nearby storehouses, which were small outbuild- ings made of adobe-like thick walls with tile roofs.

Charcoal braziers (*hibachi*) can be counted as furniture since they were portable and improved one's comfort. They were wide clay or copper urns filled with clean sand mixed with charcoal ash. Charcoal shards were added as needed to keep the immediate area warm, something like modern space heaters. Specialized hibachi (*tabako-bon*) were made with a small drawer built into the side for use in tobacco pipe smoking. An- other type was more like an enclosed stove, with a single hole at the top over which to place a copper kettle for tea water. This *shichirin* brazier had a fire door on the side through which charcoal could be added to stoke the fire.

The *kotatsu* was an ingenious device used to warm one's lower body as the family sat around a small table. A half-tatami mat would be pulled out of the floorboards and a hibachi set into the middle of the sunken area. A low table fit right over the hole and a cloth cover or futon was spread over it. People slipped their legs under the tentlike covering and thereby warmed themselves from the waist down. It was a convivial place where the family could crowd around in chilly weather to sip hot tea, eat snacks, and talk. One could slip one's hands under the cover to warm them from time to time.

Chairs had been imported from China in ancient times. They had never become popular in Japan except as thrones in the palace. Low backless stools (*agura*—"saddles with legs") were often used by daimyō, the shōgun, and imperial princes to raise themselves above their attendants. More commonly, these nobles sat on a tatami area raised a half foot above the other tatami areas. *Zabuton* (padded) cushions were also used to raise them above the crowd. During the "Christian Century" chairs became popular among converts, if for nothing else than to seat visiting priests with comfort. After the persecution and eradication of Christians in the mid-seventeenth century, the chair became a suspicious (and seditious) piece of furniture that no doubt became firewood among most families.

Tables were also often used at court and in the shōgun's castle. These were of a uniform height of about eighteen inches, made to link together. They measured about a meter square. In commoner houses, with the exception of the kotatsu table, people did not sit at tables; tables came to them. Small wooden tray-tables (about eighteen inches by a foot in area) of about six inches in height were set before each individual at mealtimes. Food was placed in small individual bowls, plates, and saucers on each tray. The culinary custom continues to be practiced in some restaurants even today in what is called the *teishoku* (special platter), which is served on an individual tray.

The fusuma sliding screens can also be described as furniture because they were often painted or otherwise decorated. Most were fitted with recessed metal or wooden handholds (*hikite*) with which to slide them on their runners. These decorations were often finely wrought pieces of artwork with intricate carving, casting, stamping, lacquer, or etching incorporated into them. Some fusuma had silk tassels fixed into the framework to act as handholds.

Standing folding screens (*byōbu*) of two or three hinged panels were decorative as well as functional room dividers. Smaller screens (*furosaki-byōbu*) were used to partition off a section of the room and to protect a shichirin tea brazier for the tea ceremony. Special single screens set into a standing wooden frame were often placed at the entrance to shield the inner apartments when the shoji was opened to admit guests from the outside. Single screens (*tsuitate*) could also be placed in such a way as to protect the rest of the room when one was grinding and watering an

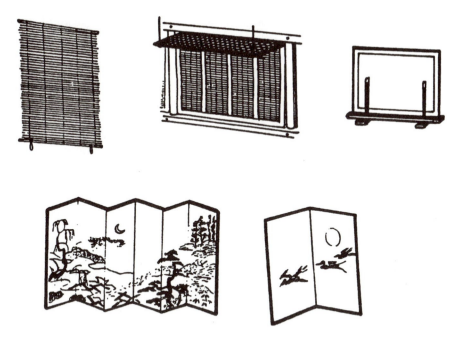

Screens (clockwise from top left): hanging horizontal reed sudare, opened by drawing screen up like Venetian blinds; mise blinds (drawn up like sudare), wooden outer screen lattice suspended by hooks from the eaves; single-panel tsuitate standing screen (panel slides between two sets of upright frames): two-panel folding standing furosaki-byobu, usually used to shelter a corner; multiple-folding standing byobu, used as a room divider. (Top row drawings by Rosie Ortiz, bottom row by Erin Farr)

inkstone. On matsuri days, decorative screens were placed outside on the engawa veranda, ostensibly to air, but in reality to allow strolling neighbors to admire one's heirlooms.

Sudare or *misu* (horizontal split bamboo hanging screens) were sometimes affixed to the eaves. They could be rolled up like Venetian blinds or unfurled to block the wind or shield a room from the sun. Other types of screens included the *kaya* (mosquito nets) and the *noren* (shop curtains). Noren were sometimes vertical bead strings (called "Chinese curtains") that separated the commercial front of chōnin houses from the rear living quarters. They were also the cloth banners, split to allow customers to walk through, that hung from the door lintel. They were emblazoned with the name or symbol of the establishment. They also served as fly screens (or so it was said).

There were several types of lanterns and lamps, though out in the countryside most people went to bed at dusk and arose at dawn, working outside when they needed light. The most common types of interior lighting were oil lamps (*todai*) and candles. Oil lamps were technologically fairly simple. They consisted of an oil reservoir into which a wick of some kind trailed. *Shokudai* (candlestands) cradled candles made of vegetable oil and sumac (or bee's) wax with paper wicks. Hand-held candlesticks (*teshoku*) were said to be the major cause of home fires, when left unattended at bedtime. Most lamps and candles needed someone to trim the wicks to keep them brightly burning. Ornamental *andon* (framed paper lanterns) gave off a diffused light that was more like a reflected glow. Special colored paper lanterns (*tsuri-andon*) were often hung from the eaves or rafters at festival times. Many of these typically decorated the Gay Licensed Quarters. Some of the round paper lanterns (*chochia*) were collapsible to be stored flat.

Another sort of interior furniture was the various boxes used to store materials. Most were simple dovetailed corner wooden affairs, but some, like the *suzuribako* (writing boxes), also served as lap desks in addition to storing one's writing materials. *Honbako* (book boxes) kept the precious printed page dry, and flat boxes with sliding lids kept the inkstones (*suzuri*) stored until use. Polished bronze mirrors (*kagami*) were often mounted onto upright wooden frames, or stored in boxes that could be propped up by the hinged lid for maximum effect.

A wide variety of baskets, bowls, urns, trays, and pitchers was made of various materials. A special "morning face" (*asagaowa*) porcelain was used as a nightjar and portable urinal. Other special ewers (*chozu-bachi*) were kept off the engawa for people to wash their hands after visiting the privy. Usually a dipper was provided to ladle water over one's hands. The ground underneath was paved with pebbles to dissipate the water.

As noted previously, Japanese did not sleep on raised beds, but rather laid thick futon quilts directly on the tatami and covered up with thinner padded futon. The portable mattresses were stuffed with cotton batting and were sewn into three gathered sections to fold into a small bundle for storing away in a closet or tansu chest. Most people did not use pillows, but because some noblewomen (and some men) wore very elaborate hairstyles, they used a special neck pillow. These blocks of wood were more like pedestals inserted under the neck to keep the head elevated and undisturbed in sleep. Some were padded with cloth, but they were nothing like the soft feather pillows developed in the West. In the frigid northern climes, some people nestled into padded *yogi*—gowns that were like sleeping bags with sleeves and neck sewn in.

Whatever was used during the night was whisked away into closets during the day to provide maximum living space. About once a week the futon were draped over a railing, beaten with a bamboo flail duster, and left out to air. In most cities there were shops which refurbished futon. This usually consisted of unsewing the quilt, washing it and the batting, and then resewing with clean or new cotton batting.

Out in the countryside the peasants sometimes stuffed the mattresses with clean straw whenever the ubiquitous lice became too prevalent. People who did not have tatami commonly built raised wooden platforms (*nando*) covered with straw mats. The whole family huddled together for warmth under straw mats, sacks, or extra clothing. Hibachi were too dangerous and expensive to keep burning all night. There was little danger from asphyxiation from the smoke since the houses were open at the roofline. What was more dangerous was a hibachi or portable candlestick being knocked over at night and setting the whole house on fire. As in the West, bedwarmers were employed to good effect. Special *anka* (irons) were filled with charcoal and used to heat the futon before bed.

Another method of warming the house just before bedtime was the bath. Much has been written about this utilitarian practice, which Japanese transformed into a social event. Most peasants could never dream of owning the deep hot water cabinets (*ōfuro*) where one could luxuriate in comfort. They were simply too expensive to heat. More commonly the evening bath was a steambath. Since minka farmhouses were very small, a medium-sized two-liter pan could be filled with boiling water, heated after the tea and before the cooking fire died. People would huddle around the steaming pan and use cereal husks sewn into cloth bags as loofah-like washcloths to scrub away sweat and accumulated dirt. They would then towel down with their personal hand towel that had been dipped into the cooling water. If they went to bed promptly they could retain much of the heat from the steam to usher them into their nightly stupor.

In the homes of the wealthy, true ōfuro were available. These were rectangular cypress tanks (taller than wide) made watertight by close fitting, resins, glues, or lacquering. Hot water was poured into the tank and people took turns sitting in the bath, not to wash, but to bake away aches accumulated during the day. People washed themselves before entering the bath, usually with splashes of water from small pots as they crouched on tiny stools over the duckboards. The cereal bran bag was used here too.

As a rule the oldest adult male soaked first, followed by sons, women, and younger women. Sometimes even lucky servants were obliged as well. Much has been written about the origins of ōfuro. Probably the best explanation is that they came from the mineral spring (*onsen*) spas that dot Japan's coastlines and mountains (see Chapter 23). Whatever the genesis, bathing took on social significance as well. In the onsen, many people bathed together, very often regardless of gender or age. In the larger towns public facilities sprang up to accommodate whole wards of people. These commercial public baths (*sento*) were sometimes divided into male and female sections, but the smaller ones could afford only one large tank, so everybody bathed together. It cost only a copper or two (for use of a towel) to enjoy a relaxing hot bath in the company of one's neighbors. The custom continues even today despite the fact that most people can now afford an ōfuro in the privacy of their own homes.

Some ōfuro had a heating stove built beneath the copper bottoms to eliminate the need to transfer hot water from a stove to the ōfuro. The most common of these were called *Gyoemon-buro*, after Ishikawa Gyoemon, who was boiled to death as punishment in Ieyasu's time. In order to protect the feet of the occupant, a wooden disk with many holes drilled into it was submerged and held down by the feet of the bather. Humorous tales abound of rustic rubes or drunken louts singeing their feet (or worse) on the copper when they misused this contraption.[6]

If we give credence to the arguments of some anthropologists and ethnologists that the more furniture and conveniences a society enjoys, the higher their standard of living, then Japan was pretty well suited in the eighteenth century. The poorest farmers and chōnin probably owned little more than the clothes on their backs, a few eating and cooking utensils, a smattering of agricultural and artisanal tools, and perhaps a minimum of other personal items (most made by themselves). But even these poor folks seemed to be much more fortunate than their counterparts in three-quarters of the world. We are told that many Chinese tenant farmers had to rent knives and hoes, the two essential implements needed to farm, cook, and make straw shoes, hats, and clothes. It should also be noted that the millions of Africans in their slave diaspora and Amerindians on the plains and in South American encomienda had much less as well.

I do not intend to make light of the drudgery and danger of Japanese peasant life. I merely wish to stress that in terms of material culture, at least, they were far better off than many other poor people of the world. Demographers and economic historians have argued convincingly that Japanese life expectancy probably indicates a higher standard of living as well.[7] Hanley has suggested that

> based on the evidence we have of Japan's material culture and level of physical well-being in the nineteenth century, it is hard to support the argument that its people were living on average a lifestyle that compared negatively with that in the countries of the West in the same century in terms of the level of physical well-being.[8]

Religious Buildings
The buildings set aside for Shintō purposes were large in total number, but very limited in actual construction. As described in Chapter 4, the shrine was usually a small rustic affair that scarcely can be described as a building at all. Often the rustic shrine consisted of a shed that housed a few relics or symbols of the

Todaiji in Nara. (Photo by Louis G. Perez)

kami. Usually the wood used to make the shed was not even stripped of bark, and not a few were little more than bunches of tree limbs lashed together to form a crude shelter for the offerings to the kami.

There were perhaps a thousand or so more substantial buildings for shrines in the entire country. Some shrines, like those at Atsuta, Izumo, Hachiman, and especially Ise, were complexes that included residences for the priests and *miko* servants. These buildings retained a distinctive architecture that included thatched or planked roofs with protruding crossed exterior beams. These buildings were usually built high off the ground and resemble the religious buildings of Southeast Asia (particularly Malaysia, Indonesia, and the littoral islands). The Ise shrine has, for centuries, been disassembled and rebuilt using identical plans, but with newly hewn and dressed *hinoki* (cypress) wood every twenty years. Only a very few hereditary carpenters are allowed to work on this most sacred of shrines, and only with closely guarded secret plans and specifications.

The wood of these shrines traditionally was left unpainted to weather naturally. During the Tokugawa period, for some reason, some of them were trimmed in vermilion paint, which is the color reserved to the imperial house.

Green is the color for Buddhist temples. The architecture of these holy buildings was Chinese in style and design. The early temples were actually built by Chinese, and Japanese carpenters emulated Korean artisans and the style of later buildings. The distinctive architectural aspects were enormous tiled roofs that turned gracefully upwards at the eaves, a raised open bay, and post and lintel exterior supports. Thick tree-sized posts that were joined to the rafters by ingenious puzzle-like wooden joints supported the massive roof. Like the Shoin open bay style, the central space could be enclosed with sliding or folding wall screens. There was also a veranda space below the eaves, but generally the central floor was not carpeted with tatami. Usually the entire flooring consisted of wide, polished planks of wood. The altar area where one or more statues of the Buddha were ensconced commonly dominated the central area. Usually the ceiling was ornately covered, often with gold leaf or other sumptuous painting, carving, or design.

Very often several outbuildings surrounded the central temple. Monks and priests lived, ate, studied, and otherwise worked in these buildings, but others were used as storehouses and sheds. A few of these storehouses were designed in such a way as to provide an ideal milieu for preserving documents and artifacts for centuries. Recent studies have shown that these ingeniously designed storehouses maintain an ideal humidity and temperature most conducive to museums and libraries. The Chinese and Koreans who built the first Buddhist temples also erected pagodas, which were the architectural expression of prayer. Like church spires and steeples, the pagoda channeled the eye and the soul upward toward heaven. In India, this edifice (*stupa*) commonly also housed religious relics and human remains. In China and therefore in Japan, it took on tower-like dimensions. Several (always an odd number) stories soared up to an ornate roof. Apartments within the pagoda were used for storage and religious ceremonies, the idea being that the lower floors were for more mundane uses, each succeeding floor being dedicated to more ephemeral and holier purposes.

All of the Buddhist buildings were laid out in a precisely symmetrical plat; everything was to balance everything else. But Zen temple complexes often incorporated rock gardens to help restore the apparent natural asymmetry and unseen balance in nature. In other words, both tried to teach and preach with architecture.

Castles   While castles are buildings of the elite, and therefore stray beyond the scope and intentions of this study, millions of lower-ranking common samurai lived in their environs, so we will deal with the topic briefly.[9]

Castle construction had long historical roots. Most in the fourteenth and fifteenth centuries scarcely deserved the name, being simple earthen redoubts surrounded by moats, ditches, and other defensive impediments. With the surge of civil war in the late fifteenth century through the sixteenth century, castle construction took on enormous proportions. Imposing stone walls, rammed earth, and deep moats surrounded the

Horyuji Pagoda near Nara. (Photo by
Louis G. Perez)

castle keep (*naikaku*) and were topped with castle towers (*tenshukaku*),
parapets, and firing stations. The area directly around the defensive
tower was called the "inner circle" (*honmaru*) and was considered the
last line of defense. A concentric ring of walls and moats created the
secondary line of defense (*ninomaru*). The daimyō and his most trusted
vassals had their residences there. The third ring (*sannomaru*) contained
most of the rest of the samurai. Construction required huge stones hewn
from mountain quarries and rolled on logs or floated on rafts for miles.
No mortar was used in the construction of the walls. Rocks were hewn
to fit precisely and were "rubbled" together, using smaller stones and
rock scree to bind the wall together.[10] Obviously, much labor was required for such construction.

In the early period, most castles were built on hilltops, partly to take
advantage of the obvious benefits of higher ground. These mountain

Marugame Castle. (Photo by Louis G. Perez)

castles (*yamajiro*) were intended to withstand only short sieges and often were used primarily as temporary redoubts and observation stations. Water supply was often an Achilles' heel since it had to be carried or pumped uphill to the castle keep. Many yamajiro were dismantled and brought down into the plains in the late sixteenth century when Oda Nobunaga forced his vassals to consolidate their many castles into a single one per domain. Small hillocks or artificially constructed hills raised the castle above the surrounding countryside in these "hilltop-plains castles" (*hirayamajiro*). More were built directly on the plains (*hirajiro*) and depended on natural defenses such as rivers, cliffs, or oceanside. Most augmented these natural barriers with concentric moats and high stone walls.

For our purposes here, the samurai elite lived secure within these imposing fortifications. Lesser warriors were housed in barracks nearby. Eventually, when daimyo demanded that their samurai live within the

Moat surrounding the Imperial Palace in Kyoto. (Photo by Louis G. Perez)

castle instead of out in their rural fiefs, samurai residential areas became more substantial and extensive. Middle-ranking warriors often were allowed freestanding Shoin style homes. Each was permitted a standard-size lot according to his social station. Common samurai were relegated to tenement-like long (*nagaya*) blockhouses similar to the chōnin apartment buildings. These buildings were usually daubed with a mud plaster and had tile roofs. As with the chōnin, each apartment had its own private doorway, but shared privies, gardens, cisterns, and even kitchens. The inhabitants were not charged for rent, housing being considered part of the samurai's due.

The samurai residences, which were kept separate and distinct from the chōnin areas, received somewhat better amenities than did those of the chōnin. For instance, streets were often paved with cobblestones and were bordered with stone gutters. Most streets were built more with common defense than convenience in mind. They were commonly gated at either end and were constructed at zigzag angles to impede the way of invaders. Stone steps were constructed at weird angles, depths, and heights to frustrate anyone who might try to run up them. Stone walls usually curled upwards toward the right to take advantage of the fact that most warriors wielded swords in their right hands. That is to say, invaders were hampered as they went upward because the walls were always on their right. Defenders had clear lines to slash because the walls were on their left as they faced downwards.

Samurai residential areas always had superior water supply and drainage because they were essential in siege warfare. Most sixteenth-century castles were built on the plains and were raised artificially to dominate the surrounding countryside. Fifteenth-century castles had been built on hilltops and were therefore subject to being isolated and easily deprived of water.

In most castle towns (see Chapter 11) the chōnin took advantage of the protection offered by the castle walls. They availed themselves of the dependable water supply systems as well as of the ready and reliable clientele for their manufactured goods and services. Most castle towns (*jokamachi*) sprang up almost like metal filings clumping around a magnet. A few, like Hiroshima, actually existed as trading centers before their citizens lured nearby daimyō into their center with a ready-made supply of food, artisans, and servants. In either case, jokamachi existed in a symbiotic relationship with the castles that they surrounded. The chōnin depended on the samurai for protection and for a steady, dependable source of trade; the samurai relied upon the chōnin to supply them with food, clothes, and other items essential for their lifestyle.

> The medieval castles were for military defense and, thus, were often poorly related to economic and traffic facilities. If the lords of these castles were defeated, or moved, the castle centers were quickly reduced to mere villages or ghost towns. Others were better situated with relation to communicative and commercial activities and, hence, survived after the loss of political and military functions as commercial towns.[11]

NOTES

1. Engelbert Kaempfer, *The History of Japan: Together with a Description of the Kingdom of Siam*, 3 vols., trans. J. G. Scheuchzer (Glasgow: James MacLehose and Sons, 1906), 2:306.

2. Edward S. Morse, *Japanese Homes and Their Surroundings*, 2nd ed. (New York: Dover, 1961), 6.

3. Ibid., 124.

4. Ibid., 9.

5. Ibid., 6.

6. One of the anti-heroes of Ippensha's *Shank's Mare* toasted a very sensitive portion of his anatomy in one hilarious (to us, not to him) episode. See also Morse's description in Morse, *Japanese Homes*, 205.

7. In particular, Robert J. Smith (an anthropologist), Thomas C. Smith, Susan B. Hanley, Kozo Yamamura, and Ann Jannatta.

8. Susan B. Hanley, *Everyday Things in Premodern Japan: The Hidden Legacy of Material Culture* (Berkeley: University of California Press, 1997), 190.

9. There is a profusion of books on the subject. See Yazaki Takeo, *Social*

Change and the City in Japan: From Earliest Times Through the Industrial Revolution (New York: Japan Publications, Inc. 1968), particularly 143–65, for an excellent concise treatment of castles.

10. For a concise description see Nakai Nobuhiko, "Commercial Change and Urban Growth in Early Modern Japan" (James L. McLain, trans.), in John W. Hall and James L. McClain, eds., *Early Modern Japan*, volume 4 in *The Cambridge History of Japan* (Cambridge: Cambridge University Press, 1991), 519–95.

11. Yazaki, *Social Change*, 130.

10

Village Life

By and large, the peasant population (see Chapter 2) of Japan lived in small to medium-sized rural villages. The Neo-Confucian ideal of rural, agricultural, self-sufficient villages ideally contained "three generations under one roof" of the "one hundred names" (*hyakusho*, the literal name for peasants). Since demographers tell us that the average life expectancy for the era was about forty years, it is possible that many homes in the villages did indeed contain a small extended family of a farmer, his wife, one or two children, and perhaps one or both of his parents.

Estimates of the number of peasant villages in the eighteenth century range upwards as high as 63,000. If one can depend on the accuracy of population estimates, Japan's population peaked and then remained constant at about 30 million for the duration of the century. Assuming that 10 percent of the population lived in the cities, then one can safely assume that the rural population remained at about 27 million. All things considered, then, the ideal small village probably did constitute one hundred peasant families with a total population of around 400 people. Each person was assigned about one *cho* of land and was assessed about one *koku* of rice as tax. In the Tokugawa lands, therefore, each village was approximately equal to all the others. It was a simplistic but effective measure of administrative streamlining. Each village contained about 400 people; the tax for each village was about 400 koku.

Without question, the lives of the peasants during the eighteenth century were harsh at best, brutal at worst. George B. Sansom's celebrated comment about the relationship between government and peasant sums it up best: "[T]he Tokugawa cared much about agriculture, but not much about the agriculturists."[1] Simply put, the Tokugawa considered the farmers to be "rice machines" that were to be fed just enough to ensure that they continued to produce the staff of life. An eighteenth-century Neo-Confucian administrator was known to maintain that "peasants are like sesame seeds; the more you squeeze both, the more production you get."[2]

By 1700 a century of institutionalized exploitation had been at work. The samurai administrators of bakufu and individual han alike tried to extract as much from the peasants as possible. They charged as much in taxes as the traffic would bear. There seemed to be a fine line between keeping the peasantry just on the brink of starvation, yet healthy and energetic enough to keep them working. Too much in taxation and the peasants might rebel, not enough and the top administrators would scream for more revenue.

In the 1580s most farmland in Japan had been classified according to fertility. Hideyoshi had forced the daimyō to survey the land, and the Tokugawa continued to use those surveys for taxation purposes. There were three types of farmland: paddy fields, upland fields, and residential plots. The first was for wet-rice agriculture, meaning that it was flat enough to hold the water necessary to grow rice. Upland meant fields too dry or too steep on which to grow rice. Other crops such as barley, wheat, millet, soybeans, sorghum, and the various and sundry vegetables, herbs, and commercial crops like rape, linseed, sesame, mulberry, tea, cotton, and flax were expected to be cultivated there.

Typically, the villages consisted of small, crudely built houses clumped together to conserve flat agricultural land. Residential land was to be kept to an absolute minimum. Usually the villages were jammed hard against the foothills or forests that served as the real boundaries of the rice fields. Rivers, streams, canals, and other watercourses dominated the life of the village since most of Japan was involved in wet-rice agriculture.

All villages were classified into three types: agricultural (*nōson*), mountain (*sanson*), and fishing (*gyoson*). About 80 percent of Japan's villages were noson. Only about 5 percent were engaged in mountain agriculture, and the rest drew their sustenance from fishing. No matter what the village crop, taxes (*kokudaka*) were calculated in rice-equivalents. In some regions, peasants could sell their crops and pay the tax in specie; in others, they were required to barter to obtain rice in order to pay the kokudaka. In some areas the daimyō wished to encourage specific commercial crops (silk, cotton, tobacco, hemp, tea, etc.), so the taxes were calculated in those products.

Virtually every village convenience was shared communally among the official members of the community. And therein is the crux of village political and social life. When the villages were officially "established" by the daimyō at the end of the sixteenth century, the farmers were also officially "recognized" as members and residents of this corporation-like administrative unit. Prior to this time, the country had been divided into a plethora of different administrative units. The old *ritsu-ryō* system had given way to semi-autonomous estates (*shōen*). These had continued to coexist with Minamoto Yoritomo's and Ashikaga Takauji's *gokenin* divisions. Often the local samurai gathered their entire extended kinship groups around them so that land was held jointly and, frequently, severally. Lord-vassal relationships were mirrored in land administration as well as in kinship relationships. Whole villages, then, in those days might contain one large fictive kinship group ruled by one man.

The daimyō who had survived the century of civil war in the early 1600s were encouraged by the Tokugawa to set up political regimes that mirrored the bakufu system of control. That is to say, the Tokugawa collected taxes in kind from the residents according to a complex and very thorough land survey. The original surveys had been conducted to determine the population and land productivity for purposes of warfare. Hideyoshi had commanded a national cadastral survey beginning about 1587, and many of the regional tax records in 1700 (indeed, in some areas until 1873) were still based on those surveys of 1587.

The governing daimyō of any particular rural area assessed kokudaka taxes collectively (*nengu*) for the entire village as the smallest administrative unit. When Hideyoshi had "frozen" society back in the 1580s, many former warriors had been demobilized and forced to return to the soil. Most of these men were (as was Hideyoshi's family) *ashigaru*. A few had risen to samurai status. These "excess" warriors were mollified in their demotions by being assigned special status as hereditary village headmen. These *gonō* (though other terms are used regionally) were allowed to keep and wear the short ceremonial sword as a badge of status. Usually, the gonō acted as official representatives to the daimyō for the village. There were many onerous responsibilities involved in village headship, but there were also perquisites.

> [M]ost village headmen employed wide discretionary powers in making decisions for their villages. They alone had legal permission to communicate directly with higher officials; often they had the power to set tax assessments on individual villagers and, as part of their customary dues, they could demand a variety of labor services from the members of the community. The most autocratic among them treated their office as an extension of their own family and property.[3]

In many villages, however, a council of village elders (*otona* or *toshiyori*) met from time to time to manage village affairs. These men were

Top: cypress hibachi brazier; footed ceramic hibachi; ceramic kamado stove.
Middle (straw products): agura camp stool; enza sitting mat; waraji sandals.
Bottom (oil lamps): shokudai; tripod; reflector pole; andon box reflector. (Top
row drawings by Chas Sima, middle row by Haley Schumaker, bottom row by
Tim Starr)

commonly the heads of the important families in the village. They served
as a council to determine tax assessments for the entire village. In some
villages, these councils were almost democratic in nature since the heads
of virtually every household sat on the council. Since rights, privileges,
and obligations were shared collectively, the designation of who quali-
fied as "regular" members was important.

The "old" families (that is, those that had lived in the village for decades, and by the eighteenth century, for over a century) were considered
to be regular members with corresponding rights, privileges, and obli-

gations. "New" landowners were often assessed taxes, but had no regular say in village government. It goes without saying that the "water-drinkers" (*mizunomi*), that is, the landless tenants and casual laborers, were considered to be transitory and at best adjunct to the village society.

> [V]illage status [was] explicitly recognized in seating arrangements, office, rank-title, and privileges with respect to dress and domestic architecture. These signs of status, which were often formal and even constitutional, were not automatically adjusted as economic status changed, and bitter quarrels sometimes erupted over the resulting discrepancies.[4]

The bakufu had organized their armies into small-unit administrative groups that simplified command and control on the battlefield. It had transferred this system to village government as well. *Gonin-gumi* (literally, **Administrative Groups** "five-man groups") were administrative units consisting of five family headmen who were mutually responsible for the conduct of each individual. The idea was that each member monitored the conduct of the others, since punishments were shared by all. In reality, it often worked exactly in reverse, since members covered up the misdeeds of other gumi members reciprocally. They became in effect ready-made peasant conspiracies. The Qing Dynasty (1644–1911) employed a similar system called *ba-jia* in China.[5] The gumi served also as natural self-help groups for corvée, water usage, and other communal tasks and privileges.

Usually every village enjoyed historical access rights to forests, water, fishing, hunting, and even swamps. The rights were managed communally, and since all of these activities were labor-intensive, the "harvesting" of these products was done communally as well. For instance, the maintenance of irrigation canals required corvée-style dredging parties that would simultaneously repair the sluices, banks, weirs, and levees. Fish and other freshwater products were shared communally. Also, gangs of workers would go up into the forests and mountains to exercise their communal foraging (*iriai*) privileges to harvest "green fertilizer," which was cut into the soil before planting. Charcoaling parties, firewood gathering, berry hunting, root and herb harvesting, sedge cutting, and various hunting tasks all were done collectively and the products shared communally. All gumi members participated in this iriai foraging collectively. Similarly, seaside "harvesting" such as seaweed gathering, salt making, and the gathering of sea urchins, cuttlefish, sardines, smelt, clams, mussels, and other shoreline products were done in this gumi.

Similarly, plowing, planting, transplanting (of rice seedlings), weeding, irrigation, harvesting, and grain processing were done collectively.

Not surprisingly, the village usually lightened the work by engaging in races and other contests. Musicians often provided a rhythmic drumbeat to accompany arduous tasks. Villages would stage festivals (*matsuri*) that combined harvest celebrations and religious ritual to appease and summon the tutelary kami. Since frequently the local kami were in fact the village ancestors, the matsuri had mixed familial, agricultural, and religious connotations.

Indeed, the matsuri corresponded to the seasonal agricultural rhythms of the region. Many rituals were familiar from one region to another, but many were specific to the locality. The carrying of an anthropomorphic kami seated on palanquins (*mikoshi*) through the village was common to most villages. So was the tossing of pounded rice balls (*mochi*), some containing coins, out to the children. Spectacular parades of flaming torches, which had their origins in parties to drive away animals, insects, or evil spirits, became common in most parts of Japan. Virtually all these village rituals began or ended at the local Shintō shrine (sometimes at the Buddhist temples as well) and were staged by the regular members of the village. The mizunomi were occasionally allowed to participate, but it was generally understood that their participation was honorary and temporary.

In many villages, the peasants were wary of traditional headmen and actually preferred a different kind of leadership:

> More exactly or ironically speaking, the more evidently incompetent and lacking in ability he was, the more popular he tended to be among his fellow villagers. Even if he was incapacitated with palsy, he could be a village headman . . . everybody knew that natural calamities were beyond the control of all human abilities and efforts. With a good-natured, generous, inarticulate old man of an old family as their headman, the villagers felt satisfied realizing that such an old man was not their chief by virtue of his ability or effectiveness. They felt relieved to know that no element of competition was included.[6]

In addition to the village council and the various task gumi, each village also commonly had a young man's association (*wakamono-gumi*). Although no specific qualifications were enforced throughout any han or region (much less the entire country), membership corresponded to being an unmarried son of a regular village member (*hon-byakusho*). Although the "young man's" title implies age restriction, in actuality, marriage and inheritance ruled. Since marriage and succession to family headship were often concomitant, a "young" man was allowed to become and remain a member until he married and/or assumed headship of his family. Young men commonly joined after being recognized as

Top: Norimono palanquin; kago open palanquin; detached tea hut (note
sliding shoji doors and tiled roof). Middle: wooden tubs and buckets around
duckboard; footed bentwood water container. Bottom: gyoemon-buro bath
with bottom-heating chamber; side-heated ōfuro bath. (Drawings by
Karen M. Bean)

adults (around age fifteen), and continued to participate if they remained
unmarried until their advanced age became a commonly acknowledged
embarrassment. After all, it would be unseemly to have a bald-pated,
spindly-legged, doddering old geezer cavorting about, nearly naked in
a *fundoshi* (loincloth), struggling to hold up his end of the village mikoshi. In some areas of the country, young, active married men were
allowed to retain membership in the group.

The wakamono-gumi often lived together in barrack-like houses. This was particularly so for second and third sons who would not inherit land or village membership. They worked as hired hands, though some would eventually set up cadet or branch households (see Chapter 18). The wakamono-gumi arranged and carried out several specific tasks within the village. Primary among these responsibilities were those associated with matsuri and other religious activities. Specific agricultural tasks were also their bailiwick. In some regions, they were responsible for communal plowing of rice fields, in others, for gathering "green" fertilizer, charcoal-making, maintaining fire watches, raising and repairing thatch roofs, digging wells, maintaining sluice gates through the night, and other such communal tasks.

In many villages there was a corresponding *musume-gumi* of young unmarried women. There was never the same group solidarity in these as in the wakamono-gumi because usually young women were betrothed early and went to serve their future in-laws (frequently in a nearby village) at a young age. The women had gender-specific tasks, of course. Cooking, childcare, sewing, textile (silk, cotton, linen) production, and such tasks are familiar to most agricultural societies throughout the world. But in Japan, the backbreaking job of rice seedling transplantation was the sole purview of women. Some anthropologists argue that the custom resulted from anatomical facility. That is, women are physically better suited for bending and stooping tasks, while men are better adapted to jobs requiring upper-body strength, such as lifting and carrying. Other anthropologists note that the Japanese themselves long argued that women's fertility mystically transferred to the rice seedlings. Therefore, the custom may be said to be religio-cultural. Whatever the case may be (perhaps a combination of empirical and mythic beliefs), women did the transplanting in almost all Japanese communities.

As noted above, most village tasks were communal ones. The building of a house required the efforts of the entire community. Gangs of young men worked under the supervision of one or two master carpenters, joiners, thatchers, sawyers, masons, and other specialists. The young men did the dragging, carrying, lifting, and other heavy unskilled work, and the specialists did the fine work. This is not particularly different from most construction crews throughout the world, but what was important in Japan was that everyone participated. Each member could therefore expect that everyone else would help him whenever his house needed building or repairing.

Again, since these tasks were considered to be properly communal, the very collectivity of the job created a social bonding experience. Beneficence and obligation were not very far apart in Japan. Thousands of household registers contain notations of what each family contributed to each task throughout the generations. If great-grandfather Yamashita received a ridgepole from the Nakamura family fifty years ago, one could be certain that when the Nakamura house needed repair, the young scion of the Yamashita clan had better be the first man to offer his services. One can safely argue that such obligation (*on*) engendered cultural and social solidarity within the village. The solidarity was maintained against all "outsiders." Indeed, Japan is well known for the strong sense of the group. The inside-outside (*uchi-soto*) binary often is taken to illogical extremes.

The obvious aliens to the village included the samurai and daimyō, of course, but also extended to the village mizunomi and any other non-member. Itinerant peddlers, seasonal workers, hired hands from other villages (including maids and soon-to-be brides who worked for a season as servant girls), troubadours, actors, wandering monks, and the like all could depend upon the villagers putting up a united front against them in any dispute. In the rare peasant uprisings (*ikki*), the social pressure to participate extended far beyond one's personal needs or fears. Not to have participated branded one in that village society as having repaid beneficence with ingratitude. The punishment of social ostracism was more horrible than anything the daimyō or samurai, or even the bakufu itself, could inflict upon the family. Occasionally it worked in reverse. Mizunomi and other newcomers were sometimes accorded village membership by virtue of their participation in dangerous village activities such as ikki.

Despite this village solidarity, however, there were very real competitions within the village and within each gumi. The smallest peasant unit was of course the *ie* (see Chapter 18) or household. Each ie competed with the others to survive and prosper. Since all village families participated in the same agricultural endeavors, raising the same crops at precisely the same times, the only way to succeed was to husband and acquire more land. Families who lost their land were likely to die out. So we may say that the very survival of the family depended on the fierce competition for land.

Land could be lost through a number of ways, most involving taxes. Since each family was assessed a specific portion of the village tax, the failure to meet one's obligation threatened every other member of one's gumi and the village at large. One could ill afford to lend rice to another family to pay their taxes lest one put one's own family at risk. Therefore, loans were usually collateralized in land. A crop failure because of sickness or other misfortune often meant the loss of one's land. The moneylender who had acquired the land usually could not afford to hire others to farm it (one of the major employments of wakamono-gumi members), so ordinarily, the family that had just lost it continued to reside on the land as tenants. Sharecropping was a precarious way of life because tenants had little protection or insurance against catastrophic loss. Village solidarity could extend only so far. Families that lost land often simply expired. Non-inheriting sons left, and even scions became extinct if they could find no land to own.

Peasant life was very harsh and precarious indeed. Much has been made by economic historians of the rigor of peasant life. To be sure, the daimyō were interested primarily in the payment of taxes and cared little for the plight of the peasant. But they could ill afford a peasant uprising because this was the primary signal to the bakufu that a daimyō had lost control of his han. In the seventeenth century, the bakufu occasionally removed the daimyō from the land in escheat privileges (reversion to the government when no direct heirs were available), but by the eighteenth century this was very rare. If a village or group of villages arose in ikki, however, the daimyō could be called to task by the bakufu, and often daimyō were forced to resign in favor of their heirs as punishment for mismanagement of their han. One must also consider that the daimyō, like the samurai class at large, really believed the morality of Neo-Confucianism, which held that the daimyō was like a paterfamilias charged by society with the benevolent protection of his children, the peasants. One can argue whether this was an effective prevention of overly harsh taxation, but there seems to be ample evidence that the combination of Neo-Confucian morality with the threat of peasant ikki kept most daimyō in line.

We must also consider that very few eighteenth-century tax rolls reflected the actual productivity of the land. Perhaps because new land surveys were very costly, time-consuming, and otherwise extremely distasteful for the daimyō, scarcely a score were even attempted among the 270-odd han during the century. Land reclamation projects, including swamp drainage, hillside terracing, and inlet landfills, all added to the amount of land under cultivation. Add in the increased productivity due to improved tools, hybrid seeds, commercial fertilizer (see Chapter 15), better irrigation methods, and introduction of cash crops, and it is apparent that the peasants seemed to be doing better in the eighteenth century than they had for over two centuries before.

It must be stressed, however, that there was a significant increase in tenancy rates. Land lost through foreclosure continued to be farmed by the same peasants, but what had changed was the concentration of land wealth in fewer hands. Gonō and other substantial families began to acquire more land than they could farm by the end of the century, and this helped to fray and sometimes destroy the village solidarity. Part of the problem might be ascribed to the rise of commercial crops, which militated against continuance of the age-old rural self-sufficiency that characterized the feudal period. As more land was acquired, so was political power augmented. The temptation to cheat one's tenants in tax assessment undoubtedly led to many problems. As landlords grew in wealth, it is not difficult to imagine that they used the power of that wealth to bribe han officials or otherwise improve their social and political standing in the village.

Evidence convinces us that most ikki were aimed at ameliorating local and specific problems having to do with local landlords and village headmen, and not with the han or bakufu officials. They often appealed to those latter officials, of course, but the primary targets of their protests were moneylenders, sake brewers, village headmen, and landlords. Often the ikki participants were content to smash into a rice storage building, raid warehouses, and seize and destroy all financial documents (loan, tax, ownership, and tenancy records). The han or bakufu officials often settled for a symbolic punishment of ikki leaders (though execution was common) because they understood that the uprisings were not aimed at the government, but at local usurers and landlords.

The bakufu was obviously very concerned that the peasants remain peaceful in their lives. It had granted the in- **Village Law** dividual daimyō the right to near-autonomy as long as the villages remained peaceful. In 1649 it had issued the Keian Proclamation, aimed at the administration of its own lands. The daimyō were encouraged to emulate these laws in their own han, and before long it became the de facto law of the peasantry throughout the land.

The thirty-two article law code demanded that peasants obey all bakufu law (whether they were aware of them or not—ignorance of the laws was no excuse or mitigation) and to pay their taxes promptly, completely, and without complaint. They were encouraged to be honest, frugal, and industrious in their lives. They were to devote themselves to their fields by day and to engage in making items necessary for their lives (straw sandals, hats, raincoats, etc.) at night. They were to live simply and frugally, avoid drinking sake or tea, and improve their lands with fertilizer and by planting trees and bamboo to protect their crops. They were not to eat rice, since it was destined for tax payment, but were to subsist on the "simple grains" of barley, wheat, millet, and sorghum. Cabbage, beans (there were over twenty varieties), peas, *daikon* (radishes), and other leaves and vegetables might supplement their diet. It should be noted that most eighteenth-century villages lived up to the bakufu ideal and were largely self-sufficient except for metal and salt.

Villages were required to maintain a message board where new laws, wanted posters, and other messages were posted. We are told that in some Kyushu villages anti-Christian edicts remained on the boards for two centuries (being periodically replaced, of course, when the weather rendered them unreadable). Curiously, wanted posters sometimes had a coin attached as an incentive reward for information. Villagers knew that to remove the coin without tendering information was punishable by death. Stories are told of minor village crises that cropped up when a coin disappeared, perhaps stolen by a vagrant or wandering minstrel. The villagers were forced to replace the coin from their own coffers.

The villages were required to maintain three separate official village registers. One listed the regular members (hyakusho) of the village by age, gender, and relationship to head of household. Births, deaths, and changes in headship or marital status had to be noted carefully. Another register listed servants working in the village at any given time, giving information on their age, gender, and from where they came. The third register was of anyone who visited the village. Traveling merchants, entertainers, artisans, priests, and the like had to be accounted for.

Village life was very carefully controlled externally, but the villagers themselves were free (a relative term) to actually administer government. No village willingly submitted itself to the scrutiny of outsiders. As much as possible, disputes were settled internally. The behavior of everyone was monitored and controlled, usually within the gonin-gumi, but ultimately throughout the entire village. Punishments were meted out communally. Restitution was the order of the day for crimes of property, though apparently these were very rare, since no one had very much and, it would have been nearly impossible to hide stolen articles because everyone knew who had what. More serious crimes of violence and passion seem to have been quite rare. Physical injury and loss of property required the entire village to adjudicate. Apparently the most severe punishment was ostracism and banishment, since it was tantamount to a death penalty.[7] Homeless people in the eighteenth century had little recourse outside of their villages. Village registers had to account for everyone, even travelers and vagabonds. Few peasants would feed or aid these castaways, and gonin-gumi would promptly report any family member who extended aid and comfort to a family member who had been banished.

Villages assessed regular members a surtax to maintain a fund for village expenses (mura-nyuyo) such as the cost of entertaining visiting han officials, maintaining roads and bridges, or traveling expenses for village headmen. Special surtaxes were leveled collectively to maintain shrines and temples and to pay for matsuri expenses. Many villages formed mutual-aid societies (ko) to provide for widows and orphans or to ameliorate some calamity in the village. Occasionally these ko became traveling funds for a few villagers to visit shrines on pilgrimages. All of these expense records were monitored very closely, and not a few headmen lost their lands or positions if they were caught in embezzlement.

All in all, peasant villages were self-sufficient, self-governing, and self-perpetuating. They were, for all intents and purposes, the loci of social, economic, cultural, and political life for eighteenth-century peasants. Scores of generations of peasantry were born, lived, and died within the confines of their home village. It was their total paradigm, their cosmos.

NOTES

1. George B. Sansom, *A History of Japan* (Stanford: Stanford University Press, 1963), vol. 2, 243.

2. Gary P. Leupp, *Servants, Shophands, and Laborers in the Cities of Tokugawa Japan* (Princeton: Princeton University Press, 1992), 7.

3. Anne Walthall, *Social Protest and Popular Culture in Eighteenth Century Japan* (Tucson: University of Arizona Press, 1986), 97.

4. Thomas C. Smith, *Nakahara: Family Farming and Population in a Japanese Village, 1717–1830* (Stanford: Stanford University Press, 1977), 115.

5. Tsuneo Sato, "Tokugawa Villages and Agriculture" (Mikiso Hane, trans.), in Chie Nakane and Shinzaburō Oishi, eds., *Tokugawa Japan: The Social and Economic Antecedents of Modern Japan* (Tokyo: University of Tokyo Press, 1990), 49.

6. Soichi Watanabe, *The Peasant Soul of Japan* (New York: St. Martin's Press, 1980), x.

7. Roger Thomas notes that the Japanese word still most commonly used for social ostracism, *mura-hachibu*, means "village ouster," reflecting its rural roots.

II

Cities

Arguably, Japan was among the world's most urbanized countries in the eighteenth century. As noted in Chapter 2, the population stabilized at about 30 million for the entire eighteenth century.[1] About 10 percent of that number were city residents. Estimates vary somewhat, but even the lowest suggest that 7–9 percent (others claim 10–12 percent) of the population lived in cities,[2] while no country in Europe had more than 2 percent. Put in another way, Susan Hanley suggests that in the eighteenth century Japan had only about 3 percent of the world's total population, but boasted 8 percent of the world's total urban population.[3]

In 1750 Japan had three of the world's five largest cities. Osaka and Kyoto each had about the same 500,000 population as Paris and London.[4] Five of Japan's cities had over 100,000, while there were only fourteen cities of that size in all of Europe.[5]

The primary reason why Japan had so many large cities was political expediency. In the first decades of the seventeenth century the Tokugawa had forced all of their vassals to concentrate their armies into one castle per han (a few were allowed more than one for administrative purposes). This practice only accelerated the trend toward military urbanization begun a century and a half before. Every castle engendered a surrounding town (*jokamachi*) to supply the samurai lodged within; some of these grew to be large cities.

Edo became Japan's largest jokamachi in the late sixteenth century. Prior to that it had already been a rather large jokamachi and **Edo** fishing town with a population of perhaps 30,000. It sat at the head

of Uraga, a large protected natural harbor in the distant east of the country. Minamoto Yoritomo had established his own bakufu in nearby Kamakura in the 1180s, and it had served as the administrative military
capital of the country until the 1330s. Edo had served as a jokamachi for
a number of Sengoku era daimyō until Hideyoshi had deeded it as a
reward for Ieyasu's loyalty in the late 1580s; the cession was also intended to keep him occupied transferring his base of operations, since
his home domain was near Nagoya. Ieyasu had moved his military headquarters there and had built a huge castle in the early 1590s. When he
gained power over the country in 1600, he had made it the capital of the
newly established Tokugawa bakufu. Thousands of his vassals moved
there, and Edo became a burgeoning metropolis. Ieyasu had rivers diverted, and the dirt from the new riverbed excavation was used to fill
in swampy areas to make residential areas. Canals were also dug for
transportation networks. The canals were faced with stones, and ramps
and docks were built to accommodate warehouses and market areas.[6]
An elaborate water supply system was made and sewer disposal was
created (see Chapter 15).

The bakufu had mandated a system called "alternate attendance"
(*sankin-kotai*) whereby daimyō were required to spend half of their time
in the shōgun's attendance in Edo, and the other half in their home castle
town. Their families were required to remain in Edo as hostages. Each
daimyō was required to bring an appropriate entourage of samurai and
servants. Most daimyō brought at least 500 samurai. Many brought more
than 1,000, and one, the Maeda, commonly brought more than 4,000![7]
The practice was intended as an indirect tax on the finances of the daimyō, but also to bring pomp and circumstance to Ieyasu's capital city.
By 1700 the population of Edo had soared to over a million. About half
the population lived there permanently; the other half was constantly
being rotated.

> This gave the city a great warrior population, pouring a huge
> amount of the total national wealth into the capital city to under-
> gird their consumptive demands. Their vast purchasing power
> drew together a concentration of merchants, artisans, temples, and
> shrines, forming a gigantic city on a scale never found before in the
> history of the world.[8]

Only about a half of the population was samurai; the other half consisted of urbanites (*chōnin*) who served them. The bakufu had over 5,000
hatamoto (bannermen) who enjoyed stipends of over 100 koku per year
(and some up to 9,500). The bakufu chief offices were staffed from the
top 200 families of these men. Another 20,000 direct retainers (*gokenin*),
with stipends of under 100 koku, staffed the other governmental posi-

tions in Edo. So perhaps 100,000 people were Tokugawa family members or their closest retainers. Another 400,000 samurai and their families were "part-time" (but often actually permanent) residents.[9]

In the early civil war period, daimyō had encouraged merchants and artisans to put down roots near their castles in order to supply their troops. Daimyō had granted them not only a dependable livelihood and a ready market, but also tax-free status, free land for home construction, and protection from the warfare that ravaged the countryside. After the bakufu had put an end to warfare, merchants and artisans needed no artificial incentives to draw them to the large cities, particularly to Edo.

The city was divided up into administrative, residential, and commercial sectors. At the center was Ieyasu's towering castle keep, which was surrounded by concentric circles of samurai *yashiki* (residences). Within the castle walls the bakufu conducted both family business and the national offices of the shōgun. Ieyasu's most trusted hereditary vassals, the (hatamoto), saw to routine governmental tasks. Ieyasu's oldest and most loyal allies (*fudai*) helped the shōgun with the administration of the country as a whole (see Chapter 3).

In the lower reaches of the city chōnin of every type were housed in their own neighborhood wards (*machi*), of which there were over 1,700 during the period. The machi were often given names that reflected who lived in the district. For example, the Kome-cho (rice ward) and the Kamiya-cho (paper dealers' ward) districts housed rice dealers and paper dealers, respectively. Other areas were named after the original village of groups of laborers who had migrated to Edo en masse.

The bakufu left the actual administration of the machi to the residents, who designated their own leaders (*nanushi* or *otona*) on much the same principle of primacy as the agrarian villages (*mura*) out in the countryside. Originally, most machi were single-profession enclaves. But as the city grew and new neighborhoods were built, dry-goods merchants tended to move into the new neighborhoods, where they established local branch stores. By the eighteenth century, the machi were integrated with all manner of artisans and merchant houses. Only fishmongers, blacksmiths and metalsmiths, and the hereditary outcaste *eta* (ritually polluted because of their involvement with death—butchery, tanning, mortuary, etc.) remained in their own distinct machi.

Most of the middle-ranking and higher samurai employed commoner servants in their households. After about 1650 the chōnin could no longer fill that need, since many hired servants themselves. An elaborate labor market had evolved to bring peasants from the surrounding area to serve in livery. Labor bosses, employment services, and surety guarantors all provided labor on annual contracts. Even children were drafted into apprentice-like servitude. Gary Leupp, who has written extensively on the subject,[10] estimates that upwards of 80 percent of all chōnin hired servants and that virtually all of the samurai did as well by the end of the era. A kind of debt peonage obligated debtors to servitude, but most servants were under free annual contracts and were protected by law. Leupp notes that many of the servant girls, and not a few boys, were subject to sexual and physical abuse. He also notes that many became involved in sexual liaisons by choice and that some lucky peasant girls managed to parlay these relationships into marriage and permanent chōnin status.

A sophisticated system of day-laborer registry (*hiyatoi-za*) was founded as early as 1655. Licenses were issued for contract labor bosses who daily formed gangs of coolie-like unskilled laborers who performed menial tasks in exchange for a little food and less pay. Gangs of these laborers slept in the open air or under bridges and flocked to construction sites in search of work.

Edo briefly copied a system of workhouses initiated in Kanazawa in 1670 whereby vagrants were provided with food and lodging as well as meager pay for such labor. Some training and apprenticeship took place there, but it was seen as a temporary stopgap manner of dealing with the burgeoning flock of vagrants made homeless by famine or natural disaster out in the countryside. When such calamities struck, peasants swarmed into the cities in search of work and food.

The chōnin often raised sums to be used as charity for these hapless folk, but the bakufu preferred to rid the city of these beggars periodically. In mid-century the bakufu mounted a serious and draconian campaign to repatriate these folk "back to their native provinces" (*hito-gaeshi*). Needless to say, the villagers back in the "native provinces" were not thrilled to see these folk return, since the villages were still reeling from the original calamity that had forced the vagrants to leave.

By 1721, the date of Edo's first citywide census, the chōnin population was numbered at some 501,000.[11] Of these, 323,000 were men. A century later the chōnin population was 545,000, but the male-female ratio had flattened out significantly to 397,000 males and 248,000 females.[12] The samurai population was about the same as the chōnin population, and the sex ratio was even more skewed toward men since few females accompanied samurai men to Edo in sankin-kotai.

Early in the seventeenth century the bakufu had designated special Licensed Quarters for prostitution, theaters, and geisha activity. This Gay Quarter (see Chapter 19) was in the lower-lying swampy areas, but was moved several times to accommodate expanding neighboring residential and commercial districts.

This tendency of Edo to develop entertainment areas and theater[s] along shorelines and near bridge abutments was also a characteristic of many other early modern cities. . . . Edo's pattern must be considered typical of an early modern form of urban development in which a commercial city is constructed around of network of canals situated on a river delta.[13]

Virtually every machi had its own parish Buddhist temple where citizens were required to register and perform rituals (*fumi-e*) annually to demonstrate that they were not Christians. The religious issue was clouded by the fact that many machi residents registered with the parish temple for administrative purposes, but actually practiced other forms of Buddhism. This was particularly so among the various Pureland sects. They didn't mind registering with a Shingon or Tendai temple for administrative purposes, but they worshipped at their own sect temples (see Chapter 4).

The machi were subdivided into even smaller sections according to familial and commercial relations. These smaller units were usually bunched around a common tutelary Shintō shrine, and the denizens often referred to the areas as *mura* (village, though it came to mean neighborhood) in the rural sense. This was partially because many of the people were of a common profession and had come to Edo from the same ancestral region or village. Many of the shrines contained their own cemeteries, thus creating a common ancestral home within the city.

Most professions had been allowed to create their own guilds (*za*) to maintain order within their commercial world. Like the medieval European guilds, the za determined prices and wages, and set policies for apprenticeship and other commercial conventions. Most machi were really controlled by the guilds, though in the mixed-profession machi, za were not as influential. The bakufu also attempted to create mura-style five-man common responsibility units (*gonin-gumi*), but they did not work very well because there were few actual administrative needs for them. In the villages, they were used to parcel out rights and obligations (particularly those relating to taxes) and to maintain the peace. There was no agricultural tax in the city, however, and the za and *machi-bugyō* (ward administrators) absorbed most administrative and judicial functions.

The city government required each machi and samurai residential district to mount night and fire watch (*jishimban* and *tsujiban*) patrols. Those services and others will be covered below (see the section on city lifestyles).

Kyoto, the home of the powerless emperor, as well as the locus of many important Buddhist temples, continued to be a very **Kyoto** large city. Also, it was strategically placed midway between the eastern and western portions of the country, as well as at the southern end of Japan's largest lake, Biwa, which was also an active trading conduit.

Kyoto was one of very few Japanese cities built on a city plat. Modeled after the Tang Chinese capital of Ch'ang-an (modern Xian) and Kyoto's predecessor, Nara, the city was constructed on a grid axis. The Imperial Palace and its tutelary temples were in the north, and the ancient commercial districts were on either side of the Kamo River, which bisected the city, running roughly north to south.

Along with its religious and ancient imperial aspects, the city was also a vibrant artisan center. In the eighteenth century it remained the center of textile production, including brocade silk, cotton (until surpassed by Ōsaka in the mid-eighteenth century), and linen. It was also famous for its metalworking, with some of the country's finest gold, silver, and copper smiths setting up shop there. Tea was grown and produced in the neighboring foothills, the picturesque tea plantations competing with hillside pottery kilns. Most of the artistic finished goods of the country were produced in the city, including musical instruments, writing and painting brushes, paper, fans, and umbrellas. It was also a publishing center (see Chapter 22), mostly of religious literature. Its easy access to the ocean and to Lake Biwa also made it a transshipment and commercial center.

Although nearby Nara had been the first Buddhist center of the country, for the next millennium Kyoto served as the headquarters for most of the major Buddhist sects in Japan. The city was dotted with some 7,000–8,000 temples. Most were very small niches throughout the city, but not a few were gigantic in size and scope, a few with towering pagodas. Incredibly, there were even more Shintō shrines, including the huge Kitano Shrine on the outskirts of the city. Indeed, sumptuous temples dominated the surrounding neighborhoods of Kyoto. Many continued to receive the beneficence and financial support of the rest of the country. The Enryaku-ji Tendai complex on Mt. Hiei above Kyoto dominated the surrounding countryside, but Nobunaga and Hideyoshi had stripped it, and all temples, of their tax land. The militant Pureland *ikko* communities surrounding Kyoto had been similarly demilitarized and were now administered by the twin temple complexes at Nishi and Higashi Hongan-ji, which were separated by only a wall in the center of Kyoto.

The bakufu maintained a branch office within the imperial city, which watched over the imperial house like a hawk. Several imperial restorations had presaged changes in government (and would again in 1868), so the bakufu was careful to keep its rivals from forming alliances with the emperor. Some 105 daimyō maintained a residence in the city,[14] but they all were also carefully watched. As in the case of the three other major cities, Nagasaki, Ōsaka, and Sendai, the bakufu administered Kyoto directly, appointing governors to watch over it. Ordinarily, the bakufu was so wary of collusion and possible alliances that it assigned

Katsura Imperial Palace Pavilion. (Photo by
Louis G. Perez)

two governors to the major cities. They were to alternate in attendance
at Edo and back in the city. So paranoid was the bakufu that the governors were not even allowed to speak to each other as they passed on
the road to and from Edo.

Ōsaka was scarcely a day's journey away from Kyoto. Its
proximity to the ancient imperial capital, along with its position   **Ōsaka**
on the Inland Sea, made it Japan's largest trading center. The
seventeenth-century European visitor Engelbert Kaempfer opined in the
quaint English translation:

[T]he Japanese call Ōsacca the universal theater of pleasure and
diversions. Plays are to be seen daily both in publick and in private
houses. Mountebanks, Jugglers, who can shew some artful tricks,
and all rary-shew people, who have either some uncommon, or

> Monstrous animal to shew, or animals taught to play tricks, resort
> thither from all parts of the Empire, being sure to get a better penny
> here than any where else.[15]

Ōsaka became a large city during Hideyoshi's time; it was his some-
time capital. It was also the largest trading port and the center of rice
exchange. Daimyō from western Japan shipped their rice to Ōsaka (via
the nearby port of Hyogo), where they "exchanged" it, or rather sold it
for money or script to be used during their sojourn in Edo. By 1720 the
city merchants were processing over 5 million koku (25 million bushels)
annually. It was also the commercial center for a host of other products
including fresh fish, fishmeal (for fertilizer), various dried marine products, lumber and other wood products, pottery, iron tools, and vegetable
lamp and cooking oil. After 1750 it dominated the cotton market as
well.[16]

Its harbor was unsuitable as a deepwater port, which became imma-
terial since the bakufu had limited the size of ships as part of its *sakoku*
policies after 1640. Hundreds of small trading ships plied its harbor, and
many more were built or repaired there. The port connected to the superior port at nearby Hyogo (modern Kōbe) by overland cartage and by
smaller trawlers.

There were very few samurai in Ōsaka. Perhaps 95 percent of its population of half a million were merchants and artisans. It was therefore
decidedly chōnin in its tastes and lifestyle. Indeed, its citizens are still
said to be the most commercial-minded people of the country. The city
was so self-conscious of its image that it developed a commerce-laced
jargon that became a distinct regional language all its own. Residents of
nearby Kyoto and Nara (let alone faraway Edo) were said to have great
difficulty in understanding the people of Ōsaka, which of course gave
the latter a distinct advantage in trading with outsiders.

Similarly, Ōsaka had by the eighteenth century developed its own
brand of entertainment and its own clothing and hairstyles. The cuisine
was said to be self-consciously distinctive as well. Residents were constantly comparing themselves to the *Edokko* (literally, "child of Edo"—it
connotes something like "typical Edoite") in a way reminiscent of the
residents of another Second City (Chicago to New York). The wealthier
chōnin developed their own self-conscious subculture, aspiring to greater
status than would ordinarily be accorded to merchants in the Neo-
Confucian philosophy of the era. They became patrons of the theater and
of other arts. Indeed,

> the ideal of the Ōsaka merchant was to retire from business at the
> earliest possible age (after successful capital accumulation) and to

delegate routine business to a trusted chief clerk. Retired merchants could then enjoy music, dance, book reading, or the tea ceremony.[17]

As suggested, by far the most important aspect of Ōsaka, indeed its raison d'être, was its rice exchange. It unintentionally became Japan's banking center as well. The bakufu had hoped to keep the 270-odd han separate in every way in order to divide and rule. It had resisted a national currency system (though it monopolized all of the gold, silver, and copper mines). This unwittingly redounded to Ōsaka's financial benefit. Along with the purchasing and transshipment of the rice of all western Japan, Ōsaka served as the center for money exchange. Specie and paper money from every han and even some still-circulating Mexican silver pesos (which had been the international commercial medium of exchange, being reliably hard-minted at 98 percent purity) and Chinese copper *cash* were exchanged for a few standard rice-backed commercial notes. Every large rice merchant house in Ōsaka maintained offices in Edo (and a few did so in Sendai and Nagasaki) where the certificates could be redeemed for credit or goods. This was, in effect, a private banking system, since all of the Ōsaka merchants honored, at a small discount, each other's rice certificates (see Chapter 16).

By the eighteenth century a kind of rice-futures commodity market had developed in Ōsaka. Rice and sake merchants (they were often the same people) bought tomorrow's rice crops at today's prices, sometimes even before they were planted. Futures were bought, sold, and traded like money and routinely appreciated at interest as well. Not surprisingly, other commercial crops such as silk, cotton, flax, linseed, rapeseed, sorghum, and all the other grains and greens were handled in similar financial transactions. The city was known as the "kitchen" of the country. Ōsaka became the center of moneylending and pawn-brokering as well.

Ōsaka was divided into za-dominated neighborhoods, each with its own temples and shrines. Since there were fewer bakufu officials than in Edo, the bakufu-appointed governors deferred to a council of machibugyō who actually administered the sprawling metropolis. As in Kyoto, the bakufu maintained two interdependent governors of the city.

Nagasaki Nagasaki was Japan's most cosmopolitan city during the eighteenth century, but even that distinction was to damn with faint praise, for Japan was officially a secluded country (sakoku). Nagasaki was also, along with Edo, Japan's most artificially established city. In 1570 the local daimyō had ceded the small fishing village to the European Society of Jesus in hopes that they would establish a Christian enclave and international trading center there. His reasoning was that if the Jesuits put down roots there, the Portuguese traders would be tempted to land their annual silk cargoes from Macao there, enabling him to profit from harbor fees. He was correct in his strategy. Within a decade the town boasted a population of over 50,000, and perhaps half of that number were Christians, practicing their faith in the seven churches established there. By 1590 it contained a Jesuit seminary, a printing press, a leprosarium, a hospital (La Santa Casa de Misericordia), and Japan's largest annual silk market.

Oda Nobunaga had seen the obvious advantages of continuing to allow the Jesuits some manner of administrative autonomy over the city provided that it paid a tributary tax. Hideyoshi had established his own secular control there in 1587, appointing its governor, but allowing the city to elect their own *machi-bugyō* (ward directors). Nagasaki had been the site of Hideyoshi's attempts to curtail the power of the European church in Japan in 1597 when he had twenty-six Christian leaders crucified on the bluff overlooking the city. Ieyasu had tightened secular control over the city, and his heirs had finally quashed the power of the Christians there in the 1620s and 1630s. After a rebellion arose in neighboring Shimabara in 1637–38, led by disaffected Christian samurai, the bakufu had eradicated Christianity in Japan. Among the anti-Christian edicts passed after 1640, the country was "closed" to foreign intercourse. Japanese were enjoined (on punishment of death) from traveling abroad, and the country was closed to foreigners except for those given express permission to trade at Nagasaki.

The resident aliens were of three nationalities: Chinese (who were by far the greatest in number), Koreans, and Dutch. They all resided in their own carefully monitored enclaves. They were tested annually by *fumi-e* ritual to ensure that they were not Roman Catholic Christian. Curiously, they were not allowed to celebrate any Catholic Christian holidays such as Easter and Christmas lest they somehow infect their Japanese servants. They were only allowed to trade in certain restricted products, and their ships were always carefully searched for weapons and other contraband. Their cargoes were purchased in lots on consignment by licensed (another bakufu unofficial commercial tax) monopoly agents.

The Dutch had been rewarded for their anti-Roman Catholicism (they had aided the bakufu by shelling the Christian-led rebels at Shimabara), being allowed annual trading visits. They were relegated to Deshima, a prison-like artificial island constructed in the center of Nagasaki harbor. A few Dutch factory traders were allowed to reside in Deshima the year round, but were restricted in their movements. Only carefully monitored Japanese were allowed to act as their caterers, servants, commercial agents, and prostitutes (Dutch wives and women were not allowed). The Dutch continued the silk monopoly, but were allowed to import a few other European goods as well. The Dutch East India Company resident was required to make an annual pilgrimage to Edo to report on recent events in the world.[18] Engelbert Kaempfer and the Swedish physician

Carl Peter Thunberg were allowed on these annual trips, providing us with much information about the material culture of the period.

There were perhaps twenty-five cities of over 30,000 in 1700, and there were over 250 jokamachi around the pri- **Other Cities** mary castles, and perhaps another 1,500 marketing or temple towns with populations in excess of 10,000.[19] Keeping all of this in mind, however, we must remember that 90 percent of the population lived out in the rural countryside (see Chapter 10).

Several of the larger han had large jokamachi, notably Hakata, Nagoya, Kamakura, Kagoshima, and Kanazawa, all with populations of over 50,000. Other market and temple towns and post stations grew to considerable size as well. Ōtsu, for example, was situated at the southern end of Lake Biwa and therefore became the center of a famed guild of itinerant merchants (the *Omi Shonin*). Sendai, north of Edo, served much the same function that Osaka did in the south. Rice and other products came into its harbor for transshipment to the hungry consumers in Edo. Ise and Izumo housed two of the nation's three most important Shintō shrines (the other being Atsuta in Nagoya) and therefore developed modest-sized cities around them that catered to the steady throng of pilgrims (see Chapter 23). Nara and the nearby Buddhist complex Horyu-ji attracted their own pilgrims, and the burial city complex of Ieyasu (who was worshipped as a deity) at Nikko also had many visitors.

Because the bakufu had instituted the "alternate attendance" (*sankin-kotai*) hostage system, many cities and towns sprang up to provide food and lodging for the hundreds of thousands of samurai on the road to and from Edo (see Chapter 23). The need to transship food and other supplies to Edo had a tremendous effect on the development of market towns as well. Obviously those towns situated at crossroads, river crossings, harbors, and other such convenient places burgeoned most of all. Not only were they the sites of permanently established markets, but they also served as convenient meeting places at which to accomplish all sorts of business.

Marriages were often arranged in these towns. Go-betweens (*nakodo*) often met the families of prospective marriage partners in the marketplace, which served as a neutral ground where one could actually catch a prearranged glimpse of bridal candidates. Villagers could often book entertainers for their matsuri in these towns. Agents were known to make the rounds there too. Some towns became famous for their short-term schools. Young farmers could receive a week's worth of education in agrarian "down times," that is, between essential farm tasks. Many youngsters helped to transport the tax rice to such towns and then stayed for a few days to brush up on the rudiments of education.

City Lifestyles

As indicated above, the cities were organized into machi neighborhoods, each almost autonomous in administration. Local temples, shrines, and *za* played important governmental roles. If the city was a jokamachi, the larger administrative unit was the preeminent daimyō. Most daimyō developed bureaucracies that consciously mimicked the bakufu. From time to time the bakufu would issue laws for its own family-controlled domains, but urged the other daimyō to pass similar laws.

The bakufu enforced Neo-Confucian social ethics in the country as a whole, so usually the laws reflected that orthodoxy. Like the peasants in their mura, the chōnin were enjoined to be frugal, industrious, and honest in their professional and personal laws. Sumptuary laws were periodically and routinely issued that forbade chōnin from wearing particular types of clothing (especially silk) and eating, drinking, and generally behaving in a manner "above their station." Merchants were instructed to accept their role in society and to behave in ways appropriate to their cosmic and social status. Fathers were instructed to protect and educate their sons in the ways of the merchant; wives were to obey their husbands; children were to love and obey their parents and provide for them in their old age; and everyone was enjoined to obey their samurai masters.

Chōnin did not pay actual taxes because the Neo-Confucians believed that the government would have been complicit in parasitic activity if it taxed commercial activity (and would have passed along the cost to the consumer). There were many fees, however. Residents paid a ground rent to the daimyō, and paid several surcharges to defray urban administrative expenses. There were fees for wells, sewage and sanitation, night watchmen (called "candle money"), police, and other city workers.

A special category of service was for night watchmen. The male residents of the machi did this duty in rotation. In addition to policing the area to keep out burglars and strangers, the watchmen sounded out the hour, using a complex system of signals that included conch horns, drums, bells, and gongs.[20]

The other mutual responsibility system in the cities was for fire protection. Each machi mounted its own fire patrol, and each house was required to keep pails of water on the roof. In early times the residents also served as "volunteer" firemen, but by this time the machi paid a kind of extortion and insurance fee to professional firemen, who were often *eta* (outcastes). Kaempfer noted that the general fear of fire had created a peculiar kind of fire protection: "[T]hey know no better remedy at present, but to pull down some of the neighbouring houses, which have not yet been reach'd, for which purpose whole companies of firemen patrol about the streets day and night."[21]

These men (*tobi*) were more dismantlers and house razers than they were firemen. Their chief duty was not to try to extinguish the blaze, but to deprive the fire of fuel. They did this by tearing down houses that were burning, to be sure, but more commonly by rapidly dismantling surrounding houses and helping residents to carry their possessions into nearby fireproof earthen sheds (*kura*).

Since Japanese houses were built in sections and usually not permanently nailed, but rather joined into place (see Chapter 9), the firemen would simply disassemble the house and move it out of harm's way. Residents who had not paid their fees or tipped adequately would see their houses destroyed with the excuse that safety required them to save other residences (that is, those of people who had paid). The job was very dangerous, which is why only the lowest level of society would do it. These men were truly acrobatic in their profession. Very often they gave demonstrations at matsuri, scrambling up and down hand-held ladders, turning somersaults, and vaulting off roofs for tips. Very often the firemen tattooed their bodies with distinctive designs and maintained their own secret subculture within each community. They attended their own temples and shrines and otherwise maintained separate neighborhoods, usually on the lowest and poorest land subject to floods, on the periphery of the cities.

Since houses were made of wood and paper, the average chōnin feared fire more than any other calamity. Machi-bugyō mounted neighborhood firewatchers who patrolled the area to force residents to extinguish all candles and fires at bedtime. Citizens could be fined or punished harshly for failure to obey the fire patrol. Houses were jammed in together in most large cities, so fire could leap from one house to the next very quickly.

In Edo fire was so common that it was cynically referred to as "Edo-blossoms" (*Edo hana*). Entire sections of Edo burned down completely virtually every twenty years. The main mansion of the daimyō of Tamba burned down no fewer than sixteen times during the Tokugawa era. The fabled Meireki fire of 1657 killed over 100,000 people and destroyed more than half of the city. Another huge fire in 1772 burned almost half the city, and another in 1788 is said to have destroyed 357,000 homes, rendering 80 percent of the city homeless. In 1720 the bakufu forced all newly constructed houses to be built with ceramic tile roofs and mud plaster walls.[22]

Every time there was a catastrophic fire, machi-bugyō, with the permission of their samurai masters, would declare areas as firebreaks. Wide cleared swaths of land were declared to be "uninhabitable," but before very long the bugyō would be bribed into granting zoning variances, or to turn a blind eye to new construction. Before long, another fire would rage through the area, and new attempts would be made to create firebreaks.

As indicated in Chapter 18, the chōnin behaved socially very much like their rural cousins. By the eighteenth century most chōnin were more than a century removed from their agrarian roots, but they continued to live in very much the same manner as if they had maintained rural identities. Indeed, many harked back to their old rural homes (*furusato*) and maintained their urban shrines and cemeteries as "branches" of the rural "trunks" (*hon*). They often gave furo-sato names to their current homes, designating them as "new" (e.g., Shin-Aoyama, Shin-Sakai).

Chōnin practiced exogenous (out of the community) marriage, though that often meant outside of the machi, but within the profession. Dowry was more common than bride-price, but the latter was not unknown, particularly between economic strata. Apprenticeship within a common profession (e.g., fishmonger, greengrocer, drygoods dealer) was the norm. Many families within a particular za were therefore interrelated, so commercial, social, economic, and even political lives were similarly intertwined. Each family maintained their *koseki* (family registers), which were required by the government anyway. Each also kept very careful records, not only of financial affairs, but also of social obligations. It was easy to discover within a day who had contributed what and how much to every communal fund.

Heads of prominent families went about the machi to collect for matsuri or other neighborhood expenses. There was no haggling; everyone knew precisely how much was due according to custom. Indeed, the collectors sometimes were placed in the position of having to refuse an "inappropriate" contribution because of the social implications. Newcomers (and there were very few of these) would be quickly put in their place by the neighbors, who would tell them what was appropriate to their station and status in the community. Although established more recently than the rural villages, the machi were closed communities with as much tradition and history as their mura analogs.

Most chōnin lived in individual apartments in blockhouses (*nagaya*) built by urban landlords. The apartments each had their own entrances, but often shared common facilities such as wells, reception rooms, gardens, kitchens (shared or used in turn), storage (*kura*), and toilets (see Chapter 15). A few wealthy merchants could afford separate houses, but the samurai, jealous of their social standing, could punish them under the ubiquitous sumptuary laws. Often the common chōnin lived in the rear of their modest shops (see Chapter 9).

Chōnin children probably enjoyed better lives than their peasant or even their samurai cousins. The making or selling of manufactured goods was infinitely less dangerous or tedious than most farm tasks. Because the bakufu and daimyō wished to keep their own samurai contented and well fed (they were, after all, armed), the cities usually fared better at the expense of the peasantry in times of famine. Ironically, one disease that seemed to hit samurai and chōnin harder was the "white rice" malady of beriberi. Because the peasants commonly ate bran-rich unpolished rice and the other grains, they received ample vitamin K. The richer folk who could afford polished white rice therefore suffered from this vitamin deficiency and developed beriberi. It was perhaps just one of nature's little ironies.

Chōnin children had their own games and amusements (see Chapter 22), but the significant advantage to living in the cities was that children were not commonly employed in hard labor or apprenticed until they were teenagers. They therefore can be said to have been the only children in Japan with a real childhood. Stories and accounts abound about the relatively carefree lives of chōnin children. Obviously the wretched urban poor (particularly the eta) who had no real skills or property suffered horribly, but evidence suggests that there were precious few of these in most cities. The bakufu imposed severe penalties on peasants who tried to flee their harsh lives for the cities.

The final category of urbanites is the samurai. It is usually assumed that they lived in high style and comfort appropriate to their high social station. This was not always true. First, their stipends were based on (by the eighteenth century) century-old ancient rice production quotas, which theoretically corresponded to the fief of their ancestors. In theory, one koku (approximately five bushels) of rice was sufficient to maintain one samurai at war for a year. Actually it was more like two koku, but even that was per capita and did not include family or vassals.

Jokamachi Samurai

Second, inflation and rice supply manipulations had at best halved the buying power of a stipend. In the seventeenth century the samurai commonly received their stipend in actual rice shares, but by the eighteenth century, they received credit vouchers instead. This was partially due to the sheer nuisance of trying to store and barter rice during the year, but it was also designed to protect the samurai, since the Neo-Confucian adage was that the samurai had so little interest in personal gain that "they did not even know the price of rice." Obviously, living in a large city was infinitely more expensive than living in a small town, so those expenses cut into their stipends. Those samurai who traveled with their daimyō to Edo were even more encumbered with expenses. Even if they lived in the blockhouse *yashiki*, they still had to maintain residences for their families back in the han jokamachi.

It is interesting to note parenthetically that many high-ranking samurai maintained two families, one "official" family in the han, and another in Edo. Diaries and letters tell us that often when a samurai returned to his han, his Edo family adopted a "new father," that is, another samurai residing in the capital with *his* daimyō! Small wonder that lineage is difficult to trace in many Edo families.

Third, the daimyō themselves were usually in tough financial straits. Various public works, such as road repair, coastal defense, post station maintenance, and so on, were mandated and assigned to the daimyō by the bakufu. Since the bakufu had no regular and systematic national taxation system, these public works assignments were financial exactions and indirect taxes. They were uniformly expensive and in addition to their regular expenses, and usually the only way to pay for them was to borrow from wealthy merchants. Added to those debts, inevitably every daimyō family had its profligate scion, mistresses, or concubine. Frequently when a reform-minded daimyō inherited, he would institute some economic program that almost always required everyone to be frugal. The way to share the economic "pinch," of course, would be to require daimyō and samurai alike to "contribute" a portion of their personal stipend to pay for reforms. A 10 percent cut in the daimyō's expenses, however, meant a night without sake; for a samurai it might mean a night without supper.

Finally, because of normal biological progression, the population increased over a century. But the samurai positions and stipends did not. Samurai were required to pass on their estates and titles undivided, but what of the noninheriting sons? Sometimes two samurai were appointed to the same job. If it carried a special grant for administrative expenses, then one could live on the stipend and the other could eke out a living on the grant. But this was not always possible. Little wonder that demographic evidence suggests that samurai practiced population control measures, especially infanticide.

Higher-ranking samurai were granted residences appropriate to their status, but the overwhelming majority of samurai (perhaps 95 percent were of medium and low-ranking status. Many of the latter lived in barracks (*yashiki*) while single, or might be granted an apartment in blockhouses, the one-story equivalents of tenements. Almost all chōnin lived in such housing, but it was not particularly appropriate to the samurai's high status. Merchants and artisans were allowed into samurai residential areas only as servants, deliverymen, or repairers.

Theoretically samurai enjoyed the right of *kirisute-gomen* ("cut and continue"), which meant that they could cut down any commoners who offended them without penalty. In reality, it was most inconvenient for a samurai to actually kill without compunction. Anyone who did so would be hard-pressed to find any chōnin who would serve, cater, provision, or, worst of all, lend to him. Therefore the punishment for such arrogant behavior was social ostracism. In practice, most daimyō proscribed such arrogant behavior and exacted fines, fees, and "apology money," paid as indemnity to the family of the deceased or injured man. Wealthy and influential merchants could pressure daimyō into exacting harsher penalties.

Daimyō passed laws modeled on bakufu codes in order to govern the samurai. Like all other members of society, they were to behave as Neo-Confucianism dictated. But since they were the moral and philosophical models for the rest of society, they were expected to set an example for propriety.

Virtually every samurai was literate, having been schooled in the literary as well as the martial arts. Samurai children **Education** spent more time in school learning to read and write than they did on fencing, riding, or archery practice. The samurai, after all, were really more bureaucrats than warriors by the eighteenth century. Less than 5 percent of them (policemen generally) used their martial training to any great extent, and many served in merchant-like positions such as quartermasters, tax collectors, and military procurers. Usually their positions required them to keep records, to adjudicate legal cases, to write letters, and generally to behave like government functionaries— in short, to be bureaucrats.

> Even though they carried swords, they were simply symbols to indicate their privileged status, and . . . swords were never to be used as weapons. Indeed, the martial arts of modern Japan were simply physical exercises and the object of artistic appreciation for samurai.[23]

Most chōnin machi had at least one informal school established and maintained by the residents themselves. In the countryside these "parish schools" (*terakoya*) were housed in the local Buddhist temple, usually the only public building in the village. Terakoya were staffed by literate monks or the occasional educated gonō peasant. They were called parish schools, but the education inculcated there was primarily of the secular and rudimentary type rather than religious. In the cities, the teachers were often lower-ranking samurai who taught to supplement their paltry stipends. The curriculum was primarily Neo-Confucianism, using moral treatises as primers. Many chōnin schools employed shop clerks to teach the use of the abacus (*soroban*) and other rudimentary forms of mathematics and bookkeeping.

Many chōnin girls were integral to their family's commercial enterprises, particularly since many young wives ran the business while their husbands were away. Not surprisingly, then, many young girls attended their own segregated classes, where they were taught the basics of mathematics, drilled in the *kana* syllabaries, and learned to read the few *kanji* necessary for the business (the kanji for "rice," "gold," "silver," "paid," etc.). Of course most girls also received some kind of training in what their families considered to be the "womanly arts," whether that meant to sew and cook, or to play musical instruments, dance, or sing. They usually did so at the feet of their older sisters, their mothers, or other female relatives. Young married women learned the craft, trade, or social graces of the family into which they had married.

For religious acolytes and monks, most larger temples and monasteries conducted religious education, but very few commoners ever matriculated, since one had to become a monk in order to take advantage of such specialized training. Virtually all monks were literate in Japanese, a few in Chinese, and even fewer in Sanskrit.

Samurai children enjoyed a very short childhood, since at about age seven or eight the males began to attend school and were expected to behave like samurai. Girls received an appropriate education to prepare them to be good samurai wives and mothers. As harsh as this may seem, European visitors compared the treatment of children very favorably to that in Europe at the time. The Jesuit Francis Caron noted in 1637:

> The parents educate their children with great care. They are not forever bawling in their ears, and they never use them roughly. When they cry they show a wonderful patience in quieting them, knowing well that young children are not of an age to profit by reprimands. This method succeeds so well, that Japanese children ten or twelve years old, behave with all the discretion and propriety of grown people. They are not sent to school till they are seven or eight years old, and they are not forced to study things for which they have no inclination.[24]

Thunberg agreed nearly a hundred years later when he said:

> I observed that the Chastisement of children was very moderate. I very seldom heard them rebuked or scolded, and hardly every saw them flogged or beaten, either in private families or on board vessels; while in more civilized and enlightened nations, these compliments abound.[25]

If we knew nothing else about Japanese society than these two observations by foreigners, it would be enough to tell us that Japan was a very special place.

NOTES

1. Bakufu census figures total 26 million commoners but did not enumerate samurai. Various studies suggest that the samurai population was about 3.7 million for most of the period. See discussion in Takeo Yazaki, *Social Change and the City in Japan: From Earliest Times Through the Industrial Revolution* (New York: Japan Publications, 1968), 140–42.

2. Nobuhiko Nakai says 5–7 percent; see Nobuhiko Nakai, "Commercial Change and Urban Growth in Early Modern Japan" (James L. McClain, trans.), in John W. Hall and James L. McClain, eds., *Early Modern Japan*, volume 4 in *The Cambridge History of Japan* (Cambridge: Cambridge University Press, 1991), 519. Hanley says 10–12 percent; see Susan B. Hanley, *Everyday Things in Premodern Japan: The Hidden Legacy of Material Culture* (Berkeley: University of California Press, 1997), 16.

3. Susan B. Hanley, "Urban Sanitation in Preindustrial Japan," *Journal of Interdisciplinary History* 18:1 (Summer 1987), 1.

4. Donald H. Shivley, "Popular Culture," in Hall and McClain, *Early Modern Japan*, 713.

5. Nakai, "Commercial Change," 519.

6. See Hidenobu Jinnai, "The Spatial Structure of Edo" (J. Victor Koschmann, trans.), in Chie Nakane and Shinzaburō Oishi, eds., *Tokugawa Japan: The Social and Economic Antecedents of Modern Japan* (Tokyo: University of Tokyo Press, 1990), 124–46, for convenient discussion.

7. Hanley, "Urban Sanitation," 4.

8. Yazaki, *Social Change*, 173.

9. Kozo Yamamura, "Samurai Income and Demographic Change: The Genealogies of Tokugawa Bannermen," in Susan B. Hanley and Arthur P. Wolf, eds., *Family and Population in East Asian History* (Stanford: Stanford University Press, 1985), 65.

10. Gary P. Leupp, *Servants, Shophands, and Laborers in the Cities of Tokugawa Japan* (Princeton: Princeton University Press, 1992).

11. Numbers are inexact since infants were often not counted and there were substantial numbers of people who had no permanent residence—day laborers, for instance. See Yazaki, *Social Change*, 141.

12. By 1867 the ratio was 119 males for each 100 women. Ibid.

13. Jinnai, "Spatial Structure," 137.

14. Katsuhisa Moriya, "Urban Networks and Information Networks" (Ronald P. Toby, trans.), in Nakane and Oishi, *Tokugawa Japan. The Social and Economic Antecedents of Modern Japan* (Tokyo: University of Tokyo Press, 1990). This number is cited on page 99, though other sources claim that the number was much smaller.

15. Engelbert Kaempfer, *The History of Japan: Together with a Description of the Kingdom of Siam*, 3 vols., trans. J. G. Scheuchzer (Glasgow: James MacLehose and Sons, 1906), 3:6.

16. See Nakai, "Commercial Change," for an excellent synopsis.

17. Hidetoshi Kato, "Japanese Popular Culture Reconsidered," in Richard G.D. Powers and Hidetoshi Kato, eds., *Handbook of Japanese Popular Culture* (Westport, CT: Greenwood Press, 1989), 303.

18. See Reinier Hesselink's charming account, "A Dutch New Year at the Shirando Academy," *Monumenta Nipponica* 50:2 (Summer 1995), 190–235.

19. Gilbert Rozman, "Edo's Importance in the Changing Tokugawa Society," *Journal of Japanese Studies* 1 (Autumn 1974), 110–11.

20. See Kaempfer, *History of Japan*, 3:5 for a list.

21. Ibid., 3:75.

22. Nakai, "Commercial Change" 576–77.

23. Kato, "Popular Culture," 303.

24. Richard Hildreth, *Japan: As It Was and Is*, 2nd ed. (Wilmington, DE: Scholarly Resources, 1973), 403.

25. Ibid., 402–3.

12

Rural Work

The work of most Japanese in the eighteenth century was that of primary agrarian production. That is, more than 90 percent of the population resided in the rural countryside and was engaged in agricultural production. Perhaps half of that agricultural effort was to provide food for itself; the other half to produce food for the 10 percent of the population that lived in its burgeoning urban sector, and to provide the necessary raw materials to make clothing, houses, tools, and other goods for the manufacturing industry. Of the other 10 percent (urban) of the population, perhaps half of them made, sold, served, and transported manufactured goods to where they could be consumed. The final 5 percent of the population managed and governed the work of everyone else.

This chapter examines how work was commonly done, the level of technologies employed, and some of the products produced. We will focus our attention first on the primary occupation of the people, food agriculture. Then, we shall deal with commercial crops. Later chapters consider the work of artisans, the movement of goods, the service industry, and, finally, management of the entire economy. Bear in mind throughout that the fundamental premise was that Japan was a rural, self-sufficient agrarian society. By the eighteenth century, that Neo-Confucian ideological construct was already showing signs of considerable wear and tear.

Many within the system saw ruptures and fractures within the body politic and had already begun to chafe at the sense of anomie and discontinuity that pervaded the economy as well as the society as a whole.

Japan was far more urban and infinitely more commercial than the seventeenth-century Neo-Confucian ideologues could have ever imagined. Among the peasantry, far more farmers were engaged in non-agricultural tasks. And even among those who continued to raise agricultural crops, a significant minority was cultivating crops that could not be consumed without considerable manufacturing endeavor. Many of the farmers growing cash crops could properly be classified as wage laborers, and many more were tenant farmers, working the fields of a landlord class.

Agriculture
Without doubt, the overwhelming majority of Japan's eighteenth-century farmers grew rice. Most of the daimyō calculated agrarian taxes based on the supposed level of production of that staple crop. Farmers who grew other crops, therefore, often had to sell their produce to buy the rice with which to pay their taxes. Some daimyō encouraged—even demanded—other crops, and therefore accepted tax payments in other commodities. By the late eighteenth century many daimyō preferred a direct cash payment. But, by and large, most farmers were actively engaged in rice production.

Ironically, not many peasants could afford to eat the rice they grew, at least in its polished (white) form. They were instructed by their daimyō to eat other grains (i.e., barley, wheat, millet, sorghum) and to turn over all their rice as tax. Even if they had some polished rice left over after taxes, most peasants had to sell that to buy other things. As we shall see shortly, other than the obvious use of rice as food, it was also used to produce sake, Japan's primary alcoholic drink.

Wet-rice agriculture was almost as old as the society. Prehistorical archeological evidence suggests that rice had been cultivated in the country for nearly two millennia. Immigrants who came from continental or littoral Asia two or three centuries before the Common Era had probably brought the technology with them. By the eighteenth century, it was central not only to the diet of Japan, but to its spiritual core as well. Many have noted the important role that rice plays in Japan's native religion, Shintō. It can also be argued that Japan's social rhythms resonated with the needs of wet-rice cultivation. The warrior-bureaucrats who consumed most of the rice produced were as tied to rice as were the farmers who grew it. The nation's financial system was based on the price of rice. The basic agricultural technologies of rice, therefore, were probably as advanced as anywhere else in the world at the time.

One might wonder why rice was so important to the Japanese. One reason was that the huge population pressures demanded a high caloric return on human effort expended. Rice is amazingly efficient, returning high yields and requiring that only about 5 percent of a crop be kept for seeds. Wheat, corn, barley, millet, and sorghum all require that 20–25 percent of the harvest be kept for seed.

A second reason is that, when polished, rice absorbs more than twice its weight in water while cooking. The high carbohydrate content of cooked rice provides abundant energy, and its sheer volume also fools the body into thinking that one's stomach is full, and therefore that one is satiated. Unfortunately, the polishing also removes the nutrient bran covering, so rice must be supplemented with vegetables and proteins in order to provide a nutritious meal.

The third reason is cultural. Rice was the diet of superior cultures on Japan's periphery for thousands of years. No doubt it was presented as a superior technological and agricultural paradigm when it came to Japan. It simply made more sense to expend one's energy growing one's food on one's own land in sedentary agriculture than roaming around hunting and gathering in competition with other hungry folk, which was an uncertain livelihood at best. In any case, by the eighteenth century rice was the staff of life.

In the early spring, farmers would repair the miniature dikes (or ridges) surrounding approximately one-quarter of their available land. After carefully plowing the earth, breaking up the clods, and removing rocks, the farmer would laboriously spade in what was called "green" fertilizer (see Chapter 15), the detritus, cut grass, and other vegetation "harvested" in nearby hills and forests. The decaying vegetation would provide the nutrients necessary to continue cultivating rice on the same ground that had produced it for hundreds of years. The fields would then be flooded with two to four inches of water.

Obviously, to saturate the soil to the extent that the field remained flooded required a great amount of water. For centuries peasants had carefully dug and maintained irrigation ditches and had developed a rather sophisticated system for water distribution. Sluice gates, bamboo conduits, and water wheels (see the discussion on agricultural tools below) were the most efficient. This technology was so essential to the cultivation of rice that breaking down the paddy ridges and opening the sluice gates at the wrong times were two of the some dozen or so "heavenly sins" mentioned in the *Kojiki*.[1] Japanese also practiced step-down terracing whereby water was sluiced down from one terraced paddy field to an adjacent lower one, and so on.

Sometimes rivers and canals were diverted to take advantage of the silting of watercourses. Areas recovered from swamp or river were often designated as "new fields" (*shinden* or *wajū*) and were exempt from taxation for up to a whole generation.[2] Such fields were also used to allow second and third sons to inherit a bit of land on their own, since only one son inherited the family farm in a system of primogeniture.[3]

Once the field had lain under this water for two or three days, farmers would then strew rice seeds kept from the previous harvest over the fields in a broadcast method. In the five or six weeks that it took for the seeds to germinate into seedlings, the farmer would prepare the other three-quarters of his paddy allotment as he had done with the seedling patch. In some areas, farmers carefully integrated other crops with rice so that they were harvesting winter wheat just days before they had to prepare the same ground for rice planting. The detritus of other crops such as wheat could also serve as green fertilizer for the rice crop.

The ground now being ready, the farmer would do something that must have seemed counterintuitive to those unacquainted with wet-rice cultivation. He would uproot the seedlings, carefully rinse the roots, and then stack them in bundles throughout the rest of the field. At this point the seedlings are of absolutely no nutritive value (except as feed to animals), so it was an act of faith to uproot one's entire crop before it had properly matured. But of course this task had become traditional and routine over time.

The seedlings were separated and laboriously transplanted, approximately three inches apart in long rows, into the waiting paddy fields. Bent at the waist, ankle-deep in filthy water, the transplanters stooped down thousands of times to plug each seedling into the muck. This back-breaking job might be done by a four- or five-person family in the day or so that the seedlings remained viable, but more commonly, gangs of peasant women did the task communally. The men went collectively up into the hills to harvest the green fertilizer but might spade it into the soil individually. Plowing and other farm tasks could be done separately, but collective teams of women almost always transplanted together (see Chapter 10). Peasants believed that women's fecundity mystically was channeled into improved fertility for the rice.

Men who were not actively involved in other agrarian tasks would toss the bunches of seedlings to the women, shore up paddy ridges, dredge irrigation canals, or provide a rhythmic accompaniment for the job. Traditional "call and response" work songs lightened the drudgery. Double-entendre calls by the men were answered rhythmically by the women to the collective enjoyment of all. Women could make ribald jokes about their sex lives or make suggestive taunts to the men; the time seemed to slip by faster, and the work seemed not as tiring. Other games and races helped to lighten the load. Often the whole village would celebrate the end of the crucial transplantation with a matsuri, and winning teams of transplanters would be feted with food and drink. Those who could still dance on tired legs did so. The kami of rice would be propitiated with gifts of pounded rice cakes (*mochi*) and sake, both products of the previous year's rice crop.

During the rest of the summer there were still hundreds of necessary tasks for the farm family. Weeding, draining, or irrigating the paddy rice fields at appropriate times, repairing dikes, dredging ditches, cultivating other crops, and the like kept the peasants always busy. The roots of the rice plants would be fertilized with collected human urine and nightsoil at appropriate times, no doubt a fetid and disagreeable task, but an essential one.

Children often were saddled with the task of keeping birds away from the ripening grain, but several ingenious scarecrows were developed as well. Dressed effigies (*kakashi*) and twirling paper owls were employed as in the West, but so were a number of "bird rattlers" (*naruko*) that were supposed to startle the birds with loud noises. One employed bamboo lengths that, when filled with water dripping from a sluice, would bang down a flat rock and then empty itself in order to start the process again. Another type, called "pulling boards" (*hiki-ita*) consisted of long lengths of twine attached to several clacking boards. One child could pull and release several strings alternately to startle birds all over the field.

Harvesting was usually done collectively, with large teams sweeping through several fields at once. The rice stalks would be cut very low to the ground using scythes and sickles. The stalks were gathered into armfuls of sheaves, using a few twisted stalks themselves as ties. The sheaves would stand out in the field to dry for a week to ten days, and then the kernels would be separated from the stalk using winnowing boards ("dragon's teeth"), or by being flailed against a stone or tree. The flails and winnow boards were ingenious inventions (see section on agricultural tools below), but harvesting still required a great deal of labor. At this point an appropriate amount of unhulled rice would be stored away in dry places to be used as seed in the next growing season.

The kernels of grain would be separated from the protective husks by a number of methods. Trampling, flailing, and stripping were all laborious and time-consuming, but essential. Commonly the grain would be tossed lightly into the air so that a slight breeze would carry away the chaff, while the kernels fell to the ground. The resulting grain was called brown rice because it was still encased in its nutrient bran covering. It could be, but was not commonly, cooked at this stage because it remained hard, did not absorb much liquid, and required much heat to prepare. It was usually polished using pebbles or bones to grind away the bran.

Highly polished white rice was the ultimate goal, since it absorbed twice its volume of liquid in cooking and was therefore more substantial as a meal. The bran was used as animal fodder. The polishing brought out rice's natural sticky, starchy quality. White rice was suitable for "binding" gruel and for rolling rice balls. It could be pounded into a gluten mass (*mochi*) or ground into flour. It could also be used to brew sake.

The rice was carefully measured and poured into woven straw bags, where it awaited the taxman. Of course we know that peasants tried to hide as much of the rice as possible during all of these harvesting phases in hopes that they could fool the samurai into thinking that the land was less productive than it really was. In most cases this hidden surplus was the difference between bare subsistence and a pitifully small improvement in the stark lives of the farmers. We also know that farmers would steal away to nearby scrubland and foothills, where they would secretly cultivate rice and other crops in hidden fields. Such was the nature of Japanese agriculture.

The rice straw could be used in several ways, but none was wasted. Some was chopped up, to be mixed with other vegetation (and the bran) to be used as silage for the very few horses and water buffalo kept in the villages. Some straw would become part of next season's fertilizer, and other amounts were woven into a profusion of artisanal products. Some was used as fuel, though it had to be mixed with other fiber, since it burned hotly but very quickly.

During the entire rice cultivation season, the farmers were also growing all sorts of other crops. Upland fields (those too steep or otherwise unsuited to wet-rice cultivation) were sown with many tuber-root vegetables (e.g., carrots, radishes, beets, potatoes). Indeed, the introduction of potatoes in the sixteenth and seventeenth centuries had been a godsend for the Japanese farmer. In particular, the sweet potato, with its very high carbohydrate content, was often the only thing that kept peasants alive during famines. One would venture to say that most peasants ate more potatoes than rice (see Chapter 7). Cabbage and other green leafy vegetables were also grown extensively, as were legumes of all sorts and several other grains.

Some southern and western areas of the country sustained two and even three crops of rice; even the most northern climes produced at least one. Of course this would have leached the soil of all nutrients, so more often than not, other crops were rotated into the rice cycles. Several strains of wheat, millet, barley, oats, and sorghum were common. Soya beans were a major source of protein, especially when made into tōfu and *shoyu* (soy sauce) (see Chapter 7). Virtually every edible root, bark, fruit, nut, berry, herb, grass, bush, and vegetable was cultivated or harvested in Japan. The country produced an astounding variety of foods.

Wheat, millet, sorghum, and barley were considered to be "dry" crops, that is, crops that did not need routine irrigation. They could also be cultivated in the uplands, and during the cold months. Some varieties were grown in winter and were ready for harvest just when rice cultivation began. The stalks of these grains were more suitable for silage and green fertilizer than for the production of woven straw products. Wheat was simpler to process after harvesting because polishing was not essential. The winter wheat was harder and therefore more difficult to grind than rice, but the flour was suitable to many more dishes than rice. Wheat flour became the major source of noodles, which were (and continue to be) very important in the lives of common people, as were wheat flour steamed buns. Buckwheat (soba) and other grain (including rice) flours were also made into noodles. Millet and barley were more commonly eaten in porridges, gruel, and soup.

Farmers very much thought of the forest as part of their world. In addition to fruits, nuts, berries, roots, and even small **Forestry** birds and animals harvested there, they depended on the forest for fuel and fertilizer as well as other wood products. The forest provided the "four trees of life": mulberry leaves for silkworms, lacquer trees, paper mulberry trees, and tea (actually a bush). Their building materials all came from the forest as well.

The real problem was that the bakufu and the daimyō also drew wealth and building supplies from the same forests. Lumber for the huge cities after 1600 strained even the huge forest of Japan. Almost 85 percent of Japan's land is heavily forested, but much of it is difficult to reach because of the mountainous terrain on which it predominated. Nevertheless, the huge ridgepoles and beams needed for castles and temples had seriously deteriorated old-growth forest stands by this time.

[T]he widespread deforestation of the early modern predation ended once and for all that long era during which the people of Japan managed their woodland loosely and exploited it freely. In the transformation that rulers and villagers achieved by the mid-eighteenth century, forests were carefully delineated and use rights clarified. The rule makers specified forms and limits of exploitation in great detail.[4]

Fallen trees and detritus from storms and high winds had been the traditional purview of villagers. But after about 1670 the bakufu, which controlled the major forests, began to forbid peasant gleaning without prior samurai inspection and authorization. Forestry inspectors came into the forests and plotted entire sections for bakufu use only. Trees were marked and registered to keep peasants from poaching.

The peasants depended on fallen limbs for firewood, and many farmers had gone into the production of charcoal as a "down-time" by-employment. Charcoal was produced on site along hillsides. Two types of charcoal were made. *Watan* was produced from several types of wood and was used for home heating and cooking, and of course was sold in nearby cities. Commercial charcoal (*kotan*) was produced from *kuri* (chestnut wood) and was used in production of metal. Charcoal was superior to even seasoned wood since it was nearly smokeless and produced an even, focused heat.

Sometimes peasants were employed by the bakufu and even some daimyō as foresters in a burgeoning new forestry after about 1680. Seed-

Two carpenters sawing planks from a dressed log in the mountains of Totomi, with Mt. Fuji in the background. Several cuts are made simultaneously to prevent warping. (Katsushika Hokusai, Japanese, 1760–1849, Mt. Fuji from the Totomi Mountains, from the series "The Thirty-Six Views of Mt. Fuji," 1823–29, woodblock print, 25.9 × 37.3 cm, Gift of Miss Katherine S. Buckingham to Clarence L. Buckingham Collection, 1925.3278, photograph © 2001, The Art Institute of Chicago, All Rights Reserved, photograph courtesy of The Art Institute of Chicago)

ling nurseries were developed on cleared forest land, and transplantation was done whenever trees were harvested. Unfortunately, peasants discovered that if the seedlings failed, the bakufu would pay day laborers to try again the next season. Peasants therefore made sure that they had continuing employment by doing the job shoddily.

The peasants were involved in much negotiation to retain their traditional rights to enter the forests (*iriai*) to gather green fertilizer and to glean firewood:

> The tension between the conflicting impulses to destroy forests for agricultural production and to maintain them for production emerged during the seventeenth century. During the eighteenth the picture was complicated by intensifying concern over scarcity of forest products, notably timber and firewood, which led forestry officials to shift their attention to wood production. The change in priorities was evident in bakufu regulations, which dwelt increasingly on managing the production of timber and fuel.[5]

One final "crop" that falls somewhere in between agriculture and artisanal activity is fishing. Being an island nation, Japan **Fishing** obviously had a long history with fishing, even longer than with sedentary agriculture, in fact. Spearing and types of gaffing are described in the ancient histories, and the folktales tell of all types of fishing even before that. Archeological evidence suggests that fish were the major protein source for most prehistoric riverine and ocean shore cultures in Japan. As suggested in Chapter 7, Japanese aversion to the eating of meat probably had more to do with the burgeoning population than with the Buddhist proscription against the killing of animals. The expanding agricultural paddy land had stripped away the forest habitat for most animals. But the eating of fish was never proscribed; cynics suggest that had it tried to forbid it, Buddhism might have failed as a religion in Japan.

The Japanese ate and otherwise used an astonishing variety of sea products, and all of them had to be harvested. Like agriculture, sea (and fresh water) products had their seasons. Particular varieties of fish were available only at certain times of the year. Fishers had to adjust to those maritime rhythms, and Shintō seemed to adjust to fishing life as well. The winter harvests were very dangerous because of the biting cold. But the late summer–early autumn harvest was perhaps even more perilous because of the typhoon season, particularly along the eastern shores. The craggy coastlines, a result of volcanic activity, made the profession a dangerous one. The tricky, rapid ocean currents and estuary flows added to the peril.

Not surprisingly, then, the primary fishing was done close to shore.

The many bays, coves, and inlets were the safest for shallow-draft ships. By the eighteenth century fishermen did not stray far from shore anyway, but that was due to the bakufu's *sakoku* edicts. A fisherman who slipped out of sight of the shore was liable for harsh punishment because it was feared (even a century later) that crypto-Christians might try to rendezvous with offshore Europeans. By this period several fishing nets had been developed; most could be handled by one ship, but several required cooperation between two or more. The most effective nets used for deepwater shellfish were trawling nets. The dragnet (*hiki-ami*) was imported from Korea after Hideyoshi's invasions in the sixteenth century. Gangs of Korean fishermen were brought as slaves to Japan, where they taught native fishers how to use the long nets in teams. Japanese had a wide variety of dipping nets (*sade-ami*), which could be maneuvered by one man using the power of a bent pole in much the same manner that farmers dipped water from wells.

Several types of divers plied the waters of protected coves to harvest oysters, clams, mussels, abalone, and the like. The most famous were the female *awabi* (abalone) divers, who have long captured the imagination of foreign men because the young women worked practically nude.

Other crustaceans were harvested in traps and pots, as were eels, octopus, and squid. Sea anemones, sea urchins, and other crustaceans were harvested along the shoreline and in tidal pools. The fish-laden ships would scurry to coastal ports to sell their catches to fish wholesalers in established markets. We are told that every evening the fish docks of Edo and Ōsaka, in particular, were like beehives as each ship jockeyed to dock only long enough to disgorge its catch. Wholesalers would row out to the ships in small skiffs and buy the whole catch before it had even hit the dock.

Seaweed, kelp, and other ocean vegetation was also harvested along the coasts and brought ashore for processing. We will follow that industry as well as the processing of other fish and marine products in Chapter 13.

Freshwater fish were abundant as well, but not to the extent of ocean fishing. Japan's rivers are mostly short and very rapid, since the distance from the mountains to the shore is relatively short. Japan has few lakes worthy of the name, and only one, Lake Biwa, is the locus of commercial fishing to any extent. Fish weirs and ladders had been employed for centuries, and there were even commercial hatcheries and fish nurseries established to increase production in many places. The Japanese carp (*koi*) were raised commercially in small ponds, as were freshwater shrimp, catfish, and other fish. Many villages cultivated fish in their water retention basins as well.

One other type of freshwater fishing should be mentioned here. The use of cormorants for commercial fishing was a picturesque and lucrative but controversial industry at the time. Cormorants were captured (or bred) and used to catch lake fish in many places, especially along the coasts of Lake Biwa, where they were immortalized by *ukiyo-e* woodblock printers of the period. The long-necked birds had a tight band slipped on their necks, which prevented them from swallowing the fish that they speared. Traces were slipped through the neck rings, and one deft fisher could manipulate up to a dozen birds from one boat. Torches were used on moonless dark nights. The light attracted the fish, and the cormorants swooped down to spear them with their beaks. The birds were reined back to the gunnels, where they would disgorge the fish that they could not swallow in exchange for the bait-sized tidbits that were their reward.

Devout Buddhists argued that forcing the birds to kill the fish created bad karma for the hapless birds. The fishers in turn argued that *their* own karma designated that they should do this, and therefore it was also part of the huge karmic fate of the cosmos (it is always easier to blame cosmic powers). Besides, cormorants were no different from dogs used in hunting, were they? The issue was never settled to anyone's satisfaction.

Most of the fish and shellfish were eaten fresh (i.e., within two days), but several more types were salted or dried to be shipped into the interior. Most mountain dwellers never tasted fresh fish. Sardines and other small fry were also dried for fertilizer. When mixed with heads, tails, bones and other fresh fish offal, these could be dried into fishmeal cakes that turned a tidy profit, considering that the ingredients would have been discarded anyway. Fish fertilizer was particularly useful for farmers growing cotton. The beaches of some relatively uninhabited islands were turned into stinking masses of drying fishmeal. Children would spend the day shooing away gulls and other shorebirds who must have thought they had died and gone to the Great Buffet in the sky.

Farmers also cultivated a variety of cash crops. The most obvious are the fiber plants necessary for clothing, such as **Cash Crops** flax for linen, cotton, mulberry leaves for silkworms, hemp and jute, and a particular type of cloth made from pounded bark. Prior to the sixteenth century peasants had worn very rough clothing made from hemp or from pounded bark. A few regions produced enough flax for linen.

Cotton had been introduced into Japan a century or so before, and by the eighteenth century it had replaced every other type of cloth for common clothing. As Susan Hanley suggests, the Sengoku daimyō were very interested in cotton for three military purposes: "Canvas was more durable than straw for sails and more resistant to weather; cotton [gun] fuses were more reliable than those made of cypress bark or bamboo;

and cotton uniforms were more durable than paper, warmer than hemp, and wore and looked better in battle."[6]

Cotton was raised commercially primarily around Ōsaka, but it could be grown in small upland fields virtually anywhere. The big problem with cotton was that it required a great deal of fertilizer, since it leached the soil of nitrogen in only one or two crops. Fishmeal, dried sardines, and improved commercial nightsoil collection in the seventeenth century made cotton a commercial crop. In 1736 the value of all the cotton that went to Ōsaka exceeded even the value of the considerable amount of rice that came there.[7]

Silk production was almost as old as rice agriculture. The technology had migrated from China in prehistorical times. Virtually any farmer could produce raw silk filament, but the production of fine textile took considerably more technology and industry. The basic requirements for elementary sericulture were simple enough. Peasants could buy cards of silkworm eggs, gather mulberry leaves (planted on the edge of fields as windbreaks), feed and nurture the worms as they developed from the eggs until they spun cocoons, and then boil the cocoons in order to extract the raw filaments. Peasant women could spin the filaments into thread at this point, but usually they sold the raw silk to artisans and bought more eggs. They could earn a modest supplement to their incomes, but few farmers would risk sericulture as anything but a sideline because it was a dangerous gamble. Virtually anything could happen along the way to doom a crop. Diseases and blights could wipe out an entire egg card or kill all of the worms before they spun their precious cocoons. Other diseases, early frosts, or typhoons might kill or blight the mulberry, and the worms would eat virtually nothing else. In short, it was a lucrative but very risky business. In the regions of the country where daimyō demanded silk as tax payment, they all too often suffered catastrophic crop failures that threatened the very lives of the poor peasants forced to raise silkworms for a living.

A very much less dangerous commercial crop was tea. By the eighteenth century Japan consumed a great deal of tea. It was by far the most popular drink in the country. Even poor peasants could afford the few coppers necessary to buy poor quality teas. Except for a very small amount of special blends imported from China, the country grew as much as it needed, and indeed probably exported as much (via the Dutch) as it imported.

As noted in Chapter 7, tea drinking and cultivation were a millennium old in Japan. The less bitter blends of the twelfth century brought by the the priest Myoe had made the drink tremendously popular. In addition to the traditional Zen tea ceremony (*chanoyu*), tea was enjoyed as a social and comestible product. The Chinese infused tea leaves in very hot water; the Japanese style was originally to grind the tea into a powder and to whisk the powder into hot water. The froth was allowed to settle before it was drunk.[8] But for the last century or so, Japanese also steeped leaves in hot water like the Chinese but preferred to let the water cool a little after it had boiled. Special "hot water coolers" (*yu-zamashi*) were developed to accommodate this custom, which was said to make the tea less bitter.[9]

Tea was grown on foothill terraces or other well-drained land. It grew best in the foggy climes, in long rows of bushes that hugged the contours of the southern (for the morning sun) side of the foothills. Tea bushes grew from transplanted cuttings of older bushes; a bush older than about ten years was considered to be worn out. The leaves were plucked by hand, the "younger" higher leaves being most prized. The lower leaves as well as the attached stems were of inferior grade. The bush continued to sprout leaves after each picking, so the harvest was really a periodical gleaning.

The leaves were washed and steamed, then baked or "fired" in iron roasting pans. During the firing, the leaves were massaged and rolled to insure uniform cooking and to sear in the natural oils. The fired leaves are cooled by fanning and then slowly roasted over a low heat. The lesser grades often required two roastings to properly settle the oils. They were then spread out to dry in the sun. The very best hybrids and finest "tender" cuttings were sealed hermetically into lacquered jars. The inferior grades were packed into pottery, wooden, or cloth containers, depending on the whimsy of merchants and their customers, all of whom swore that their choice preserved or enhanced the quality and taste of the tea. The wise producer acceded to every wish and preference.[10]

Agricultural Tools and Products

Most tools employed by farmers were rudimentary in technology. By the eighteenth century virtually every farmer owned or shared an iron-tipped plow. Many did not own an animal to pull the plow, however. Horses and water buffaloes were expensive to buy and to maintain. The small garden-sized plots of most peasants could not sustain an animal throughout the year. The cost of the necessary food and silage was beyond the means of the ordinary farmer. Since Buddhism proscribed the eating of meat, a farmer could not supplement his diet or his income by raising an extra animal to butcher. Japanese did not generally consume milk products either. Frequently, an animal could be owned collectively and shared throughout the year. Poorer peasants were forced to pull the plows themselves, obviously a backbreaking job.

Various iron-bladed hoes (*kuwa*) and spades were available and used for a variety of farm tasks. The *kusakezuri-kuwa* was the most common one used for weeding. *Itaguwa* were used for furrowing and plowing. *Karagumwa* used small thick blades for clearing land, and the three-pronged *Bitchu-guwa* could be used to turn the soil (laboriously) like a plow. Virtually every family owned a sickle because they could be used for so many farm tasks besides rice harvesting, such as clearing brush, trimming trees and bushes, and chopping straw and sedge. A few families obtained long-handled scythes, but in the eighteenth century they were not common. Various knives were used for many purposes. Japanese food, like Chinese food, was chopped into small pieces in order to save on the fuel to cook it, and also to pickle it.

Every village had one or two men who were specialists in carpentry (see Chapter 13). Very often they plied these skills as by-employment to their main agricultural livelihood, but some of the larger villages had full-time professional carpenters. Some of these peasant artisans doubled as thatchers, but more frequently there were men who did that as their sideline exclusively. Thatchers (see Chapter 9) took teams of young men out to gather sedge, which was cut into uniform lengths and then allowed to dry for a week or so. Then the young men would hoist the straw up onto the roof as the thatcher wedged it into the roof and then trimmed it to provide maximum protection and drainage. Thatchers used razor-sharp knives and fulcrum shears to ply their trade.

Almost every medium-sized village had a blacksmith; some smaller villages shared one between two or three villages. These men created an enormous variety of iron products with an astoundingly small kit of tools. Compared to Longfellow's Village Smithy, the eighteenth-century Japanese artisan looked like an itinerant tinsmith. A standard hollowed rock forge with a small leather hand-bellows, two or three iron mallets, a small anvil, and a bucket of water were sufficient to turn out most of what the farmers needed. Since Japanese did not iron-shoe their animals, and since they did not require large iron pieces such as barrel or wagon wheel hoops, the smithy could concentrate heat and energy on very small pieces indeed. The basic needs were knives, hoes, spades, plow tips, hammers, saw blades, sickles, scythes, food choppers, and a few other odds and ends. These could be produced rather easily using only pig-iron ingots and charcoal. Japan had very little iron ore and even less coal, so it had to adjust.

Most other farm implements were made of wood or straw. Buckets, pails, barrels, casks, and handles of every sort were, as in Europe and the Americas, fashioned by coopers out of wood. Virtually none of them ever employed iron hoops for the barrels; plaited straw ropes were used instead. Almost anyone with rudimentary knowledge of woodworking tools could make rain clogs (*geta*). These consisted of a plain eight-inch plank of paulownia wood with two grooves cut into one side. Two pieces of wood were hammered into the grooves perpendicularly, and then a hole was drilled into the plank at one end. Two short lengths of straw rope were knotted together at one end and the loose ends threaded through the hole in the wood. The loose ends were then looped and the

Tools. Top: bitchu-kuwa hoe; sickle; "dragon's teeth" grain flail. Second row: reed sieve; sedge grain scoop and winnow. Third row: wood plane, carpenter's inked string. Bottom: handsaw. (Drawings by Edward Lee)

ends fastened to the side of the plank, one on either side. The geta was then kept on the foot by threading the ropes between the great and second toe. The two pieces of wood elevated one above the mud or snow, and the foot was kept relatively dry.

The Japanese did not use large tables or, indeed, much wooden furniture in their homes, so there was no real need for such craftsmen in ordinary villages. The only other major employment for carpenters was

Cooper constructing a large wooden vat for storing brewed sake using very simple tools. View from Fujimigahara in Owari. (Katsushika Hokusai, Japanese, 1760–1849, Fujimi-ga-hara [Fuji-view Field] in Owari Province, Edo period, 1830–32, woodblock, 25.4 × 37.15 cm, Clarence L. Buckingham Collection, 1925.3229, photograph © 2001, The Art Institute of Chicago, All Rights Reserved, photograph courtesy of The Art Institute of Chicago)

in house construction (see Chapter 9), and for the wood joinery that went into the interior furnishings.

Almost all farmers made straw products whenever they were not actively engaged in other agricultural tasks. The rice straw was woven into an astonishing number of things. Straw sandals (*waraji*) were woven at night or during the down-times of the agricultural rhythms. Traditionally, they were supposed to be the first task of the New Year. Waraji were simply coils of braided straw that served as a rough shoe sole. They were fastened to the feet with a thong that fit between the great and second toe and with braids of straw that looped through the sole and tied at the ankle. A finer woven sandal (*zori*) was intended to be worn inside the house. These had only the toe thong, since they were intended to be slipped on and off at will. Straw boots (*waragutsu*) were also made for houses that had packed dirt (*doma*) floors. Thicker snow boots (*yukigutsu*) were made for walking through the deep snow in the far northwest corner of Honshu. Flat straw platform snowshoes were also manufactured.

Raincoats (*mino*) and snowcoats (really essentially the same thing) were made by peasants for their own use as well. These were simply rows of straw sewn into hemp coats to provide a surprisingly waterproof coat that shed the rain very well. Conical sedge hats (*ami-gasa*), straw seat cushions (*enza*), wadded sitting mats (*okidatami*), sleeping mats (*shikidatami*), woven rice bags, and straw ropes were made virtually by everyone. All that was needed was some kind of cutting tool and some dexterous hands. Sedge products like baskets and hats were a little more complicated, but not by much.

Clothing, on the other hand, required much more expertise. By the eighteenth century almost every village produced enough cotton for its own clothing needs. The cotton was carded and stripped of seeds by hand. The strands were twisted into simple thread in roughly the same manner used by eighteenth-century American rural women. Thread could be dyed using any one of scores of homemade natural vegetable dyes. Cloth was woven on simple looms. Since the Japanese kimono (see Chapter 8) could be easily fashioned into a one-size-fits-all generic garment, there was no real need for tailors. The length could be altered somewhat with simple basting stitches, and the width was adjusted by the simple technique of wrapping the body to fit. It also helped that the Japanese were of a common racial stock, so the differences in body sizes of adults were minimal. Clothing producers used little more than fulcrum shears, needles (produced in the cities), a spinning wheel, and a simple loom.

Flails and grain winnows were simple but ingenious tools. The flails are familiar to most fans of martial arts movies. The so-called nunchucks used by Kung-fu Shaolin priests in combat are grain flails. One simply attaches two wooden poles together end to end with a rope (few were linked by chains). One then grasps one pole and swings the other through the air to flail (hence the name) the grain stalks on the ground. The accumulated force of the flail was some twenty times what one could bring to bear with only one pole, and it had the added advantage that the flail rarely cracked or broke as a single pole would do from the torque on the handle. Another common way to remove the grain from the stalks was to take two cooking chopsticks (a foot longer than the standard ones used for eating) and then run the stalks between the two, flailing away from the body in a stripping motion. This was relatively simple in terms of technology, but it was very tiring.

Stalks could also be whipped against an upright pole, a handy tree, or rock. The problem with this method was that it threw the kernels a distance from the flailer and there would be some difficulty rounding them all up unless one did this in a room or other enclosed space. A better device was a "dragon's teeth" winnow. The first ones were simple enough: V-shaped notches could be cut into a plank of wood, which would be made to stand upright with the row of sawlike teeth pointing upwards. A flailer could then lay a sheaf of rice (or wheat, millet, barley, or sorghum) across it, then pull the grain spears rapidly through the row of teeth. Old, dulled saws (sharp ones would cut the stalks) were sometimes mounted on planks, and eventually craftsmen began to construct a more U-shaped row of teeth since that did not cut the straw as much. By the eighteenth century every village owned at least one "dragon's teeth" contraption which was shared communally.

Grindstones could be small, hand-operated horizontal pestle-and-mortar affairs, but most villages had large communal ones. The larger prototypes came from China. They were basically two wheels of coarse granite or other abrasive stone. One wheel would be mounted horizontally as the base with a pole anchored in the center. The other smaller wheel would then be mounted on a horizontal axis attached to the base wheel's upright pole. The upper grindstone wheel would roll on the base, turning in a tight circle, grinding the grain between the two wheels. Pushing the top wheel around would operate the machine by the axis. The longer the axis, the less energy needed to push the wheel, but the greater circumference one needed to walk around. Obviously a horse or buffalo could be prodded or led around that circle and the job could be accomplished sooner and with less human power. The first grinding produced very coarse grist, which could be ground even finer into flour with each subsequent pass of the wheel. Small children could be trained to scoop the grist behind the wheel for the next pass, and the child could prod the animal along with a few kindly whacks on the rump while simultaneously scooping the grist.

Another major agrarian tool was the waterwheel (*noria*). This required communal effort and a considerable outlay of rural capital to buy, construct, and maintain in good working order. The basic principle is that of a paddleboat propeller. A log was mounted horizontally as the axis for the wheel onto a sturdy frame of double uprights at each end of the axis. The wheel was constructed of a dozen or so spokes radiating from the center. Concave scoops were mounted at the ends of the spokes. People would then turn the wheel by "climbing" it endlessly. As the people-engines trod on the ends of the spokes, the scoops would ladle up the water and then carry it to the top of the wheel as it turned, and then deposit it with a splash on the other side of the wheel. In this manner, a continual (at least as long as someone "climbed" the wheel) stream of water could be pumped from a ditch onto a higher paddy field.

Some farmers had to make do with the laborious pole dipper. This was a water bail attached by rope to a long pole wedged into the ground. The operator used the springlike tension in the bent pole to rhythmically dip water from a pond to a higher field. Obviously this was labor-intensive and required long sessions to bail sufficient water to flood even a very small field. Such pole ladles were used in shallow wells, though some well pails were hauled up by the rope, pulling hand-over-hand. Only very few hand-cranked well rope contraptions were ever found in rural areas, though they were common in urban areas where the wells were much deeper.

Similarly, the ubiquitous one-man one-wheel barrow of China was scarcely used in Japan, though people and animals drew two-wheeled carts. Carriages and dray wagons were primarily urban conveniences. Two-man palanquins were common on the major highways, but no one used them in the rural areas unless a daimyō was visiting.

These palanquins were of two main types. The *kago* was a basketlike contraption that was suspended from a pole carried by two or more porters. The multicarrier types had two poles. If there were more than two carriers, one or more could compensate for the weight by shifting to the back when going uphill or to the front when going down. The rider sat cross-legged at the bottom of the basket, which could be quite uncomfortable on long trips. The other type, the *norimono*, was more like a small cage, which had a solid, flat floor on which to sit. These were mounted on top of a packhorse, or rather on top of the bags and other luggage strapped on the horse. Almost no wheeled carriages plied the rural roads, because although the roadbed was hard-packed and generally well maintained, the rains would quickly turn the dirt into mire. There were no wagon ruts in rural Japan. Two-wheel oxcarts had been used to transport people back in the Heian era, but they had almost disappeared except in Kyoto.

Perhaps we should also consider here stream and river crossing

A woman in a Norimono palanquin prepares a kiseru tobacco pipe; the tabako-bon carrier is in front of her, within the Norimono. The servant kneels with a lighted wick, ready to light the pipe. The bamboo screen along the carrying pole would drape down to provide the rider with privacy. Woodblock print by Ishikawa Toyonobu. (Courtesy of Asia Library, University of Michigan)

Example of late-eighteenth-century bridge construction. Artist of print unknown. (Courtesy of Asia Library, University of Michigan)

"tools." There were three types in the countryside. Bridges of all types were constructed or thrown across narrow streams. Trees were sometimes felled or dragged across a small stream, and then trimmed of branches and bark to serve as balance beams. Grappling ladder ropes could be suspended over deeper and longer spaces, and trestle bridges were constructed from time to time. The latter would almost inevitably be washed away by the gushes of water that scoured most river canyons in times of heavy rains or snowmelt. Stout stone arched bridges were more common close to and within the larger towns and cities. A few picturesque steeply humped "turtle" bridges (looking like upside-down U's) could be found, chiefly near large Buddhist temple complexes. These were Chinese and Korean in origin, and the Japanese found them to be quaint but not very practical, because they were slippery even when completely dry.

The second type of fording "tool" was the rope ferry. These appeared to be simplicity itself because they required only two working parts. One needed some kind of float, such as a boat or a raft on (or in) which to place the cargo. By stretching a stout rope across the water, anchored to firm objects on either side, the ferryman could simply pull the ferry across to the other side. Obviously, over a swift-running stream (which most of Japan's rivers were) this was trickier than first imagined. A man would have to be very strong to keep a boat, even one firmly tethered to the rope, moving across the strong current. In Japan the remedy was to "sling" the boat at an oblique angle that took advantage of the current rather than fighting against it. The boat could be hauled upriver a short way on one side in the shallow water, then "slung" down to the other side in a similar manner. Obviously this required more than one or two men to operate. Usually a horse on either side was used to haul the ferry upriver after each crossing.

The third fording method was the use of sure-footed horses or men to carry goods and people across water. This could only be accomplished in shallow, wide flooded areas, and not in swift-running deep rivers. A final method was to wait until the flood had receded and then cross on one's own power.

NOTES

1. See Donald Philippi, ed. and trans., *The Kojiki* (Princeton: Princeton University Press, 1968), for the other social "sins."

2. See Tsuneo Sato, "Tokugawa Villages and Agriculture" (Mikiso Hane, trans.), in Chie Nakane and Shinzaburō Oishi, eds., *Tokugawa Japan: The Social and Economic Antecedents of Modern Japan* (Tokyo: University of Tokyo Press, 1990), 37–80, for an excellent discussion.

3. See Thomas C. Smith, *Nakahara: Family Farming and Population in a Japanese*

Village, 1717–1830 (Stanford: Stanford University Press, 1977), for an interesting discussion, particularly p. 33.

4. Conrad Totman, *The Green Archipelago: Forestry in Preindustrial Japan* (Berkeley: University of California Press, 1989), 113.

5. Ibid., 97.

6. Susan B. Hanley, "Tokugawa Society: Material Culture, Standard of Living, and Life-Styles," in John W. Hall and James L. McClain, eds., *Early Modern Japan*, volume 4 in *The Cambridge History of Japan* (Cambridge: Cambridge University Press, 1991), 689.

7. Ibid., 689.

8. See Engelbert Kaempfer, *The History of Japan: Together with a Description of the Kingdom of Siam*, 3 vols., trans. J. G. Scheuchzer (Glasgow: James MacLehose and Sons, 1906), 3:238 for description.

9. See Basil Hall Chamberlain, *Japanese Things* (Rutland, VT: Tuttle, 1971), 454.

10. Compare ibid., 450–54, and Kaempfer, *History of Japan*, 3:224–42.

13

Urban Work

In the larger cities, particularly in the jokamachi and six or seven metropolises, work was much different. Here the artisans worked with more skill and at a much more leisurely pace. Of course their work was tied to the market as much as was the piecework of smaller towns, but many of these items were much more refined and "manufactured." Without question, a large percentage of chōnin workers were involved in semiskilled labor, but the elite artisans predominated.

The latter made an astonishing variety of goods. We can only scratch the surface here, but perhaps we should focus on items more common to Japan than to European and American cities at the same time. That is, we will mention, but we will not spend much time with, the largely urbanized work of artisans who made everyday essentials such as kitchen utensils, simple tools and furniture, textiles, and common clothing. We will concern ourselves here with lacquers, cloisonné and other jewelry makers, theatrical, musical, and military product producers, and the like.

Japanese pottery was world renowned even in eighteenth-century sakoku seclusion. It had never attained the **Pottery and** high artistry of the Chinese and Korean kaolin porcelains, **Ceramics** but it had developed artistic and technologic expertise of a different sort. The Japanese prized the rough-glazed rustic style made famous by *raku* and *mashiko* artisans. These styles had their origins in the Zen *chanoyu* tea bowls imported from Korea in the sixteenth century. Their hillside kilns, hard by the clay pits around Kyoto, Nikko, and other regions, turned out hundreds of pots, bowls, vases, and other pieces of utilitarian pottery, but also a great number of artistic objects as well.

We should note here that Japanese eating customs highly influenced the types of bowls and plates that were produced. The Japanese were accustomed to having each side dish served individually in tiny saucers and plates rather than bunched together on large plates. It has been suggested that this is probably because they wished to appreciate each food separately and individually, but many stews were prepared as well, particularly in the New Year celebrations. Others have argued that the small dishes facilitate offerings to the kami, but this is problematic too. Regardless of the reason, the fact that the Japanese preferred to eat in this way created a tremendous market for miniature-sized dishes. These were very often glazed ceramics, but there were many lacquered wooden ones, as well as straw baskets and platters. Each person being served separately, there was a need for individual serving trays. These were actually tiny tables with short legs, set before each guest seated on the floor. Most tray-tables were made of lacquered wood.

Jewelry

Jewelry was often lacquered as well. The Japanese also improved on a continental Asian process commonly called cloisonné. This involves beating gold and silver into etched designs cut into common metals. These jewelry pieces are then lacquered. Brooches, pins, and other pieces became very popular abroad as well. Artisans developed very sophisticated inlays and carvings for sword and quiver covers as well as a thousand other decorated objects. The portable Buddhist home altars (*Butsudan*) were similarly inlaid with nacre, lacquered (especially in silver and gold), and decorated. The area around the jokamachi Hikone on Lake Biwa specialized in these altars, which were then sold all over Japan by the fabled *Omi Shonin* itinerant traders.

A few words should be said about other jewelry manufacturing here. The famous women divers brought up pearls cultivated in oysters. Abalone mother-of-pearl (nacre) divers also harvested shellfish that were carved into beautiful shapes. The Japanese are also famous for lacquered carved miniatures. Tiny animals, people, Buddhas, and other figurines were carved from bits of whalebone, ivory, wood, and other materials and then were lacquered into amulets, fobs, portable shrines, and other bric-a-brac. Particularly popular were drawstring pulls (*net-suke*) for tobacco pouches and silk purses. Artisans carved fanciful shapes and decorations for other art objects, such as sword hilt guards (*tsuba*).

These and other miniaturizing tendencies of Japanese gave testimony to the comment by the nineteenth-century Japanophile Basil Hall Chamberlain that "the Japanese genius touches perfection in small things."[1]

Oil lanterns (clockwise from top left): hanging metal "pierced wick" todai lamp; covered ceramic "pierced wick" table lamp; cochia lacquered hand-held "walking" or palanquin lamp; "corner" andon standing lamp with waxed paper winged reflectors. (Drawings by Jennifer Mool)

Skilled craftsmen, mostly in Kyoto, but a few through-out the rest of the country, manufactured a profusion of musical instruments. Many of these were also artfully painted, lacquered, inlaid, and carved. Biwa lutes, sami-sen, and other stringed instruments were very popular, as were various flutes. By far the most common instruments were drums.

Musical and Theatrical Products

Most were small, hand-held (single bongo-like) drums that accompanied the three major theater genre performances (Bunraku, Kabuki, and Noh), but there were many large drums as well. The drums known as *taiko* were titanic, requiring groups of drummers to play them. Special woods were grown and shaped for these drums, and the skins of animals were employed for the heads.

Artisans produced a profusion of items for use in the theater. The most elaborate, in terms of both production and aesthetics, was the manufacture of puppets for Bunraku. Perhaps more accurately, the major products were the heads and hands of the puppets, because the bodies were basically frames on which to drape costumes. As noted in Chapter 22, a team of three men manipulated the puppets. One apprentice managed the right hand and another the feet. Master puppeteers used one hand to manipulate the puppet's left hand, and the other to manage the head.

Puppet hands were made in several different styles depending on their function. One-piece hands were for show; others with a thumb and a single moveable finger were for holding scarves, pieces of paper, and the like. Occasionally a fully articulated hand with several joints was used to actually express emotion in a kind of body language, especially in dance. There were artisans who specialized in the carving of hands alone. Obviously the multijointed varieties took much skill and much time to make. The artistry and technique became so highly developed that in the twentieth century, makers of prosthetic devices came to study with Bunraku hand artisans.

Surpassing that expertise were the artisans who made puppet heads. Heads were carefully carved from a single block of special wood, which was split in half to better hollow out the interior. The interior portion of the face received almost as much attention as the outer part. Toggles and strings were rigged so that the puppeteer could manipulate the movement of several parts of the face. Eyes were made to roll, to blink, and even to move independently of each other to create the expression of extreme rage and frustration: the cross-eyed stare. Eyebrows could arch and knit, lips could be parted to bare teeth, and tongues could even protrude. All of these could be done simultaneously to effect a startling approximation of reality. An ingenious device was developed whereby a head would have a protruding pin mounted on the lower lip. The puppeteer could snag a scarf to the pin and create the sensuous and very suggestive illusion that the woman (most commonly) was biting the cloth in the throes of sexual ecstasy, a common theatrical convention.

Of course the exterior of the face received much loving care in construction, but the faces were really quite standard in physiognomy in terms of character genre. Most young women looked quite similar, as did old people, heroes, villains, and the like. In most cases the characters

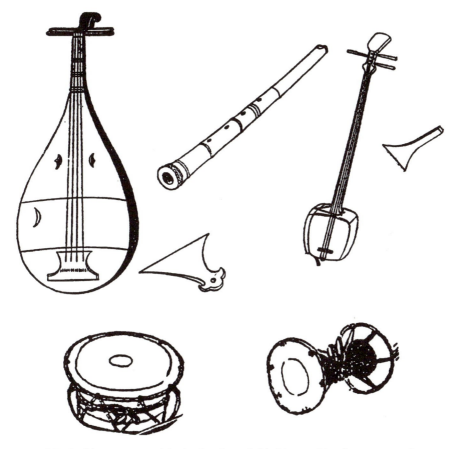

Musical instruments (clockwise from left): biwa with plectrum; reed
shakuhachi flute; three-string samisen with plectrum; two hand drums.
(Drawings by Tim Starr)

were differentiated by costume and hairdressing rather than by facial
differences.

The backs of the heads were fairly standard since most were covered
by wigs, scarves, and hats. Nevertheless, head carvers carefully matched
the halves to be sure that the essence and spirit of the "personality" were
complete and pristine. Naturally, head makers knew a great many different arts such as carving, shaping, painting, mechanical construction,
and, of course, repair and maintenance. A sophisticated head took
months to make, but could last for decades.

Similarly, skillful artisans created Noh and Gagaku (an ancient court
dance) masks. Rarely did the artisans of one genre participate in manufacturing objects for another. Most artisans were attached to theater

companies and manufactured products only for their own. Noh and Ga-gaku masks did not have any mechanical parts but were just as aesthetically sophisticated in their appearance. Like Bunraku, the masks were of conventional type according to the age, gender, and character of the role.

In all the theatrical genres, costumers and hairdressers were very important as well. Silk workers produced an endless supply of sumptuous costumes, some artfully dyed, others embroidered, and yet others painted. All theater must constantly stretch the conventions of style to new heights, and must also approximate the past in costume. The costumers in Kabuki in particular were artists more than artisans.

Similarly, hairdressers had to keep constantly inventing fanciful new styles and designs, particularly for the *onna-gata* (female impersonators). Most actors wore several wigs during a performance, and virtually all were made of human hair, since there were far more humans than horses in Japan to provide the hair. In most wigs, each hair was individually painstakingly sewn (and then knotted into place) into a silk skullcap that could be removed in the wink of an eye. The wigs were styled into place in much the same way that humans had their hair dressed. That is to say, the styles could be changed and were not totally immobilized. They therefore required occasional dressing and adjustment.

As noted in Chapter 22, the actors and puppets became trendsetters, style mavens, and clotheshorses. But of course it was the costumers and hairdressers who actually created the new rages; the actors and puppets merely wore them.

Wooden Products Japanese joinery, cabinetry, and carved wood products were of very high quality. Some joining pegs were used in constructing these products, but iron nails were very rare indeed. Most objects such as trunks, cabinets, and the like were ingeniously cut to fit closely together with dovetail flanges, tabs, inserts, and other interlocking devices that required only a little glue. Even ordinary boxes, barrels, pails, and casks were made with tongue-in-groove technology. One piece interlocked with the next by sliding into grooved recesses.

In terms of woodwork in general, as in the other professions, the Japanese worked wonders with relatively few and relatively low technology tools. The carpenter's toolbox contained only a few small tools and looked paltry and amateurish compared with the standard kit in the West. Few European carpenters of the time would venture out on a job without two or more each of hammers, saws, planes, drills, and knives, not to mention pencils, chalk, measuring tapes, plumb lines, levels, T squares, and barrels of nails. A Japanese carpenter made do with one small saw, a knife, a hammer that also served as a plane and as a measure, a length of chalked line that also served as a plumb line and level, and a handful of wooden or bamboo pegs. Similarly, a workman's bench in the West was cluttered with clamps, vises, glue pots, and other aids. In Japan, straw twine and glue sufficed.

In Japan scaffolding was quickly constructed of a few dozen lengths of stout but lightweight bamboo and a score of short straw ropes with which to lash them together. Japanese workmen of all types worked nearly naked except in the coldest weather. Most wore only split-toed anklet (tabi) socks on their feet and therefore were able to scramble up scaffolding like monkeys, lacking only a prehensile tail. Even stone-workers and masons wore practically no protective clothing, shoes, or helmets. Indeed, several European observers commented that Japanese workmen looked more like beggars than skilled craftsmen.

Japanese carpenters never developed the long water-driven bandsaws of sawmills, nor did they employ large sanders or box planes. Virtually all woodwork was done with small-tooth handsaws that were labor-intensive and very tedious to use, but turned out pieces that needed almost no sanding. Planks were planed with adze-like hatchets, but were made remarkably smooth and true by simple, small, short strokes. The secret was perhaps that virtually everything was standard in size. Cross-beams, ridgepoles, and house column uprights were massive and heavy, requiring but little outside dressing. Virtually every other house plank was relatively thin and narrow, more like lathing and wainscoting than the standard Western two-by-fours and the even heftier four-by-sixes. Most housing construction was easily planned and joined because the fusuma and tatami frames were identical in size. No window joinery was needed because inner fusuma were of translucent paper. There were no frilly cupolas, gables, dormers, spires, and epis to the roofs as in the West. All rooms were standard rectangles, measured in tatami mats. All walls were load-bearing outer shells supported by standard columns. There were no inner walls since the standard fusuma served as sliding room dividers. Few measurements were necessary; houses and most buildings were designed much like the so-called prefabricated models of the mid-twentieth-century American cookie cutter tract houses.

Almost no houses were made of brick or stone. Mud wattling was sometimes smeared over bamboo latticework to effect a kind of stucco exterior, but virtually no cement or mortar was used in house construction. Even stone buildings and walls, primarily in castle construction, were not mortared. Stones were hewn to fit together closely, or small stone shards were used to "rubble" together interlocking larger stones. Stonemasons took much more time preparing and dressing stone than they did in actual construction. Outer walls were often made of rammed-earth blocks held together by the weight of facing stones.

Other than wood frames and tatami mats, the other major component of most houses was roofing. A few single homes still had thatch roofs,

Wooden objects. Top: wheeled wooden cart; camp stool; traveling lacquered dressing case with pull drawers and locking over-door. Middle: wooden pillow topped with cloth cushion; Ema (horse) praying fetish; wooden carrying tray. Bottom: lacquered inro medicine case with five stacking drawers, tied with silk cord and held with netsuke fob; two-drawer makeup chest with bronze kagami mirror; serving honzen tray-table. (Drawings by Haley Schumaker)

but the typical urban longhouse tenements almost all had shingle or tile roofs by the eighteenth century. Dried (not fired) clay tile became very popular because construction was cheap and they offered more protection in the event of a fire.

Brewing   Japanese did not grow grapes for wine,[2] distill grain mash for whiskey, or brew beer. Virtually the only alcohol made was brewed sake. It is called "rice wine" by some because the brewing and fermenting were similar to grape wine production. Its production is more similar to that of tequila from the maguey cactus in Mexico. A rice mash was brewed with small amounts of wheat or millet;

yeast was introduced and the mash was allowed to ferment. The sake was strained, decanted, and cleared at various steps, and the final clear liquid was stored in wooden casks until potable.

Sake technology had come to Japan from China, probably as early as did wet-rice cultivation techniques. By the eighth century it was so ingrained (pun intentional) into Japanese life that it had been incorporated into the *Kojiki* and *Nihon Shoki* histories and was part of Shintō ritual. A millennium later, sake was a very lucrative business. Many large rice merchants invested heavily in sake brewing, and they became, along with independent brewers, moneylenders as well. The bakufu tried desperately to keep sake out of the hands of the peasants, but virtually every village brewed a few casks for use in matsuri and other rituals. Village brewers who could only take the time to do so during the winter months of inactivity were called "one hundred–day men" (*hyakunichi-otoko*) after the December through March brewing time. Most of the production was done in the larger cities. Not surprisingly, the "kitchen" of the country, Ōsaka, led in production.

Another liquor called *shochu* was popular, particularly among rural brewers. It was brewed from rice and wheat and fermented with potato juice. It is similar to the Mexican pulque stage in tequila in that the alcohol content can vary wildly from one batch to another, so much so that it is occasionally poisonous.

Another form of brewing was not for alcohol, but for *shoyu*, what is known in the West as soy sauce. This concoction had come to Japan from China (a familiar phrase), but rather later than sake. This was something of a minor by-product of tofu and miso paste production. The latter two are produced from the soya bean. The Japanese had long used soybeans for food, and it was an excellent by-season crop because it restored nutrients to rice-leached soil. The beans had to be soaked in water for long periods because they are extremely hard to chew and are very bitter to eat naturally.

For miso, the beans are boiled for several hours, mixed with salt and *koji* wheat malt, and then allowed to ferment in wooden vats for months. The decomposed grit can be formed into a thick paste which is then diluted in small amounts with water into the salty, cloudy soup that is familiar to most diners in Japanese restaurants today. A preliminary stage produces a vile-smelling food called *natto* that can be eaten as a condiment or snack by people without a sensitive sense of smell. Since natto is "predigested" by enzyme action, it became an excellent baby food as well.

Tofu is manufactured by boiling the beans and skimming off the froth, which is then allowed to congeal. The amorphous rubbery substance is cut into slabs and eaten as is, in soups, or with sauces, vegetables, and spices added. Tofu can also be sun-dried, and the chewy, leathery strips can be kept for long periods. Tofu is very high in protein and absorbs the taste of any liquid.

Shoyu is actually as much wheat as it is soy in content. Soybeans are boiled until soft and then blended with an equal amount of wheat grist. The mixture is cooked and fermented for a day. An equal amount of salt is added and then diluted with enough water to equal two and a half times the original volume of the mixture. The admixture is stirred several times a day for two weeks or so and then allowed to sit covered for two to three months. The final stage is to decant and strain. The resulting dark liquid was used full-strength or diluted as a cooking, marinating, and dipping sauce. Until the late eighteenth century there was no regular method to control the quality of the shoyu. At that time, the major brewer Kikkoman discovered "quality control" methods, and shoyu became quite popular even among the poor peasants.

Military Products   Although Japan had remained isolated and "closed" for more than a half-century before 1700, it still continued to produce some military products. Also, despite being at peace since about 1640, artisans still continued to manufacture swords, bows, arrows, dirks, and other killing weapons. Because the country had been at war sporadically for almost five centuries, from the 1150s to the 1640s, the military artisans were quite proficient. Indeed, many historians have suggested that Japan very well may have invented tensile steel for use in sword making.

The sword became much more than the horrible killing machine that it clearly was. It took on an identity as the "soul" of the samurai. The sword became invested with all sorts of mystical and quasi-religious beliefs. Artistically, it became a hallmark of Japanese artisanship. "As an art object it is unmatched—its finely polished steel surface has an intrinsic beauty unique among objects made of steel. The deep lustre and bewitching variations in the crystalline structure of the surface steel have been likened to the beauty of the glaze on ceramics."[3]

Swords that had come to Japan from China and Korea were in many ways more like European swords than like the Japanese curved blade (*katana*) that came to be associated with the medieval samurai. The katana was very much a hybrid of many Asian styles. By the late thirteenth century Japan produced arguably the finest swords in the world. They became a major export to China and the rest of Asia, bringing very handsome prices.

Japan has very little iron ore and even less high quality hard coal. This paucity of raw materials, ironically, probably led to the development of carbon steel. Early on the iron swords made in Japan simply were inferior to Korean swords, so Japanese iron workers experimented with all sorts of metal alloys and smithing techniques in order to improve the native blades. They happened on the "double-back" method, which although time-consuming, tedious, and very labor-intensive, produced a superior product.

Simply put, the sword was the product of perhaps twenty different firings. Each time the iron was heated to nearly a white-hot temperature, then the metal was folded back on itself and the halves fused together by being pounded with a heavy maul hammer. It was then cooled in water and the process repeated. Each time the iron was heated, it burned out more impurities in the metal, a process that accomplished in months what could be done in minutes by the Bessemer converter technology five centuries later. And each time the metal was hammered into itself, it actually fused molecules together, rendering the iron into steel. Later, the finest smiths experimented with combining this very hard steel with "softer" steel to make the blade into a composite that could hold a razor-keen edge, yet was flexible enough to absorb tremendous torque without bending or cracking. The entire process took on a religious aspect. Shintō priests were called in at critical junctures in the production to ritually purify the blade.

The inner core (*shingane*) was the product of five or six foldings and therefore was relatively low in carbon content. The "skin" (*hadagane*) that was fused and welded over the shingane core had been folded perhaps as many as twenty times (creating more than one million layers!) and therefore was very high in carbon. When this had been accomplished, the blade was painted with a secret concoction of clay and ashes spread thicker on the back of the blade and thinner along the single cutting edge.

The blades were then polished and honed for months until they were considered completed. Commissioned swords were then tested before they were delivered to their new owners. The best way to test the new sword, of course, was on the human body. Obviously, there were not many volunteers for this task, so sword testers bought the bodies of condemned prisoners. Swords were ranked on their proficiency in cutting through limbs, torsos, and even groups of torsos. A sword that could cut through three or four bodies in one swipe was obviously very sharp and powerful indeed. The results of these tests would be engraved on the blade itself as a gruesome advertisement.

Swords also took on a mystical quality, and stories abounded of their magical qualities. Swords from the fourteenth century still continue to hold an edge six centuries later. Not surprisingly, samurai took to naming their swords, much as in Arthurian legends. They became family heirlooms.

In the eighteenth century the killing power of the katana was no longer as essential as it had been a century or two before. In fact, it had become a social symbol, and few samurai could afford to commission a superior new blade. Obviously, such a blade took a long time to make. Estimates of the cost of a new top-line blade run as high as the equivalent of three years of an average samurai's annual stipend. Most blades were passed on to one's successor along with one's inherited position and stipend. It was a badge of status. Swords were still being produced in the eighteenth century, but most were of distinctly inferior quality. Most of the new production was for ceremonial purposes. A young samurai, particularly one who would not inherit his father's stipend, would often be given a new sword at his coming-of-age ceremony. Swords were also commissioned as prizes for martial arts tournaments and as ceremonial status symbols for sumo wrestlers (*rikishi*) and the like.

The companion short-sword (*wakizashi*) or dirk, worn by every samurai, was typically about eighteen inches long. Since the katana was a two-handed sword, very few warriors fought with the dirk. The wakizashi purportedly was to be used for only two things. First, it was used to take the head of a defeated foe as a war prize. This was done ceremoniously and very carefully to avoid damaging the head, since one's reward was contingent on the level of the foe vanquished. Second, the dirk was appropriate for taking one's own life in the gruesome but honored *hara-kiri* ("belly slitting") or *seppuku* (ritual suicide).

Many ex-samurai (*gonō*) who had been decommissioned in Hideyoshi's time were allowed to wear the single wakizashi as a symbol of their status as hereditary village headmen. Toward the end of the period, the bakufu and some daimyō invested the wealthiest merchants with wakizashi as special status in recognition of their "service." Usually the service recognized was a special "gift" or forgiveness of a large debt owed by the daimyō or bakufu to the merchant.

The wakizashi did not have to withstand the tremendous torque of a two-handed slash, so the blade was usually vastly inferior to that of the katana. In the eighteenth century probably three times as many wakizashi were made as good katana.

Two centuries before, Japanese ironworkers had been kept busy turning out thousands of other killing tools. Spears, halberds, arrowheads, and the vicious-looking "sleeve entanglers" (multibarbed tips mounted on long poles that were intended to hook a samurai off his horse) were produced to arm the foot soldiers (*ashigaru*) of the day. Most of these iron pieces were of very inferior quality.

The Japanese never developed the huge shields used in European jousting and warfare. Similarly, Japanese armor was distinctly different as well. Infinitely more flexible and lighter, the Japanese type was not made in sheets of metal. Instead, it was constructed of small pieces of iron and lacquered leather sewn together with silk. The tightly sewn segments were nearly impervious to sword cuts, spear thrusts, or arrows. Huge epaulets and wide-brimmed sloping helmets served as an additional protection for the dangerously unarmored neck and face.

In defense of a flight of arrows, a samurai typically hunched his shoulders and scrunched his head down much like a turtle, and he was nearly impervious. Because samurai were mounted warriors, the armor flared out to serve as a skirt protection for the groin and thighs. The arms and lower legs were wrapped in separate armor pieces that were strapped snuggly to the limbs to provide as much mobility as protection. The entire suit weighed perhaps thirty pounds (compared to the European suit, which weighed up to four times more). In the late sixteenth century solid pieces of iron were fashioned into breastplates to protect against musket shot. That often added another ten pounds. Solid iron helmets were created, as were iron masks to protect the face against cannon shrapnel.

Armor was produced by a host of artisans, each with their own specialties. Blacksmiths turned out the small curved pieces of iron in various shapes and sizes according to where they would fit in the suit of armor. Other artisans lacquered the iron and leather pieces, and still others assembled and sewed the parts together. By the eighteenth century, armor was not very practical for a bureaucrat, so lighter versions were substituted. Since armor was only used for ceremonial purposes, virtually everyone had lightweight armor made. The principle was the same, but the iron was replaced with lacquered wood instead. Armor artisans were allowed to express their aesthetic sensibilities through the use of lacquered designs and colored silks. Edo armories were especially famous for their fine handiwork. Special armor was developed to be used in the *kendo* martial art of mock sword fighting.

Japanese longbows were justly famous for their strength and accuracy. The double-curved short bows and crossbows of the Mongol invaders of the late thirteenth century were probably more powerful, but the Japanese rejected technological innovation in favor of their traditional longbows. These curious killing machines were seven to nine feet long, made of laminated wood. The bow was held, not in the middle as is common everywhere else in the world, but further down to take advantage of the severe arch. They were made to be fired from horseback (hence the length), though in the sixteenth century flanks of *ashigaru* archers were used to good effect. The arrows typically were six inches shorter than European arrows and were fletched with three feathers rather than four.

Unlike sword fighting, which became passé by the eighteenth century, archery remained quite popular. The bakufu encouraged archery contests to maintain the martial spirit of the samurai. Archery artisans therefore remained busy turning out fine bows and arrows. Similarly, makers of wooden and bamboo swords used in *kendo* prospered as well. In both cases, these artisans worked with various woods to make laminates that were bound together by resins and lacquer.

Another military industry that survived (but only barely) into the eighteenth century was the production of firearms. Within a decade of the introduction of the clumsy arquebus from Portugal in the 1540s, Japanese artisans were making models superior to their European analogs. Japan's superior iron technology and the traditional sense of miniaturization were both brought to bear to improve the weapon. The same could not be said of Japanese cannon casters, however, partially because Europeans kept the fine art of bronze casting secret from the Japanese, for obvious reasons. Portuguese, Spanish, and Dutch ships would have lost their supremacy if the Japanese had ever mastered the art of cannon construction.

Curiously, the Japanese had stopped production of most firearms by the early eighteenth century. Historians disagree over why this was so.[4] Perhaps it was a conscious attempt to stop the proliferation of military technology and return the samurai to the rustic ideal of *bushido* ("the way of the warrior"). Perhaps it was to concentrate the few cannon and arquebus, still closely guarded in locked armories, in the hands of the bakufu. Whatever the reasons, armories became museums rather than manufacturers of firearms. Some arquebuses were manufactured for a type of firearm martial art that employed them. Not many were used in hunting since the Japanese did not eat much meat. Besides, the sport of hawking took care of those who had such bloodthirsty urges. At the end of the eighteenth century, a few bakufu bureaucrats were allowed to experiment once again with cannon casting, but it never amounted to much.

Perhaps one final military product should be included here. Sword hilt guards (*tsuba*) were obviously important to the effectiveness of the weapon. Hilts were four to six inches long because they were intended for a two-handed grip. The guards were much smaller than the European kind, being only about two to three inches in diameter and intended to guard only against an enemy's blade sliding down one's own toward the hands. By the seventeenth century these tsuba had become lavish artistic pieces. Fanciful metal filigree, carving, etching, and lacquering made the tsuba into gorgeous art objects. Chōnin aficionados began to collect them in the early eighteenth century, and by the end of the period there was a thriving business in "harvesting" them from destitute samurai. Along with the tobacco pouch fobs (netsuke), tsuba have continued to be prized art objects among serious collectors.

NOTES

1. Basil Hall Chamberlain, *Japanese Things* (Rutland, VT: Tuttle, 1971), 34.

2. Except briefly by the Portuguese in the area around Nagasaki during the late sixteenth century.

3. Victor Harris, "Japanese Swords," in Michael D. Coe, ed., *Swords and Hilt Weapons* (London: Barnes and Noble, 1993), 43.

4. See Noel Perrin's *Giving Up the Gun: Japan's Reversion to the Sword, 1543–1879* (Boulder: Shambhala, 1980).

14

Cottage Industries

People who lived in towns larger than the agrarian villages did work that was closely related to agricultural work. They often took raw materials produced by farmers and turned them into finished goods. Some peasants, in fact, commuted to these nearby towns to do day-work, or took materials home as "cottage industry" handiwork. The most common such work was silk production. Peasant girls, for example, would work all day in "silk sheds," which were little more than thatched outdoor canopies, constructed to handle what were essentially outdoor tasks out of the hot sun or the rain.

Similarly, rural day-workers made umbrellas, folding fans, paper products, or other goods that did not require much skill or specialized expertise in these medium-sized towns. The important factors here were cheap, often off-season labor, and a nearby supply of raw materials. Often, the male relatives of these young single women sold and transported the raw materials to the towns. Split bamboo, mulberry (leaves for silkworms, bark for paper), straw, sedge, and a number of forest products kept the young women at work.

Village girls processed the raw silk into finished goods in the semi-rural silk sheds. It was here that the dangerous and smelly boiling of cocoons was done. The cocoons were boiled in large cauldrons that required a substantial amount of fuel. Therefore it was economical to keep the water boiling for several batches rather than just a scattered few in a village. Young girls would snatch the boiled cocoons out of the water, and then tease

Silk Production

out the filament ends while they were still very hot and wet. Girls would constantly scald their hands and arms, and many became sick from the noxious odor of boiled worms.

Other, more skilled workers then twisted the silk filaments into thread and wound them onto spools that could be dyed together in large batches. Weaving was often done indoors, but sometimes was also done in these sheds, which were built close to the fast-running streams that were necessary for washing the silk as it was woven. Most commonly the very specialized textile work was done in larger cities in larger indoor manufacturing shops. Embroidery was slow, painstaking work and was usually done after the kimono had already been cut into shape. The making of embroidered sashes (*obi*) was also done in such factories.

Cotton
Cotton production revolutionized the textile and clothing industries in Japan. The fiber plant had been imported to Japan in the sixteenth century. By this period it had taken over as the major and most common cheap textile for the common people. In fact, by mid-century cotton overtook and surpassed even rice as the major commodity transshipped through Osaka.

The simple means of cotton processing and production involved carding, ginning, and twisting of thread in preparation for weaving. The simple horizontal (*izaribata*) looms could be operated by anyone with a modicum of dexterity. In the early part of the century a new "tall loom" (*takabata*) was developed in the Osaka area. It proved to be three to four times more productive, but required two workers, whereas the izaribata could be managed by one person alone.

Not surprisingly, then, the izaribata continued to be used by individual weavers, usually those who wove as by-employment and cottage industrial work. During the period "putting-out" piecework (*dashibata*) systems thrived. Entrepreneurs supplied thread to individual weavers who then produced piecework on their own looms. Some suppliers even rented looms to pieceworkers. Labor bosses sometimes formed weaving companies by training dexterous indentured workers (*hōkōnin*), but these folk did not have much incentive to produce quality goods unless they could buy their freedom by doing so. A few signed contracts to win their freedom by paying off their debts with deferred wages.

The takabata were used in factory-like settings. In the Nishijin cotton industrial center in Kyoto there were reputed to be over 100,000 weavers, most working in tandem in shops that employed fifty weavers or more. Most were part of a factory system (*uchibata*) where weavers were required to sign annual contracts.[1]

Cloth Dyeing
By the eighteenth century Japan had developed hundreds of dyestuffs and several score of dying methods. All required a dependable fast-moving stream or river in which to rinse the cloth after each application of color. Therefore, not surpris-

Woman engaged in weaving while child plays beneath the loom. (Suzuki Harunobu, Japanese, c. 1725–70, Throwing the shuttle, 1765, woodblock, 27.62 × 20.64 cm, Clarence L. Buckingham Collection, 1937.21, photograph © 2001, The Art Institute of Chicago, All Rights Reserved, photograph courtesy of The Art Institute of Chicago)

ingly, most dyeing was done in semi-rural districts, very often next to rivers descending from the surrounding mountains.

Japanese had learned several dyeing methods from Chinese and Korean artisans, but there had been domestic dyeing for centuries before. Once indigo extraction had been mastered in Japan, it became the single most common method, since it "set" into the very molecules of the cloth and therefore had a tremendous dye-life. Archeologists have uncovered indigo-dyed cloth buried for over a thousand years that still retains the distinctive blue coloring.

The simplest type of dyeing was soaking cloth directly in a brewed slurry of leaves, roots, or other raw vegetable dye plants. Depending on the dye, the cloth might be dipped and rinsed several times in order to best set the color into the cloth. Some dyes required boiling the cloth in the dye concoction. Vegetable dyes after a time were mixed with other materials such as charcoal soot, lye, plum vinegar, ground minerals, and alum. The combinations allowed the dyers to change not only the color, but also the texture of cloth. Primary colors could be faded to various more subtle shades. All concoctions dyed the cloth a uniform color. One had to use another method if one wished to have more than one color, or wished to make patterns or other designs.

The next step up in terms of technology was to tie-dye (*kokechi*). One bunched the cloth and tied it tightly so that the dye did not permeate into the bound areas. A skillful artisan could make intricate designs and patterns by retying and redyeing in several steps of bunching, gathering, pleating, winding, and tying the fabric. A further advance in terms of technology was to paint designs directly on the cloth after the fabric had been dyed. Stencils could be used to apply paint in patterns.

Another more sophisticated practice was to use one of the various "resist" methods, which were reverse variants of painting or printing. This entailed anointing the cloth with a substance that made it resist dyeing, hence the name. Rice paste (*kyokechi*) and waxes (*rokechi*) were applied to the cloth in patterns and then the cloth was dyed. Once the "resist" potion was removed, areas where the dye had not penetrated would appear. So, instead of drawing in color, the resist method blocked out areas not to be dyed. Obviously this was time-consuming and tedious since the resist had to be applied and removed by hand. Even cut stencils (*kata-zome*) required substantial handwork that was often beyond the capabilities of ordinary dyers. Similarly, woodblock printing took considerable artistic as well as artisanal skills.

By the eighteenth century Japanese had solved many of the problems of dye production by compartmentalizing the various tasks and functions. Unskilled apprentices did all of the heavy lifting and the tedious tasks such as drawing water, emptying vats, stirring cauldrons, rinsing, and spreading the cloth to dry. Skilled artisans specialized in specific phases such as printing, drawing, applying or removing resist, tie-dyeing, mixing and blending colors, and so on. The result was a stunning variety of prints, patterns, and fading that is rarely surpassed even now.

Embroidery As in the rest of the world, sewing designs into cloth produced a striking effect in even the most common fabric. Japanese learned the tricks of the trade from Chinese and Korean masters but after a time surpassed the continental methods. Employing the standard methods of painting or stenciling designs, Japanese began to use lacquer and foil to enhance the embroidery as well. Foil decorating (*surihaku*) improved on the gold and silver dust paints used in the rest of Asia by impressing the foil directly into the fibers of the cloth. Lacquer and glue concoctions kept the foil stable and resistant to normal wear and tear. Incorporating embroidery within the surihaku foil print enhanced the design even more. Gold and silver threads were used, as were several types, textures, and thicknesses of dyed thread.

The painstaking and time-consuming work involved made embroidered fabrics the most expensive in Japan. Few chōnin ever saw an embroidered gown except at the theater or on the backs of the geisha. But many chōnin women produced the gorgeous material. A skilled embroiderer in Kyoto or Ōsaka, where most of the work was produced, could make a tidy living indeed. Stories are told about whole families of women who specialized in the art and founded matriarchal enterprises where they plied their craft and kept their secrets for generations. It is said that poor young women with proven dexterity were adopted into the families, often marrying sons or nephews of the matriarchal embroiderer.

The fine sedge and straw work artisans applied their skills to fundamentally raw materials. In addition to the straw shoes, hats, raincoats, ropes, mats, and bags produced in the rural areas, chōnin straw workers made a number of impor-

Straw and Bamboo

tant products as well. Particularly important were the straw mat (*tatami*) makers. They wove very tight, uniform-stitched lengths of carpeting which were then padded and tightly stretched over wooden frames. In each region of Japan, the tatami were made in uniform sizes (commonly two meters long, one meter wide) which then became the standard for all construction (see Chapter 9) in that region. Rooms were therefore standardized in size, measured by the number and pattern of tatami mats. The springy mats were very comfortable to sit or sleep on and lasted for years. Worn tatami were cheap to repair, but usually were replaced with an identical-sized mat from an area that did not experience as much traffic.

Ordinary undecorated tatami were cheap enough so that virtually every chōnin could afford enough to cover the floors of at least one or two rooms. Wealthy chōnin and village headmen could afford to have the tatami decorated with brocaded silk seams. Virtually every samurai house was outfitted with tatami. Mud and water stains were easy to clean, but because shoes and geta tore the sedge and seam tapes, Japanese became accustomed to removing their shoes upon entering a house carpeted with tatami.

Interior sliding screens (*fusuma*) were also made in interchangeable, uniform sizes. These were wooden frames covered with thick translucent

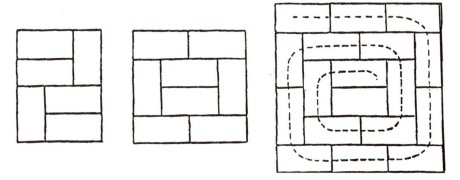

Tatami arrangement patterns: six-mat; eight-mat; the rotation pattern for an eighteen-mat room to even wear pattern. (Drawings by Louis G. Perez)

paper, which could then be decorated with artistic paintings. The outer wall sliding screens (*amado*) were made of wood frames over thick sedge mats or thin sheets of veneered wood. The artisans who specialized in these fusuma often constructed the entire screens, though some merely assembled the various parts.

Paper   Papermaking was another skilled occupation that worked with various raw materials gathered in the rural areas. According to folklore, the Korean monk Docho had brought both papermaking and brush-making to Japan in 610 C.E., but papermaking undoubtedly had come more than a century before. In many areas of the country peasants made rough sheets of paper during the winter as a kind of cottage by-employment. They would collect a few hundred sheets and then would take them to the many "paper fairs" where they would be sold to traveling wholesalers. The fairs were called *ni-shichi* (two-seven) because they were commonly held on days of the month ending with the numbers two or seven (2, 7, 12, 17, 22, and 27).

By the eighteenth century the better paper (*washi*) was made in the semi-rural small towns where whole gangs of peasant-artisans would work together in a kind of a proto-factory. It was hard work, mainly because the best paper was manufactured in very cold water, so the workers spent a great deal of time with their hands or feet in frigid mountain streams.

A particular type of mulberry (*kozo*) was grown as a commercial crop. Meter-long wands of saplings were stripped of their bark, which was pulped into a thick colloidal suspension. The process involved several stages when the cellulose slurry was bleached with lye and washed repeatedly. A vegetable glue was added to "firm up" the liquid, and the final step was to sieve the slurry into thin sheets, which were then dried on polished planks of wood in the sun. The best paper required very cold water rinses, so the frigid streams below melting snow packs in the northwest became the primary centers for paper production. There were hundreds of uses for paper beyond those functions commonly found in the West. Japan is probably the first country to commonly use cheap paper for disposable tissue. The Jesuit friars of the sixteenth century even sent back samples of the stuff to astound their friends in Europe. We are told that one Japanese "embassy" sent by a Japanese Christian daimyō to Europe in the early seventeenth century caused small riots wherever they went. An account says that when the Japanese happened to blow their noses into the tissues and then dispose of them, crowds of Europeans fought to recover the curiosities.

Folding and "palm-frond" (so-called because they were so shaped) fans, umbrellas, hats, clothing, and even shoes were made of lacquered paper. A particular type of very strong twine was made of paper also.

A substantial use of paper was for the manufacture of umbrellas and fans. Umbrellas allegedly were brought to Japan **Umbrellas** in 570 c.e. as a gift to the emperor from Korea. Generically, **and Fans** umbrellas (*kasa*) were made of split bamboo ribs radiating from a bamboo or wooden core. Thick paper was glued to the bamboo ribs, and then the whole was either oiled or lacquered to make it waterproof. The first kasa were permanently extended, but Japanese later developed a collapsing model. The latter were manufactured to create permanent pleats in the paper between the ribs so that the umbrella could be folded and collapsed around the handle. A simple cloth sash could be slipped down to keep the umbrella folded until it needed to be unfurled. The heavier models (*amakasa*) were for rain, and there were lighter translucent parasols (*higasa*) as well.[2]

In the eighteenth century both styles were highly decorated with geometric patterns and fanciful paintings. A particular design called "snake-eye" (*janome-gasa*) left the center unpainted, surrounded by a red or blue painted border. Another style had two concentric circles painted to resemble a bull's-eye. These latter were very common at the hot spring *onsen* and at inns along the main highways. They were decoratively gay in color and design as well as functional conveniences for the guests to shade themselves from the sun or keep themselves dry during a downpour.

Most umbrellas were produced by the "putting-out" cottage industry. Peasants would provide the split bamboo and wooden handles; paper, lacquer, oil, glue, and paint dealers each would supply the other essential products. Agents would supply all these essentials to individual artisans, peasants, and chōnin who laboriously fashioned them into the finished umbrellas in their homes. The petty producers bought the materials on consignment and then sold the umbrellas to the agents.

The system rarely involved the exchange of much money. Most trans-

A rainy day. Left to right: three men share an umbrella, a poor fisherman, and an umbrella salesman. Woodblock print by Utagawa Kuniyoshi. (Courtesy of Asia Library, University of Michigan)

actions were done on credit. Very often one set of cottage industrial workers produced "raw" unfinished umbrella skeletons, another set papered them, and a third oiled, lacquered, or painted them. The entire process could take weeks, since the glues, paints, and waterproofing oils had to season and dry on the paper before the next process could be started. In many ways the whole manufacturing process was a disjointed, but long, continuous assembly line from raw materials to finished goods.

The same could be said of fan makers. The manufacturers specialized in the many tasks as well. Like umbrellas, the first fans were single-piece (*uchiwa*) and were permanently extended. They resembled the palm fronds with which peasants in southern China and Southeast Asia wafted the air around them in the torpid, stultifying heat of the tropics. Peacock feathers from India and Persia could also have been models for the original fans that came to Japan from the rest of Asia. It is generally acknowledged that the folding collapsible fan (*ogi* or *sensu*) was invented in medieval Japan, some claim by the widow of the warrior Atsumori while she lived in Miei-do temple.[3]

No one knows precisely, but perhaps the collapsible umbrella gave some anonymous artisan the idea to apply the same basic principle to fans. Fans were technologically simpler to make than umbrellas, of course. The fan required only a single linchpin to anchor the radial ribs because a fan is a mere half-circle (actually, some fans could be made into full circles). Fans require heavier paper folds that allow it to hold its shape, whether extended or collapsed.

Most fans were made of the same materials as umbrellas, but some were made of costlier specialized materials. Whalebone and metal ribs were used to manufacture sturdy war fans (*gunsen* or *tessen*) that were used for signaling troops. These fans were very large (so that they could be seen from great distances), waterproofed, and had distinct colored signals painted on each side. They were used much like the signal flags used on ships until relatively recently. Daimyō continued to employ special battle standard fans (*gunbai uchiwa*) that were carried by their samurai vassals as if on parade during the *sankin-kotai* journeys to and from Edo.

The fan ribs were made of many different materials including split bamboo, animal bone or horn, or a fragrant wood such as cedar or sandal. Artisans carved beautiful designs and shapes to make even the most utilitarian fan a work of art. Several types of paper were employed, and some were even made of lacquered silk or painted with gold or silver paint.

More delicate fans were used by dancers of all kinds to convey nonverbal messages. A panoply of emotions and ideas could be signaled by the deft and graceful movement of the fan. One may well imagine the range of signals that could be flashed by a coquettish young woman to a male admirer. Fans were also used to convey written messages as well. Fans were manufactured that featured a blank white paper surface upon which a message could be written; the fan was closed to hide the message, and then secretly passed to someone else. It is said that young men bought the same type of fan that was often carried by young geisha, the better to exchange surreptitiously to send clandestine messages. Many a Kabuki or Bunraku plot turned on the wrong person picking up a fan-message intended for someone else. The same type of "blank" fan was sometimes used by daimyō to send a message to a miscreant samurai ordering him to commit hara-kiri. Obviously the message was more important than the medium here, but one can imagine the various emotions that might play over the mind simply because one was handed a closed fan.

Many fans were printed with road maps or written road guides and were sold in shops along the major sankin-kotai highways. They gave valuable information including distances between post stations, fees and costs at most inns, and suggestions of good places to eat.[4] It became a courtesy to people traveling in the opposite direction to leave the fan/ map/guide at an inn when one was finished with it.

Fans were among the most valuable exports that were traded for Chinese, Korean, or Dutch products. Virtually every ship manifest during the eighteenth century contained several gross of fans. They became very popular, and therefore very costly, in Amsterdam, and scarcely a Dutch museum can be found without a representative collection. Had the bakufu wanted to increase trade (it decidedly did not), fan artisans might have become as common as waraji makers, and there were millions of those.

Over the centuries fans were used in hundreds of different ways. They were standard equipment for the kitchen, since charcoal burned much hotter and more efficiently when fanned. A fan was necessary to rapidly cool freshly cooked rice when making such dishes as sushi. Fans were standard accoutrements (*rikyū ogi*) for the chanoyu (tea ceremony), and also for Kabuki (*maiogi*) and Noh (*chūkei*) dancers. Every monk carried a fan, which was used to beat the rhythm for chanting sutras. Sumo referees signaled the start of a match with rigid fans (*gampi uchiwa*). Restaurants and sake shops in the large cities used them for advertisement as well as occasionally writing the day's specialties as kind of a mobile menu carte. Many advertisement fans for the theater were decorated with *ukiyo-e* woodblock prints.[5]

Lacquer   Japanese have been known for the quality of their lacquerware for centuries. The process probably came (as did many Japanese technologies) from China and Korea, but one type (*urushi*) was used back in the prehistoric Jōmon era.[6] There were several types of common lacquer, but all required a great deal of skill. Most were extracted from the sap of the *urushi-no-ki* (literally, "lacquer tree"). The tree is of the sumac family, and the sap was as poisonous when absorbed topically as it was if ingested internally. Even a casual handling of the sap during its decoction would result in a serious skin rash. Similarly, the fumes of the rendering process were caustic and could be fatal if one did not ventilate the room. Needless to say, the process was done with great care, and always in the open air.

Virtually anything could be, and was, lacquered. The most common were wood, leather, pottery, paper, and cloth. The process started with the distillation of the lacquer itself, which was a dangerous (poisonous) process. Several coatings of the varnish-like liquid hardened into a shell that transparently preserved the grain, painting, or carving of the base underneath.

Artisans experimented with colored lacquers, the most popular being red and black, but there was a genre (*maki-e*) that used gold and silver dust as well. Ordinary wood and clay vases, dishes, and utensils became beautiful but very durable pieces that were very easy to clean and maintain. By the eighteenth century, lacquerware pieces were a major export, especially to Europe via the Dutch at Deshima. In fact, the lacquering process came to be known as (and is still called) Japanning.

In Japan tanning was considered at best a necessary evil. Buddhism forbade killing any animals, so, except for fish, the **Leather** Japanese did not eat animal flesh. But society had to dispose of the bodies of those animals that had died naturally. As with human remains, the people charged with this task were the outcastes, called *eta* (literally, "abundant pollution") or *hinin* ("non-people"). These unfortunates were probably descendents of war captives (usually Koreans), but were often also former prisoners, absconders, or criminals, as well as the deformed or leprous. They were felt to be ritually unclean, morally base, and probably damned by their karma earned in evil former lives. They were therefore morticians, executioners, and leather-workers (also night-soil collectors). Curiously, some of the straw workers (tatami, waraji, etc.) were eta, as were many firemen. Eta were more common in the southwest than in Edo and the northern cities.

Technically, then, any animal whose hide was to be tanned into leather was supposed to have died naturally. We are told that in at least a few tanning areas Buddhist priests were wont to drop by to be sure that animals were not being killed for their hides. In most places, we suspect that a few animals might have met unexpected and quite unnatural deaths. This is so particularly with cats, whose hide was used as drumheads and for the resonating boxes of samisens. One cannot imagine tanners sitting around for a cat to cough up his ninth life before they could fill an order for cat skin.

As in the rest of the world, everybody wants leather, but no one wants it processed in his or her environs. The process is horribly noxious, and the streams used for washing away offal are polluted for miles downstream. Suet and tallow can be rendered, but there was no great resale market in Japan because of the Buddhist proscription against killing and the Shintō blood pollution taboos. Most Japanese used vegetable oils for their cooking and lamps. Even candles were made of vegetable wax. But since there were no real alternatives to leather for some things (saddles, reins, and other horse "furniture," for example), tanning was a necessary evil.

The Japanese made very fine leather from all kinds of animal hides. Horse leather was particularly prized for armor since the samurai believed that the courage of their war steeds remained imbued in the leather. The tanning process was similar to the methods used in the West, except that human urine was often used to bleach color in the leather. Potash lye was toxic, of course, so the Japanese often used leaching ponds to dehydrate the offending slurry. Most leatherwork was done in fairly close proximity to the tanning yards. The Japanese dyed, lacquered, and tooled leather before it went out to be further worked by eta craftsmen. Military boots were occasionally made of leather, but very few common Japanese wore leather shoes. As indicated, most leather went into tack for horses. The Japanese saddles were distinctive from most Western analogs. They were often leather-covered wooden forms. By the eighteenth century the country had been at peace for nearly a century, so probably more people rode in *kago* (palanquins) than astride a horse. Even when they did ride, they mounted from the right side of the horse, and then sat as a cross-legged passenger while the real horseman walked ahead leading the animal by the reins.

Purses, wallets, and personal pouches were made of textiles (often silk), so very little leather actually ever touched human skin. Even armor, quivers, and shields made of leather were usually lacquered. In the case of armor and helmets made of leather, they were always lined with silk or cotton.

NOTES

1. The cotton industry is best covered by William Hauser in *Economic Institutional Change in Tokugawa Japan: Osaka and the Kinai Cotton Trade* (Cambridge: Cambridge University Press, 1974), but there is a nice shorter discussion in Satoru Nakamura, "The Development of Rural Industry" (J. Victor Koschmann, trans.), in Chie Nakane and Shinzaburō Oishi, eds., *Tokugawa Japan: The Social and Economic Antecedents of Modern Japan* (Tokyo: University of Tokyo Press, 1990), 81–96, particularly 85–87.

2. See Frederic de Garis, *We Japanese: Being Description of Many of the Customs, Manners, Ceremonies, Festivals, Arts, and Crafts of the Japanese, Besides Numerous Other Subjects*, 3 vols. (Yokohama: Yamagata Press, 1949), 1:150.

3. Chamberlain so suggests; see Basil Hall Chamberlain, *Japanese Things* (Rutland, VT: Tuttle, 1971), 156.

4. Richard Hildreth, *Japan: As It Was and Is*, 2nd ed. (Wilmington, DE: Scholarly Resources, 1973), 285.

5. Two excellent studies are Julia Hutt and Helene Alexander, *Ogi: A History of the Japanese Fan* (New York: Dauphin Publishers, 1992), and Neville John Irons, *Fans of Imperial Japan* (Berlin: Kaiserreich Kunst, 1982).

6. Louis-Frédéric, *Daily Life in Japan at the Time of the Samurai, 1185–1603*, trans. Eileen M. Lowe (New York: Praeger Books, 1972), 144.

15

Nightsoil

The most important difference between waste disposal in Japan and in the West was that human excreta was not regarded as something that one paid to have removed, but rather as a product with a positive economic value.[1]

Nightsoil (the term is a British Victorian Age euphemism for human excrement) played an unusually important role in agriculture and material culture in Japan during this period. Not much has been published in English on this topic. With a few notable exceptions,[2] the primary academic work remains untranslated in Japanese.

"Harvesting" of nightsoil and its use as a commercial fertilizer was at the very nexus of a rapidly changing society in the eighteenth century. The burgeoning urban centers of the early part of the century necessitated a systematic regime for the removal of human excrement. Without such a system, the teeming populations in jokamachi, temple towns, and administrative cities would have rapidly polluted their own water supply, the almost inevitable result being the spread of one water-borne epidemic or another, which of course was one of Thomas Malthus' "natural checks" on population growth.

Concomitantly, the surrounding agricultural areas would have been hard-put to produce enough vegetables and green groceries to feed these swelling cities without a dependable supply of cheap, readily available commercial fertilizer. The nature of contemporary transportation made the safe delivery of fresh produce from distant agricultural areas at reasonable prices extremely unlikely. Perhaps this would have radically changed the diet of urban dwellers.

In terms of social systems, the "ladlers' guilds" that developed among nightsoil collectors led to a distinct socioeconomic accommodation among samurai, chōnin, and the lowest, poorest segment of society, the outcaste hinin (or eta). Indeed, the largely hinin wholesale brokers of nightsoil and urine became wealthy and influential leaders of their own sub-social communities at the periphery of Japan's three largest cities, Edo, Ōsaka, and Kyoto. If for no other reasons than these three considerations of urban hygiene and health, nightsoil as a commercial "cash crop," and the attendant social changes engendered by the rise of ladlers' guilds, the study of nightsoil collection in eighteenth-century Japan would be worthy of considerably more study.

Almost from the advent of sedentary wet-rice paddy cultivation in Japan, the use of nightsoil as a fertilizer was a necessary evil. The prehistorical agricultural "missionaries" from the Asian continent who introduced this labor-intensive and technologically sophisticated crop probably instructed their Japanese pupils on the judicious use of nutrient-rich human excrement as fertilizer. The high population density required an almost constant use of the land to grow rice, which, in addition to being labor-intensive, is also very high on return of nutrients and calories for expended labor energy, producing thirty to fifty grains of rice for every seed planted.[3] If constantly in use to grow rice, the soil could very quickly lose its fecundity. Crop rotation was practiced sporadically, but not systematically, much less scientifically. Obviously, rice farmers were forced to enrich the soil or face starvation. The Chinese or Koreans who taught the Japanese to grow rice must have also suggested that nightsoil was a ready, dependable, cheap, natural, and renewable source of fertilizer. Nightsoil is used as fertilizer in almost all paddy rice cultivation throughout Asia. Virtually everywhere, when the society progresses beyond the "slash and burn" technology of agriculture, nightsoil becomes a natural fertilizer.[4]

There are intimations of the use of nightsoil as fertilizer in the ancient oral chronicles that were later incorporated into the *Kojiki* and *Nihongi*. Indeed, there is a kami of nightsoil mentioned therein. It has even been suggested that human excreta received a prominent place in the creation story of Japan precisely because they were an important aspect of the early Japanese agricultural society. Shinto deals with excreta as ritual pollutants precisely because they were an integral part of Japanese life.

Collection of nightsoil on most farms was not an accidental and incidental task, but a purposeful and important part of the agricultural rhythms of the society. Instead of defecating into privy pits dug into the ground, as is done in most rural areas around the world, the Japanese either sank wooden casks into the ground, or carefully lined the privy holes with clay to collect the excreta. The solid feces were winnowed from the slurry and allowed to ferment, usually for at least a month.[5] Urine was often stored separately and used to "ripen" compost pits of agricultural waste. We now know that urine is a chemical "activator" or reagent necessary to the decomposition of green plants if one is to create good humus quickly.[6]

While women readied the ground for the transplantation of the young rice seedlings, men would venture into the forest to "harvest" woodland grass, shrubs, fallen leaves, and other decaying detritus. This green fertilizer, called *karashiki* in Japan, was mixed judiciously, in a rather sophisticated formula, with "cured" or fermented nightsoil to enrich the soil around the seedlings. The Swedish physician Carl Peter Thunberg, who visited Japan in June 1775 as part of the Dutch enclave at Deshima in Nagasaki, describes the ladling of the liquid fertilizer directly on the roots of rice plants as a "method which avoids the waste incident to spreading the manure on unplanted fields, to be dried up by the sun, or to lose by evaporation its volatile salts and oily particles."[7]

The "green" *karashiki* and nightsoil mixture could also be mixed with ashes, garbage, fish oil, and later pressed rapeseed or dried sardines, and then cut into the soil before the flooding process preparatory to seeding.[8]

The agricultural manuals that circulated throughout Japan beginning in the fifteenth century and proliferated through the mid-nineteenth century[9] all featured, in prominent places, tips on nightsoil collecting, winnowing (new inventions for primary-site separation of feces from urine in cunningly designed privy furniture), curing, mixing, and application of fertilizer.

By and large, however, the application of nightsoil as a fertilizer was an individual, isolated, and rural task. Nightsoil was seen as an essential though relatively minor part of the common agricultural tasks of the average farmer. Since these farms were small and self-sufficient affairs, the average household grew little more than was necessary to appease tax collectors and to keep itself fed and clothed at a rudimentary level.

Most farmers had their own tiny kitchen gardens where they lovingly cultivated the few vegetables that brightened their otherwise drab subsistence diets. The use of nightsoil fertilizer in these gardens was common. The agricultural manuals often advised peasants to locate their privies in areas convenient to the inhabitants (and down-wind in the prevailing rural breezes), but also close to the "curing" tanks and kitchen gardens.

As long as Japan remained a rural, self-sufficient, agricultural economy, the use of nightsoil as fertilizer would have remained an individual, rural, and "low-tech" affair. What changed the nature of the technology was the rapid and almost endemic urbanization engendered by the rise of castle towns (*jokamachi*).

Urban Water Supply

The rapid urbanization created tremendous problems in this area. Edo in particular encountered serious problems because it burgeoned into the largest city in the world in less than a half-century. These were problems that Ōsaka and Kyoto had more leisure time to solve given their slower and therefore more manageable rate of urbanization. Tokugawa Ieyasu himself early on presciently anticipated the urbanization sprawl and the attendant water supply problem. He commissioned one of his top military engineers to draft a plan and then construct the famous Kanda water system. The early system employed open trenches that tapped into the nearby Inokashira spring east of Edo and relied primarily on gravity feed for some forty miles of irrigation canals with some 3,663 subsidiary ducts. Later the mains were improved into water conduits of squared wooden sluices, hollowed bamboo, and eventually even some fired clay tiles. As the city grew to outstrip the water supply, the Tama River system was added, and eventually four more water systems were built and maintained. All accounts agree that the amount of fresh water was sufficient for the needs of the 1 million inhabitants.

The real problem was keeping the water pure and unpolluted by human wastes. Even amateur historians are familiar with the horrid story of European water systems in large cities. Flushing excreta into the Thames River solved the problems of the residents upstream but caused horrendous difficulties to the poor souls who resided downstream. The rivers and canals of most large cities in this period (Paris, Copenhagen, Delhi, and Beijing, to name but the most obvious) were open sewers. Those citizens who did not have direct access to waterways routinely flung the contents of slop jars out into the street.

Even if we consider only the aesthetic and olfactory aspects, this was a huge problem. But when one considers the attendant hygienic risks, this rapidly and repeatedly becomes the breeding ground for a horrendous catastrophe. Epidemics of typhus, typhoid, cholera, dysentery, and other water-borne diseases were common and predictable. They were practically unavoidable and therefore endemic.

In Japan, however, although such epidemics were not unknown (except typhus and cholera, which arrived in the nineteenth century with the Europeans), they were rarer and much less catastrophic than in London, Paris, or other large European cities. A late nineteenth-century European observer suggested that

> those diseases which at home are attributed to bad drainage, imperfect closets, and the like seem to be unknown or rare, and this freedom from such complaints is probably due to the fact that ex-

crementitious matter is carried out of the city by men who utilize it for farms or ricefields.[10]

Also, the relative lack of disease can be attributed to Japan's preoccupation with ritual and actual pollution within the Shintō religion. That is, Japanese from early on adopted much more stringent personal hygienic practices, such as washing the hands, rinsing of the mouth, and of course the popularity of bathing, though we must observe that bathing in what seem to be ubiquitous *ōfuro* (deep hot baths) is only a recent tradition. Prior to the early nineteenth century, home ōfuro were very uncommon.[11] Bathing at hot springs was a popular medicinal regimen that became common in terms of pilgrimages and therefore tourism. *Sento* (public baths) in large cities sometimes included deep hot ōfuro, but bathing was usually done communally.[12] We have ample descriptions of traditional ōfuro in the travel literature of the eighteenth and nineteenth centuries, notably *Shank's Mare*.[13] More common were steam baths that needed very little water and little fuel to heat them if used in confined spaces. The steam would open the pores and loosen the accumulated dirt on the surface of the skin. Strategically placed sloshes of water or judicious use of a damp towel then wiped the dirt away. Also, Japanese only ate their vegetables cooked or pickled, they maintained individual sets of eating utensils that were not shared, and they commonly drank water only after it had been boiled, usually in tea.[14]

The very concept of purity in Shintō and the collective responsibility caused by population pressures kept the Japanese from polluting their running streams of water as well. Hanley reminds us that one of the fundamental differences between the West and Japan is that in Japan "human excrement was an economic good."[15]

Fairly early on, most cities worthy of the name came to grips with the removal of urban excreta. It was one thing for nightsoil to collect for the greater good of the peasant family, but what of the urban chōnin who did not farm? If left to their own devices, chōnin would probably have done what most urbanites did in Europe and America: fling it away as far as possible and let someone else deal with the problem. Japan's long history of communalism and collective responsibility made this solution difficult.

The Nightsoil Trade

The solution arrived at was almost too simple: hire some poor person to take it away. In many cases, peasants in the nearby environs could be easily and cheaply hired to do this disagreeable task. The peasants, in addition to the by-employment wage, also got to keep the nightsoil and use it on their own fields. Perhaps whole villages took advantage of this double boon: lots of people producing fertilizer for them *and* paying them to cart it away! For the poor peasants it must have been like finding lost coins on the road.

Perhaps somewhere along the way the chōnin realized that the peasants seemed only too happy to take this odious offal away. Perhaps the peasants themselves gave away the game when they appeared eagerly with their buckets and ladles even on frosty winter mornings. Perhaps the competition of rival villages who came to get their share tipped off the chōnin. We know of several cases when melees resulted when rival groups vied for the right to collect it. In any case, by the early sixteenth century it had become customary for nightsoil ladlers, as they came to be called, to present a few vegetables as *Orei* ("thank money") at the time of collection, or more commonly as New Year's gifts. Before long, the game was up and chōnin began to charge peasants for the privilege. As strange as this would seem, Western societies have long had garbage collectors, metal scroungers, rag pickers, bone men, and suet and candlewax collectors, all of whom profited by their municipal service.

By the time that Edo became the largest city in the world (probably about 1650), nightsoil collection had become serious business. The bakufu, in typically bureaucratic fashion, tried to regulate it and therefore issued edicts to control the collection of nightsoil. Only peasants could engage in the practice, though it is hard to imagine that there were very many chōnin, much less samurai applicants for the job. This was mainly to keep the merchants from gaining some kind of profit from the enterprise. Contracts had to be employed. Landowners and landlords were judged to be the owners of the solid feces, but the renters and residents continued to "own" their own urine.

This decision was the result of several lawsuits by tenants who had argued that they actually "produced" nightsoil and that the landlords did nothing but collect the product of their ardent endeavors. The bakufu, in Solomon-like wisdom, was lucky that solids could be (and routinely were) separated from liquids, otherwise undoubtedly they would have sliced the baby in two to keep the peace. Ōsaka has a similar history of nightsoil collection, except that its population was nearly 90 percent chōnin, since very few samurai lived there.[16]

The most astute of the peasantry found that they could continue to benefit from the nightsoil without ever actually having to touch it. They hired the poorest and lowest social segment of society to do the dirty deed. Many of these hapless fellows were the "usual suspects" of any society: the ne'er-do-wells. Other sorts were absconding peasants, criminals, and of course the outcastes: the eta or hinin. Hinin, then, became the primary actual collectors, though at first the peasants, and of course some merchants, directly benefited. Before very long, gigantic networks of collection, fermentation, distribution, transportation, and even retail sales quickly developed. Huge barges were engaged to ship the nightsoil, and something like tankers transported the urine as far away as the cotton fields of the Kinai.

Within a generation, however, the eta ladlers realized that they had a near-monopoly on the actual collection of nightsoil. They formed ladlers' guilds that successfully negotiated higher wages, long-term contracts, and eventually monopolies. These guilds tried at various times to organize price controls and to present a united front among all nightsoil workers and dealers. Occasionally they resorted to violence, extortion, and intimidation, hiring young toughs to impose their ideas on others.[17]

The collection, fermentation, transportation, and sale of nightsoil were by the mid-eighteenth century at the very nexus of Japanese society. The removal of the excreta was an obvious boon to urban society.

Nightsoil at the Nexus

The European Jesuit priest Joao Rodrigues, who visited Japan in the late sixteenth and early seventeenth century, noted in one of his letters that Japanese privies were much different from those of Europe:

> The interior of the privies is kept extremely clean and a perfume-pan and new paper cut for use are placed there. The privy is always clean without any bad smell, for when the guests depart the man in charge cleans it out if necessary and strews clean sand so that the place is left as [if] it had never been used. A ewer of clean water and other things needed for washing the hands are found nearby.[18]

Even if only for aesthetic reasons, without a modern sewage treatment system, the collection was a convenience for which most societies would gladly pay. And because the collection and removal did not involve the water conduits, this solved the problem of possible pollution of the freshwater supply. The implications for the hygiene and health of the city dwellers are readily apparent to us now, but it was important to the contemporary citizenry and their administrators as well. One cannot even hazard a guess as to how many lives were saved by this simple solution to human waste disposal.

Furthermore, the transportation and sale of the nightsoil as fertilizer made the immediate environs much more fecund. The agricultural production of almost every crop was greater in the environs of Edo than in virtually any other region of Japan. I think that we can safely say that this was in large part directly due to nightsoil used as fertilizer. This was part of an environmental cycle, of course. More nightsoil, more crops, therefore more food sold in Edo, therefore better nutrition, therefore more population, therefore more nightsoil.

The supply and demand were inextricably linked and mutually perpetuating. It can be argued that the rise of some cash crops—cotton, for instance—could not have been possible without a steady, dependable supply of cheap commercial fertilizer. Nightsoil was essential to growing cotton until other commercial fertilizers such as pressed rapeseed, sesame seed, and dried fish cakes came to be used.[19]

One indication of the importance of nightsoil as a commodity is the rising cost of nightsoil, both at the point of collection and at the locus of actual use. We have only scattered anecdotal information about "cost" at the early stage of this commodity because people were being paid to cart it away. We have many documents that record an individual peasant or a village bringing a few daikon, some mochi, or some miso as Orei at New Year's. But this could be interpreted as thanks for the opportunity of the employment, not the product.[20]

By the mid-seventeenth century we can see that the chōnin landlords were no longer paying to have the excreta removed, that is, judging that the right to keep the nightsoil was sufficient payment for services rendered. Collectors began to invent new schemes by which to get more business, including washing out the privies after the nightsoil had been removed. Others provided "gifts" of scrap paper for privy use.

Increasingly more common, from the late seventeenth century on, were contracts that specified how many radishes, melons, sweet potatoes, or other green groceries were due to the landlords and daimyō in payment for the amount of nightsoil collected. Before long, cash payments in specie were demanded. We have several receipts indicating that the landlord of a ten-family longhouse tenement (*nagaya*) was paid one ryō, which was the specie equivalent of a koku (5 bushels) of hulled polished rice, the amount of rice estimated as necessary to feed one adult male for a year. To put this into perspective, two ryō was the average annual wage of a day laborer in Edo and equal to the average monthly income of most common samurai.

Contracts for entire machi were signed for ten-year terms that commonly averaged *hundreds* of ryō per annum. It is alleged, though it is probably hyperbole, that the barges of nightsoil leaving Edo harbor were worth more than the annual kokudaka of some smaller daimyō. It was said that "the people of Edo receive [food] with their mouths and contribute [fertilizer] with their buttocks."[21] Which brings us to the most logical conclusion that nightsoil was "graded" in terms of its worth.

Whenever males and females had separate privies, the nightsoil of men was sold for up to 50 percent more than that of females.[22] Nightsoil of common chōnin ranked only slightly above that of the ladlers themselves, though it may be assumed that the latter did not pay for their own production. Samurai yashiki privies were next, the women's quarters followed in gradation, followed by the inner quarters of hatamoto and other important samurai. The Licensed Quarters of theaters, geisha, prostitutes, tea houses, and restaurants produced the highest quality, and therefore more expensive nightsoil. This was allegedly due to the diet of all those people. Nowhere does it say so, but I would suppose that the diet of the common peasants was such that their produce would have ranked lowest of all.

We should say something here about roadside nightsoil. Because of sankin-kotai and the increasing popularity of religious pilgrimages, there was always a host of people traveling along the highways. Constantine Vaporis has told us much about the post towns and the corvée labor assigned to maintain them.[23] Others have told us that young children and old men were assigned the task by these villagers of collecting the droppings of the horses used to maintain the extensive transportation and communication system of post roads: "All the manure of the animals kept was carefully preserved, old men and children following the horses of travelers, with a shell fastened to the end of a stick, and a basket in which to put whatever they collected."[24]

We are told that enterprising peasants devised a system to collect human excreta as well. Wooden casks were sunk into the ground near the clumps of trees that were planted at fixed intervals as distance markers.[25] These containers were emptied regularly by the post station villagers and used to supplement their own fertilizer. There are reported instances when ladlers' guilds tried to take over these roadside collection stations, but the villagers fought, sometimes literally, to retain their monopolies. The ladlers did, however, often break into the roadside inn business. They managed to convince the landlords and innkeepers to allow professional ladlers to do the job. Of course, since this excrement was the product of daimyō, hatamoto, samurai, and other well-fed people, it sold for handsome prices.

It is hard to overemphasize the importance of nightsoil collection for the agricultural productivity of the period. Sufficient vegetables for the immense population of Edo could not possibly have been provided without the advent of this commercial fertilizer. The effect of nightsoil fertilizer on the growth of cash crops such as cotton is, or should be, self-evident. I will make no claims as to its resulting effect on the growth of a Japanese national economy here except to say that it was perhaps Japan's third national commodity after rice and cotton.

NOTES

1. Susan B. Hanley, "Urban Sanitation in Preindustrial Japan," *Journal of Interdisciplinary History* 18:1 (Summer 1987), 1–26.

2. See ibid and a handful of other publications by Hanley, including *Everyday Things in Premodern Japan: The Hidden Legacy of Material Culture* (Berkeley: University of California Press, 1997); "Tokugawa Society: Material Culture, Standard of Living, and Life-Styles," in John Whitney Hall and James L. McClain, eds., *Early Modern Japan*, volume 4 in *The Cambridge History of Japan* (Cambridge: Cam-

bridge University Press, 1997), 660–705; and "A High Standard of Living in Nineteenth Century Japan: Fact or Fantasy?," *Journal of Economic History* 43:1 (March 1983). Also, Anne Walthall, "Village Networks: Sodai and the Sale of Edo Nightsoil," *Monumenta Nipponica* 43:3 (Autumn 1988), 279–303. Ann Bowman Jannetta, in her *Epidemics and Mortality in Early Modern Japan* (Princeton: Princeton University Press, 1987), also has a section on nightsoil collection.

3. Toshio Furushima, "The Village and Agriculture During the Edo Period" (James McClain, trans.), in Hall and McClain, *Early Modern Japan*, 478–518.

4. Ibid., 505.

5. Surprisingly, when allowed to ferment for more than thirty days, most of the harmful bacteria have been consumed by "good" bacteria, and the result is a nearly inert (in terms of human pathogens) substance that has actually been nutrient-enriched by the fermentation process.

6. Furushima, "Village and Agriculture," 507–8.

7. Quoted in Richard Hildreth, *Japan: As It Was and Is* (Wilmington, DE: Scholarly Resources, 1973), 404 (originally published in Boston by Phillips, Sampson and Co. in 1855).

8. Tsuneo Sato, "Tokugawa Villages and Agriculture" (Mikiso Hane, trans.), in Chie Nakane and Shinzaburō Oishi, eds., *Tokugawa Japan: The Social and Economic Antecedents of Modern Japan* (Tokyo: University of Tokyo Press, 1990), 70.

9. Jennifer Robertson, "Japanese Farm Manuals: A Literature of Discovery," *Peasant Studies* 11 (Spring 1984), 169–94.

10. Edward S. Morse, *Japan, Day by Day*, 2 vols. (Boston: Houghton Mifflin, 1917), 1:23.

11. Hanley, "Urban Sanitation," 20.

12. Ibid., 21.

13. Jippensha Ikku, *Hizakurige or Shank's Mare*, trans. Thomas Satchell (Rutland, VT: Tuttle, 1960).

14. Hanley, "Urban Sanitation," 20.

15. Hanley, *Everyday Things*, 117.

16. Walthall, "Village Networks," 290–94.

17. Ibid., 295–96.

18. Quoted and translated by Michael Cooper, ed., *They Came to Japan: An Anthology of European Reports on Japan, 1543–1640* (Berkeley: University of California Press, 1965), 221.

19. Furushima, "Village and Agriculture," 513–14. See also William B. Hauser, *Economic Institutional Change in Tokugawa Japan: Osaka and the Kinai Cotton Trade* (Cambridge: Cambridge University Press, 1974).

20. Walthall, "Village Networks," 294.

21. Ibid., 296.

22. Edward G. Seidensticker, *Low City, High City: Tokyo from Edo to the Earthquake* (New York: Knopf, 1983), 283.

23. Constantine N. Vaporis, "Post Stations and Assisting Villages: Corvee Labor and Peasant Contention," *Monumenta Nipponica* 41:4 (Winter 1986), 377–414.

24. Thunberg, quoted in Hildreth, *Japan*, 405.

25. Ibid., 395. Also, Engelbert Kaempfer, *The History of Japan: Together with a Description of the Kingdom of Siam*, 3 vols., trans. J. G. Scheuchzer (Glasgow: James MacLehose and Sons, 1906), 2:294.

16

Trade

The merchants of the Edo period had a feeling of crisis. They never knew when they might become bankrupt, however large their businesses. This must have seemed almost natural, given the nature of commerce.[1]

Without doubt, the least understood aspect of the society was the economy. The bakufu by turns tried to stifle, then to encourage, and finally to manage trade throughout the country. When each government policy led to unforeseen and unintended results, the bureaucrats would shift emphasis to a reverse course. Commodity prices and interest rates fluctuated at every turn. The merchants, who could have been the natural allies of the bakufu, were forced to be its most wary adversaries.

Much of the confusion can be traced directly to the bakufu's obsession with Neo-Confucianism. Because that philosophy seemed to be such a perfect fit for the baku-han system in terms of social and political control, it was never apparent that the economic aspects of the system could be flawed. Hideyoshi and Ieyasu had recognized that to freeze the society in terms of vertical social mobility was to preserve the political status quo. Eternal social strata based on occupation separated military and administrative power from the power of the land, and in turn from economic wealth. The basis for this separation was morality. The social classes were "natural" divisions determined by function and contribution to society. The selfless administrators governed hapless childlike farmers and protected them from rapacious parasitic merchants. Peasants and artisans were productive; bureaucrats were moral managers and protectors; merchants were greedy.

It was natural and appropriate that the managers tax the productivity of the farmers and craftsmen in payment for the function of government. But to tax the merchant was to share and collaborate in the nefarious activities that sapped the lifeblood of the producers. Any tax on trade would inevitably be passed on to both producer and consumer, so the bakufu was forbidden to tax the merchants by its own moral philosophy. Not that the merchants were clamoring to pay their share of taxes; on the contrary, they probably would have evaded taxes just as the peasants did. But, since they were constantly reviled and hounded by the bakufu, many merchants became adversaries and saboteurs of the system.

By nature, petty merchants are social conservatives. Any disruption in the social fabric threatens business. Small traders cannot afford long disruptions in trade. They have very little capital, usually working on small profit margins and living from hand to mouth. They are natural and integral parts of the communities that they serve. The smallest economic waves drown the petty merchant because he depends on his customers and suppliers as much as they depend on him. He cannot gouge his customers with inflated prices during times of want because he depends on their trade throughout the year. Cheat someone this month, they find another merchant the next. Honesty and compassion are more than just lip service; they are watchwords to live by.

The petty chōnin were given a stake in their own governance by virtue of the fact that the bakufu allowed them some measure of self-governance in their neighborhoods. The bakufu quickly tired of trying to manage the everyday lives of the plebeian city folk. So the samurai bureaucrats appointed responsible merchants to adjudicate the routine matters within the wards (*machi*) of the major cities controlled by the bakufu. These leaders (*machi-doshiyori* or *nanushi*) were often elected within the machi from among representatives of the five-man mutual-responsibility groups (*gonin-gumi*) that mirrored rural village governance models (see Chapter 11).

During the period, therefore, the petty chōnin obeyed the laws and cooperated with their customers and governors as best they could. No doubt, if the bigger merchant houses could have been similarly incorporated into the macroeconomic life of the society, the economy of the time would not have been as chaotic and schizophrenic as it was.

Official Agents   The bakufu was a direct result of a century of military necessity. The governing bodies (see Chapter 3) were extensions of military units. Similarly, the economic affairs of the bakufu and most of the daimyō governments that emulated it were outgrowths of military systems of organization. As the Tokugawa had grown in land and power, its simple supply organization had become more and more complex. Quasi-samurai quartermasters took on larger tasks in order to keep the Tokugawa forces fed, clothed, and equipped. Some of these bakufu intendants became commercial agents themselves or made deals with wholesalers and substantial merchants. In order to ensure supplies and manage prices, the bakufu made licensed monopoly agreements with wholesale merchants. These official purveyors (*goyō shonin*) were given pride of place in the new merchant residence wards (machi).

Other official wholesalers (*ton'ya*) entered an uneasy and precarious relationship with the bakufu. Their commercial ties to the bakufu gave them ample opportunities to make large fortunes on the increased scale of trade alone. Even keeping profit margins very low, the huge amounts of commodities involved allowed any ton'ya considerable leverage to determine prices and therefore to manage the microeconomy of the surrounding countryside. But because they were never very far from the watchful gaze of the bakufu itself, the ton'ya had to walk a precarious fine line in every endeavor. Any ton'ya who prospered "unduly" or seemingly disproportionately from the current financial situation was in danger of being dispossessed as an example to other merchants. Also, since their accumulated wealth was always a temptation to the bakufu, a merchant was always in danger of being required to provide a "forced loan" (*goyō-kin*) to alleviate bakufu financial straits.

Most of these loans were never repaid, and the very few that were did not accrue interest payments. Sometimes the license fees (*myoga-kin*) would be raised without warning, and the ton'ya could scarcely pass on these costs easily since they were under the constant scrutiny of the bakufu. In medieval times the Kamakura and Muromachi bakufus had both experimented with "Acts of Grace" (*tokusei*). When the uproar from indebted samurai vassals became a cacophony, the bakufu would arbitrarily cancel all samurai debts and force moneylenders and pawnbrokers to restore property seized by loan default. The bakufu itself benefited from these tokusei since the government was usually itself deeply in debt to moneylenders. The obvious (to us, not, apparently, to either bakufu) result was not just ruined merchants and moneylenders. That would have been of little concern to the samurai. What was worse, however, was that merchants had long memories and refused to grant credit or lend money until the previously cancelled debt was repaid. The financial community was small enough that if the merchants kept faith with each other, no one would lend money to a samurai who still owed money to another merchant.

Failing that, interest rates would skyrocket as money became scarce. The wealthy simply hung on to their money until economic times became better. Every tokusei resulted in an even worse economic period than the era of indebtedness that had preceded it. The Tokugawa were generally aware that tokusei did not work in the long run, but occasionally their samurai would force them into granting one. Forced loans and other economic extortion schemes were similarly temporary palliatives that exacerbated the financial woes of the society.

One must also factor in the fact that there was not a real national economy anyway. There were nearly three hundred microeconomies, one for each semi-autonomous han. All were interrelated, to be sure, but there was no real overriding national integration. That too was a result of Tokugawa political policies. The baku-han system purposefully kept the various han independent and separate in order to avoid political alliances. The Tokugawa feared every type of social, economic, religious, and familial integration lest it lead to military alliance. Even the trusted Fudai daimyō were not encouraged to create any financial links and rationalizations. Each daimyō had his own financial agents, wholesalers, and ton'ya. Often many of the ton'ya themselves were interrelated by marriage or some other form of social cohesion, but they maintained independent and separate relationships with individual daimyō.

Every daimyō was required after 1635 or so to make pilgrimage-like trips to Edo as part of the hostage and "alternate attendance" (sankin-kotai) system (see Chapter 3). The trips themselves and the long periods that the daimyō were required to spend in attendance in Edo caused considerable economic hardship. The maintenance of two separate residences for the daimyō's family and entourage was financially crippling alone. But the fact that the daimyō were forced upon the Edo economy for sustenance was even worse. The Tōzama daimyō from the outreaches of the country were hard-pressed to supply themselves with food and clothes from their distant domains. The simple cost of shipping and storing sufficient rice for hundreds of miles was prohibitive.

The remedy was for the daimyō to "sell" his rice to wholesalers in Ōsaka or Sendai (for northern daimyō) and then use the money to pay for expenses while in Edo. Obviously, this gave those Ōsaka and Sendai wholesalers tremendous financial leverage. In some ways, it was the best of all worlds for these financial magnates. They set the price when they bought and when they sold. In both cases Adam Smith's "invisible hand" determined the rates. In Ōsaka, all the daimyō brought in their rice when the regional supply was at its highest: after the autumn harvest. The daimyō, in turn, bought rice when and where it was in greatest demand: in Edo during the rest of the year. Only the wrath and arbitrary whim of the bakufu kept prices somewhat in line. The Tokugawa also had to deal with the Ōsaka and Sendai rice ton'ya, so a modicum of financial restraint was necessary.

By 1715 there were 5,655 ton'ya in Ōsaka alone. In addition there were 8,765 private rice brokers (*nakagai*) and 2,343 independent agents, as well as 481 goyō shonin private purveyors to castles. Obviously the plethora of official and private dealers formed a power financial base in this city alone.[2]

Added to these economic problems were the badly mis- understood and mismanaged bakufu financial policies. At **Fiscal Follies** each shogunal succession, another group of government advisors came to the fore. Each new group would rush to initiate new financial reforms in order to remedy the mistakes of its predecessors. At three significant junctures during the eighteenth century, new national economic policies created tremendous turmoil in the entire country. Two so-called reforms restored the old conservative moralistic Neo-Confucian controls that sought to return the society to its agrarian rural twelfth- century Sung Chinese antecedents.

Each reform enjoined the society to be frugal. Samurai administrators were urged to retrench financially in their own households and to save whenever possible in their public policies. The top bakufu bureaucrats sought to set an example for everyone by imposing a 10 percent recision on their own stipends. Everyone was urged to do the same. A 10 percent cut in the budget of a hatamoto meant that their wives could not buy another kimono for a month. For the lower-ranking samurai, however, a proportionate recision meant that his family could not afford to eat polished rice for a week every month. This was hardly the remedy for the financial problems of the nation.

Usually the reforms also required merchants to roll back their prices and to cut interest rates. As in the above example, the wealthy Ōsaka ton'ya might be temporarily inconvenienced, at least until they could squeeze the poorer merchants and peasants beneath them. The bakufu was also particularly fond of making an example of a few rich merchants, as much for circus as for reform. The most egregiously wealthy mer- chants would have their wealth confiscated and displayed for all to see the cause of the nation's financial misfortunes. There were plenty of those types around. It is estimated that in the mid-century there were no less than 200 ton'ya with annual incomes equal to those of many daimyō. A few of them could be dispossessed, and the bakufu reformers expected that the others would fall into line and the economy thereby be reformed.

It was all so simple: why hadn't anyone thought of this before? A month later, when the prices and interest rates had risen precipitously, the answer should have been obvious. It *had* been though of, and it did not work. Nevertheless, the reformers kept to their programs, no doubt reasoning that the reforms needed more impetus. So a few more mer- chants were dispossessed or forced to "loan" money (*goyō kin*) to the government. Before long, however, the money simply ceased to exist. Coins disappeared into backyard caches, costly clothing seemed to dis- solve, riotous parties and sumptuous feasts vanished, and even the Kabuki and Bunraku theaters seemed to become noticeably more spare in their costumes. Prominent people walked to work instead of taking palanquins, young blades stayed at home instead of cavorting at the Licensed Quarters, women dressed in plain monochrome kimonos, and musicians seemed to have vanished into thin air. And yet, the price of rice did not drop, and loans were even dearer than ever.

Eventually, some minor indication was given that no more extortion and dispossessions could be expected. The crisis had passed momentarily, and things returned to normal. Prices usually dropped slightly as rice hoarders broke into their caches, and interest rates eased. The bakufu bureaucrats convinced themselves that their policies had triumphed. In reality, nothing had changed. In fact, very often interest rates remained high because the moneylenders risked as little as possible for fear that another round of fiscal follies was in the offing.

Evidence suggests that the merchants saw these periodic fiscal retrenchments and dispossessions as a cost of doing business. The few times that the bakufu adopted policies of taxing and encouraging commerce caused a hailstorm of moral indignation from the true believers in Neo-Confucianism. One attempt by the bakufu reformer Tanuma Okitsugu was aborted by outraged moralists. It did not help much that Tanuma was apparently personally corrupt, although perhaps no more so than many of the moralist administrators. But he was publicly disgraced as much for his moral turpitude as for his "immoral" financial reforms.

National Commerce   As suggested, eighteenth-century society was not really integrated into a national economic system except through the rice exchange necessitated by sankin-kotai. The primary locus of this exchange was in Ōsaka. During the period, there were at least 4,500 ton'ya in that city alone. Perhaps one-quarter were directly involved in rice exchange. At least one hundred of the daimyō had their own rice ton'ya established there. Estimates of the annual amount of rice that passed through Ōsaka range as high as 10 million bushels.

The system has been accurately characterized as a rice exchange because very little of the rice that entered Ōsaka's port was consumed there. Most of it was brought by wholesalers who stored it there temporarily until it was transshipped to whereever it was needed. In reality, rice was exchanged for paper. Daimyō received vouchers or letters of credit that could be exchanged for goods and services in Edo. Since each han issued its own paper money (see section on money below) called *hansatsu*, the wholesale merchants had to convert this too into credit to be used in Edo.

The primary rice market in Ōsaka was situated in Dojima, which gave its name to the whole trade. Economic historians claim that Dojima became the locus of the world's first commodities futures market, thirteen decades ahead of Chicago (1865). It was a complex system, which shall be considerably simplified here. Basically, there were two kinds of rice in the system. "True rice" (*shomai*) was that which had been actually bought, delivered, and rested in Dojima storehouses. This was the staff of life for Japan. Some was consumed in Ōsaka, some was turned into sake there, but most of it was eventually shipped to Edo.

"Paper rice" (*choaimai*) was grain to be delivered in the future. The crop could be "purchased" on paper, that is, with no money changing hands. When the price and the date of delivery had been recorded, the *right* to possess it could be sold, traded, or used as collateral for loans. All such commercial activities existed only on paper until the rice was actually delivered.

As in the West two centuries later, commodities could be purchased "on margin," that is, with only a small part of the actual money ever being encumbered. "Trading on the margin" meant that financiers could stretch their actual cash into ten to fifteen times its actual worth, as long as they completed the trades on the right to purchase before the money actually came due. When *choaimai* was actually delivered it magically turned into *shomai* ("true rice").

Not surprisingly, the bakufu was very uncomfortable with anything that it could not actually see (much less understand), so occasionally it would attempt to stop this Dojima trade. But since it existed only on paper and in the minds and mutual trust of the exchangers, the bakufu could do little to stop or impede it. Also, it quickly discovered that the long-term futures market actually helped to stabilize price fluctuations, so it turned a blind eye to the practice as long as no one complained, and of course, as long as the Dojima traders greased their palms from time to time.

Not surprisingly, the Dojima exchange evolved into the major monetary exchange as well. Money, rice futures, vouchers, and other financial instruments were themselves traded, bought, exchanged, bartered, and collateralized for loans. Most of the futures, in fact, were collateralized and highly "leveraged," in the parlance of Wall Street two centuries later. Most large loans were floated in Ōsaka since there was nowhere else that very large sums accumulated. Many daimyō and even the bakufu itself arranged most of its loans there. Not surprisingly, these loans were usually repaid with interest, and scarcely anyone even whispered the word *tokusei*, even in jest. No one could afford to be ostracized by the Dojima bankers. The earthy adage of the era suggested that "when Dojima men fart, even the shōgun smiles and claims it smells sweet."

The Tokugawa monetary system was nearly as chaotic as the baku-han political system. Officially, the bakufu had arrogated **Money** the right of minting to itself. It had seized all of the gold, silver,

Yamada Hagaki privately issued note,
Japan's oldest paper money, circa 1600

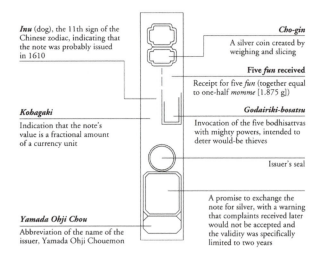

Inu (dog), the 11th sign of the Chinese zodiac, indicating that the note was probably issued in 1610

Cho-gin
A silver coin created by weighing and slicing

Five fun received
Receipt for five *fun* (together equal to one-half *momme* [1.875 g])

Kohagaki
Indication that the note's value is a fractional amount of a currency unit

Godairiki-bosatsu
Invocation of the five bodhisattvas with mighty powers, intended to deter would-be thieves

Issuer's seal

A promise to exchange the note for silver, with a warning that complaints received later would not be accepted and the validity was specifically limited to two years

Yamada Ohji Chou
Abbreviation of the name of the issuer, Yamada Ohji Chouemon

Yamada Hagaki, Japan's first paper money. (Courtesy of the Bank of Japan, Institute for Monetary and Economic Studies)

and copper mines in the country and denied anyone else the right to circulate or coin specie. It had attempted to collect all the Chinese copper cash that was the common money (along with weights of specie) in Hideyoshi's time. Although the bakufu ostensibly controlled all foreign trade, in reality it allowed the daimyō of Tsushima to trade with "offshore" islands, meaning Korea. Similarly, it allowed Satsuma to carry on trade with the Ryukyus.[3] In both cases, copper Chinese cash filtered into the country from these sources, and after a time the Tokugawa turned a blind eye to the unofficial specie.

"Cash," after all, was very much like copper pennies in the West. Worth very little, they were more like small bits of copper that greased the wheels of commerce throughout the country. The coins were round with square holes in the center through which a string was laced. A string of one hundred cash became a unit of currency, though they were often "discounted" to ninety-five or even fewer per string. Occasionally strings were broken up to be used as tips, alms, or small gifts for beggars and children. They could just as easily be restrung into collections of ten, twenty, or a hundred.

The bakufu coined chunks of gold and silver into a rather complex and cumbersome system of exchange. A tenth of an ounce of silver was something like a dime (called *bu*). Larger coins were denominated by weight. The largest silver "coin" was actually about the size of a human hand and called *koban*, though a full ounce of gold was called ryō and was technically equal to a koku of rice (about five dry bushels).

The bakufu would have preferred that no paper money circulate since it made a profit from time to time by debasing the coinage. This usually resulted in a spate of inflation, of which the bakufu claimed not to understand either cause or effect. From time to time, however, the bakufu would relax its prohibition on paper money, usually after someone had, quite coincidentally, made a large gift to the bakufu. In point of fact, virtually every han issued its own paper money (hatsatsu), which was convertible only within the han itself.

The Dojima exchange bankers accepted virtually every kind of money, some of which had to be deeply discounted, of course. The money exchange was a very lucrative business indeed. Coupled with these various notes, the Dojima issued rice vouchers, as noted above. These were redeemed at branch offices in Edo, and could be "spent" on credit in the shops, restaurants, and inns along the roads to Edo. So if there was anything that remotely resembled a national currency, it was these rice vouchers. The Dojima agents had branch offices in Sendai, the other rice exchange in the north.

The Shonin That is not to say that the entire country was financially dysfunctional, at least not always and not uniformly. In large part, the petty merchants (*shonin*) went about their business with circumspection. For the most part, the shonin bought agricultural goods in agrarian areas and transported them to urban areas of demand, where they sold them at a profit. Similarly, the shonin made arrangements to buy manufactured goods or to provide services to whoever wanted or needed them. Peasants bought the absolute necessities and made do with scant luxuries like a few sips of sake or a few mouthfuls of white polished rice at the matsuri. The chōnin went about their lives and livelihoods with few cares because the shonin performed their tasks and services honestly and diligently.

Many petty shonin joined guild-like associations (*kobuna-kama*) for mutual protection. These organizations were modeled on the rice ton'ya guilds and were intended to share costs and risks among many members. Most petty shonin bought from the wholesalers associated with their guilds and borrowed money from the kobuna-kama itself. They were obliged to pay annual license fees (*unjō-kin*) to their city administration.

A few groups plied their products on a national scale. The fabled Omi Shonin of petty merchants located along the shores of Lake Biwa ranged far to the north and west in search of customers. Traders in specialty items such as silk and other textiles, gold, silver, iron products and tools, religious accoutrements, rare spices, sugar, perfumes, and the like had to roam far afield to sell their wares. Many relied upon cheap lodgings at temples and shrines; many others flocked to the more inexpensive hostels along the sankin-kotai highways. They took advantage of roadside food stalls and cheap restaurants in the larger cities, but many more had to rely on some manner of barter in the countless villages where they plied their trade. Village registers, which had to list all visitors, suggest that many peddlers passed through.

Within the cities, the shonin mostly waited for customers to come to their tiny shops. Most lived in the dank rooms behind their simple shops. Only a very few could afford homes separate from their shops. The shonin had to make occasional trips to their suppliers to buy more merchandise. Most had made arrangements with artisans for a steady supply of manufactured goods. Dealers in items that were manufactured at the periphery of the cities had to go there to purchase supplies. Such items as textiles, leather, bamboo, and straw products had to be situated near streams or raw materials. A number of items also were sold at semiannual fairs, and so wholesalers went there to buy them. Pottery, silk, indigo, cotton, and paper were such products.

Greengrocers and fishmongers were required to arise early to buy their supplies at central markets and then hurry home to sell them before the heat of the day wilted or spoiled their wares. Because there was no refrigeration, chōnin bought their food provisions daily. Restaurants often had them delivered. There were hundreds of other specialty shonin—dealers in salt, sake, sugar, charcoal, rice, paper, cooking and lamp oil, soy sauce (shoyu), cutlery, pottery, and tofu to name only a few. Other dry goods merchants stocked a profusion of nonperishable necessities of life such as needles, thread, thimbles, flint, fans, umbrellas, candles, pots, and pans, to name but a few.

Wholesalers, agents, and suppliers of all types abounded in the larger cities. Though not commonly considered a trading commodity, human excrement (see Chapter 15) was collected and sold to outlying farmers. Caterers, procurers, and labor agents dealt in human labor of every stripe and description. Gangs of construction workers, carpenters, smiths, masons, bearers, horse handlers, carters, and the like were commonly organized by labor agents and bosses.[4] Traders in sex abounded in even the small towns. Prostitution and other sexual entertainment (see Chapters 20 and 22) were considered commerce, even if it was in human misery.

As suggested (in Chapter 18), the needs of a shonin house created a very different system of inheritance than was common in the villages or among the samurai. A merchant had to perpetuate the business at the expense of blood ties. A shonin could ill afford to have the business pass to an adolescent or an incompetent heir. Therefore, a shonin often adopted capable apprentices or clerks, and more often that not, would apprentice his own children to other shonin shops. "Succession went to the most able, though care was taken to ensure that a comfortable life was possible for those with no responsibility in the business. With the ever-present danger of bankruptcy, an inflexible pattern of inheritance was not inappropriate."[5]

In short, the urban economies were vibrant and essential during the period. By and large, the society was well served by its merchant class. When left to their own devices, the shonin prospered. When harassed and disturbed, they endured. For the most part, the lives of the shonin were infinitely better than the lives of the average peasant if for no other reason than that they were not routinely and rapaciously taxed by the samurai.

Curiously, the urban shonin were caught between a bumbling, incompetent samurai class of administrators and an equally moralistic peasantry who believed that the shonin were no better than lice, fleas, and other parasites. The moralistic preaching of the samurai class had permeated the minds of the farmers, who

> reasoned that commercial policies were wrong if they harmed many for the sake of the few. They concentrated on an empirical definition of evil—to threaten the livelihood of others in achieving a benefit for oneself. Perceiving self-interest (greed) as a deliberate attempt to ignore the effect of one's actions on others, they expected their rulers to condemn and rectify such behavior. In the end, they

applied their determination of moral standards not only to merchants but to government officials.[6]

NOTES

1. Shoichi Watanabe, *The Peasant Soul of Japan* (New York: St. Martin's Press, 1980), 168.

2. Ian Martin Ropke, *Historical Dictionary of Osaka and Kyoto* (Lanham, MD: Scarecrow Press, 1999).

3. See Ronald P. Toby, *State and Diplomacy in Early Modern Japan: Asia in the Development of the Tokugawa Bakufu* (Princeton: Princeton University Press, 1984), 7.

4. See Gary P. Leupp, *Servants, Shophands, and Laborers in the Cities of Tokugawa Japan* (Princeton: Princeton University Press, 1992).

5. Watanabe, *Peasant Soul*, 169.

6. Anne Walthall, *Social Protest and Popular Culture in Eighteenth Century Japan* (Tucson: University of Arizona Press, 1986), 86–87.

17

Customs

To most Westerners the Japanese customs regarding names seem to be at best confusing, and at worst perverse. Names were much more malleable and transitory than is normal and natural in the West. In Neo-Confucianism, one is charged to "rectify name and reality." The idea is that names are symbolic as well as indications of aspiration. Not surprisingly, if one felt that one had changed in temperament, goal, or essence, one should indicate that change symbolically by changing one's name. Names were magical as well as symbolic. It was not unusual for a man of substance, then, to undergo many changes of identity as he went through life.

In the eighteenth century only the samurai and some of the wealthiest *chōnin* and peasant gonō were allowed to keep what would be considered a surname or family name. As with other sumptuary laws, the intent was to differentiate the noble from the base-born.

Villagers were commonly known only by a *tsusho* or *zokumyō*, both of which mean "common name." Unfortunately, the system of tsusho names was usually quite conventional and therefore might cause some confusion without the benefit of a surname. The firstborn son was almost always named Taro ("big boy") or Ichiro ("first boy"), the second Jiro ("second son"), and the third Saburo ("third son"). Since most families did the same, the resulting comedy of errors was reminiscent of Charlie Chan's "Number One Son." The various Taro were often differentiated within the village by some sort of descriptor ("big-foot," "red nose," "tall," etc.) or patronymic ("Taro's son"). In the market towns, if one had to differentiate one peasant from another, a merchant might refer to one by one's village, such as Murayama ("Mountain Village") Taro, or according to one's special occupation ("rice-mat Jiro," "sedge-hat Saburo," etc.).

To confuse the issue even more, custom dictated that in order to fool the evil spirits, who might like to carry off a precocious youngster, babies would be given an infant name (*yomyō*). It was reasoned that the kami were much less likely to bother a brat named Stinky or Carbuncle than one named Bright or Precious. The name was something like a nickname that disappeared as the child grew older. In some regions, particularly in the cities, the yomyō were more like the numbering of children (Taro, Jiro, etc.) and then were replaced with a more auspicious name like Hajime ("Commencement") or Akira ("The Bright One") at the child's coming-of-age ceremony.

In the eighteenth century girls were often named according to some aspiration of the parent in much the same manner that Western girls were named after Biblical literary figures or feminine aspirations, for example, Hope, Esperanza, Faith, Maria, Dorcas, Huldah, or Portia, Regan, and even Ophelia. This system of female names (*yobi-na*) took on flights of fancy as girls were named Haru (Spring), Kiku (Chrysanthemum), or Mitsu (Abundance). Toward the end of the century it became common to add the honorific prefix "Ō" to the name to make the little darling "Honorable Filial Piety" (Ōko). The suffix "child" (*ko*) was also attached to create a fanciful name such as "Honorable Silver Girl" (Ōginko).

For most villagers the lack of a surname never really hindered them much since villages were small (around 400 people) enough so that everyone knew immediately which "Red-cheeked Ichiro" one meant. In the city neighborhoods, the same held true since the machi were more like urban villages than modern cities. Most chōnin knew who Jinja-mae Taro ("the Taro who lives in front of the shrine") and Yamashita Ōhanako ("Honorable Flower Child who lives at the foot of the mountain") were. Obviously, the names trip off the tongue better in Japanese than in English. They are similar enough to Western usage ("Pegleg Pete," "Long John Silver," or "One-eyed Jack") to make them less exotic to us than one would think after first impression.

Samurai and gonō village headmen were entitled to surnames, but even they were descriptive of one's home province (Mutsu, Date, Akita), much as Western names indicated former village, town, or occupation (Cooper, Smith, Weaver, etc.). The very oldest and most prestigious (Fujiwara and Minamoto) derived from the old noble (*kabane* or *muraji*) titles. By the eighteenth century most samurai surnames (*uji* or *myōji*) were the product of a curious honorific practice that allowed one to attain a portion of one's feudal lord's name at investiture. A daimyō named

Yamamoto (Mountain Base) might allow his samurai vassal the com-memorative Yamashita (Foothill) or Yamamura (Mountain Village). The vassal, if he became a powerful man himself, might pass on a portion of his name to his own vassal.

A few rich chōnin were allowed to create their own surnames as a reward for a "gift" to a daimyō or to the bakufu itself. Ironically (and parenthetically), when commoners were given the right to choose sur-names for themselves in the 1870s, many chose Tokugawa and Matsu-daira, the two names most commonly used by the shōguns. No one was foolish enough to assume the name of the imperial house (Yamato).

If the system had been limited to the above conventions, it would be simple enough to trace family lineages. But Japanese had several more naming systems. The poetic identity (*Gō*) was similar enough to Western pen names (Mark Twain or George Sand) to understand without much difficulty. Posthumous names for emperors (*okuri-na*) are similarly un-derstandable, though most European kings assumed their reign names (Louis XIV, Henry VIII) upon accession rather than in death. Buddhist posthumous names (*hōmyō* or *kaimyō*) were originally assigned only to the founders of sects, important temple abbots, and the like, but even-tually everyone who had a Buddhist funeral was granted such an ap-pellation.

More confusing, however, was a penchant for changing one's name to change one's luck, or to indicate a change of vassalage (rare in the eigh-teenth century), residence, or adoption into another family. As noted in Chapter 18, families often adopted the husband of a daughter as the family scion. Most often the young man assumed the name of his wife's family, but sometimes a conflation of both names was allowed. A Yamamoto adopted into the Matsumura family could become a Yama-matsu. A man could assume a new surname to symbolically commem-orate a change in social or economic station. Or one might honor one's teacher by assuming a portion of his name.[1]

Much has been written about the Japanese penchant for in-scribing their bodies with elaborate and fanciful tattoos (*ire-*   **Tattoos** *zumi*). Indeed, the very first historical document that refers directly and explicitly to Japanese customs mentions tattoos. The third-century Chinese *History of the Wei* (*Wei-chih*) notes that the Japanese common people covered their bodies with intricate tattoos. The quasi-Caucasian Ainu people tattooed the mouths of young girls by slicing and then rubbing wood ash into the wounds.

Evidence indicates that such body decorations became passé and dé-classé by the eighth century, and certainly by the eighteenth they were appropriate and common only in very few instances and social quarters. Tattooing had long been used to brand criminals permanently as part of their ostracism. It was common enough to brand a miscreant with his crime upon his forehead.

Many within the criminal underclass, which often mixed freely with the eta-hinin outcastes, were fond of showing their contempt for society by embellishing their tattoos. By the mid-seventeenth century almost every fireman, carter, tanner, and carpenter began his apprenticeship with a symbolic tattoo. The multicolored tattoos took on the importance and symbolic honor of chevrons as indicators of one's rise within the professional fraternity. Many men crowned their careers when they underwent a costly, painful, and time-consuming torso tattoo. Entire scenes from Japanese classic warrior tales were embellished over the stomach, chest, and back of the proud master fireman.

The process was as slow and laborious as it was painful, and even dangerous. The principal technique was to inscribe the area with a pattern of tiny surface pinpricks, into which vegetable dyes were daubed. In order to ensure uniform coloration, only small, discrete areas could be tattooed at one time and then allowed to heal and then scab over. Two or three tattoos therefore could be in progress simultaneously, each in a different stage of preparation.

Many tattoo artists, for many can truly be said to have attained that designation, prescribed special secret concoctions, balms, baths, and ointments that helped speed up the healing process or intensify the color of the tattoo. Many of these artisans formed their own guilds and secret societies to preserve their craft. The societies and the tattoo process itself took on mystical and pseudo-religious proportions. Within the underclass demimonde tattoo artists were held in high social esteem and usually enjoyed a comfortable existence. Tattoos remained a powerful symbol throughout the era and endured into the twenty-first century within the *yakuza* criminal underworld.

Gambling   Much consideration was given to whether this topic more properly belongs in Chapter 22. As we shall see, it might have been discussed in Chapter 4 because of its origins rather than its later practice. It appears here because it is deemed to be more custom than anything else.

Gambling can be said to have originated from oracle and divination practices. The casting of bones, amulets, lots, and other shamanic indicators predicted fortune as much as it interpreted cosmic phenomena. As such, such formulaic rituals can easily be translated into gambling in one form or another. Wagering on physical bouts and contests was similarly deemed to give insight into the world of the unknown. Sumo and archery were both vested with shamanic charisma since both apparently were based as much on esprit as on strength, technique, or prowess. A gentle breeze could waft the flight of an arrow; a slippery bit of clay could turn the ankle of the most stalwart wrestler. Such contests seemed to be expressions of the ineffable and esoteric. Indeed, Shintō shrines very often staged such contests as appropriate manifestations of the kami.

It is no accident or coincidence that in almost every language and society one expresses the sense of chance as an opportunity to "change one's fortune" or one's luck. Winners thank their "lucky stars" (astrology at its core), the "gods," "Lady Luck," or some other metaphoric expression of fate. In Japan, the sometimes perversely capricious kami were thought to influence human life through gambling.

In many societies gambling occurs most often among the classes that can afford it least. Mafia, yakuza, and (most perversely) even state-run lotteries sap the finances of the very poorest of the poor. In eighteenth-century Japan, this was decidedly not the case. This was partially due to the Neo-Confucian moralities that were the order of the day. Samurai administrators made certain that the childlike peasants would never succumb to such vices through a network of paternalistic moral laws. The punishments for gambling were so draconian that it was practically unknown in the provinces. Peasants and touts alike were cut down on the spot if they were even suspected of gambling. Families could lose everything if any member was involved.

Curiously, a tontine-like game developed in the countryside but was allowed and even encouraged because the chance was disguised or nullified by rules of mutual support. Mutual-aid societies (*ko*) required a small annual payment from each "player." Each year one or two "winners" were designated and allowed to collect all the fees with the understanding that everyone would get a turn at "winning." The funds were intended to cover the costs of a pilgrimage, usually to an appropriate shrine or temple, very often to the Grand Shrine at Ise. The only real element of chance in a mutual-aid ko, however, was if a "winner" were to become ill, die, or otherwise be unable to use the funds for the intended reasons. Ko that tended toward gambling were shut down quickly by the authorities, and anyone involved was harshly and quickly punished.

In the cities, however, gambling thrived among all classes. Most took place within the Licensed Quarters, where all sorts of games were rife in every brothel, teashop, and sake shop. A kind of dice was used, as were cards. Geisha and prostitutes were often used as shills and touts to bring their customers into rigged games.

Interspersed within the ubiquitous noodle, riceball, and grilled snack stalls were various games of chance. Mini-archery games were the most popular since they were technologically (and logically) simplistic. The Japanese did not develop darts or play games in which balls are thrown until the late nineteenth and twentieth centuries, with the advent of baseball. Wooden ring and beanbag tossing were common, as was a game similar to skittles.

There was an innocuous common drinking "game." Games similar to British "forfeits" were played virtually everywhere. The latter were similar to the "paper-rock-scissors" of Western children except that a single index finger was extended to indicate a gun rather than the two-finger scissors as in the West.

Enough Kabuki and Bunraku plays contain evidence of extensive gambling to suggest that the chōnin quarters were rife with the vice. Predictably, a species of debt collector developed to serve the gambling enterprises. Samurai and sumo *rikishi* down on their luck naturally gravitated toward such sidelines. Pawnbrokers became very common as well. The bakufu frowned on samurai pawning their swords since these were symbols of class and station as well as family heirlooms.

Fortune-Telling   In a society where shamanic divination was traditionally accepted, it is not too surprising that various kinds of fortune-telling would be common and popular. The female shamanic *miko* were intrinsic to Shintō. Virtually every village worthy of the name had at least one diviner. Most were older unmarried females whose schtick was to fall into a trance in order to "channel" the voices of the kami and one's ancestors.

A profusion of Korean shamanic diviners migrated or were captured by the forces of Hideyoshi in the 1590s, giving rise to an even more exotic genre of fortune-tellers. There were also groups of charlatans of every stripe including pseudo-phrenologists (who "read" the shape of one's skull), and "readers" of every omen (tea dregs, animal entrails, and even chicken excrement) and sign. They tended to congregate in the (temporarily) dry river beds of every large town and city, where the eta resided.

Many of the Eastern European or Western Asian accoutrements of the craft never migrated as far as Japan. Crystal balls and pyramids never seemed to appear in Japan. A tarot-like card system developed, probably from Korea. The symbols and omens are even more esoteric than tarot.

The Taoist *I Ching*, on the other hand, became very popular in Japan. It is based on the precepts of magic numerology. The sixty-four possible combinations of six lines of solid or segmented lines (the same as casting six sets of three coins: heads or tails) were called hexagrams. Each was keyed to a specific cryptic divination in the *I Ching*. Practitioners also used yarrow sticks to accomplish the same casting of lots. A similar fortune-telling device was available at most temples. For a few coppers one could select a numbered chopstick from a proffered covered container. The number corresponded to one of the Taoist hexagrams, or sometimes to a supposedly Buddhist secret symbol (often written in pseudo-Sanskrit) indicating the "path" of one's luck or fortune. Since most people were illiterate, in some temples tightly rolled scraps of paper contained magical symbols to "tell" one's fate. Sutra fragments were often substituted for the Taoist hexagrams.

Most commonly one's "fortune" contained ominous warnings of approaching evil that one could avoid by purchasing a cheap amulet or talisman from the selfsame seer. Many of the esoteric and magical symbols of Shintō and Buddhism were used in these amulets. At least the poor peasants did not expect to be procuring a splinter of the Old Rugged Cross, but they were often sold shards of Buddha's bones or snippets of his hair. Since the Grand Shrine at Ise was disassembled and burned every twenty years, to be totally replaced, charlatans (and not a few monks, priests, and nuns) sold tiny vials said to contain the actual ashes of the old shrine.

As with most Japanese technologies, medicine had its origins and influences in China, most often via Korea. The basic   **Medicine** philosophical foundations of medicine involved the idea that the body was matter influenced by cosmic and natural energies called *chi*. Chi flowed through everything, including all of nature. The natural channels of chi currents kept the body animated and nourished in much the same manner that Europeans believed that humors coursed through the body. When these channels were blocked, chi energy was pent up and denied to portions of the body. One could unblock the flow through the use of finger pressure, massage, ointment, and heat, and through the application of other stimuli such as needles inserted into the skin topically.

Acupuncture (*hariryōyi*), massage, and moxa (*moe-kusa*; burning of medicine topically on the skin) were the most common exterior remedies for sickness and injury. Medical practitioners inserted hairlike iron, silver, copper, and more rarely gold needles into specific points along the axial avenues or channels that freed up the movement of chi. Deep and sometimes painful massages were used to similarly unblock the channels and to stimulate the movement of chi.

Similarly, small herbal concoctions were burned directly on the skin (moxa) to dilate the interior channel. Kaempfer noted, "I found the backs of the Japanese . . . of both sexes so full of scars and marks of former exulcerations, that one would imagine they had undergone a most severe whipping."[2]

This moxabustion or moxacautery could also involve "cupping" whereby glass globules could be cupped to the skin. This involved burning a tiny bit of desiccated herb on the skin and then immediately covering it with a glass cup. The combustion of the moxa created a vacuum as the oxygen was consumed within the cup, causing the skin to pucker. It was believed that the cup also sucked up internal impediments that had blocked the channels of chi.

In terms of internal medicinal pharmacopoeia, Japanese had experimented with various natural concoctions for centuries. The Chinese pharmacopoeia was vastly more sophisticated, partially owing to the Taoist obsession with the elixirs of immortality and sexual potency. Chinese and Korean medical practitioners had brought this pseudo-science to Japan throughout the years. Virtually every Japanese acolyte and monk who had journeyed to China (or even India) in search of enlightenment returned to Japan with a trunk full of Chinese herbs and liquors. Indeed, tea came to Japan as such an elixir. Lest a Westerner scoff, Chinese had discovered medicines such as quinine and digitalis centuries before Western scientists. Also, Japanese, Koreans, and Chinese scarcely ever imagined that lancing and bleeding could cure patients. There is evidence that the use of maggots to debride necrotic tissue and the use of leeches to drain hematomae both came to the West from China.

In eighteenth-century Japan, most medicine worthy of the name was practiced rather than administered. Just as there was no licensing of physicians and surgeons in the West until it became a revenue and social control measure, "doctors" in Japan were really just practitioners and purveyors. In many cases, the "craft" was an inherited one much in the manner of any other artisanal esoteric skill. Families practiced their medical arts together with pharmacists and concocters.

Thousands of herbs, grasses, roots, and animal parts (especially blood, sweat, semen, urine, excrement, and venom) were gathered and processed. Desiccation, distillation, grinding, cooking, brewing, pickling, and virtually every other method of combination were used in secret formulae. Most were little more than quack nostrums similar to Western snake oil, but not a few apparently were effective when used for particular symptoms. If for no other medicinal reasons, a healthy dose of a diuretic, colonic lavage, or purgative seemed to have worked wonders simply because the patient rarely continued to complain of minor symptoms for fear that another dose was forthcoming.

Scores of pharmaceutical manuals were printed during the period, and many more almanacs contained medical advice as well. The bakufu finally became convinced that the Dutch practiced a curious, though apparently efficacious method of medicine. In the early eighteenth century they relaxed their ban on publishing books on Western topics to allow manuals of *Rangaku* ("Dutch Studies") medical science. Particularly popular were books on surgery. The Chinese Taoist religions forbade such invasive therapy since the body must be maintained complete for spiritual regeneration. By the eighteenth century Europeans had overcome a similar proscription against "mutilating" of the body and had surged ahead in this aspect of medicine. Japanese doctors in Nagasaki had observed Dutch surgery and became convinced that it had application in their own practices. The bakufu finally agreed after some members of the Tokugawa family were apparently cured by Dutch physicians and surgeons.

Commoners in Japan, of course, had no such recourse. They patronized native medical practitioners. Some had recourse to shamans, and it must be said that both seemed equally efficacious (or ineffective), just as in America at the time. Hospitals were almost unknown, and the few that operated (no pun) were more in the realm of leper hostels or parturition huts.

Midwifery was not as highly developed an art as in the West. Most women could aid younger women during delivery, but the practice commonly remained securely within the extended family, without recourse to village specialists. As in the rest of the world, birth was still accomplished with the help of gravity. Medical science had not "progressed" to the point where women were laid on their backs for the convenience of the doctor, but to the detriment of the mother. The woman in labor perched or squatted on a low stool, and another woman supported her from behind until the baby's head appeared. Mothers remained seated after birth to help with the delivery of the placenta and were only allowed to lie down after they had suckled the baby for the first time.

It was at this critical juncture that infanticide, if it was contemplated, was done. The earthen bowl that was used to give the baby its first bath could also be used to "send it back to Buddha"[3] by drowning. As noted in Chapter 2, not only females were killed; if the birth order was inappropriate, or one already had too many boys, male babies were sometimes killed as well. Reprehensible and disgusting as this is to our sensibilities and morality, the Japanese had little if any moral aversion to the practice. It was one of the major methods of family planning.

Another medical method was, as in the European spa, to "take the waters." Japan's numerous geothermal vents produced thousands of natural hot springs (*onsen*) that were convenient to virtually everyone in the country. Onsen geysers and pools of hot springs were most common along Japan's long rocky coastline, but onsen were quite common in the mountains as well. The onsen in the mountains were even more popular than the coastal ones because of the precipitated minerals coursing through the water.

Sulfurous springs were particularly popular because the belching sulfur was deemed to be medicinal as well. Hundreds of ailments and discomforts were believed to be treatable by extended stays in onsen. The water was usually very hot indeed, and long soaks are now known to be efficacious for rheumatism, arthritis, and various other diseases and maladies of the skeletal joints. Obviously, only the wealthy could afford extended stays, though some of the mutual-aid *ko* societies intended the funds to be used for onsen. Onsen near major pilgrimage sites obviously did very well, since two tasks could be accomplished in one fell swoop.

Inns and hostels sprouted around the onsen, which became a major medicinal and tourist industry during the century. Many onsen inns specialized in therapeutic diets and other medicinal regimens. Most also could readily cater to other human needs as well. Prostitutes were often employed as masseuses (and masseurs as well if one's tastes ran in that direction), and virtually every inn had entertainment of some kind. The term *onsen-geisha* came to mean prostitute, since most of the entertainers made a living in that manner as well as by singing or dancing.

Pets   Pets, as in the West, and as the Japanese in the twenty-first century understand the term, were practically unknown in the countryside. Many farm families kept dogs, cats, ducks, chickens, and geese, but they were considered tools as much as living beings. Buddhism forbade the killing of animals, even for food. However, many Japanese ate all of the above, but not in their regular diet. Dogs and cats served as protectors and as mousers. Chickens, ducks, and geese produced eggs and devoured many noxious insects and worms that fed on the ripening grain. Anyone who has lived around ducks and geese knows that they are excellent "alarms" against trespassers as well. One is more likely to slip by an alert dog than by a protective gander.

Some daimyō still kept hawks for sport, and many Japanese kept singing birds and crickets for companionship. The Japanese carp (*koi*) was perhaps as much a pet as anything else. Koi can be trained to eat from one's fingers and apparently like to be stroked and petted. Many were raised for food, of course, but few people mixed the two purposes. It is universally difficult to eat one's animal friends. It is generally better to munch on an anonymous species. Most temples kept koi as pond decorations and as symbols of the commonality of human and animal life. Monkeys, being so similar to humans, were also kept around remote temples.

In the large cities, small dogs imported from China and Korea became the rage as pets among wealthy chōnin women toward the end of the century. Wealthy matrons could be seen walking the little dears on leashes late in the evenings along the canals. It probably was also a convenient excuse to get out of the house and to show off new kimonos and other finery.

Surprisingly, the most feared animal in Japan was not the rare wildcat, the few poisonous snakes, the ubiquitous snapping turtles (perhaps the peripatetic mosquito?), or any other feral animals. It was the fox, which was believed to be a manifestation of demons and goblins (*tengu*). It was thought that demons passed easily into the bodies of foxes, and because those sly creatures were always in the environs of humans, they then could jump into humans too. The myth was curiously wrapped up in the Inari rice shrines where foxes were symbols of kami that protected the crop by snacking on small rodents. No one in his or her right mind, however, was ever recorded as having tempted fate by making a fox into a pet. It would be as crazy and as dangerous for a Transylvanian to keep bats as pets in the same era. In Japan bats were not harbingers of evil, but owls often were so considered.

Almost nothing better distinguishes and caricatures Japanese these days (except perhaps a camera dangling around **Greetings** one's neck) than their system of greetings. By the eighteenth century it was formalized almost to the point of ritual. The modern bow probably originated much before then, but in this period there were even more gradations than there are today.

The symbolic act of bowing one's head probably comes from a self-abasement to the spirits. To bow or to prostrate oneself before a deity is almost as natural as falling silent when one approaches any religious site. It is an acknowledgment of respect, awe, fear, and dread. To do so before one's human superior seems to be just as natural. Some have argued that it is also a ceremonial exposing the vulnerable nape of the neck to a warrior to indicate that one comes in peace. Extending (or raising, like the Native American Indians) an empty right hand is similarly a symbol of peace, as is the joining of both hands in supplication as in India, Thailand, and other littoral Asian societies.

In eighteenth-century Japan commoners were said to bob the head to virtually everyone as a greeting. A deeper bow was owed to the village headman, a priest, nun, or other person worthy of respect. An approaching samurai was another thing altogether. If one was mounted, one had to immediately dismount and drop to one's knees. The forehead had to touch the ground in obeisance if one did not wish to risk a swift sword slash. Even when a samurai allowed one to look upon him, the peasant dared not risk meeting the samurai's gaze with his own. So wide was the social chasm between samurai and peasant that the former felt violated by the stare of the latter. Samurai still maintained the right of *kirisute-gomen* ("cut with impunity"), but very few actually did so since the paperwork and criminal investigations were so worrisome.

Obviously, although chōnin technically ranked even below peasants, not much business could have been accomplished if the chōnin had to behave in such an obsequious manner. When a samurai stepped into a merchant shop (and most avoided doing that by sending their servants), the merchant would be expected to bow and scrape like a lowly peasant, but on the street, most chōnin only nodded or looked away studiously as if they had not noticed that a samurai was walking by.

On the main roads, a single samurai would be accorded a deep bow, but when samurai were aggregated into huge parades on the sankin-kotai voyages to and from Edo, most commoners dropped into the dust. Marching samurai oozed testosterone that made punishment of offensive behavior on the part of commoners obligatory lest one's peers think one unmanly.

Woman were expected to bow to everyone, even their husbands, fathers, and parents-in-law. The female bow was supposed to be graceful and demure. Young women were taught to bow in a kind of coquettish sideways simper while covering their lower face with an unfurled fan. Serving girls were required to proffer the serving tray as they extended their bodies in a kind of cat-stretch while on their knees. At snack stalls, a cursory bow would suffice. Rumor has it that geisha were taught upwards of twenty different bows, each appropriate to the station of one's customers and to the occasion. Even common prostitutes were expected to know at least a dozen bows.

NOTES

1. See Basil Hall Chamberlain, *Japanese Things* (Rutland, VT: Tuttle, 1971), 344–48 for an informative, if sardonic, discussion.

2. Engelbert Kaempfer, *The History of Japan: Together with a Description of the Kingdom of Siam*, 3 vols., trans. J. G. Scheuchzer (Glasgow: James MacLehose and Sons, 1906), 3:282.

3. Peasants sometimes referred to infanticide as "thinning the crop" (*mabiki*).

18

Family

The family in eighteenth-century Japan was an amalgam of traditional culture and of a recent legal innovation. Prior to about the fifteenth century, the family was an extended fictive kinship idea that had served social, economic, religious, political, military, and cultural needs. The ancient idea of *uji* designation corresponded to old northern European fictive kinship groups called tribes or clans. Usually patriarchal, the family encompassed real and fictional kin and often economic and military allies. Family membership was both natal and customary. Distant relatives who lived in family compounds were accepted as part of the family, while children born into the family but now residing elsewhere were not. Servants, spouses, concubines, in-laws, apprentices, and all sorts of people who would not be considered part of the family in Western societies were quite often considered to be full-fledged members in Japan.

That had changed during and after the Sengoku era. Hideyoshi and Ieyasu incorporated the Neo-Confucian worldview into Japanese society, and therefore families became more narrowly defined. Part of the new definition had to do with co-sanguine ideas of shared blood, but it also had much to do with administrative units. After about 1600, the household or *ie* became the newly defined family.

The household was conceived to be the corporate body, and its members were expected to sacrifice personal desires and accept all major decisions of the household head. The headship passed to one child, in principle the eldest son of the incumbent, to whom both authority and property were transferred.[1]

The origins of the ie were to be found in the samurai patrimony. A samurai's title and status passed on to his legal heir whether related by blood or not. Since samurai status was originally attached to land grants (or administrative-tax rights), it was much simpler and more efficient to limit the number of families and titles to correspond to the amount of land to be divided. By 1600 the Tokugawa samurai all resided in administrative cities, usually castle towns. They were paid, not in a share of spoils (there being no warfare), but in a stipend which represented a share of the tax rice collected by the daimyō. The title, status, administrative position, and stipend were all represented by the household and were indivisible. Only one incumbent, only one heir, only one head of household existed at any given time.

In terms of governmental and judicial administration, only the ie existed. The head of the ie spoke for the household; individual members were just that. The ie continued until there was no one to inherit property or title. Scrupulous family registers (*koseki*) had to be maintained as legal documents. People could enter the ie by birth, marriage, or adoption. They could leave by death, disinheritance, and marriage outside the ie.

Since this ie system apparently worked so well administratively for the samurai, the bakufu transferred the idea to the peasantry as well. The Neo-Confucian paradigm miniaturized the samurai ie to fit peasant realities. They too inherited title (*hyakusho*), status, and the small pieces of paddy land as property. The ie inherited all. The head of the household was its representative; it was up to him to perpetuate the household and to pass it on, undivided, to his heir.

The family, then, no longer really existed; only the household did. The family existed only to serve and perpetuate the household. Heirs therefore had to be obtained. The simplest way was through sexual procreation, but other means were available and legal. Heirs could be adopted.

Adoption   Adoption seems to be a common idea in most societies, but the Japanese definition was nearly unique. Childless household heads could adopt the sons of relatives, and nephew adoption is the most common in Japanese history. In the Western and Chinese customs this would preserve the idea of bloodline, that is, that the father and heir should share common ancestry. But in Japan after 1600 or so, the continuation of the ie was much more important than blood relationship. Therefore, since women could not inherit headship (this came out of the need to preserve undivided estates during the centuries of feudal warfare), they were technically cut out of the equation, except that in Japan they could be the conduits for inheritance. Often an ie head adopted his son-in-law as his heir. The husband of his daughter could not inherit in his own natal family (to avoid the concentration of land); so he would jettison his own name and assume that of his father-in-law. It was not unknown for inheritance to skip a generation. That is, the grandson of an ie head (himself without a son) would adopt one of his own grandsons (the one that did not stand to inherit the headship from his own father).

Childless couples sometimes adopted an unrelated young married couple to be their heirs. Other unrelated young men could also be adopted, but they had to be without prospect of inheritance through their own natal families. Complications arose when a scion died and the second son was forced to renounce his adoption into another family in order to assume the headship of his natal family. Needless to say, attempts to trace lineage in Japan are very complicated. That fact did not seem to bother the Japanese in the eighteenth century, and truth be told, it does not apparently trouble them even 200 years later.

Within chōnin merchant households the already complex adoption system was further complicated by the needs of the business. Because the merchant needed to be assured that an adult male could succeed him in business at any time, and thereby protect the family inheritance through financial acumen, he often could not wait until his own son became an adult. By the eighteenth century a new system was in place in most of the larger cities. A merchant's son would be apprenticed (*detchi*) to another merchant household, and the household head in turn would adopt his chief clerk (*banto*) as his own heir.

Boys (and often girls as well) were apprenticed as detchi at the age of seven and went to live with other merchant families. They would receive room and board, one or two sets of clothes per year, and often a little spending money. In return they would serve their masters, first by drudgery, eventually being allowed to train in the specialty of the business concern. After twenty years or so, they could be adopted as heirs or would be set up in business in a cadet or branch (*bunke*) business. In the meantime, the young man's natal family was doing the same with another set of detchi. Young boys were therefore dispossessed of their birthrights before they were even born. Often, however, the adopted heir would in turn adopt the natural son of his adopted father, and thereby continue the bloodline, but also assure that the business would always be run by an adult.

The custom had obvious advantages in nurturing and perpetuating the business. One did not have to depend on the vagaries of heredity and hope that one's sons would be capable and intelligent. That was someone else's problem. Better to groom one's heir, winnowing out any feeble-minded or incompetent apprentices and selecting the best.

Artisans and other occupations followed a similar custom as well. One nineteenth-century European observer noted, "[T]his is it which explains such apparent anomalies as a distinguished painter, potter, actor, or what-not, almost always having a son distinguished in the same line: he has simply adopted his best pupil. It also explains the fact of Japanese families not dying out."[2]

Marriage   It goes without saying that the more "natural" and normal perpetuation of the family was through marriage and sexual procreation. But again, marriage must be interpreted in a manner somewhat different from Western and Christian customs.

As in the feudal West, marriage was not seen as the union of two people in love, nor even as a permanent monogamous estate. Marriage was a social, and sometimes political, military, economic, or religious combination of two corporations (usually called families). Men who would be allied with other men frequently "cemented" the alliance through marriage. Specific arrangements (prenuptial agreements?) were made for dispossession of property in cases of divorce or the birth of children (which affected, the division of property). All in all, it was a legal arrangement for goals other than emotional or sexual gratification.

In Japan, as in many societies, "trial" marriages were fairly common. Prospective brides came to live with the family of the boy and some sexual experimentation was allowed, it generally being understood that if pregnancy resulted, the wedding ceremony would follow immediately. Commonly, the young girl served the patriarchal family as a servant for a year until her first menses at about age thirteen or fourteen. If the arrangement did not suit both parties, then the girl would return home and could be betrothed and married to another without any stigma due to the loss of virginity. In the countryside in particular, young people were allowed some premarital license, and not much stock was placed in bridal virginity. What was important was proved fecundity, namely, pregnancy. That was, after all, the purpose of the marriage, to produce children and therefore heirs.

Among the samurai, however, more attention was paid to chastity before marriage, and prospective brides could be and sometimes were rejected if they were not virgins. More often, however, this was ignored and the marriage was carried on.

Among peasants, the only ceremony was the traditional *sansankudo* ("three sips from three cups"), which is descriptive of the simple ritual. The bride and groom exchanged three thimble-sized sake cups in turn, which were consumed in three sips each. Upon completion of this public ceremony, the couple was considered married, and everyone at the wedding then celebrated the union with food and drink, the bridal couple thereafter being quite ignored.

Among samurai and some chōnin of substance, the ritual extended to a week of ceremony. A go-between (*nakodo*) made the actual match after investigating each prospective family's history, financial standing, social reputation, and even the possibility of some hereditary disease. The nakodo acted as guarantor should either family be displeased after the wedding. Often an *omiai* (literally, "see-meet") was arranged to assure both parties that the other did not have two heads or was otherwise unsuitable. At that point either party could abort the proceedings without much loss of face.

If both parties were agreeable, a betrothal was announced and there would be a *yuino* (exchange of gifts), since both dowry and bride-price were common in Japan, depending on the relative social and economic station of the respective families. Sometimes the gifts were converted to actual money (*jisankin*). The sansankudo was performed as in the simple peasant wedding.

Commonly the bride wore a white kimono (as well as a peculiar triangular hat that was supposed to hide the "horns of jealousy"), white being the color of death and mourning. This symbolized that the bride had died to her natal family. To assure everyone of that symbolism, the bride's name was blotted out of the *koseki* (family register) and then was entered into that of her husband's. That ceremony was commonly done on the third day after the marriage and was called "returning home" (*sato-gaeri*) when she was formally received in her natal home as a guest. Of course if the husband-to-be were about to be adopted into his wife's household, all of the wedding rituals would be altered, since the bride was to remain at home.

It is important to note that many people were never allowed to marry. This was one method of birth control to avoid excess children who could not inherit. Second and third sons, if they could not form cadet houses (easier among merchants than among samurai and peasants who could not subdivide their patrimony), were doomed to a netherworld. Not surprisingly, many hired out as seasonal workers or left home for some uncertain life elsewhere. During warfare, these were the men who filled the ranks of ashigaru. Many became sailors, monks, itinerant merchants, and the like. Young women who did not marry often joined the ranks of servant girls, or sadly, of prostitutes and geisha.

Marriage was a significant social threshold for everyone concerned. Frequently, when a young man married and brought his wife home, his father would "retire" (*inkyo*) from the active headship of the ie. Symbolically, the "old" head and his wife would move out of the main room of the house, exchanging rooms with the "new" head and his new wife. At this time, any remaining siblings in the house would move out as well. Obviously this was a rupture in the old social order, one which was not taken lightly.

It allowed the brother who could not stay permanently to leave at an age when, through apprenticeship or service to an employer, he might establish himself elsewhere in life and eventually marry. [A]lso, since it was not always certain which brother was to inherit, until a marriage in fact had occurred, the quick departure of the others may have been partly a way of avoiding bitterness in the family after the parents' choice became known.[3]

Divorce In Japan, divorce was possible without the attendant social and economic catastrophes that characterized it in other societies, China, for example. Men could divorce their wives relatively easily and on very minor pretexts. Incompatibility may accurately characterize most grounds for divorce in eighteenth-century Japan. That included such problems as the new bride being "lazy," too talkative, or inconsiderate, but most of all "childless." What this really meant was that she had not given birth to a boy within a reasonable time (usually two years). She was then unceremoniously returned to her natal family. If this were done, any dowry had to be returned with her, so this often served as a deterrent to divorce.

Since children were the property of the household patriarchy, a divorced woman returned to her natal household without them. But, being childless, she was unencumbered and could therefore be married off relatively easily. More commonly, returned wives were sold into concubinage or prostitution.

Not surprisingly, it was more difficult for women to divorce their husbands. If her natal family was more prominent than her husband's family, however, the divorce became much easier. A woman could divorce a husband who had gone insane, who had become a criminal, or, rarer, who abused her or the children. A divorce was often granted for those men who had renounced the world and had become Buddhist monks. Also, there was a little-used escape at Kamakura. Since 1285 the Zen temple of Tokei-ji was known as the "divorce temple" because wives who could abscond there were given sanctuary and, if they remained cloistered there for three years (later reduced to two years), they would be granted a divorce by the bakufu. There were rarely more than twenty or thirty women there at any given time, so it was perhaps the epitome of the exception that proved the rule.

Childless widows could and did remarry. Widows with children had to remain in the households of their deceased husband if they wanted to remain with their children. Among the chōnin and peasantry, divorce and widow remarriage were much more common than within the samurai class. There was scarcely a rural village that did not contain several women who had been married more than once.

NOTES

1. Robert J. Smith, *Ancestor Worship in Contemporary Japan* (Stanford: Stanford University Press, 1974), 33.

2. Basil Hall Chamberlain, *Japanese Things* (Rutland, VT: Tuttle, 1971), 17.

3. Thomas C. Smith, *Nakahara: Family Farming and Population in a Japanese Village, 1717–1830* (Stanford: Stanford University Press, 1977), 134.

19

Sex

[I]n the samurai class, the wife's infidelity was harshly punished, most often either by divorce or repudiation, in the other classes, nobles or farmers, it was of no consequence, so long as the fact was kept secret, so as to prevent the husband from losing face.[1]

European visitors to Japan in the sixteenth century were astounded with Japanese sexual mores (or more accurately, their apparent lack of them). We can understand why the Jesuit priests were so scandalized by the Japanese casual indifference to the "sanctity of marriage" and to the lack of social disapproval of male homosexuality, but even the lusty sailors, soldiers, and merchants of every European nationality marveled at Japan's apparent lack of sexual shame. Letters, diaries, and histories were full of European shock at the sight of mixed bathing, open prostitution (of both sexes), common pederasty between Buddhist monks and their juvenile acolytes, transvestism in the Kabuki theater, and seemingly total disregard for premarital and extramarital sexual practices.

Perhaps because Shintō had no strictures against sexual expression, and because Buddhism is a renunciatory religious philosophy, Japan did not concern itself with sex as "sin" as does the monotheistic Judeo-Christian and Islamic West. Neo-Confucianism in China contained strictures against homosexuality, but they were largely ignored in Japan. Shintō is more concerned with what is ritually appropriate versus that which is polluting. Except for an implied condemnation of incest, Shintō viewed sexuality as natural, normal, and appropriate human behavior. The Shintō quasi-historical canons, the *Kojiki* and *Nihon Shoki*, are replete with references to all sorts of sexual expression, but one would search in vain for any suggestion that any of it was "bad" or "evil."

To be sure both Confucianism and the twelfth-century Neo-Confucian reformist Chu Hsi preached that there should be ideal human relationships, among them that of marriage partners. But because the Chinese were more concerned with etiquette and propriety, and because the need for family continuity was paramount, extramarital sex and consensual premarital sexual experimentation were not particularly a problem.

Buddhism in its origins had some strict laws about sexuality, but one must remember that it taught that the world was illusory and that *any* emotional attachment was counter to one's salvation. Any sex, then, was part of the emotional attachment that bound one inexorably to the wheel of painful life. As it was practiced in China, Buddhism maintained the practice of celibacy among the priesthood, but in some sects in Japan this too was jettisoned and priests were encouraged to marry and to pass on their religious duties to their sons.

Homosexuality   Homosexuality in medieval Japan was tolerated to such an extent that Japanese scarcely were surprised when they encountered it. That does not hold true for the Europeans who encountered it in the sixteenth century. The Jesuit Alejandro Valignano could not even use the word pederasty, referring to it as "the sin that does not bear mentioning."[2] Another priest, Francesco Carletti, said about it, "[T]his country is more plentifully supplied than any other with those sort of means of gratifying the passion for sexual indulgence, just as it abounds in every other sort of vice, in which it surpasses every other place in the world."[3] Whether this was mere hyperbole or whether Carletti had kept his eyes glued shut during the long ocean voyage from Portugal, Japan shocked these pious men with its blatant tolerance for sexual gratification of all sorts and stripes.

During the medieval period, priests were enjoined from marriage in most sects, but it was fairly common to engage in homosexual sex with other monks. Young acolytes called *chigo* became lovers. Among the samurai class "it was frequently proclaimed that love for a woman was an effeminate failing. In both cloister and barracks, the love of man for man was more than mere sexual gratification. Ideally, at least, it was based on a lasting relationship of loyalty and devotion."[4]

Anecdotally, we are told that male homosexuality among the samurai class during the century-long Sengoku civil war period was so common that it became the norm among fighting men. It was certainly very popular in most of the burgeoning castle towns of the late fifteenth through the sixteenth centuries. Male prostitutes were commonly available in most inns. The bakufu's only real concern was that homosexual liaisons sometimes led to social disruption. They also tried to prevent the kidnapping of young boys to be enslaved in sexual servitude. Otherwise they considered the practice between consenting adults nothing with which to be concerned.

Apparently it was so common that the Neo-Confucian philosophers did not even mention it much in their treatises. The bakufu did not make it illegal, and the only mention of it in their moral edicts and sumptuary laws had to do with any brawls or public disturbances outside homosexual brothels or at the stage doors of Kabuki theaters. The terms "night friend" (*yoru no tomo*) and "beloved boy" (*chōdō*) were common enough to be instantly recognized by most people.

If common Japanese were neither shocked nor particularly offended by the idea of male homosexuality, the Europeans who came to Japan certainly were. The Jesuits who came in the sixteenth century, as noted above, were astounded that it was so common and so accepted by society. In the eighteenth century, Kaempfer recounted with obvious distaste entering one of the last stations before Edo along the Tokaido and seeing

> nine or ten neat houses, or booths, before each of which sate [*sic*] one, two, or three young boys, often to twelve years of age, well dress'd, with their faces painted, and feminine gestures, kept by their lew'd and cruel masters for the secret pleasures and entertainment of rich travelers, the Japanese being very much addicted to this vice.[5]

Finally, homosexuality among the denizens of the theater was a common thing. As noted in the section on Kabuki, the origins of that genre were, at least in part, based in female prostitution. The authorities tried to limit this behavior because of the brawls among their male customers. The bakufu forbade women as actors, but before long the young Kabuki actors that played feminine roles were also involved in prostitution. Feminine roles are traditionally played by a professional class known as *onnagata*, and although many of those actors were exclusively heterosexual, many were practicing homosexuals. We are told of frequent brawls among their competing male customers, and not a few suicides were attributed to some unrequited gay love.

We have little information about female homosexuality, but we would be foolish to think that it occurred less in eighteenth-century Japan than anywhere else. Nevertheless, it was neither as celebrated nor as overt as male homosexuality was during the period. Gary Leupp's work on homosexuality in the period suggests that lesbianism was common behind closed doors but was never commercialized as male homosexuality was.

                            Heterosexual practices are the subject of much of Jap-
Heterosexuality   anese literature. Allusions and euphemisms abound in
                            court poetic anthologies, and the topic is perhaps the
overriding driving force in such eleventh-century classics as *The Tale of
Genji* and *The Pillow Book of Sei Shonagon*. Premarital and extramarital
sexual affairs are rife throughout the literature. Diaries, letters, and war
tales would be incomplete without frank and honest mention of such
human behavior. What is of importance here, however, is that sex is
considered natural, normal, and inexorable among humans. These acts
are occasionally condemned because they caused some inappropriate
emotional or social (even political) attachments or actions. Men and
women could have sex, as long as it did not interfere with their other
social roles. A man could take concubines and often was encouraged to
do so for both sexual and procreational purposes. A problem might ensue, however, if he grew too fond of his sexual partner and ignored his
filial, familial, paternal, social, political, economic, or marital obligations.
The *giri-ninjo* dichotomy that is the nexus of many Kabuki and Bunraku
plays was a problem *not* because of the sex, but because of the inappropriate emotional attachment.[6]

We must hasten to say that heterosexual activity, despite the apparent
Japanese sense of natural license, has its own consequences, namely,
pregnancy. For this reason we find that abortion and infanticide were
quite common in Japan (see Chapter 2).

A chapter on sex would not be complete without further discussion of
prostitution and, of course, the obsession of men throughout the world:
the geisha. Prostitution and the so-called Gay Quarters (the innuendo
was not recognized by the Victorians who encountered the "licensed
districts" in the nineteenth century) were tolerated by the Tokugawa
bakufu not to regulate morality, but to control and even profit from
them.

The presence of camp followers long preceded the American Civil War
General Joseph Hooker who gave his name to the profession. Virtually
every samurai band attracted and patronized prostitutes as sexual release and gratification for men who were separated from their wives and
consorts for long periods of time. Most daimyō recognized that prostitution was at worst a necessary evil in castle towns. Most attempted to
control rather than to preclude it. Young women were obtained for the
licensed castle brothels by procurers who kidnapped or purchased them
from their families. The many young widows (since the endemic warfare
frequently made them so), when they could not make another marriage,
frequently became concubines and prostitutes.

Lest one think that prostitution was a "victimless crime" during the
time, we must hasten to note that while it was not a crime in the legal
sense, most prostitutes *were* victimized since they were sold into sexual

slavery by men. We should also note, however, that prostitution was an economic institution that had very little in the way of social (and almost no moral) stigma. Women could be "redeemed" by lovers or relatives who could repay their "contract" obligations to the procurers or brothels. Kaempfer noted that "after having serv'd their time if they are married, the guilt of their past life [is] by no means laid to their charge, but to that of their parents and relations, who sold them for so scandalous a way of getting a livelihood in their Infancy, before they were able to chuse a more honest one."[7]

The Tokugawa Bakufu from time to time attempted to suppress prostitution, sometimes in search of a social morality, but more often because the brothels were often a nuisance to their neighbors, as well as a perpetual threat to the peace. The bakufu decided fairly early on to tightly control and restrict prostitution to Licensed Quarters. Brothels were allowed to exist as long as their owners promised to police the area and to keep the peace. Licenses were issued (sold) which eventually became hidden revenue for the bakufu coffers. High fences were built around the area, and all customers were disarmed and very carefully controlled. In the bakufu's capital, Edo, the quarters were called the Yoshiwara after the "reed field" wasteland that it inhabited. In Kyoto the area was called Shimabara. Hideyoshi had concentrated the brothels of Kyoto there as early as 1589. Most medium to large cities had such a quarter; some, like Ōsaka, had more than one. Guidebooks tell us that in 1700 there were 308 officially sanctioned prostitutes in Kyoto, 760 in Ōsaka, and 1,750 in Edo. By 1780 the number in Edo had increased to 2,900, and in 1799 it had nearly doubled to 4,972.[8] One must remember that this did not include the unlicensed ones that inhabited public baths, massage parlors, teahouses, and sake shops! Donald Shively reminds us that prostitution was so common in Japan that there are over 500 euphemisms in the Japanese language for the word prostitute.[9]

The quarters became a demimonde of entertainers, musicians, purveyors of food and liquor, actors, prostitutes, maids, geisha (more below), and of course the male customers of every economic and social stripe imaginable. Technically, only the chōnin were supposed to be allowed into the quarters, but samurai and even daimyō came in disguise. Indeed, sedge hats and headscarves (because of the distinctive samurai hairstyles) were rented at the entrance to the quarters, and checkrooms were provided to store the swords of the warriors. We are told of countless covered carriages (transportation of the haughty daimyō) parked just outside the gates as their passengers spent an evening of revelry inside.

Scores of food stalls, liquor shops, and musicians' stages crowded among the sometimes opulently appointed brothels, and there was a lively business in curios, clothes, books, and everything else imaginable (and some unimaginable) within the "nightless city." In fact, the ukiyo-e woodblock prints were named after the term ukiyo or "floating world." Often unofficial theaters crept into the quarters. Not surprisingly, their plays were more bawdy and risqué than those of the official Kabuki and Bunraku theaters, which were relegated to their own quarter.

Prostitutes were ranked and graded by their stylish young and rich customers, and most guidebooks had convenient pages of rankings for every brothel. Ironically, some young wags began to call the rankings by the same names given to bakufu samurai ranks. The fees were graded to those rankings, so, not surprisingly, much money changed hands as bribes to better the rankings. Similar rankings were printed monthly for Kabuki actors and for geisha.

Geisha   Geisha ("artistes") were not necessarily prostitutes. But, like prostitutes, they were indentured servants, sold to geisha masters by their parents. Much conjecture and argument continue about the origins of geisha, but most scholars agree that they were accomplished entertainers and not sexual servants. Prior to the early sixteenth century geisha had in fact been a male occupation limited to those who had been schooled in the traditional dance and musical forms of the court. Later, more and more women were introduced into the profession, and before very long they predominated. In the early eighteenth century they were frequently found in the prostitutes' quarter, where the geisha entertained and the prostitutes plied their trade in close proximity. In 1779 the bakufu tried again to legislate public morality by legalizing the geisha. Typically, the bakufu sold licenses (a way to regularize and also to tax another morally questionable occupation) to the geisha "stables" (sumo houses were also called stables) or houses but specified that they had to be outside the Gay Quarters.

Young apprentice girls (*hangyoku* or *maiko*) were indentured for terms of five to ten years with an "advance" on their eventual wages made to their parents. In reality, because the girls were charged for their upkeep, including music and dance lessons, musical instruments, clothing, and so on, they were indentured for life. Some of the most popular geisha could earn enough fees to redeem their contracts, and wealthy patrons could and did redeem them as well. The top geisha could often open their own houses and would purchase young girls for the trade.

The geisha underwent years of training in makeup, music (dance, singing, and playing instruments), poetry, calligraphy, and most of all in stylish etiquette. Their ultimate goal was to attract men who would sometimes pay huge fees for their services. The apprentices would serve the geisha until they were gradually groomed to become full-fledged geisha. Geisha were not obligated to have sex with the men who paid for their services, but of course this could and did occur. With the exception of their first coital experience, these sexual encounters were the right and privilege of the geisha themselves. The first vaginal penetration, however, was a commercial arrangement. Customers vied for the opportunity to "deflower the maiden" and paid high fees for the privilege. Thereafter, the geisha arranged and conducted her own affairs, usually with the eventual goal of gaining a wealthy patron to buy out her contract and then perhaps set her up with her own business.

Like actors and prostitutes (and ironically their samurai betters), geisha were ranked, and their fees corresponded to their ranks. It was seen as socially prestigious to hire geisha to entertain at one's parties, and no self-respecting chōnin merchant would entertain his friends and customers without them. Restaurant waitresses and the apprentice geisha would do the actual serving, but the geisha would sing, dance, recite poetry, and converse with the men, pouring their drinks, lighting their pipes, and simpering at their attempts at humor.

Geisha dressed distinctively. They wore elaborate coiffures replete with expensive lacquered and tortoiseshell combs. Certain styles and colors of kimono were reserved for geisha, and the maiko apprentices wore styles designed to distinguish them from the full-fledged geisha. Traditionally, geisha wore the kimono obi tied elaborately, but differently than ordinary women and also from prostitutes (who tied it simply in the front for quick disrobing).

Geisha were, along with the top onna-gata, the epitome of womanhood in eighteenth-century Japan. Curiously, both were asexual beings. The former were professional entertainers whose sexuality might be coveted, but was usually distantly unattainable. The onna gata were sexless because they were men masquerading as women, but as such, because they were artistes, they established femininity for real women.

NOTES

1. Louis-Frédéric, *Daily Life in Japan at the Time of the Samurai, 1185–1603*, trans. Eileen M. Lowe (New York: Praeger Books, 1972), 58.

2. Michael Cooper, ed., *They Came to Japan: An Anthology of European Reports on Japan, 1543–1640* (Berkeley: University of California Press, 1965), 47.

3. Ibid., 65.

4. Oliver Statler, *Japanese Inn* (New York: Random House, 1961), 159.

5. Engelbert Kaempfer, *The History of Japan: Together with a Description of the Kingdom of Siam*, 3 vols., trans. J. G. Scheuchzer (Glasgow: James MacLehose and Sons, 1906), 3:53.

6. Briefly, *giri* was the duty and obligation due to society; *ninjo* was human emotion.

7. Kaempfer, *History of Japan*, 2:84.

8. Nishiyama Matsunosuke, *Edo Culture: Daily Life and Diversions in Urban Japan, 1600–1868*, ed. and trans. Gerald Groemer (Honolulu: University of Hawaii Press, 1997).

9. Donald H. Shivley, "Popular Culture," in John W. Hall and James L.

McClain, eds., *Early Modern Japan*, volume 4 in *The Cambridge History of Japan* (Cambridge: Cambridge University Press, 1991), 748. The Anthropologist Jim Stanlaw contends that there are probably as many such euphemisms in English. I will take his word.

20

Women

Although we have endeavored to incorporate women within the main body of this examination of the eighteenth century, this chapter considers a few aspects of the lives of women that do not fit very well elsewhere. We trust that this will in no way marginalize their essential contributions to the society and culture.

As with their male counterparts, commoner women did not figure much in the considerations of the samurai administrators that dominated so much of the culture in the eighteenth century. The literate elite scarcely alluded to them at all, and if they did, it was mainly in a pejorative sense. When the annual sumptuary regulations referred specifically to women it was because the government wished to instruct their menfolk on how women were best to be handled. Often the regulations warned against wives who squandered their family's meager income on frivolous pursuits and needless luxuries. It was as if women as a whole were spoiled, willful children who needed to be managed and protected from their own base excesses.

The most famous treatise on Tokugawa era women is commonly attributed to Kaibara Ekiken, who must be otherwise considered a friend and apologist of the common people. This moralist tract, "Greater Learning for Women" (*Onna Daigaku*), was penned during the time when the Neo-Confucian philosophers were trying desperately to reform Japanese society. They had witnessed the debauchery of the chōnin (e.g., Gay Quarters) and even the samurai classes at the expense of the poor farmers. As a group they sought to elucidate the moral errors of the times and to appeal to the consciences of the samurai elite as well. They felt that Neo-Confucian morality needed to be restored at the very core of society, and they therefore admonished all segments of society to return to the "propriety" and morality of the Confucian sages.

With that in mind, it should come as no surprise that Kaibara's treatise on women began with a brief explication of the proper role and status of women in a moral society: "Seeing that it is a girl's destiny, on reaching womanhood, to go to a new home, and live in submission to her father-in-law and mother-in-law, it is even more incumbent upon her than it is on a boy to receive with all reverence her parent's instructions."[1]

As noted in the discussion on Neo-Confucianism in Chapter 4, the dominant sociopolitical philosophy of the twelfth-century Chinese philosopher Chu Hsi (Shushi in Japan) held that all human relationships were microcosms of the cosmic and hierarchical natural laws that governed the universe. Women appeared in this cosmic paradigm only as second-class citizens, and then really only in relationship to their husbands. It was implied that a woman had Three Obediences in her life course. As a child she was to be obedient to her father; as a wife she owed fealty to her husband; and as a widow she was to obey her adult son. The Taoist cum Neo-Confucian verities of the cosmic nature of the genders held that women were intellectually and morally incompetent and must therefore be protected by men. Also, women were deemed to be not only morally incompetent by Neo-Confucianism, but were also considered the source of emotional attachment, the only "sin" in Buddhism. Not only were women intrinsically immoral (perhaps amoral is more apt), therefore, but they were also the cause of immorality in men. Witness Kaibara's explanation: "The five worst maladies that afflict the female mind are: indocility, discontent, slander, jealousy, and silliness. Without any doubt, these five maladies infest seven or eight out of every ten women, and it is from these that arises the inferiority of women to men."[2]

Obviously, any social philosophy that began its consideration of women in this manner had little—and cold—comfort to give them in terms of their normal expected relations with men. They were admonished to be long-suffering, forgiving, patient, honest, circumspect, industrious, modest, thrifty, and obedient—in short, to exemplify all those ideals that leaders advocate in their pets, their children, and their servants.

It does little good here to harp on just how terrible women were treated except to note that they usually triumphed in this adversity by using the weapons of the weak. Successful and influential women usually used their supposed weaknesses to control weak-minded men. If they were deemed to be overly emotional, they used emotion to gain what they wanted. If they were esteemed for their physical beauty, they forced men to suffer in order to win their favors. If they were expected to be silly and incompetent in dealing with business matters, they bested the male merchant by employing wiles and intelligence that were never to be expected of a woman. The strong do not need to pout or sulk until they attain their goals. In short, women used what few powers were allotted to them.

Ironically, of the four official socioeconomic classes of the era, women in the top class suffered the most. That is partially because they were held to a higher moral standard than their peasant and choñin sisters, but it was also due to the nature of their husbands' work. Samurai men produced nothing but administration, and that required a fair amount of technical education. Even if a samurai woman could learn to read and write the very complex Sino-Japanese orthography (and many did), she never would be allowed to apply her learning to the actual work of government.

Choñin women in general, however, often worked side by side with their menfolk in artisanal and business endeavors. Few artisan-class women were allowed to ply their husband's or their father's trade if those jobs happened to be public and required physical strength. But women excelled in arts and crafts that required dexterity, ingenuity, and aesthetic sensibility. The cottage industries of papermaking, textile design and production, fan and umbrella making, embroidery, lacquer (though less so), carving, etching, sewing, weaving, and the like did not require much strength or endurance, but did call for skill and dexterity. And since these tasks could be done indoors away from the prying eyes of the public, no one ever need know who actually designed or produced these goods.

We have ample (if anecdotal) evidence that many artisans were actually women, and that often women also assumed many traditionally male roles for their men who either could not or would not handle such tasks. Many accounts tell of women who sold, bought, collected debts, and kept the accounts of artisan families. Doting fathers often trained their daughters in their craft, especially those who were only children. Most often artisans with no sons adopted a promising apprentice, but usually that boy became heir to the household only after he had married the daughter. Hen-pecked husbands were common stock characters in the theater, so much so that only a few words of dialogue were necessary to establish that it was not that rare to have women running their own households.

Perhaps even more commonly, merchant women played substantial roles in the business affairs of their families. The fabled Omi Shonin, itinerant peddlers and merchants who plied the many towns along the shore of Lake Biwa, were away for long periods. Naturally, mothers, wives, and daughters often kept the business alive at home while husbands, sons, and fathers roamed the country in search of trade. Again, the theater is rife with women who were agents, sellers, and even wholesalers. Inheritance documents also prove that women often actually had run the business for years due to the absence or incompetence of their men.

Many young women worked as maids, waitresses, or "hostesses" in the public restaurants, tea and sake shops, and theaters in the Licensed Quarters of the large cities. Many women made a living wage as hairdressers for the prostitutes, geisha, and wealthy chonin (and even some samurai) women.

It was considered a plum position for chonin girls to serve as a maid to a samurai family for a couple of years before marriage. This was seen as a type of "finishing" school for these young girls because it made them much more attractive as wives to have served in livery. The idea was that the very proximity to the samurai trained a young chonin girl to be more refined, more moral, and more elegant. Obviously, since the samurai knew this as well, they did not have to pay these young maids very much at all, rarely more than room and board, to achieve this distinction. Linguists tell us that the accent of Edo samurai (*Edo-ben*) became something of the standard speech for the entire country because young chonin women returned to their households to teach their own children how to speak "correctly."[3]

Peasant Women   Similarly, peasant women were very important to agricultural endeavors. They were often in the fields alongside the men. For certain tasks, women were in fact preferred over men. Transplantation of rice seedlings is one of the obvious agrarian tasks, but several other cottage industrial and by-employment jobs were traditionally done by women. Unmarried daughters often took paying jobs when they were not needed in the family plots. Not all of these jobs were as maids, either. Many were in the silk sheds, or in the embroidery, weaving, and tailoring establishments of the fan, umbrella, and paper making factories. The obligatory village registers that listed "outsiders" and also family members who were routinely working outside of the village gave ample evidence that young women were very important to the livelihood of most peasant families.

A negative reinforcement of this idea that peasant girls were important to the family is the fact that registered births in most villages very nearly fit the demographic ideal of reproduction. That is to say, we know that infanticide was routinely practiced as a method of population control (see Chapters 2 and 18) as well as to improve the economic lot of village households. If significantly fewer girls than boys were registered as live births, we might suspect that girls were being disproportionately killed at birth. That does not appear to be the case, suggesting that families valued girls nearly as much as boys. This may be partially explained by the fact that adoption of sons-in-law was common in Japan. But other evidence proves conclusively, it seems to me, that the lot of young women was not significantly worse than the lot of young men. One should hasten to say, of course, that the lives of all peasants were fairly bleak, but at least young women did not suffer as much prejudice as did their samurai sisters. This is undoubtedly so because they could produce and pull their own weight.

Unfortunately, that was not the case with many young women in times of bad economic fortune, particularly in famines. When economic disaster hit, many young farm girls were "contracted," which really means enslaved, into prostitution. Urban procurers would flock to the countryside whenever famine reared its ugly head. They brought with them ready cash or credit which was paid to the farm family as an "advance" on the salaries of daughters enlisted to work for "a season" as a prostitute or a geisha.

In reality, for most girls, that season stretched on for years. Girls would be charged for their food, clothes, housing, and upkeep. Seldom did their portion of their fees even cover expenses. Unless they could convince some (lecherous) benefactor to purchase their contract, that is, to repay the "advance," they were enslaved in sexual debt peonage for life. Ironically, even as sexual slaves, young girls were looked upon as something of a family asset, perverse as that may seem. One hears of peasants who held out hope until there was none, and then sold off the daughter as a last resort. Enough laudatory stories were written of "filial" daughters who saved their family's farm by sacrificing their own bodies.

A very few geisha, and even fewer prostitutes, ever managed to prosper and rise to positions of social influence. Those that did were the social lionesses of the demimonde Gay Quarters, but they were the exceptions that proved the rule. Thousands of young women lived miserable lives. A few married in middle age, often as the second or third wife (really a concubine) of a wealthy merchant, sometimes as a replacement mother for orphaned children.

Without doubt, the lives of Japanese women were dreary ones. One cannot be certain that their lot was worse than that of their European, African, Asian, and American cousins at a comparable era. But it is particularly galling to read the following institutionalized moral admonition of Kaibara:

> A woman . . . must look to her husband as her lord, and must serve him with all worship and reverence, not despising or thinking lightly of him. The great life-long duty of a woman is obedience. . . . A woman should look on her husband as if he were Heaven

itself, and never weary of thinking how she may yield to her husband, and thus escape celestial castigation.[4]

NOTES

1. A convenient, though partial, translation is found in Basil Hall Chamberlain, *Japanese Things: Being Notes on Various Subjects Connected with Japan* (Rutland, VT: Tuttle, 1971), 502.

2. Ibid., 507.

3. The claim is made by both Gary Leupp, *Servants, Shophands, and Laborers in the Cities of Tokugawa Japan* (Princeton: Princeton University Press, 1992), and Matsunosuke Nishiyama *Edo Culture: Daily Life and Diversions in Urban Japan, 1600–1868*, ed. and trans. Gerald Groemer (Honolulu: University of Hawaii Press, 1997), 45.

4. Chamberlain, *Japanese Things*, 505.

21

Amusements

Amusements and leisure pastimes were rare things for most adults because life was very harsh for most of the country. Among peasants, the only "leisure" time between the never-ending agrarian tasks was spent making items to ease their lives somewhat. Weaving straw and reed baskets, sandals, hats, raincoats, fish weirs, and various mats took up much of the time during the winter. A few peasants made fans, umbrellas, or other bamboo and paper items to sell at the market, but most farmers made only things that they could use themselves. The only real leisure for farmers was at the various holidays (*matsuri*) held at harvest times, at the New Year, and to honor the tutelary kami. Farmers might have a bit of fun when they went to the nearby market towns or when they went by obligation to perform the annual anti-Christian ritual of icon-treading (*fumi-e*) at the local Buddhist temple.

Peasant children were allowed a bit of fun before or after their seemingly endless farm chores. One can imagine most children made up games of tag, chase, racing, throwing, catching, swimming, snow sliding, and the like. Children being alike all over the world, it is difficult to imagine youngsters not catching and torturing smaller children or small animals, fish, toads, birds, and insects. In the spring and summer children made a special game of catching and fighting dragonflies (tethered with silk thread). In the autumn, children played with fireflies and crickets. The latter's chirps (*mushi-kiki*) were considered to be soothing and "lucky." Tiny bamboo cages were made for captured crickets, and small birds were kept for their music as well. A curious practice was capturing birds to be sold to pious Buddhists to set free. Rows upon rows of cages of birds were stacked along the paths to every temple. Pilgrims could purchase a bird, along with their incense and votive placards (see Chapter 4), and then release it along with their prayers. It was thought that the bird would carry the prayer to Buddha.

Children played a counting game much like the Western paper-scissors-rock game, and a game similar to marbles was played with chestnuts. Tree swings, stilt walking (more common in cities), balance games on log bridges, rock-skipping, hide-and-seek, capture the flag, and other such games familiar to children the world over all were played in the countryside.

Farm children were often given small carved toys by doting relatives; parents could not do so because it was felt that they would "spoil" their own children. Whistles, flutes, whirligigs, tops, dolls, spears, butterfly and fish nets, and other ingeniously wrought items were to be found everywhere. Curiously, bows and arrows were seldom found in the countryside because these were believed to be the sole purview of the samurai. Documents have been found where tax-collecting samurai would confiscate even toy bows and arrows because the farmers were "not to be armed."

A game of "knocks" (*nekki*) was played whereby a pointed stick was stuck into the ground and then children took turns trying to knock it over by throwing sticks at it. Kites were made for the spring and autumn winds, but they never much developed into the sport of kite fighting (see below) in the countryside, probably because they might endanger the rice plants during the competitions.

Children often played *mekakushi*, a kind of blind man's buff, as well as *onigokko*, which is something like Red Rover in that one child tries to catch out another as groups of children run from one side to another.[1] Another common game, *fukuwarai*, was much like pin the tail on the donkey. Blindfolded children tried to arrange pieces of paper cut in the shapes of eyes, nose, and mouth into a drawn outline of a face.

At the annual matsuri, young men would band together to carry the kami palanquins (*mikoshi*) and there would be games and contests to test their mettle. Wrestling (see discussion of sumo, below) matches and tugs-of-war were common. The latter game was played so that neither team would lose. Teams would struggle against each other, but when one side seemed about to win, men from the winning team would scramble to join the rope of the other team to even out the contest. The match ended when the rope broke and everyone tumbled down laughing, assured that everyone had won and no one had lost.

Thumb wrestling was popular at matsuri also. Two opponents would clasp fingers tightly in a kind of a handshake, and then struggle to see who could pin the other's thumb. A kind of leg wrestling (until recently

Top: three types of stone lanterns; gorinto stupa with Sanskrit characters representing (top to bottom) emptiness, wind, fire, water, and earth). Middle: kiseru pipe on tabako-ire pouch; tabako-bon hibachi box. Bottom: child's top and various kites. (Top row drawings by Sheila Myers, middle row by Rachel Smith, bottom row by Matthew Nitsch)

known commonly in the West as Indian wrestling) was played to lock the opponent's leg against one's own. A curious game to lift one's opponent off his feet while standing back to back was also popular.

Samurai
Amusements

Surprisingly, the class that enjoyed the most amusements and games were the samurai. Many of the games developed from martial exercises and training, but many were borrowed from the courtiers of ancient Heian. Most samurai played *go* (or *igo*), which is a warrior's strategy game that can be enormously complex and time-consuming. The principle of the game is to surround the opponent's stones (black or white) with one's own and thereby immobilize or "freeze" them in place. In another version called "five of the same" (*gomoku narabe*) players tried to be the first to arrange five of their stones in a row while blocking their opponent from doing the same. Many samurai preferred *shogi*, which is very similar to Western chess (probably both originated in India or Persia) involving twenty pieces per side on eighty-one squares (nine rows of nine). Captured pieces could be employed by the victor, and the pieces equivalent to pawns could be "promoted" to acquire more move possibilities.

The more refined samurai borrowed parlor games from the courtiers. *Hana-garuda* (flower-cards) were very popular among the intelligentsia. There were forty-eight cards in the deck, divided into four suits of twelve cards: a bird, flower, butterfly, and poem for each of the twelve months. Another card game required one to remember allusions to one hundred famous poems (the equivalent of Authors). Incense and perfume games (*kiki-ko*) remained popular among the elite. Contestants would be challenged to name the ingredients of blended odors. Sessions of linked *renga* (see Chapter 22) poetry contests continued to be held. One poet would write two lines of poetry; the next poet would have to respond with a matching coupling line employing complex rules of literary and historical allusion appropriate to the season, mood, time of day, and historical era.

There was a plethora of "Zen-influenced" pastimes and amusements. The spare and unadorned rusticity of Zen tastes made popular such arts as flower arrangement, tea appreciation, rock gardening, the miniaturization of all things, and an appreciation for the nebulous, implied, and suggested meaning in art. There were several schools of *hanado*, "the way of flowers." Chief among them was *ikebana*, which employed strict rules and conventions for flower arrangement. Neo-Confucianism also influenced ikebana to recreate the cosmos in flowers, with different spaces and elements to represent heaven, the earth, and man. *Chanoyu* enthusiasts went to amazing extremes to develop their appreciation for the art of tea. Costly tea vessels, caddies, whisks, braziers, and even architecture were employed to create the rough and rustic aesthetic of tea. Hideyoshi, who was an aficionado, spent a fortune acquiring Korean and Chinese tea bowls; indeed, it is said that he continued the trade with China more for its tea utensils than for the sumptuous silk. It is perhaps only a slight exaggeration. In the eighteenth century virtually every samurai and most wealthy merchants and *gonō* had at least a rudimentary knowledge of chanoyu. Also, it was one of the few artistic pastimes women as well as men could excel in and enjoy together.

Bonsai, the "art of torturing small plants," as one Western wag described it, involved the careful sculpting of dwarfed trees into the "artistic ideal." Great care and husbandry went into this obsession. Years and even decades were spent coaxing and disciplining the tree's growth until the tiny specimens resembled ancient Chinese paintings. Some enthusiasts incorporated bonsai into rock gardens where "glimpses of nature" were created using the essential elements of earth, stone, water, and vegetation in very small places. The most famous rock gardens were in the Ryōanji, Daitokuji, and Kinkakuji temples in Kyoto, but virtually every samurai, wealthy chōnin, and many gonō boasted their own meticulously wrought backyard gardens. The ultimate goal was the recreation of rustic nature surrounding a consciously unadorned weathered and wizened tea hut, all in the space of a small urban lot. Fortunes were spent in the acquisition of weathered Buddhist stone lanterns, rock bridges, and even distinctively shaped rocks. Vegetation could be sculpted and trained to grow in the "natural" state depicted in Zen landscapes.

The graphic arts of the samurai included *Shodo* (calligraphy), which became an avocation for thousands of enthusiasts. Because the Sino-Japanese orthography was largely ideographic in origin, the writing lent itself to flowing line and artistic depiction of mood and style. Sumptuous paper and lustrous ink (see Chapter 13) were laboriously hand-made, as were the scores of variously sized brushes necessary to create a good "hand."

Sung era Chinese painting and calligraphy heavily influenced *sumi-e* (ink-wash painting). Splashes, blots, and ink washes (hence the name) were used to suggest the nebulous and amorphic flash of intuition that was the goal of all Zen meditation (*zazen*). Westerners who saw sumi-e in the sixteenth century were puzzled by its lack of detail. Those who saw it in the nineteenth century were enchanted by its use of blank (negative) space. Often, it was argued by the painters themselves, the lack of ink expressed much more than form and line created by ink. More ornate and sumptuous artistic styles vied with sumi-e. Their work incorporated vibrant primary colors, including the use of gold and silver dust imbedded or mixed into paint and lacquer. These latter paintings were also very popular in the decoration of daimyō residences and even the shōgun's castle and the emperor's palace. The sumi-e style continued to predominate in temple decorations. We will reserve consideration of the most popular form of painting (*ukiyo-e*) for Chapter 22.

There were several ball games. The oldest, called *kemari*, probably came from China via Korea during the sixth century. A court was marked out with four "trees" in the corners (representing the four seasons and four directions), and participants would vie to keep a deerskin and bamboo ball aloft without using the hands. Westerners familiar with hackey-sack would recognize the game, but young men rarely "won" these contests because the judges preferred style and grace to athletic ability. The premise was that the players were keeping harmony and balance (the ball) in nature (the court). A stick of incense was burned as a timer for the game.[2]

There was a kind of field hockey or pell-mell (*gichiyo*) adapted from mounted polo (*dakyu*). Dakyu was played with seven mounted men per side. The mallets were like lacrosse sticks with small nets mounted on the ends. The object of the first half of the game was to carry, toss, and deposit the team's colored wooden balls into a small (about eighteen inches in diameter) net goal while simultaneously trying to keep the opponents from doing the same. In the second half, both teams would scramble after one ball (much like Indian polo). The first team to score a goal won.[3] There was a similar game played with battledores that tried to keep the shuttlecock (*hanetsuki*) aloft between teams. It was similar to badminton, with many more players and without the net.

Another mounted sport was dog-shooting (*inu-omono*). Mounted archers would surround a dog and shoot rounds of padded arrows in turn to hone their archery skills. Another mounted archery "sport" was *Yabusame*,[4] which was usually staged at the Shintō shrines dedicated to the kami of war, Hachiman, particularly after 1725.[5] Mounted archers would gallop full-speed down approach lanes to fire arrows at small narrow targets. This took tremendous skills (in both horsemanship and archery) and concentration. Winners were said to "be at one with Hachiman."

Other amusements were similarly related to war skills. *Tori-awase* (cockfighting) and *inu-awase* (dog fighting) had obvious battlefield origins. So too did *chikara-ishi*, which consisted of bouts of strength: lifting boulders, bales of rice, or barrels of sake. The art of "sword pulling" (*tachikaki*) was practiced by many samurai. The idea was to simultaneously draw the sword from the scabbard and deal a lethal blow in one swift, smooth motion. Archery on foot (*kyujutsu*), as opposed to the Yabusame mounted variety, horsemanship (*bajutsu*), horseracing (*keiba*), arquebus gunnery (*Hojutsu*), and foot racing through obstacle courses were similarly martial in origins.[6]

Sumo (literally, "simple dance") was similarly martial in origin, but it was also couched in the Shintō religion. The traditions go back to prehistorical times, sumo being mentioned in the *Kojiki*. It began not as a

Top: three sumo rikishi (opening ceremony with sword, with decorative mawashi loincloth, traditional crouch). Bottom: traditional shoulder-pole water carrier. (Top row drawings by Michael Perillo, bottom row by Rachel Smith)

sport, but rather as an oracle. It was thought that the kami would "answer" questions by favoring one wrestler over another. Shamans presided over the matches, which were usually held on shrine grounds. A simple circle was drawn in the dirt, and the first wrestler pushed out of the circle was deemed to have lost. Throughout the feudal period warriors tested their mettle against opponents, and sometimes "battles" were settled without bloodshed through a wrestling match. Daimyō encouraged sumo for the mental as well as physical training of their samurai.

By the fifteenth century sumo bouts and whole tournaments had become systematic and regular. The various holds, pulls, and throws, trips, and other maneuvers were martial in origin, but much of the Shintō influence could be seen in the use of salt as a purifying agent, the fact that the judges (*gyoji*) dressed as Shintō priests (but holding a war fan to signal decisions), and the way that tournament tents were decorated like shrines. By the late sixteenth century sumo had become an amusement and also the source of wagers. Virtually every matsuri staged a tournament or exhibition.

Most daimyō staged tournaments in their own domains. Oda Nobunaga staged huge tournaments, as did Hideyoshi and Ieyasu. By the late seventeenth century troupes of professional sumo wrestlers (*rikishi*) were organized into houses (*beya*) that staged tournaments in all the major cities. Precise rules were established, professional judges were trained and sanctioned, and sumo took on all the trappings of a sport. In 1717 special programs were printed for the tournaments and elaborate rituals were codified for the tournaments.

By the 1740s regular bouts were scheduled in Edo twice per year, and other tournaments were held in the Horie gay quarters in Ōsaka and the Shiogawara machi of Kyoto. The traditional rituals of hand clapping to attract the attention of the kami and foot stamping to drive away evil spirits now became stylized and obligatory. At the beginning of each day's matches, the wrestlers would parade in a circle, each costumed in a silk apron sumptuously embroidered with the crest of their patron daimyō.

About that time a system of ranks was developed. The top three ranks (*sanyaku*), *ozeki*, *sekiwake*, and *komusubi* (Grand Champion *yokozuna* became a "super" rank in the nineteenth century), shared the proceeds of the entrance fees but provided for the upkeep of the lower ranking rikishi (*maku-uchi*) until they could fight their way up into the sanyaku. Former champions were allowed to maintain something of their status, acting as sumo elders. By 1780 there were thirty-six sumo beya training houses, and an association was formed to include the Ōsaka and Kyoto rikishi as well.

Strapping young men were recruited and carefully groomed for the sport. By the end of the eighteenth century rikishi were pampered entertainers, chosen for their size, but selected for their agility and strength. Special diets added prodigious girth, but shortened the lives of these giants.

To include the so-called martial arts in this chapter is somewhat misleading because they were more a **The Martial Arts** way of life than amusements. Still, they were not really tied to religion per se, though some of the martial arts schools created their own mental philosophies that borrowed extensively from Shintō, Zen, and other sects of Buddhism.

The martial arts also had some of their origins in warfare, but not generally from the samurai class. The samurai developed *kendo*, the art of fencing with bamboo (*shinai*) or wooden swords (*bokken*), and the art of sword pulling from their martial training, but the so-called empty-hand techniques were developed by the unarmed ashigaru and warrior monks. Because Hideyoshi's "sword hunt" had disarmed the ashigaru in 1587, and because Buddhist monks were forbidden to continue the warlike ways they followed in the fifteenth and sixteenth centuries, both needed to develop self-defense methods to protect themselves.

The origins of karate, jiu-jitsu, judo, Aikido, sojutsu, nagewaza, atewaza, hapkido, and the other martial arts are clouded in secrecy and myth. Each boasted a charismatic founder who gathered disciples and acolytes in tiny enclaves in temples and shrines hidden away from samurai spies. Some scholars have attributed the beginnings of the empty-hand adepts to the lay Pureland Buddhist warrior villages (*ikko*) north of Kyoto. Others suggest that many were followers of the thirteenth-century priest Nichiren.

By the mid-eighteenth century kendo had become a very popular pastime. Over a hundred schools flourished, and several refinements were made in the martial art. First, because fencing with actual katana blades was very dangerous, the bakufu made that practice illegal. Solid wood swords (bokken) and split bamboo (shinai) models were developed, as were several pieces of specially designed kendo armor. Most schools developed their own training exercises (*kata*), and by the end of the period inter-school tournaments were staged as well.

NOTES

1. William R. May, "Sports," in Richard G.D. Powers and Hidetoshi Kato, eds., *Handbook of Japanese Popular Culture* (Westport, CT: Greenwood Press, 1989), 169.

2. See Chamberlain's colorfully ironic description of the sport in Basil Hall Chamberlain, *Japanese Things* (Rutland, VT: Tuttle, 1971), 384.

3. See Reinier Hesselink, "The Warrior's Prayer: Tokugawa Yoshimune Revives the Yabusame Ceremony," *Journal of Asian Martial Arts* 4:4 (1995), 41–49.

    4. Ibid., 45.
    5. See May, "Sports."
    6. See various sports as described in the *Kodansha Encyclopedia of Japan* (Tokyo: Kodansha, 1989).

22

Chōnin Amusements

In the cities, the wealthy chōnin aped the style and taste of their samurai betters. But most of the chōnin pastimes and amusements were of the common people. Chōnin children typically had a bit more leisure time than peasant children did, but not the open fields, rivers, and beaches on which to play. Because the cities were full of artisans and tools, manufactured toys were much more common. Battledores and shuttlecock (something like badminton without the net), croquet-like balls and mallets, spinning tops, and whirligigs were much more common, as were dolls and other girls' toys. There were also several ball games borrowed from the samurai.

Most chōnin children were apprenticed at a rather early age, but the brief period before that must have been filled with the usual games played by city children all over the world. Tag, hide-and-seek in the gloaming, walking on stilts, capture the flag, wrestling, jostling, and the usual torture of small children, animals, fish, insects, and birds were probably as common in the cities as in the countryside. Flying kites was a favorite pastime in the breezy spring and late autumn. Adults became involved in kite fighting (*tako*), which only minimally resembled the idyllic children's pastime. Ground glass was glued to the lead strings of the aerodynamically designed kites in order to cut the strings of one's opponents. Tournaments (more like medieval jousts) stretched into days, and large amounts of money were wagered. Teams composed of entire machi would march off as if to war with battle flags and drums. The battlefield was a riot of colors as teams all dressed in the same colors maneuvered around the pitch. The kites themselves were probably the most elaborate and highly developed in the world. Some were actually long chains of companion kites linked together and controlled by teams. Fanciful birds and mythical animals were recreated in balsa and paper. Geometric shapes of all sorts were created, and some had long strings of firecrackers attached.

A few chōnin men learned to play samurai games such as *shogi* and *go*. In fact, some government-sponsored academies sprang up that allowed some chōnin to join. Various card and dice games were played in the parlor. Among the most popular was *sugoroku*, which is like backgammon. But the games that became popular were those of the pleasure quarters and of the matsuri. Within the bustling Licensed Quarters, which came alive only at night, purveyors and caterers crowded their stalls and carts between the brothels, tea and sake shops, restaurants, and curio shops. Many games of chance were invented, and virtually every space was jammed with the hucksters, shills, and confidence men that flocked to fleece the unwary in any gathering. These stalls and carts vied for space with sellers of curios, amulets, and souvenirs. The paths to shrines and temples were lined with such colorful stalls.

The large cities of Edo, Ōsaka, and Kyoto were complexes of self-contained urban neighborhoods (see Chapter 11) that were very much like urban villages. Each ward (machi), with its own distinctive profession, also had local kami enshrined and attached to parish Buddhist temples (see Chapter 4). Each machi therefore had its own matsuri. A resident of Edo could practically attend a different matsuri every day since there were over four hundred temples in the city. Most of the food, sake, and gaming stalls were temporary, erected for the length of the matsuri, but many of the curio and amulet shops were permanent. The streets leading into the shrines and temples were ablaze with festive torchlight. The denizens of the machi crowded through the lanes, but stopped to buy, eat, drink, and gamble on their way to the matsuri. Many of the food and sake merchants, and perhaps all of the curio and amulet sellers, were linked to wholesalers and the artisans who made their products. It is no exaggeration to say that eighteenth-century society, at least in the cities, was a commercial and consumer-oriented one.

In Gion, a central commercial district of Kyoto, the matsuri took on enormous proportions. When the country was "secluded" (*sakoku*) in 1612, the merchants adopted a maritime theme to the festival that recalled the free-booting days when Japanese merchants sailed throughout Asia in search of trade. The masts of former trading ships (now decommissioned and illegal) were mounted on floats (*hoko*) and decorated lavishly. "Gion matsuri was invented partly as a humble resistance against a new foreign (or anti-foreign) policy, and partly as nostalgic sentimentalism on the part of the merchants."[1]

In other machi, the floats took on a very different and sometimes dangerous incarnation. Disgruntled young men would sometimes purposely steer hoko or mikoshi into the homes or shops of hated merchants. Merchants who had not contributed appropriately to the matsuri funds, or who had reputations of being mean-spirited to their apprentices, often sustained substantial damage to their homes or shops. And since the kami within the mikoshi were actually controlling the path of the parade, no one could be faulted for the damage. The young men (as well as bystanders) consumed copious amounts of sake, and very often it was the only time when people could vent a little "steam" in their lives. Merchants noticed that when they donated several casks of sake, or plenty of *mochi* or other foods for the revelers, their shops would not be damaged. Surely it was merely a mysterious coincidence: the kami had been appeased.

Perhaps the single most dominant artistic style of the period involved as much craft as it did art. The *ukiyo-e* ("pictures of the floating world") woodblock prints involved the artist who drew the original picture, the artisan who carved the succession of woodblocks, and even the printer who carefully matched up the colored overlays, all to produce a succession of identical pictures. This was perhaps the most commercial of the art genres since the reproduction of many copies of the artwork was as much the intention as was the creation of the original piece of art. Woodblock printing probably originated in Korea and was used there and later in Japan to produce copies of Buddhist sutras. In eighteenth-century Japan the subjects of the prints were activities and denizens of the Licensed Quarters. Prints were commissioned as theater playbills, advertisements, illustrations for cheap books, and curios and souvenirs. Ukiyo-e masters such as Utamaro and Hiroshige earned a substantial living and left an astounding corpus of lively prints.

Woodblock printing was applied to the publishing of books as well. Hideyoshi's warriors had brought back moveable-type printing presses from their invasion of Korea, and the Jesuit padres had imported at least one printing press in the 1590s, but woodblock became the predominant method of printing by the eighteenth century.

Publishing and Reading

Written literature had a long, rich tradition in Japan. The early religio-historical tomes *Kojiki*, and *Nihon-shoki* led to imperial poetic anthologies, diaries (*nikki*), and other forms of prose literature. During the feudal centuries Buddhist writing remained popular, as did the warrior tales. But the height of common popular literature awaited the late seventeenth century and the whole of the eighteenth century. Reading became the pastime of a large portion of the literate populace.

Perhaps a few words on literacy are appropriate here. Although the written language (see Chapter 5) was difficult to master, virtually the

entire male samurai class was literate. Part of that is due the Neo-
Confucian philosophy adopted as a ruling ideology by Hideyoshi and
Ieyasu in the late sixteenth century. Samurai needed to become literate
in order to take on the role of the moral sage in society. Philosophers
preached the need for a balance of the literary and military arts (*bun-bu*)
within the ruling class. They wrote long treatises for the moral edification
of the samurai. These were published by the bakufu for distribution and
for use as elementary primers.

Every daimyō maintained a han school for the education of his samurai. Similarly, chōnin and rich peasants founded parish schools (*terakoya*), named for the temple buildings that housed them and not for the
religious education that they employed. It has been suggested that there
were upwards of 80,000 terakoya throughout the country by the middle
of the nineteenth century. Estimates of literacy are notoriously inaccurate, but some scholars claim that male literacy approached 25 percent
at the end of the eighteenth century. Female literacy, which was not
encouraged by the government, was probably a fifth of that.

Whatever the truth about literacy in the nation as a whole, it is clear
that within the cities it was the norm rather than the exception. We can
measure that with some degree of confidence when we consider the records of publication. Since sixteenth-century Kyoto was the religious center of the country, it is easy to see why there were already several
publishers established there. By 1700 or so there were 536 in Kyoto, 564
in Ōsaka, and 493 in Edo. By 1800 there were still 494 in Kyoto, 504 in
Ōsaka, and 917 in the largest city in the world, Edo. In a publishing
survey report to the bakufu in 1692 there were over 7,300 titles of books
in print. Estimates suggest that for the next century over 200 titles per
year were added to those totals. By the end of the eighteenth century
there were 183 bookstores (many publishing their own books) and seventeen rental libraries in Kyoto alone. In 1808 there were 656 bookstores
and over a hundred libraries in Edo.

Because books were still expensive to publish, and therefore to purchase, many bookstores rented books by the week and even sent out
agents to the machi to encourage rentals. The common fee was 10 percent
of the cost of the book for a five-day rental. A common publishing run
from one set of woodblocks was about 300, but some titles sold up to
4,000 copies. In addition to books, a number of smaller pieces were published. *Kawaraban* ("tile prints") were something like broadside newspapers. Printed from clay blocks (some from woodblocks too) and selling
for a few coppers, they announced news of fires, earthquakes, and other
calamities but also informed the public about politics, gossip, and even
some foreign news. Some, called *fusetsu-dome*, translated annual reports
from the Dutch. More commonly they announced new Kabuki productions or advertised new merchandise at local stores. *Egoyomi* calendars

were published listing the "lucky" days of the year as well as those days unsuitable for certain tasks, rituals, or journeys. Also common were *mek-uragoyomi* or *nanbugoyomi*, which were rebus-picture calendars for those who could not read characters. But the height of publication began in the late seventeenth century.

The early part of the century witnessed an explosion of popular literature within the large cities of Japan. This was a result of many things, including the burgeoning population in Edo, the growth of wealth and leisure time among the chōnin, the increased popularity of the various forms of theater, as well as the rise of woodblock printing.

Popular Literature

A form of literary narrative called "diversionary stories" (*otogi-zōshi*) became popular in the first quarter of the century.[2] These short stories, fables, fairy tales, and romantic episodes were descendants from those told by wandering minstrels, itinerant priests, and beggars. Enterprising publishers garnered all they could and printed them up in cheap booklets that sold for a few coppers in virtually every market town worthy of the name. Many were printed in the kana syllabary, which made them available to most people, even those who knew very few kanji. Bastardized or abbreviated tales from the classics were fodder as well, but most of the tales were written especially for this lively trade.

A related genre was the *ukiyo-zōshi* (tales of the floating world), which included a great variety of popular literature. The works of the playwright Chikamatsu Monzaemon (1653–1724) and the poet Matsuo Basho (1644–84) are included in this group as well as the exemplary tales of Ihara Saikaku (1662–93). Chikamatsu wrote for both the Kabuki and Bunraku theater (see below). Basho became the foremost haiku poet, wandering about in the country and producing a prodigious number of poems throughout his short life. Saikaku began to publish short stories about the chōnin lifestyle. He wrote a score of these anthologies in which he described the sex lives, romances, and other foibles of city folk. Indeed, he invented the term *koshoku* (to love life) to describe the riotous and ribald lives of chōnin. The term commonly meant to enjoy sex. The books were full of comedy and sex (including homosexuality) and were increasingly written in the simple syllabary *kana* for the semi-literate reader.

The ukiyo-zōshi genre was further divided into types of writing which included humorous (*kokkeibon*), erotic tales of the pleasure quarters (*sharebon*), and "tales of human affection" (*ninjōbon*). Pornographic picture books (*shunga*), collected theatrical playbooks, collected *haikai* poetry books, and the so-called smelly books (*kusa-zōshi*), which were something like modern *Manga* comic books, all sold thousands of copies among the lowly chōnin.

All of these were written for entertainment rather than for personal, intellectual, or spiritual edification. As the century progressed the commoner literature flourished. Colorful illustrations and book covers were printed on woodblocks, and by the end of the period urban Japan was arguably the most "papered" (if not lettered) society in the world.

Those who could not afford to buy formal books either bought installments or rented books by the week. Scarcely a barbershop, teahouse, café, or brothel could be found without stacks of cheap booklets for customers to while away the hours. If the wills and estate lists of rural village leaders are an accurate indication, the rural areas of Japan enjoyed the popular literature as well.

There were other literary conventions as well. A number of manuals were written on virtually every subject, including business methods, food preparation, calligraphy, painting, flower arrangement, tea ceremony, home and garden decoration, clothing (making and repair), and even special books for young women on home economics topics. One title, *Higher Learning for Women* (*Onna Daigaku*), was first published in 1715 but had several publication runs throughout the century and into the next. It no doubt was purchased for young brides-to-be to inform them of their roles in life. Similarly, there were also *shunga* ("pictures of spring") books which were little better than pornography, although they might be considered marriage manuals since they featured cartoon-like depictions of sundry sex acts with genitalia exaggerated in size lest the viewer mistake what was being depicted.

One of the more popular literary genres in the countryside was agricultural manuals (*nōsho*) that depicted the latest advances in planting, irrigation, animal husbandry, hybrid seeds, new fertilizers, forestry, and even new recipes. Each contained at least elementary almanac agricultural calendars (on the proper days to plant, fertilize, etc.), but also often had sections on morality. Farmers were told moral tales about peasants who were frugal, filial, industrious, and patient and who therefore prospered. One manual, *The Comprehensive Agricultural Collection* (*Nōgyo-zenshu*), was first published in 1697 and went through five editions and was still in print late into the 1750s. There were others specializing in commercial crops such as cotton, silk, tobacco, rapeseed, linseed, and paper and lacquer forestry.[3]

There can be little doubt that the eighteenth century saw the birth of reading as a popular pastime for even the common people. Diaries and wills attest to the popularity of books, as long lists survive that indicate that virtually every household had a small or modest library.

The Performing Arts

As noted above, Japan was a highly literate country in the eighteenth century. Much of that literacy can be attributed to the popularity of storytelling and the performing arts in general. Japan has a long and rich tradition of oral history. Long before the Chinese orthography came to the country, raconteurs and missionaries developed the art of storytelling. In the eighth century missionaries (*ubasoku*) roamed the countryside armed with long horizontal scrolls (*emakimono*) illustrating the teachings of Buddhism. The monks would chant the story as they unrolled the scrolls, often beating time on a drum. Secular troubadours and raconteurs similarly roamed the country; some accompanied themselves on the lute (biwa), which gave its name to their genre, *biwa-hoshi*. They chanted chapters or popular sections from *Genji monogatari* (Tale of Genji) or the warrior tales (*gunki-monogatari*) of the *Heike monogatari* (Tale of the Heike), *Taiheiki monogatari* (Tale of Taiheiki), or *Azuma kagami monogatari* (Great Eastern Mirror Tale). Other oral literary forms remained popular. Imaginary or fanciful tales (*otogi-zoshi*), narratives to accompany dance (*kowakamai*), and historical tales (*rekishi-monogatari*) all had their audiences.

Within the cities, vaudeville-like theaters were established for narrative tales (*yose*), *manzai* (risqué dialogue), and *rakugo* (comic storytelling). Typically, the bakufu had tried to suppress these amusements, but again discovered that if licensed (another unofficial tax) and controlled, even the more salacious aspects of the amusements were innocuous.[4] The same could be said of a curious all-female transvestite revue called Takurazuka and other risqué entertainments.

Other performing arts such as music and dance were artfully incorporated into the three genres of theater, but several types of dance continued to exist in the eighteenth century. The most formal was *bugaku*, which is called court dance. As such, it probably was as Chinese in origin as it was Japanese. In fact, it was divided into three distinct forms. *Sahō no mai* ("dancing to the left of the Emperor") employed only *Tōgaku*, the music of the eighth-century Tang Dynasty in China; *Uhō semai no mai* ("dancing on the right") employed *Komagaku* from ancient Korea and *Kagura*, which was Shintō and Japanese folk music. Bugaku was performed by richly costumed dancers wearing masks. The sahou dancers wore red and uhou wore blue or green costumes.

There are also Shintō dances, most of them incorporated into matsuri. A few recreate stories of creation from the *Kojiki*. The oldest is Kagura, which recreates a story from the *Kojiki* when dancers lured the Sun Goddess, Amaterasu-omi-kami, from her cave and restored sunlight after the world's first night. It is performed annually at the Ise Imperial Shrine.

In the countryside folk dances abounded, but they were uniformly very simple musically, with rudimentary steps and rhythm. The most common was the *bon-odori*, which was a dance to welcome the returning (*okaeri*) spirits of the dead during the late summer festival of *Obon*. Harvest dances were common as well.

Music in eighteenth-century Japan was as different from Western music as can be imagined. Indeed, a nineteenth-century British jingoist, reluctant even to use the word "music" to "denote the strummings and squealings of Orientals,[5] opined that "the effect of Japanese music is not to soothe, but to exasperate beyond all endurance the European breast."[6]

But Japanese had heard Western music, or at least the Roman Catholic liturgical variety in the sixteenth century, and they were not enraptured with it either. Perhaps if they had heard Mozart they might have thought differently. In any case, in Japan, the seven-note musical scale was reduced to five notes (numbers four and seven are removed) and therefore called *pentatonic*. Also, Japanese musical notations do not contain musical notes, but mnemonic notations (but perhaps Western "notes" are as well) instead, for compositions were memorized rather than sight-read. Most music was meant as accompaniment to other performing activities and therefore never became "popular" to the extent that people went about whistling or humming familiar tunes.

Rhythm was very important in Japanese music because it was often considered metronomic in character. Buddhist chants are "scored" with drums or bells for rhythm, and most dances are limned by only one or two instruments. The Japanese did not invent many of their instruments. Most of those that many would consider traditional Japanese instruments originated elsewhere in Asia. The multistringed horizontal harp called the *koto* was imported fairly early on from China but was changed somewhat by Yatsuhashi, called the Father of Modern Japanese Music, in the 1630s. The strings are not tuned in the Western sense, but are adjusted for each performance by the artist, who manipulates bridge-like frets to alter the plucked length and therefore the tone of each string.

The three-string *samisen* was imported from Okinawa (with possible Chinese origins) at the beginning of the eighteenth century. It is shaped and plucked like a banjo, though the musician varies the pitch by plucking the flatted strings. The lute-like *biwa*, though relatively rare at the beginning of the eighteenth century, eventually became the favorite of most troubadours, very much like the European lute or the American guitar. There are a number of flutes, which produce shrill, ethereal tones. The *hichiriki* is a double-reed flute seven inches long with seven finger holes on the front and two on the back. The *shakuhachi* is an end-blown bamboo flute almost two feet long with only five finger holes—four in front, one in back. The *fue* is played horizontally like a Western flute. The *sho* is a reed mouth organ with seventeen vertical bamboo pipes (like a miniature pipe organ).

There are numerous drums in Japanese music; the most spectacular being the great drums (*taiko*), which vary from the "small" (about three feet in diameter) to the truly gigantic, which range as large as eight feet in diameter. The latter require as much physical strength and stamina as musicianship. Other instruments included gongs, cymbals, bells, and clacking blocks of wood. One may say that the human voice also became

Three women playing music: two with the three-string samisen, one sitting on a tatami playing the koto. Note the elaborate hairdressing and kimonos. In the foreground is a lacquered makeup chest and a ceramic brazier (hibachi); in the upper right are a bound book and book chest. Woodblock print by Ishikawa Toyonobu. (Courtesy of Asia Library, University of Michigan)

an instrument in rhythmic chants, shouts, and yells, all of which seemed discordant and cacophonous to Europeans accustomed to the melodic blending of notes in "true" harmony. No wonder that the acerbic Chamberlain sniffed, "[M]ay all the samisens and kotos, and other native instruments of music be turned into firewood to warm the poor, when— if at no previous period in their existence—they will subserve a purpose indisputably useful."[7]

Noh Theater Several distinct theatrical traditions evolved variously from traveling troubadours, itinerant monks and storytellers, jugglers, puppeteers, dancers, and other entertainers who flocked to matsuri throughout the country. Among the three most popular genres, Noh was certainly the most formal and "proper." Kabuki and joruri-bunraku were more popular among the common people, particularly the chōnin in the cities.

Noh traced its origins to the formal dance rituals within the imperial court. It shares the slow rhythmic dance styles with *bugaku* as well as the use of masks for the actors. The theatrical themes are from Buddhist cautionary tales. The formalized conventions require an opening introductory scene wherein the principal character (*shite*) appears first as a ghost relating his personal story as a cautionary moral tale. Noh was supported and subsidized by the bakufu because the performances were thought to edify. Virtually every city had its Noh stage, usually on the grounds of the main Shinto shrine. The long recitations were delivered in rhythmic chants accompanied by off-stage drums and chorus. The principal actors "danced" their roles to give visual effect to the performance since other body movement was very slow and stylized. The dances involved very little body movement except for the stamping of the feet. Arm and head movements were very limited. On the other hand, the *kyōgen* playlet interludes between Noh scenes were as lively and ribald as Noh was proper and static.

The kyōgen were most likely early attempts by minor actors to entertain the audience while the major actors changed costumes between scenes. Kyōgen involved ribald visual puns and slapstick comedy, sometimes even satirizing the foregoing Noh scene. By the eighteenth century, the kyogen had become more popular and prominent than the Noh plays themselves. Audiences "forced" the theatrical companies to include more and longer kyōgen performances but maintained a few snippets of Noh to keep the government censors appeased. By the mid-eighteenth century Noh found itself a distant third to the other theatrical genres in terms of popularity but maintained its government subsidies. In fact, during the century Noh was performed mainly in the daimyō and shōgunal courts, though occasionally performances were staged at major Shintō shrines.

Noh stage (from left): actors' quarters; covered entryway; main stage. Traditional pine tree scenery is shown at the rear of the stage; musicians and chanters sit to the right in the railing area. (Drawing by Brian Novotny)

Traditionally, Kabuki was said to have its origin in 1603 when a woman named Ōkuni from Izumo staged a series of **Kabuki** dances in the dry Kamo riverbed at Shijo Avenue in Kyoto. She supposedly first performed her *kabuki-odori*, derived from the processional dancing (*furyu-odori*) before Noh performances. She claimed to be raising funds for the Izumo Shrine, but everyone knew that the dances were to advertise her band of prostitute-dancers.

For the next thirty years or so various Kabuki troupes toured the countryside around Kyoto. The bakufu tried to ban Kabuki in an attempt to stop the brawls that resulted when customers fought over the prostitutes. The ban was circumvented all over the country, so the bakufu in 1629 ruled that women could no longer perform, instituting what was called *wakashu*, or "boy's style." Young men were allowed to play women's roles as long as they shaved their forelocks (which they covered with purple scarves) and dressed in men's clothing. Before long, however, wakashu had become as licentious as Ōkuni's prostitute Kabuki, becoming an avenue for pederasty and homosexual sex in general. The actors who specialized in women's roles (*onna-gata*) were often young male prostitutes. Before long, their customers again became involved in brawls as they vied for their favorites' attentions and services after performances.

The bakufu continued to try to legislate morality within the theater by subsidizing and licensing "moral" troupes and theaters. By 1700 there

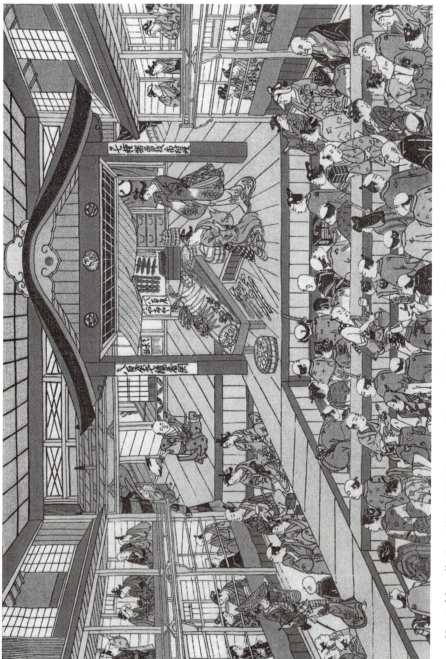

Vegetable-seller's stall in Kabuki scene. Hanamichi from lower left to center. Note the food and tea sellers in the foreground boxes and the number of swords worn by audience members, indicating the attendance of samurai. Woodblock print by Keisai Eisen. (Courtesy of Asia Library, University of Michigan)

were four official theater companies in Edo alone. This number was reduced to three in 1714 as a punishment for a sexual affair between the dashing actor Ikushima Shingoro and the shogunal lady-in-waiting Ejima. Ikushima's theater was razed as a lesson to other Kabuki actors.[8]

During the eighteenth century there were several officially sanctioned theaters in the large cities as well as a plethora of smaller theater companies (*ko-shibai* or "little playhouses"), repertory companies (*hyakunichi-shibai*—literally, "One Hundred Plays"), and literally thousands of *miyagi-shibai*—Shrine Precinct playhouses. The latter were licensed and supervised by local shrines or temples, or by the *machi-bugyō* within the cities. In addition, many villages mounted their own amateur productions, having purchased costumes and playbooks from the professional theater companies.

Several acting styles were popular during the day. "Sentimental" (*wagoto*) style was employed in emotional romantic scenes; the "rough" style (*aragoto*) involved acrobatics; and a genre known as "scandal style" (*sewagoto*) was employed commonly in the fast-paced comedic scenes. The eighteenth century saw the development of exaggerated extended poses (*mie*) when actors would hold a pose for dramatic effect.

Elaborate and lavish costumes became the norm. Brightly colored lush silks and sumptuous brocades attracted the attention of the crowds. Makeup evolved as well. The traditional whiteface (borrowed from the principal Noh masks) was limned with bright colors to emphasize and exaggerate facial expressions. By the eighteenth century certain conventions had been accepted for makeup: red colors were to emphasize anger; only heroes used blue facial lines.

There was a narrator who filled in historical and theatrical gaps to clarify and expand upon the actors' lines. He sat with the musicians to the side of the stage. The standard musical instruments were biwa, drums, gongs, and flutes (particularly *shakuhachi* because of its eerie, ghostly sound). Wooden blocks were clacked to emphasize movement or dramatic juncture. Virtually every play had several dance and acrobatic scenes. Some specialized in acrobatic fight scenes that were artfully choreographed. The actors were assisted while on stage by men "behind the black curtain" (*kuromaku*) who wore black gauze over their heads and torsos. This was to allow actors to undergo costume and even body-form changes without having to leave the stage. Costumes were designed that could be quickly reversed, torn away, or unsnapped to reveal a strikingly different appearance.

The themes of the plays were Neo-Confucian moralistic in content, with implicit Buddhist understanding of life. The typical story involved chōnin struggling with the pressures of social obligation (*giri*), as they became involved in love affairs (*ninjo*) that inevitably doomed both lovers. Love-suicide (*shinju*) of the star-crossed lovers was often the remedy until life began to imitate art too often. The bakufu banned shinju as a theatrical device and audiences were admonished not to emulate the characters that were punished for their sexual indiscretions with financial and social catastrophe.

The popular playwrights, especially Chikamatsu Monzaemon, made a handsome living churning out new scripts for Kabuki (and Bunraku; see below). Social satire was popular for a while until the bakufu banned the very mention of actual people or incidents in the 1730s. Historical dramas had been popular all along, but now farces and ghost fantasy tales became popular as well.

The major Kabuki companies signed their major actors for eleven-month contracts. The traditional debut of new plays "showing the face" (*kaomise*) came in the eleventh month. After a short run, the major theatrical magazines (*hyobanki*) reviewed the plays, and financial backing was obtained from wealthy patrons. At the same time, admission prices were set for the season, based on the ratings. Month-long theater runs were staged in the first, third, and fifth months. There was also a short midsummer run during the sixth month when junior actors and understudies played the roles. The ninth month was for visiting "guest" actors from Ōsaka and Kyoto. The Edo actors, in turn, went to other venues to extend their popularity (and that of the year's productions) to other cities. The season ended around the time of the Obon festival with "farewell" productions, and then the new season began in the eleventh month.

A major actor made a huge salary based on his popularity from the previous season. The major companies vied with each other to sign the most popular ones, and financial backers often tied their support to the actors employed. The *hyobanki* (theatrical magazine) reviews (see section on publishing and reading, above) therefore became very important, and it is clear that many bribes were paid to keep plays and actors high in the rankings.

The plays themselves were marathon performances that frequently lasted all day. Meals, light snacks, and drinks of all kinds were served during the performances. Wealthy patrons purchased the choice block audience areas (since there were no actual "seats") and used them to entertain their family, friends, and clients. The performance resembled the matsuri fair, with minor characters competing with the noisy talk of the audience and vendors. The attention of the audience would be riveted when major actors entered the scene, but wandered when minor characters dominated the stage.

The staging itself was quite sophisticated, but this is understandable since each theater had to compete with others in order to prosper. Revolving stages, drop scenery, stage trapdoors, elevators, scenery mounted on wheels, and quick costume changes (often right on stage) were common. The stage itself improved on the standard three-wall Western techniques. The *hanamichi* ("flower path") was a long ramp from behind and through the audience and was used to presage new scenes and to give major actors a long entry to strut before the audience. The audience would applaud and call out the names of their favorites as they strolled along the hanamichi, and no one seemed to mind very much (except the minor actors then on stage) that the attention of the audience shifted there. Indeed, some actors had it written into their contract to change their entries from the side or trapdoor to the hanamichi for maximum exposure. Playwrights would be recalled to rewrite scenes to accommodate new hanamichi entries.

Theater companies advertised heavily using ukiyo-e woodblock prints of famous scenes as playbills. Actors were encouraged to engage in sexual affairs and to spend lavishly on geisha and prostitutes to remain in the public eye. Many restaurants paid to have actors dine at their establishments. They became social lions. Indeed, the "floating world" of the entertainment quarters took on a surreal quality where wealthy chōnin (and sometimes thinly disguised daimyō and samurai) mixed with top actors, high-ranking geisha, and prostitutes in this nocturnal demimonde. Occasionally, when scandals became too common, the bakufu or local daimyō would send in censors, and a few samurai would be humiliated, a few chōnin dispossessed (sometimes publicly so), and a few theater owners fined or admonished, all to the entertainment of the general populace. Chōnin, men and women alike, took their sartorial cues from actors. "[T]he stage became a showroom for the display of what was new in fashion—clothing design and fabrics, weaving, dyeing, embroidery, hairstyles, combs, bodkins, makeup, and personal ornamentation."[9]

The actors were organized into feudal-like hierarchies. Top actors would flounce around with huge entourages and would ceremoniously adopt theatrical heirs who took their "father's" name upon retirement. These theatrical pedigrees were constantly published and elaborated upon by the hyobanki. By the end of the eighteenth century particular roles were reserved to specific theatrical lineages, and each family developed stylistic devices limited to family tradition. An actor from one hierarchy would never dream of employing the costume, makeup, or acting techniques of another.

Puppetry, like Kabuki, had its roots in the medieval period. Itinerant entertainers plied their craft in the cities and villages, **Bunraku** often employing crude stick-like puppets. This evolved into *joruri* puppetry, which became increasingly popular as time passed. Often joruri benefited from the occasional government bans against human theatrical companies. The bakufu preferred puppets to actual actors because there was an obvious lack of prostitution involved. Also, it may be said that because the puppet, not the puppeteer, is the focus of attention, the artiste did not become the "star," as happened with Kabuki actors. Also, puppets became crowd favorites because they could do things on stage that were impossible for human actors, such as being decapitated, flying, and transforming into other animals. Puppets could also say things for which actors would be imprisoned.

At about the same time that Kabuki became wildly popular, joruri evolved into classic Bunraku. Bunraku shared many of the same plays (and theaters), and other forms of cross-fertilization were common. It is said that actors often aped puppet movement and that puppeteers employed the exaggerated dramatic mie long before it was used by actors. Costumes and makeup conventions of each genre influenced the other.

By the eighteenth century Bunraku puppets were about one-third life-size and the major character puppets were manipulated by three men. The master puppeteer operated the head and left arm of the puppet, another man manipulated the right arm, and a third man moved the feet. Obviously this required a careful choreography of motion to approximate human movement for the puppet. The puppeteers wore the black gauze *kuromaku* of the scenery assistants of Kabuki and seemed to blend and disappear into the scenery. Occasionally, exceptionally adept master puppeteers were allowed to appear barefaced without the gauze covering, but this honor was quite rare until the nineteenth century. Typically the head artiste wore high *geta* (platform shoes) that allowed him to tower over the other puppeteers (since he had to manipulate the head) and which he stamped to give effect to the movement of the puppet's feet.

Puppet heads were marvels of engineering. Carved by artisans from a single piece of wood, they were hollowed out to provide ingenious devices that allowed the eyelids to close, the eyeballs to rotate (one of the dramatic poses indicating frustrated rage was to cross the eyes), lips to purse, teeth to be bared, and eyebrows to arch. Artful wigs, often made with human hair, were attached, vivid features were painted, and sumptuous costumes were employed to make the puppets very lifelike. The hands were fashioned to allow many functions. Separate hands might be used to hold objects, wave, gesticulate, or caress. Various feet similarly could be used for different effects. No feet were actually provided for female puppets since their gowns were floor-length. The puppeteers simulated knees and elbows beneath the costumes.

There were no actual puppet bodies. The costumes were fashioned to give corporeal shape to the puppet and were complete ensembles. When the puppet needed to change costumes, the head was removed and put onto another costumed body. Puppets could therefore quickly age or be transformed into animals by simply transferring the head while retaining the rest of the puppet's body.

Unlike in Kabuki, the puppet-actors did not "talk." All dialogue was delivered by one stage-side narrator who changed the timbre and cadence of his voice to allow for the differences of male-female, old-young styles of speech. The musical accompaniment was similar to that of Kabuki.

During the eighteenth century the theater became a very important influence in the lives of commoners, chōnin and peasant alike. Donald Shivley called it "a classroom" that

> taught through performances and also through the many different publications of joruri, texts, synopses of kabuki plays, and many genres of storybooks that drew their material from the stage. The theater taught historical name and facts, however unreliably. More important, it taught the common people a consciousness of the past and the culture's inherited traditions.[10]

NOTES

1. Hidetoshi Katō, "Japanese Popular Culture Reconsidered," in Richard G.D. Powers and Hidetoshi Katō, eds., *Handbook of Japanese Popular Culture* (Westport, CT: Greenwood Press, 1989), 301.

2. There are hundreds of books on Japanese literature. The best expository writing is without doubt the works of Donald Keene. An excellent concise treatment can be found in the *Kodansha Encyclopedia of Japan.*

3. See Tsuneo Sato, "Tokugawa Villages and Agriculture" (Mikiso Hane, trans.) in Chie Nakane and Shinzaburō Oishi, eds., *Tokugawa Japan: The Social and Economic Antecedents of Modern Japan* (Tokyo: University of Tokyo Press, 1990), 74–75, for a list of manuals.

4. Muneo Jay Yoshikawa, "Popular Performing Arts: Manzai and Rakugo," in Powers and Hidetoshi, *Handbook of Japanese Popular Culture*, 76.

5. Basil Hall Chamberlain, *Japanese Things* (Rutland, VT: Tuttle, 1971), 339.

6. Ibid., 342.

7. Ibid., 344.

8. See descriptions in Donald H. Shivley, "Popular Culture," in John W. Hall and James L. McClain, eds., *Early Modern Japan*, volume 4 in *The Cambridge History of Japan* (Cambridge: Cambridge University Press, 1991), 706–69, and Moriya Katsuhisa, "Urban Networks and Information Networks" (Ronald P. Toby, trans.) in Nakane and Oishi, *Tokugawa Japan*, 97–123.

9. Shivley, "Popular Culture," 759.

10. Ibid., 758–59.

23

Travel

Despite an abundance of laws that made it difficult, Japanese in the eighteenth century did a great deal of traveling. The bakufu forbade the permanent movement of people in order to "freeze" the status quo in the early seventeenth century. The reasoning was that there would be much fewer of the wrenching social disturbances that had plagued the sixteenth century if everyone could be forced to stay where they were. The bakufu meant this in both the physical and the social sense. People were forbidden to change residence, occupation, or social class. Harsh penalties were meted out against peasants absconding from their agrarian obligations; even people who aided them in any way were executed. Peasants who had to travel even short distances were required to show signed permission (*orai-tegata*) from the village headman to anyone who challenged them.

Similarly, the bakufu intended to erect barriers between the various han domains to make any attempt at military or economic coalition very difficult, if not impossible. They took care to position traditional enemies in close proximity and posted their families and most trusted vassals in between as well. All of the roads were tightly controlled to make easy movement throughout the country worrisome and difficult. Barrier gates and checkpoints dotted all major roads. These guard stations were placed at all the natural choke points—at mountain passes, narrow valleys, and where the mountains met the coastline.

Added to those political constraints, Japan's physical topography made travel difficult and even dangerous. The country was formed by tremendous geological uplift due to volcanic activity, which had created craggy coastlines and steep mountains. Even volcanoes that had been dormant for decades and even centuries would occasionally rumble and spew out lava and ash. The streams were narrow, short, and very rapid compared to the long, wide, meandering rivers of continental Asia. Therefore, not many Japanese rivers were suited to boat traffic, and many had gouged deep canyons that made normal crossings perilous.

Since the country was insular, the Japanese had long ago mastered small boat transportation. The rocky volcanic coastline made this kind of transportation risky, but the extensive coastline was dotted with many coves and natural harbors. The short offshore land shelf, powerful currents, tricky river deltas, monsoon winds, rip-tides, whirlpools, an occasional typhoon, and even tsunami tidal waves made sea travel dangerous. Coupled with these natural impediments, the Tokugawa had begun a conscious effort to isolate the country from the rest of the world beginning in 1612 and culminating in the *sakoku* ("closed country") edicts of the 1640s.

In addition to strict laws against travel abroad, to disappear from view of those on land made sea travelers liable to execution upon return. The bakufu had severely limited the construction of oceangoing vessels. Large, deep-draft, sternpost rudder ships were forbidden to assure that Japanese would not be able to sneak away to rendezvous with any European ships. So profound was the bakufu's fear of collusion between crypto-Christian converts and foreign powers (all allegedly controlled by the Pope through his Spanish and Portuguese subjects) that it had decided to hermetically seal the country.

Yet, the bakufu had in effect sabotaged its own restrictions against travel by way of its "alternate attendance" (*sankin-kotai*) hostage system. In order to control the powerful warlords, the bakufu required that their immediate families remain as hostages in Edo as guarantors of the daimyō's good behavior. Every daimyo was also required to spend half of his time in his han capital and the other half in attendance of the shōgun in Edo. Those who lived only a few days from Edo could spend six months in each place; those who resided further would alternate years.

This system was born mostly as a result of Tokugawa paranoia, but it was also intended to force financial ruin on the warlords. The cost of maintaining two separate residences was exacerbated by the travel logistics. Traveling with an appropriate entourage was expensive enough, but imagine the cost of housing and feeding them miles away from one's natural food supply. To transport sufficient rice was prohibitively expensive because one would have to bring enough food to feed the porters as well. Most daimyōs took the other alternative: bringing rice to Ōsaka or Sendai and absorbing the lesser expense of rice exchange. In that way, daimyō saved on the full cost of transportation to and storage for a year in Edo (for the unintended social and economic effects, see Chapter 16).

The bakufu developed an elaborate and extensive post station system to deal with the sudden increase in the number of travelers. Many cities and towns sprang up to provide food and lodging for the hundreds of thousands of samurai on the road to and from Edo. There were five officially designated highways for sankin-kotai, the most famous being the Tokaidō (Great Eastern Way), which went through Kyoto and Nagoya on the way to Edo. No fewer than fifty-three post stations were established on the Tokaidō.[1] Nearby daimyō were required to provide horses and bearers to serve official traffic as part of their corvée obligations. Virtually every han had such a system within its borders for military and strategic reasons anyway. Daimyō were limited as to which official road they could take, and when they could travel. The Tokaidō was by far the most commonly used since the road skirted the eastern seaboard between Kyoto and Edo, passing through perhaps 60 percent of the urban population.

On the major roads small hillocks were planted with firs along the way, partly to act as shady rest stops, but also to mark the distance to the center of Edo. All distances were measured from the bridge (Nihonbashi) opposite the entrance to the Tokugawa castle. Heaps of sand were piled along the way to be spread over wet patches on the road. Peasants who lived nearby were forced to service the roads as part of their collective corvée labor obligations (*sukegō*).

Bakufu officials and their entourages (including baggage and products on their way to the shogun) were conveyed free of charge on the road. Daimyō, merchants, and other travelers were allowed to hire horses and bearers at fees set by the bakufu. There were also a number of postal and message systems that carried letters at very rapid speed. Normal messages were conveyed on the thrice-monthly express (*sando hikyaku*), which took about a week from Kyoto to Edo; by the end of the eighteenth century it was commonly three and a half days. More urgent messages could reach Edo in only a day, riders stopping only to change horses (like a Pony Express) along the way. The messengers carried the missives in ornate lacquered boxes and rang bells along the way to warn other travelers to give way. There was also another hikyaku system operated by the daimyō related to the Tokugawa (*shimpan*). It left from Wakayama on the fifth, fifteenth, and twenty-fifth of each month and returned from Edo on the tenth, twentieth, and thirtieth. The system was also called the "seven ri" (*shichiri hikyaku*) system because each post station was seven *ri* (about 17.5 miles) apart.[2] There were over a hundred private express systems, many with set schedules, but most departing when they had a load sufficient to cover costs.[3]

Bakufu officials and the daimyō entourages could only stay at inns designated by the bakufu, where they could be watched by bakufu censors, who were actually spies. Several inspection stations along the way monitored the sankin-kotai traffic. One, at the narrows at Hakone near Mt. Fuji, was enjoined to "watch for women going out and guns coming into" the capital. The daimyō were required to leave their families as hostages in Edo, and since guns were very carefully restricted, it stands to reason that if a daimyo wished to start a rebellion, he would want to get his family out, hence the inspection for women leaving the city and guns entering it. Written passports (*tegata*) were issued by the bakufu and had to be carried by travelers at all times. Certain checkpoints were notorious for their rude and harassing treatment of women travelers. No doubt the bakufu encouraged such treatment since they expected women to remain as hostages and guarantors for their menfolk.

Since the sankin-kotai entourages of the major daimyō were quite large, they were scheduled two or three days apart to allow the inns and post stations time to recover from one before the next one came along. Signboards along the roads informed the traveler which groups were scheduled. The packhorse handlers (*mago*) were required to pass on such information. A total of 159 daimyō were required to use the Tokaido, 37 the Oshukaidō, 34 the Nakasendo, 25 the Mitokaidō, and 3 the Koshukaidō.[4]

Previously, the only normal accommodations for travelers were in Buddhist temples. Since Japanese did not require permanent beds (see Chapter 9), travelers could, in theory, carry their own bedding. All they then needed was a sheltered flat place to sleep. Every temple had plenty of those. A few coppers (as a donation, of course) would usually suffice to obtain a sleeping place, a few more for the skimpy meals that monks commonly ate. But what was one to do with a horde of a thousand arrogant samurai? No temple could be expected to cope with such throngs of people.

Licensed (again, a hidden and unofficial tax on commerce) hostlers were allowed to establish official inns at these post stations. At first, these inns were more like official government hostels than hotels. Bakufu officials could expect little more than a dry futon in a crowded room, a nearby privy, perhaps bathing facilities, and a communal kitchen. By the eighteenth century, however, the inns were considerably more plush and accommodating. Virtually every inn could provide an escalating level of service commensurate with one's ability to pay.

Inns
The typical inn in the eighteenth century (if there was any such thing) was a complex arrangement for the traveler's comfort.[5] The main room was bare of furniture, as was every Japanese room except the kitchen and bath. It was commonly open on at least three sides in good weather, the center being carpeted with sedge mats (*tatami*), and the outer veranda portion floored with polished planks. Those

travelers who were in a hurry, stopping only for a quick meal, especially at midday, could sit on the veranda. Those who meant to tarry awhile sat on the tatami (actually on their haunches, since Japanese do not usually sit with legs dangling as in the West).

When travelers arrived at dusk, often they were dragged in by young maids who came out into the street to lure them in.[6] Travelers were often greeted with a moist towel with which to wipe the grime of the road off their faces and hands. Unless he had special culinary delicacies in mind, the traveler was served what everyone else ate. Before the meal, however, a cup of tea or at least hot water was proffered.

Small, short-legged individual table-trays laden with food were brought by servants and placed before each customer. Each victual was served in a small individual dish. A common meal (see Chapter 7) consisted of three essential elements: rice, pickled vegetables, and clear broth soup. A small piece of broiled fish or eel might be added as well as hot sake, at additional cost of course. Local delicacies were available, and virtually every inn specialized in snacks or special dishes such as broiled skewers of fish, sautéed or boiled vegetables, hearty stews, porridges and gruels, rice crackers or cakes (*mochi*), some fruits (always peeled, often stewed, broiled, dried, or candied, but never whole), and various marine products, fresh (mussels, clams, oysters, sea urchins) and dried (cuttlefish, octopus, abalone, etc.).

After a meal, traditionally terminated by the rice course, the customer could lounge while a bath was readied. While he waited, he might take a few puffs from a proffered miniscule tobacco pipe (called "one puff"). The bath might be a communal one, but usually was a cabinet full of scalding water (see Chapter 9) wherein one could ease away the pains of travel. Customers were often offered the use of a short kimono (*yutaka*) after the bath. Since most Japanese retired shortly after sunset, travelers retired to a bed fashioned from cotton-stuffed futon with perhaps a hard pillow to keep their coiffure intact.

Most maids in the inns also served as prostitutes (a separate charge, of course), but if that was not the case, the inn manager could make arrangements of that sort from nearby brothels. Every post town was rife with such arrangements. It was not only accepted, but also expected that the male traveler had healthy sexual appetites, which could not be normally sated since their wives and concubines did not travel with them. Homosexual male prostitutes and young attractive boys could also be procured for those with "different" tastes. None of these special arrangements were received with moral condemnation or, indeed, the least bit of shock or surprise on the part of the hostlers. Male chastity, if there were such a thing in eighteenth-century Japan, would have been unusual and probably viewed with some suspicion by that society.

Breakfast was much less leisurely than dinner and usually consisted similarly of rice, pickles, and soup. Often rice or other grains were cooked in a thick gruel, and steamed wheat (or rice) buns flavored with sweet bean paste were offered at breakfast. The midday meal was the least substantial of all. A bowl of rice or hot noodles along with hot tea sufficed for most travelers. Many skipped this meal altogether.

More leisurely travelers, pilgrims, for example, might sojourn for more than one night, but most travelers were in a hurry to be on their way. They would settle their bills and be off. Curiously, there was a custom in some areas where travelers would leave small gifts for the innkeepers, unlike in the West, where travelers sometimes take towels, stationery, and ashtrays as souvenirs. Fans, handkerchiefs, and hand towels were common as gifts of appreciation. There were small shops along the road to buy such trifles and curios. Wealthy travelers commonly had their own servants clean the room and put away the bedding before they left.

Most of the post stations became thriving towns, with inns, restaurants, sake shops, and other establishments, many selling locally produced specialties to travelers.

> As one reads old guidebooks, it sometimes seems that the Tokaidō must have been lined with shops from one end to the other, each hawking a local specialty . . . even lesser wares were faithfully cataloged in the guidebooks, and a knowledgeable traveler could recite his way from one end of the highway to the other by naming the local specialties instead of the towns and villages.[7]

Pilgrimage Travel for religious purposes had a long and very rich tradition in Japan. Apart from the occasional monk who traveled to China in search of revealed truth and instruction,[8] there is a long history of Japanese traveling to holy sites in Japan. By the eighteenth century there was a plethora of well-established pilgrimage routes. The most famous and perhaps the most spiritually prestigious site was the Shintō shrine at Ise.

Many daimyō, while on sankin-kotai, would make a side-trip there at least once in their lives. The bakufu at first required special permission, but after a time turned a blind eye to this common occurrence. Wealthy chōnin also managed to wrangle a written passport from a machi-bugyō in order to pray for some medical miracle. After a time, a regular rotation system developed for substantial citizens of the larger cities to make the trip. Even in the villages, mutual-aid societies often "invested" leftover funds to allow a chosen few farmers to make the journey. By the eighteenth century special lotteries were established whereby everyone contributed a few coppers and a few winners would have enough to make the pilgrimage. More commonly, the "winners" were designated long before, and every *ie* head would receive a turn. No doubt many—and perhaps even most—of the pilgrims were devout in their spiritual intentions, but one wag has suggested that "a pilgrimage was an excuse for a journey, and a journey was an excuse for a spree."[9]

Pilgrims would dress in special white robes and sedge hats, and would carry straw sandals and walking sticks. Often, monks would ink a magic Sanskrit letter on the pilgrim's robe. Pilgrims were expected to buy talismans and amulets for their family, friends, and neighbors. Perhaps this contributed to the Japanese mania for purchasing armloads of souvenirs (*omiyage*) at virtually every shrine, temple, hotel, or resort that they happen to pause at for a few seconds.

At several times during the century a kind of madness overtook entire regions, when whole villages would spontaneously set off for Ise. In the space of two months (April 9 to May 29, 1705), for instance, an astounding 3,620,000 visited Ise. This was more than 12 percent of the total population of Japan![10] These outbursts of religious hysteria frightened the daimyō and bakufu, of course, but since they were never destructive or politically dangerous, the peasants would usually only be admonished to come to their senses and allowed to return home peacefully. When these mass pilgrimages happened, the entire region might flock to the roads to offer food, sake, a few coppers, towels, and other gifts to complete strangers. Inns and restaurants sometimes even spontaneously offered cut-rate or even free accommodations, and virtually all the temples along the way threw their doors open to act as hostels for the devout.

Inquiries were made by government officials to see what had set off these manias, and it was discovered that often the story was the same. Amulets would rain down upon a village from "out of the blue." No one could say what caused this magic, but perhaps the bureaucrats should have been looking for travel agents and touts from inns who might have happened to be lurking in the environs.

There were a number of other pilgrimage sites. In the eighteenth century it was common to see roving bands of professional pilgrims. Most were monks on their way to fulfill an obligatory round of pilgrimages, but there were also people who spent their entire lives wandering from one holy place to another, surviving by begging from other pilgrims or ordinary travelers on the road.[11] Mountain religious ascetics (*yamabushi*) traveled around, blowing conch horns, clashing cymbals, and beating drums to announce their arrival to other pilgrims, who were expected to donate some alms. There were even troupes of nuns similarly engaged in pilgrimage. Most were probably devoutly intent on their spiritual quest, but we are told of some, called *bikuni*, who were little more than wandering beggars and prostitutes. Kaempfer describes a horde of beggars: "In some places they and their fathers accost travelers in company with a troop of bikunis, and with their rattling, singing, trumpeting, chattering, and crying, make such a frightful noise as would make one mad or deaf."[12]

The fact that these wandering monks and beggars were even allowed to proceed along the roads is testament to how common pilgrimage was in eighteenth-century Japan. The samurai guards at checkpoints let them through without many problems as long as they were dressed as pilgrims and seemed to be behaving themselves.

Innkeepers tried to keep these bands of professionals away from their customers, but occasionally even these most commercial-minded of men would feed a lot of them with leftovers, and might even allow them to sleep on the veranda in inclement weather. Otherwise, the bikuni and their ilk had to resort to shrines and temples for lodging.

NOTES

1. There were fifty stations on the Nakasendo, and twenty-five each on the Mitokaidō, Koshukaidō, and Oshubaidō routes. See Takeo Yazaki, *Social Change and the City in Japan: From Earliest Times Through the Industrial Revolution*, trans. David L. Swain (Tokyo: Japan Publications, 1968), 133–135, for an excellent discussion.

2. A *ri* was 2.5 miles.

3. See Katsuhisa Moriya, "Urban Networks and Information Networks" (Ronald P. Toby, trans.), in Chie Nakane and Shinzaburō Oishi, eds., *Tokugawa Japan: The Social and Economic Antecedents of Modern Japan* (Tokyo: University of Tokyo Press, 1990), 97–123, for an excellent synopsis.

4. Yazaki, *Social Change*, 135.

5. Jippensha Ikku, *Hizakurige or Shank's Mare*, trans. Thomas Satchell (Rutland, VT: Tuttle, 1960), is invaluable for descriptions, but there are many other accounts, including those by Kaempfer, Thunberg, and others.

6. See Ikku, *Shank's Mare*, for a number of hilarious accounts of travelers being wrestled willy-nilly into inns and restaurants.

7. Oliver Statler, *Japanese Inn* (New York: Random House, 1961), 154.

8. There are scores of records about such travel. The most famous is recounted by Edwin O. Reischauer, *Ennin's Travels in Tang China* (New York: Ronald Press, 1955).

9. Statler, *Japanese Inn*, 168.

10. See account in ibid., 178.

11. Ikku, *Shank's Mare*, recounts several encounters with these folk, as does Kaempfer.

12. Engelbert Kaempfer, *The History of Japan: Together with a Description of the Kingdom of Siam*, 3 vols., trans. J. G. Scheuchzer (Glasgow: James MacLehose and Sons, 1906), 2:342.

Glossary

Agemono   vegetable oil deep-fry cooking

Agura   "saddles with legs"; stools

Ainu   a native people, culturally distinct from Japanese

Ajinomoto   peppered spice and MSG, used as a condiment

Aki no higan   autumnal equinox (*see also* haru no higan)

Aki no shinichi   festival to honor local spirits, October

Ama-cha   licoriced tea

Amado   residential exterior sliding screens

Amakasa   lacquered rain umbrella

Ami-gasa   conical split sedge hat

Andon   framed paper lantern

Anka   iron bed warmers

Aragoto   "rough" style of Kabuki acting, acrobatic

Asagaowa   "morning face"; porcelain night or slop jar

Ashigaru   "foot" soldier; non-samurai

Awabi   abalone

Ayu   "sweet fish"

Bajutsu   dressage-like horsemanship

Bakufu   "tent government"; generic name for feudal military government

Baku-han   name given for mixed administration of bakufu and domain

Banto   chief clerk

Benihana   safflower

Benjo   "place for business"; euphemism for toilet
Bento   box lunch
Beya   sumo training schools
Bikuni   female wandering nuns, sometimes also prostitutes
Bitchu-guwa   split-pronged hoe used for hand plowing
Biwa   three-stringed lute
Biwa-hoshi   minstrel chanters accompanying themselves on biwa
Boddhisatva   Buddhist "saints"
Bokken   solid wooden swords used in kendo (*see also* shinai)
Bon-odori   dance performed at Obon Festival
Bonsai   miniaturizing plants
Botamochi   pounded rice cakes covered with sweet bean paste
Bu   martial arts (*see also* bun)
Bu   silver coin
Bugaku   court dance genre
Bugyō   title of ministerial-level administrators
Buke shohatto   Regulations for Military Houses (1615)
Buku   abstention period after funeral (*see also* imi); taboo
Bun   literary arts (*see also* bu)
Bun-bu   unity of literary and martial arts
Bunke   branch or cadet family
Bunraku   puppet theater evolved from joruri
Bushidō   "the way of the warrior"; mystical belief system
Butsudan   "Buddha shelf"; Buddhist home ritual niche (*see also* kami-dana)
Byōbu   folding room screens
Cha-dansu   tea chest
Chakaiseki ryori   "tea and stones in one's pockets"; vegetarian meal traditionally served to Buddhist monks
Chanko-nabe   hotpot stew made for sumo wrestlers
Chanoyu   "way of tea" ceremony
Chawan   personal-sized meal bowls
Chazuke   hot tea and rice dish
Chi   energy in Taoist ideology
Chigaidana   split-level shelves in tokonoma area (*see also* usu kasumi-dana)
Chigō   homosexual lovers (*see also* yoru no tomo; and chōdō)
Chikara-ishi   bouts of strength, lifting rocks, etc.
Chō   measurement of land
Choaimai   "paper rice"; designation used in Dojima Osaka rice trade (*see also* shomai)
Chochia   round paper lantern
Cho-dansu   trunk for accounting books
Chōdō   "beloved boy"; homosexual lover (*see also* yoru no tomo; chigo)

Chōnin   urbanites; city common people
Chonmage   traditional samurai topknot hairstyle
Chozu-ba   "washing place"; euphemism for toilet
Chozu-bachi   water ewer
Chūjiki   "mid-meal"; lunch
Chūkei   fan used in Noh
Daikan   Tokugawa intendant administrators
Daikon   large white radish
Daimyō   feudal warlord
Dakyu   horse-mounted polo
Dashibata   "putting-out" piecework system, particularly in clothing
     production
Desu   verb ending
Detchi   apprentice
Dogi   padded under-jacket
Doma   packed earth floor in minka farmers' cottages
Donburi   a bowl of steamed rice served with egg and other toppings
Donjon   castle tower
Eboshi   samurai silk hat
Edo-ben   accent of Edo people
Edo-hana   "Flowers of Edo"; euphemism for fire
Edokko   "child of Edo" (or "typical Edo person")
Egoyomi   printed calendars
Ema   votive placards in Shintō
Emakimono   horizontal scroll
Engawa   open wooden-plank veranda running around a house
Enza   woven straw cushion
Eta   "abundant pollution"; hereditary outcastes (*see also* hinin)
Etui   decorative needle cases
Feng shui   "Wind and water"; Chinese geomancy
Fudai   "hereditary" daimyo most loyal to Tokugawa
Fue   flute
Fugu   blowfish
Fuku wa uchi   "in with good luck"; ritual at setsubun (*see also* oni wa
     soto)
Fukuwarai   a children's game like pin the tail on the donkey
Fumi-e   "picture treading"; symbolic stepping on icons and pictures to
     prove one is not a Christian
Fundoshi   men's loincloth underwear
Furosaki-byobu   partition screens
Furusato   "old home" ones; native home
Furyu-odori   ancient gagaku-like court dance
Fusetsu-dome   newspapers of translated Dutch news
Fusuma   residential interior sliding screens

Futon   cotton-quilted coverlet or mattress

Gampi uchiwa   fan used in Sumo

Geisha   professional female entertainers

Genkan   entry hallway

Genpuku   boy's coming-of-age forelock shaving ceremony

Geta   rain clogs; elevated wooden shoes

Getabako   box to hold geta rain clogs

Gichiyo   a game like pell-mell

Giri   duty and obligation (*see also* ninjo)

Go   checkers-like game (*see also* igo)

Gō   poetic name

Gohan-mono   generic name for foods consisting mainly of steamed rice

Gokenin   feudal vassal

Gomoku narabe   "five of the same"; a simplified game of go

Gonin-gumi   "five-person group"; mutual-responsibility administrative group

Gonō   hereditary rich peasant class, often former ashigaru

Gōso   "appeals by force"; peasant uprising (*see also* ikki)

Goyō kin   monopoly license payments

Goyō shonin   official purveyors, monopoly merchants (*see also* ton'ya)

Gunbai uchiwa   battle standard war fan

Gunki-monogatari   "warrior tales"

Gunsen   war fan (*see also* tessen)

Gyoemon-buro   hot bath cabinet with copper bottom to heat water directly from below

Gyoji   sumo referees

Gyoji ryori   special foods prepared for matsuri

Gyoson   fishing village designation (*see also* sanson; nōson)

Habakari   "reserve"; euphemism for toilet

Hachi   tiny bowls for one-serving dishes

Hachimaki   headband

Hadagane   "skin" steel used in making swords (*see also* shingane)

Haiden   "worship sanctuary" in Shintō (*see also* honden)

Haikai   poetic convention

Haka mairi   obligatory visits to a grave

Hakama   samurai silk trousers

Han   domain of a daimyō

Hana matsuri   Flower Festival, late April

Hanado   "way of flowers"; art of flower arranging (*see also* ikebana)

Hana-garuda   card game using flowers instead of suits

Hanamichi   "flower path"; theatrical entryway through the crowd in Kabuki

Hanetsuki   battledore and shuttlecock

Hangyoku   apprentice geisha (*see also* maiko)

Haniwa clay funerary figurines
Hanko portable name seal
Hansatsu "domain money"; paper currency printed by domains
Haori samurai coat
Happi short coat-robe
Hara-gake women's pinafore
Hara-kiri "belly slitting"; ritual suicide (*see also* seppuku)
Harebi "shining days"; special auspicious days
Hari-kuyo ritual for "broken things"
Hariyōyi acupuncture
Haru Basho Spring Sumo Tournament
Haru no higan vernal equinox (*see also* aki no higan)
Haru no shanichi festival to propitiate local spirits
Hashi chopsticks
Hashi-arai "wash chopsticks"; a meal-ending soup
Hatamoto "house men"; one's closest vassals
Hatsu uma "First Horse" festival, usually in early spring
Heino-bunri separation of social classes in the Tokugawa era
Hibachi charcoal brazier
Hichiriki horizontal flute
Hie an edible grass
Higasa parasol
Hiki-ami dragnet used for fishing
Hiki-ita "pulling boards" used to scare away birds from fields (*see also* naruko)
Hikite handholds for sliding screens
Hina matsuri Doll Festival in May
Hinin "nonperson"; hereditary outcaste (*see also* eta)
Hinoki cypress
Hiragana "round" written syllabary
Hito-gaeshi forced repatriation of peasants away from Edo
Hitsu small chest
Hitsugi coffin
Hiyatoi-za day-laborer registry
Hojutsu arquebus gunnery
Hoko matsuri floats
Hōkōnin indentured workers
Hōmyō Buddhist posthumous name (*see also* kaimyō)
Honbako book box
Hon-byakusho "real" peasants; regular members of a village
Honden "holy of holies" sanctuary in Shintō (*see also* haiden)
Honzen lacquered wooden tray
Honzen ryori banquet-style cuisine served on lacquered wooden trays
Hyakusho "hundred names"; generic name for peasants

Hyakunichi-otoko   "100-day men"; part-time sake brewers
Hyakunichi-shibai   "100 Playhouses"; repertoire Kabuki houses
Hyobanki   theatrical magazines that rated Kabuki actors and plays
Ichiju-issai   "one soup—one vegetable," in addition to rice; a standard
   meal
Ie   household; the official extended family designation
Igo   checkers-like game (*see also* go)
Ihai   commemorative funerary tablets printed with kaimyo
Ikebana   flower arrangement
Ikki   peasant uprising
Ikko   "Single Purpose" Pureland warriors in the sixteenth century
Imi   mourning period (*see also* buku)
Inari   fox spirit, associated with agriculture
Inkyo   aged head of household retires in favor of heir
Inro   miniature chest or box
Inu-awase   dog fighting for sport
Inu-omono   a samurai game of shooting padded arrows at dogs
Irezumi   tattoo
Iriai   traditional village foraging rights
Irori   open-hearth fireplace used in minka
Itaguwa   plowing or furrowing hoe
Izaribata   simple horizontal loom
Janome-gasa   "snake-eye" umbrella print decoration
Jisankin   money in place of ritual exchange of marriage gifts
Jishimban   urban night patrols (*see also* tsuijiban) and firewatch
Jōdō   Pureland Buddhist sect (*see also* Jōdō-shinshū)
Jōdō-shinshū   "True" Pureland Buddhist Sect (*see also* Jōdō)
Jokamachi   "castle towns" urban areas around castles
Jōmon   prehistoric, neolithic nomadic culture (c. 2,000–250 B.C.E.)
Joruri   chanting puppetry; evolved into Bunraku
Joya   expulsion of evil
Juban   open kosode-like shirt
Kabane   ancient system of court ranks
Kabuki   theatrical genre involving music, acting, and dance
Kabuki-odori   Kabuki dances
Kagami   mirror; a Shinto fetish representing Amaterasu, the Sun God-
   dess
Kago   basket palanquin, carried primarily suspended between two or
   more palanquin carriers or hung off the side of a horse (*see also* no-
   rimono)
Kagura   music of ancient Shinto ritual; also, a Shinto dance that tells
   the tale of creation
Kaimyō   posthumous Buddhist name painted on ihai (*see also* hōmyō)
Kaiseki ryori   snacks cuisine

Kakashi   scarecrow

Kakure kurishitan   "hidden" Christians

Kama   rice pot

Kamadō   earthen adobe-like stove

Kami   spirit or tutelary god in Shinto

Kamidana   "spirit shelf"; home Shinto shrine (*see also* butsudan)

Kamikaze   "divine winds"; typhoons that drove off the Mongols in the thirteenth century

Kamoi   recessed runners for fusuma, shoji, or amado sliding screens

Kana   one of two written Japanese syllabaries

Kanji   Chinese written character

Kanto   Eastern Plain, area around Edo-Tokyo

Kaomise   "showing the face"; debut season of Kabuki

Kappo   overcoat

Kara kami   "Chinese paper" used to fit into sliding screens

Kara-age   food rolled in arrowroot starch and then fried

Karaguwa   hoe used for clearing brush

Karashiki   "green" fertilizer; compost

Kariage   Scything Festival, August

Karma   dependent causality; actions that influence new incarnation

Kasa   oiled paper umbrella

Kata   "form" or exercise in martial arts

Katakana   "angular" written syllabary

Katana   curved blade sword

Kata-zome   dyeing stencils

Katsuobushi   dried bonito flakes (in soup)

Kawaraban   "tile prints"; newspapers printed from ceramic tiles

Kaya   mosquito net

Kazari-kugi   decorative iron nails used in tokonoma (recessed nook)

Keiba   horseracing

Keigo   honorific language

Kemari   kickball; hackey-sack

Ken   linear measurement, approximately two yards

Kendo   martial art of bamboo or wooden sword fencing

Kiki-ko   game of perfume identification

Kimchee   Korean pickled cabbage

Kimono   generic robe fastened with obi

Kinai   the area in central Honshu, around Kyoto-Ōsaka

Kinchaku   women's charm bag

Kirisute-gomen   "cut and continue"; the right of samurai to cut down commoners

Kirizuma   gabled sedge roof style

Kiseru   tiny "one-puff" clay tobacco pipes

Ko   lottery-like mutual-aid society

Koban   coin equal to a ryō or a koku of rice
Kobuna-kama   guild-like association of merchants
Kofun   "tomb" people, ancestors of Japanese (c. 250–500 C.E.)
Koi   Japanese carp
Koji   wheat malt used in brewing sake and shoyu
Koka   "back frame"; euphemism for toilet
Kokechi   tie-dye
Kokkeobon   humorous books, genre of published literature
Koku   dry measurement, approximately five bushels
Kokudaka   "in-kind" portion of crop paid as tax (*see also* nengu)
Kokugaku   "native school" of study
Kokuso   "domain-wide petition"
Komagaku   music of ancient Korean court
Kombu   edible kelp
Komezu   rice vinegar
Komusubi   third rank of ancient sumo
Koseki   family register
Ko-shibai   "little playhouses"; private, unsanctioned Kabuki theatrical
   houses
Koshi-maki   short kimono; women's underwear
Koshoku   "to love life"; euphemism used by Ihara Saikaku for sex act
Kosode   kimono robe
Kōtan   chestnut charcoal used for metalworking (*see also* watan)
Kotatsu   sunken charcoal heater covered by table
Koto   multistringed horizontal harp
Koto hajime   "Beginning of Things"; preparations for New Year's
Kowakamai   narrative dance genre
Kozo   a type of mulberry used for papermaking
Kun-yomi   "native" pronunciation of kanji (*see also* on-yomi)
Kura   earthen storehouse
Kura biraki   airing out earthen storehouses; done traditionally after
   New Year's
Kuri   chestnut
Kuromaku   "black curtain"; the black-clad assistants in Kabuki
Kuruma tansu   storage trunks on wheels
Kusakezuri-kuwa   weeding hoe
Kusa-zōshi   "smelly books"; cheap genre of published literature
Kusuri-dansu   medicine chest
Kutsunugi-ishi   "stone for removing shoes"; front door step
Kuwa   hoe
Kyahan   leggings
Kyōgen   theatrical playlets between Noh scenes
Kyokechi   rice paste used in dyeing
kyujutsu   archery

Kyusu teapot

Mabiki "thinning out"; euphemism for infanticide for population control

Machi residential ward; kanji character also pronounced "cho"

Machi-bugyō residential administrator

Machi-doshiyori ward elder or leader (*see also* nanushi)

Mago packhorse handlers

Maigo-fuda children's identification tag

Maiko apprentice geisha (*see also* hangyoku)

Maiogi fan used in Kabuki

Maki-e gold or silver lacquer

Makimono vertical silk hanging scrolls

Makisu split bamboo mats for rolling sushi

Maku-uchi lower ranks of ancient sumo

Mamori-fude children's amulet

Manaita cutting board

Manga comic books (twentieth century)

Manju steamed buns, often stuffed with fillings

Manzai risqué dialogue entertainment

Mashiko a type of ceramic

Masu verb ending

Matsuri village festival

Mayuharai girls' coming-of-age eyebrows shaving ceremony

Mayuzumi artificially drawn eyebrows

Mekakushi children's game, something like blind man's buff

Mekuragoyomi rebus calendars (*see also* nanbugoyomi)

Menrui noodle dishes

Metsuke system of Tokugawa spies

Mie exaggerated pose in Kabuki acting

Miko "spiritual children"; shamans or Shinto attendants

Mikoshi Shinto kami palanquin; "god float"

Minka "folk houses"; traditional single-room straw peasant houses

Mino straw raincoats

Mirin sweetened cooking sake

Miso fermented soybean, used in soup

Misu split bamboo screens (*see also* sudare)

Miyagi-shibai Shrine Precinct Kabuki playhouse

Mizunomi "water drinkers"; tenant farmers or landless peasants

Mochi sweet pounded rice

Moe-kusa "burning medicine"; moxabustion

Momohiki women's tight breeches

Mompe women's flared working trousers

Mon circular decorative patches worn like coats of arms on kimono

Moshiogusa a type of seaweed used to produce salt

Motoyui   plaited string for gathering up samurai chonmage topknot
Moxa   "burning medicine" topically on the skin (*see also* Moe-kusa)
Mugi-cha   wheat "tea"
Mura   village
Murakata ikki   peasant uprising against village leaders
Mura-nyuyo   village collective administrative expenses
Muraji   ancient system of political ranks
Mushi-kiki   chirping of insects
Mushi okuri   ritual to drive away insects
Mushimono   steamed food
Musume-gumi   village association of young women
Myoga-kin   "forced loan"; a kind of unofficial extortion from merchants
Myōji   surname, family name
Nabe   generic name for large metal stew pots
Nabe ryori   hotpot stews
Nagamochi-kuruma   "car for durables"; trunks with wheels in which to
    store things to be whisked out to kura in threat of fire
Nagashikan   steamers for food
Nagaya   "longhouse"; urban tenement
Naikaku   castle keep
Nakagai   private rice brokers, not officially sanctioned by government
Nakodo   marriage go-between; matchmaker
Nanakusa   "seven herbs"; used generically for "normal" herbs
Nanbugoyomi   rebus calendars (*see also* mekuragoyomi)
Nando   raised sleeping platform
Nanushi   ward elder or leader (*see also* machi-doshiyori)
Naruko   "bird rattlers" used to scare away birds from fields (*see also*
    hiki-ita)
Natto   fermented, partially decomposed soybeans
Nekki   "knocks"; a childrens' stick game
Nengō   reign or period dating names
Nengu   total tax for village (*see also* kokudaka)
Nenju gyoji   a yearlong system of religious observances
Nerimono   ground foods rolled into balls, floured or battered, then
    cooked
Netsuke   drawstring pulls or fobs, collected as curios
Nichiren shoshu   militant Buddhist sect
Niiname sai   First Fruits Festival, August
Nikki   diary
Nimono   stew
Ninjō   human emotion (*see also* giri)
Ninjōbon   "tales of human affection"; genre of published literature
Ni-shichi   "two-seven"; system for market rotation
Nogyo-zenshu   *The Comprehensive Agricultural Collection*

Noh traditional Japanese dance-theater genre

Noren horizontal shop curtain

Nori sheets of dried edible seaweed

Nori-maki seaweed-wrapped sushi rolls, cut into slices

Norimono cagelike palanquin, carried primarily suspended between two or more carriers or hung off the side of a horse (*see also* kago)

Norito Shintō chants or prayers

Nōsho agricultural printed manuals

Nōson agricultural village designation (*see also* sanson; gyoson)

Obi cloth sash used to fasten kimono

Obon festival in August when spirits of the dead return home to visit

Ochazuke tea-rice, a concoction made by pouring green tea over rice (*see also* chazuke)

Ōfuro hot water bath cabinet

Ogi folding collapsible fan (*see also* sensu)

Ohaguro tooth-blackening cosmetic

Oharai Grand Purification Ceremony, end of June

Ōkaeri "to return"; refers to returning spirits at Obon

Okidatami wadded straw sitting mat

Okuri-na posthumous imperial name

Omi shonin itinerant peddlers around Lake Biwa

Omiai "look-meet" arranged prenuptial meeting

Omiyage travel souvenir or gift

On sense of social obligation

Onigiri seaweed-wrapped rice balls

Onigokko children's game, something like Red Rover

Oni wa soto "out with the demons"; ritual at setsubun (*see also* fuku wa uchi)

Onnade "women's hand" style of writing

Onna gata female impersonator roles in Kabuki

Onsen hot spring inn

On-yomi "Chinese" pronunciation of kanji (*see also* kun-yomi)

Orai-tegata written travel pass

Orei "thanks"; a tip, gratuity, or bribe

Oroshigane metal grater

Oshiire cupboards with sliding doors

Oshire-isho-dansu chest for storing futon, pillows, etc.

Oshiroi face powder made of white clay and rice flour

Oshogatsu New Year's celebration

Osonae "honorable offering" made in Shintō

Otearai "hand-washing"; euphemism for toilet

Otogi-zōshi "diversionary stories," "fanciful tales"; genre of published literature

Otona village elder (*see also* toshiyori)

Otsuya family funerary wake or vigil
Ozeki top rank of ancient sumo
Patchi panties, women's underwear
Raku a type of ceramic
Rakugo comic storytelling entertainment
Ramen Chinese-style vermicelli
Ramma lintel area above fusuma sliding screens
Rangaku "Dutch Studies", generally used to indicate Western learning
Reikin "thank money"; a kind of extortion; informal tax on trade
Rekishi-monogatari "historical narrative"
Renga linked poetry
Rikishi sumo wrestler
Rikyū ogi fan used for chanoyu
Ritsu-ryō Heian era system of government, based on Chinese Tang model
Rōjū "senior councilors"; top administrators in the Tokugawa bakufu
Rokechi wax used in dyeing
Roma-ji Roman letters
Rōnin "wave man"; masterless samurai
Ryō gold coin equal in value to a koku of rice
Ryokan urban inns
Sade-ami dipping net used for fishing
Sahō no mai "dancing on the left (of the Emperor)"; genre of ancient court dance
Sakaki evergreen tree used in Shintō rituals
Sakazuki thimble-size sake cups
Sake fermented "rice wine"
Sakoku "closed country"; Tokugawa seclusion edicts (1640–1868)
Samurai "servant"; a designation for "warrior"
Sando hikyaku "thrice monthly express"; a postal delivery system
Sankin-kotai "alternate attendance" hostage system
Sansankudo "three sips from three cups"; marriage ritual
Sanson mountain village designation (*see also* nōson; gyoson)
Sanyaku top three ranks (ozeki, sekiwake, and komusubi) of ancient sumo
Sara large platter
Sashimi raw fish slices
Sashimi-bocho thin slicing knife (used to make sashimi)
Sato-gaeri bride's first ritual return to natal household
Seii-tai-shōgun "Barbarian-Subduing Generalissimo" title of head Kamakura, Muromachi, or Tokugawa bakufu
Sekiwake second rank of ancient sumo
Senbei baked rice crackers
Sengoku "Warring States" period of civil war, 1467–1570

Sensu folding collapsible fan (*see also* ogi)

Sento public bath

Seppuku ritual suicide (*see also* hara-kiri)

Setsu twenty-four "seasons" (six per season)

Setsubun first day of spring

Setsu-in euphemism for toilet

Sewa-goto "scandal" style of Kabuki acting—comedic

Shakuhachi end-blown bamboo flute

Sharebon erotic tales of the pleasure quarters; genre of published literature

Shichiri hikyaku "seven ri" postal delivery system

Shichirin charcoal brazier with side door to load fuel

Shikaidai wooden shelf in genkan entryway

Shikidatami woven straw sleeping mat

Shimenawa "Do not return rope," Shintō fetish; straw rope used to designate holy sites

Shimpan domains related to the Tokugawa house

Shinai split bamboo swords used in kendō (*see also* bokken)

Shinden "new fields"; reclaimed land, often tax-free (*see also* waju)

Shingaku "Heart Learning"; religious sect founded by Ishida Baigan, popular among chōnin

Shingane inner core of steel used to make swords (*see also* hadagane)

Shinju love-suicide

Shintō "The Way of the Gods"

Shirumono generic name for soup

Shirushi-banten happi coats worn by commercial clerks to advertise their store

Shitagi silk underwear

Shita-jime hip sash; women's underwear

Shita-obi "under the sash"; loincloth

Shite principal Noh character

Sho mouth organ with seventeen vertical pipes

Shochu fermented drink made from rice, wheat, potato, and other products

Shodo calligraphy

Shōen administrative tax-free manor

Shogi chess-like board game

Shoji sliding inner screens

Shojin ryori vegetarian cuisine

Shokudai candlestand

Shomai "true rice"; designation used in Dojima Ōsaka rice trade (*see also* choaimai)

Shonin merchant

Shoshū jiin-hatto Regulations for Shrines and Temples

Sho-tansu   trunk for writing materials

Shoyu   soy sauce

Shukaku   Harvest Festival, September

Shunga   "spring pictures"; pornographic genre of published literature

Shushi   Neo-Confucianism of the twelfth-century Chinese writer Chu Hsi

Shūso   petition to government

Soba   buckwheat noodles

Sodegaki   bamboo lattice

Somen   vermicelli

Soroban   Abacus

Soto   "outside"

Suage   fried foods, without batter

Sudare   split bamboo screens (*see also* misu)

Sugoroku   board game like backgammon

Suijin   water spirit

Suiton   dumplings

Sukegō   corvée labor obligations

Sukiyaki   beef hotpot stew

Sumi-e   ink-wash painting

Sumo   "simple dance" form of Japanese wrestling

Sunomono   mixed dishes served with vinegared rice

Suribachi   scored mortar (*see also* surikogi)

Surihaku   foil application to textiles

Surikogi   pestle (*see also* suribachi)

Sushi   vinegared rice, served with bits of raw fish

Suso-yoke   women's hip apron

Suzuri   inkstone

Suzuri-bako   box for writing materials

Ta ue   "Up to the fields"; festival for rice planting

Tabako-bon   combination tobacco storage and ashtray

Tabako-ire   cloth tobacco pouch

Tabi   split-toed socks that fasten at the ankle

Tachikaki   art of sword pulling

Tai   small-fry fish

Taigi-mibun   behavior appropriate to one's status

Taiko   giant drums

Takabata   "tall loom"

Tako   kite fighting

Tanabata   Star Festival (Vega and Altair), July

Tango no sekku   Boys' Festival in May

Tansu   wooden or rattan chest

Tatami   straw mats

Tatate   portable ink and brush sets carried by store clerks

Tegato   travel pass
Teishoku   special platter
Tekko   cotton or hemp mittens
Temoto-dansu   whatnot chest—literally, "at hand chest"
Tempura   battered, fried vegetables
Tengu   long-nosed goblin
Tenugi   towel/scarf
Terakoya   "parish school"; neighborhood informal school
Terauke seido   "temple surety system" used to register all citizens to ensure that they were not practicing Christianity and performed fumi-e
Teriyaki   marinated meat, grilled
Teshoku   hand-held candlestick
Tessen   war fan (*see also* gunsen)
Tobi   "dismantlers"; workers who pulled houses down before fire could reach them
Tobukuro   closet to house amado sliding screens
Todai   oil lamp
Tofu   soy curd
Tōgaku   music of Tang Dynasty court
Tokkuri   tall porcelain sake bottles for warming
Toko-bashira   vertical post that forms tokonoma recessed nook
Tokonoma   recessed interior nook
Tokusei   "act of grace"; debt cancellation
Ton'ya   official wholesalers (*see also* goyō shonin)
Tori-awase   cockfighting
Torii   crossbeam Shintō gateway
Toshiyori   elder (*see also* otona)
Tozama   "outsider"; daimyo least trustworthy to Tokugawa
Tsuba   sword hilt guards, collected as curios
Tsuitate   single upright screens
Tsujiban   urban night patrols (*see also* jishimban) and firewatch
Tsukemono   pickled vegetables
Tsukimi   Moon Viewing Festival, August
Tsukimi dango   rice spear dumplings
Tsuri-andon   colored paper lanterns
Tsusho   common or given name (*see also* Zokumyō)
Ubasoku   itinerant lay Buddhist preachers
Uchi   "inside"
Uchibata   factory system in textiles
Uchi-kowashi   "bash-up" peasant uprising (*see also* ikki)
Uchi-soto   "in versus out"; method of differentiating "us versus them"
Uchiwa   rigid, single-piece fan
Udon   thick wheat noodles

Uhō semai no mai   "dancing on the right (of the Emperor)"; genre of
   ancient court dance
Uji   fictive kinship group, clan
Ukiyo-e   "floating world pictures"; woodblock prints
Ukiyo-zōshi   "floating world stories"; genre of published literature
Umeboshi   pickled plum
Unjō-kin   annual license fee paid by merchants to city administration
Urushi   a type of lacquer
Urushi-no-ki   lacquer tree
Usu kasumi-dana   "thin mist shelf"; split-level shelves in tokonoma
   area (*see also* chigaidana)
Usuba-bocho   metal vegetable chopper
Uwagi   silk padded robes
Wagoto   "sentimental" style of Kabuki acting
Wajū   reclaimed land, often tax-free (*see also* shinden)
Wakadoshiyori   "junior councilors"; second most important adminis-
   trators in Tokugawa bakufu
Wakamono-gumi   "young man's association"; village mutual assistance
   group
Wakashu   "boy's style" of Kabuki acting
Wakizashi   short sword or dirk
Wan   large Chinese-style soup bowl
Waragutsu   straw snow boots for horses
Waraji   straw sandals (*see also* zori)
Wasabi   green horseradish used as a condiment
Washi   fine quality paper
Watan   oak or hardwood charcoal used for cooking (*see also* kōtan)
Yabusame   horse-mounted archery
Yakimochi   grilled hard bread
Yakimono   grilled skewers of tidbits
Yakitori   "grilled chicken"; any kind of grilled skewered meat
Yakuza   Organized crime syndicate
Yamabushi   "mountain men"; religious ascetics
Yamato   name commonly used for the Japanese people
Yashiki   mansion, residence
Yatate   portable ink and writing brush
Yayoi   prehistoric agricultural culture (c. 250 B.C.E.–250 C.E.)
Yen-riko   "reserve"; euphemism for toilet
Yoben   "place for business"; euphemism for toilet
Yobi-na   names for females
Yogi   nightclothes; also, sleeping bag–like gowns; futon with sleeves
Yokan   bean paste jelly
Yokozuna   "super" rank of modern sumo
Yomyō   infant name

Yoru no tomo   "night friend"; homosexual lover (*see also* chigo; chōdō)

Yose   narrative tale entertainment

Yosemono   gelatined foods

Yosemine   nipped sedge roof style

Yoshi-do   summer reed sliding screens

Yuino   exchange of marriage gifts

Yukigutsu   straw snowshoes

Yutaka   short cotton bathrobe

Yu-zamashi   "hot water cooler," used to cool boiled water for chanoyu tea ceremony

Za   guilds of artisans or merchants

Zabuton   padded cushions

Zaru   bamboo woven baskets

Zazen   Zen meditation

Zen   small personal tray-tables

Zokumyō   common or given name (*see also* tsushu)

Zonī   special vegetable stews eaten at New Year's

Zori   fine straw sandals (*see also* waraji)

Zosui   rice gruel

Bibliography

Akai, Tatsuroo. "The Common People and Painting" (Timothy Clark, trans.). In Chie Nakane and Shinzaburō, Oishi eds., *Tokugawa Japan: The Social and Economic Antecedents of Modern Japan*. Tokyo: University of Tokyo Press, 1990. 167–91.

Beasley, William. *Japan Encounters the Barbarian: Japanese Travelers in America and Europe*. New Haven: Yale University Press, 1995.

Borton, Hugh. *Peasant Uprisings in Japan of the Tokugawa Period*. New York: Paragon Books, 1968.

Brandon, Reiko Mochinaga. *Country Textiles of Japan: The Art of Tsutsugaki*. New York: Weatherhill, 1986.

Bush, Lewis. *Japanalia: A Concise Cyclopaedia*. Tokyo: Tokyo News Service, 1965.

Chamberlain, Basil Hall. *Japanese Things*. Rutland, VT: Tuttle, 1971.

Coaldrake, William H. "Edo Architecture and Tokugawa Law." *Monumenta Nipponica* 36 (1981), 235–84.

Cooper, Michael, ed. *They Came to Japan: An Anthology of European Reports on Japan, 1543–1640*. Berkeley: University of California Press, 1965.

Crawcour, E. Sydney. "Kawamura Zuiken: A Seventeenth Century Entrepreneur." *Transactions of the Asiatic Society of Japan*, 3rd Series, 9 (1966), 1–23.

Dalby, Liza Crihfield. *Kimono: Fashioning Culture*. New Haven: Yale University Press, 1993.

de Garis, Frederic. *We Japanese: Being Description of Many of the Customs, Manners, Ceremonies, Festivals, Arts, and Crafts of the Japanese, Besides Numerous Other Subjects*. 3 vols. Yokohama: Yamagata Press, 1949.

Dunn, Charles J. *Everyday Life in Traditional Japan*. Tokyo: Tuttle, 1969.

Earhart, H. Byron. *Religion in the Japanese Experience: Sources and Interpretations*. 2nd ed. London: Wadsworth Publishing, 1997.

Elison, George, and Bardwell L. Smith, eds. *Warlords, Artists, and Commoners: Japan in the Sixteenth Century*. Honolulu: University of Hawaii Press, 1981.

Elisonas, Jurgis. "The Inseparable Trinity: Japan's Relations with China and Korea." In John W. Hall and James L. McClain, eds., *Early Modern Japan*, volume 4 in *The Cambridge History of Japan*, Cambridge: Cambridge University Press, 1991, 235–300.

Eng, Robert Y., and Thomas C. Smith. "Peasant Families and Population Control in Eighteenth Century Japan." *Journal of Interdisciplinary History* 6:3 (Winter 1976).

Feeney, Griffirth, and Hamano Kiyoshi. "Rice Price Fluctuation and Fertility in Late Tokugawa Japan." *Journal of Japanese Studies* 16:1 (Winter 1990), 1–30.

Foard, James H. "The Boundaries of Compassion: Buddhism and National Tradition in Japanese Pilgrimages." *Journal of Asian Studies* 41 (1982), 231–51.

Furushima, Toshio. "The Village and Agriculture During the Edo Period" (James L. McClain, trans.). In John W. Hall and James L. McClain, eds., *Early Modern Japan*, volume 4 in *The Cambridge History of Japan*. Cambridge: Cambridge University Press, 1991. 478–518.

Gerstle, Andrew, ed. *Eighteenth Century Japan: Culture and Society*. Sydney: Allen and Unwin, 1989.

Gunji, Masakatsu. "Kabuki and Its Social Background" (Andrew L. Markus, trans.). In Chie Nakane and Shinzaburō Oishi, eds., *Tokugawa Japan: The Social and Economic Antecedents of Modern Japan*. Tokyo: University of Tokyo Press, 1990. 192–212.

Hall, John W. "The Castletown and Japan's Modern Urbanization." *Far Eastern Quarterly* 15 (1955), 37–56.

———. "Japanese Feudal Laws (Tokugawa Legislation)." In *Transactions of the Asiatic Society of Japan*, 38 (1959) and 41 (1962).

Hall, John W., and James L. McClain, eds. *Early Modern Japan*, volume 4 in *The Cambridge History of Japan*. Cambridge: Cambridge University Press, 1991.

Hall, John W., Keiji Nagahara, and Kozo Yamamura, eds. *Japan Before Tokugawa*. Princeton: Princeton University Press, 1981.

Hanley, Susan B. *Everyday Things in Premodern Japan: The Hidden Legacy of Material Culture*. Berkeley: University of California Press, 1997.

———. "Family and Fertility in Four Tokugawa Villages." In Susan B. Hanley and Arthur P. Wolf, eds., *Family and Population in East Asian History*. Stanford: Stanford University Press, 1985. 197–228.

———. "A High Standard of Living in Nineteenth Century Japan: Fact or Fantasy?" *Journal of Economic History* 43:1 (March 1983).

———. "Tokugawa Society: Material Culture, Standard of Living, and Life-Styles." In John W. Hall and James L. McClain, eds., *Early Modern Japan*, volume 4 in *The Cambridge History of Japan*. Cambridge: Cambridge University Press, 1997. 660–705.

———. "Urban Sanitation in Preindustrial Japan." *Journal of Interdisciplinary History* 18:1 (Summer 1987), 1–26.

Hanley, Susan B., and Arthur P. Wolf, eds. *Family and Population in East Asian History*. Stanford: Stanford University Press, 1985.

Hanley, Susan B., and Kozo Yamamura. *Economic and Demographic Change in Preindustrial Japan, 1600–1868*. Princeton: Princeton University Press, 1977.

Harris, Victor. "Japanese Swords." In Michael D. Coe, eds., *Swords and Hilt Weapons*. London: Barnes and Noble, 1993.

Hauser, William B. *Economic Institutional Change in Tokugawa Japan: Osaka and the Kinai Cotton Trade*. Cambridge: Cambridge University Press, 1974.

Hayami, Akira. "The Demographic Analysis of a Village in Tokugawa Japan: Kando-Shinden of Owari Province, 1778–1871." *Keio Economic Studies* 5 (1968).

Hearn, Lafcadio. *Writings from Japan*. Harmondsworth: Penguin, 1984.

Hesselink, Reinier H. "A Dutch New Year at the Shirando Academy." *Monumenta Nipponica* 50:2 (Summer 1995), 190–235.

———. "The Warrior's Prayer: Tokugawa Yoshimune Revives the Yabusame Ceremony." *Journal of Asian Martial Arts* 4:4 (1995), 41–49.

Hildreth, Richard. *Japan: As It Was and Is*. 2nd ed. Wilmington, DE: Scholarly Resources, 1973.

Hutt, Julia, and Helene Alexander. *Ogi: A History of the Japanese Fan*. New York: Dauphin Publishers, 1992.

Ikku, Jippensha. *Hizakurige or Shank's Mare*. Trans. Thomas Satchell. Rutland, VT: Tuttle, 1960.

Irons, Neville John. *Fans of Imperial Japan*. Berlin: Kaiserreich Kunst, 1982.

Ishimoto, Tatsuo and Kiyoko Ishimoto. *The Japanese House: Its Interior and Exterior*. New York: Crown, 1963.

Jannetta, Ann Bowman. *Epidemics and Mortality in Early Modern Japan*. Princeton: Princeton University Press, 1987.

Jannetta, Ann Bowman, and Samuel H. Preston. "Two Centuries of Mortality Changes in Central Japan: The Evidence from a Temple Death Register." *Population Studies* 45 (1991), 433–36.

Jinnai, Hidenobu. "The Spatial Structure of Edo" (J. Victor Koschmann, trans.). In Chie Nakane and Shinzaburō Oishi, eds., *Tokugawa Japan: The Social and Economic Antecedents of Modern Japan*. Tokyo: University of Tokyo Press, 1990. 124–46.

Kaempfer, Engelbert. *The History of Japan: Together with a Description of the Kingdom of Siam*. 3 vols. Trans. J. G. Scheuchzer. Glasgow: James MacLehose and Sons, 1906.

Kalland, Arne, and John Pederson. "Famine and Population in Fukuoka Domain During the Tokugawa Period." *Journal of Japanese Studies* 10:1 (Winter 1984).

Kamachi, Noriko. *Culture and Customs of Japan*. Westport, CT: Greenwood Press, 1999.

Katō, Hidetoshi. "Japanese Popular Culture Reconsidered." In Richard G.D. Powers and Hidetoshi Katō, eds., *Handbook of Japanese Popular Culture*. Westport, CT: Greenwood Press, 1989.

Kee II Choi. "Technological Diffusion in Agriculture Under the Bakuhan System." *Journal of Asian Studies* 30 (August 1971), 749–59.

Koizumi, Kazuko. *Traditional Japanese Furniture*. Trans. Alfred Birnbaum. Tokyo: Kodansha International, 1986.

LaFleur, William R. *Liquid Life: Abortion and Buddhism in Japan*. Princeton: Princeton University Press, 1992.

Leupp, Gary P. *Servants, Shophands, and Laborers in the Cities of Tokugawa Japan.* Princeton: Princeton University Press, 1992.

Louis-Frédéric. *Daily Life in Japan at the Time of the Samurai, 1185–1603.* Trans. Eileen M. Lowe. New York: Praeger Books, 1972.

Malm, William P. *Japanese Music and Musical Instruments.* Tokyo: Tokyo University Press, 1959.

May, William R. "Sports." In Richard G.D. Powers and Hidetoshi Katō, eds., *Handbook of Japanese Popular Culture.* Westport, CT: Greenwood Press, 1989.

McClain, James L. *Kanazawa: A Seventeenth Century Japanese Castle Town.* New Haven: Yale University Press, 1982.

Miller, Roy Andrew. *Nihongo: In Defence of Japanese.* London: Athlone Press, 1986.

Moriya, Katsuhisa. "Urban Networks and Information Networks" (Ronald P. Toby, trans.). In Chie Nakane and Shinzaburō Oishi, eds., *Tokugawa Japan: The Social and Economic Antecedents of Modern Japan* Tokyo: University of Tokyo Press, 1990. 97–123.

Morris, Dana, and Thomas C. Smith. "Fertility and Mortality in an Outcaste Village in Japan, 1750–1869." In Susan B. Hanley and Arthur P. Wolf, eds., *Family and Population in East Asian History.* Stanford: Stanford University Press, 1985. 229–46.

Morse, Edward S. *Japan, Day by Day.* 2 vols. Boston: Houghton Mifflin, 1917.

———. *Japanese Homes and Their Surroundings.* 2nd ed. New York: Dover, 1961.

Najita, Tetsuo. "History and Nature in Eighteenth Century Tokugawa Thought." In John W. Hall and James L. McClain, eds., *Early Modern Japan*, volume 4 in *The Cambridge History of Japan.* Cambridge: Cambridge University Press, 1991. 596–659.

———. *Visions of Virtue in Tokugawa Japan: The Kaitokudo, Merchant Academy of Osaka.* Chicago: University of Chicago, 1987.

Nakai, Nobuhiko. "Commercial Change and Urban Growth in Early Modern Japan" (James L. McClain, trans.) In John W. Hall and James L. McClain, eds., *Early Modern Japan*, volume 4 in *The Cambridge History of Japan.* Cambridge: Cambridge University Press, 1991. 519–95.

Nakamura, Satoru. "The Development of Rural Industry" (J. Victor Koschmann, trans.). In Chie Nakane and Shinzaburō Oishi, eds., *Tokugawa Japan: The Social and Economic Antecedents of Modern Japan.* Tokyo: University of Tokyo Press, 1990. 81–96.

Nakane, Chie. "Tokugawa Society" (Susan Murata, trans.). In Chie Nakane and Shinzaburō Oishi, eds., *Tokugawa Japan: The Social and Economic Antecedents of Modern Japan.* Tokyo: University of Tokyo Press, 1990. 213–31.

Nakane, Chie and Shinzaburō Oishi, eds. *Tokugawa Japan: The Social and Economic Antecedents of Modern Japan.* Tokyo: University of Tokyo Press, 1990.

Nishiyama, Matsunosuke. *Edo Culture: Daily Life and Diversions in Urban Japan, 1600–1868.* Ed. and trans. Gerald Groemer. Honolulu: University of Hawaii Press, 1997.

Oishi, Shinzaburō. "The Bakuhan System" (Mikiso Hane, trans.). In Chie Nakane and Shinzaburō Oishi, eds., *Tokugawa Japan: The Social and Economic Antecedents of Modern Japan.* Tokyo: University of Tokyo Press, 1990. 11–36.

Perrin, Noel. *Giving Up the Gun: Japan's Reversion to the Sword, 1543–1879.* Boulder: Shambhala, 1980.

Philippi, Donald L., ed. and trans. *The Kojiki*. Princeton: Princeton University Press, 1968.

Powers, Richard G.D., and Hidetoshi Katō, eds. *Handbook of Japanese Popular Culture*. Westport, CT: Greenwood Press, 1989.

Reischauer, Edwin O. *Ennin's Travels in Tang China*. New York: Ronald Press, 1955.

Robertson, Jennifer. "Japanese Farm Manuals: A Literature of Discovery." *Peasant Studies* 11 (Spring 1984), 169–94.

———. "Sexy Rice: Plant Gender, Farm Manuals, and Grass-Root Nativism." *Monumenta Nipponica* 39:3 (Autumn 1984), 233–60.

Robinson, B. W. *Arms and Armour of Old Japan*. London: Scribner's, 1951.

Ropke, Ian Martin. *Historical Dictionary of Ōsaka and Kyoto*. Lanham, MD: Scarecrow Press, 1999.

Rozman, Gilbert. "Edo's Importance in the Changing Tokugawa Society." *Journal of Japanese Studies* 1 (Autumn 1974).

Sakudo, Yotaro. "The Management Practices of Family Business" (William B. Hauser, trans.). In Chie Nakane and Shinzaburō Oishi, eds., *Tokugawa Japan: The Social and Economic Antecedents of Modern Japan*. Tokyo: University of Tokyo Press, 1990. 147–66.

Sansom, George B. *An Historical Grammar of Japanese*. Tokyo: Tuttle, 1928.

———. *A History of Japan*. Vol. 2. Stanford: Stanford University Press, 1963.

Sato, Tsuneo. "Tokugawa Villages and Agriculture" (Mikiso Hane, trans.). In Chie Nakane and Shinzaburō Oishi, eds., *Tokugawa Japan: The Social and Economic Antecedents of Modern Japan*. Tokyo: University of Tokyo Press, 1990. 37–80.

Seidensticker, Edward G. *Low City, High City: Tokyo from Edo to the Earthquake*. New York: Knopf, 1983.

Shivley, Donald H. "Popular Culture." In John W. Hall and James L. McClain, eds., *Early Modern Japan*, volume 4 in *The Cambridge History of Japan*. Cambridge: Cambridge University Press, 1991. 706–69.

Smith, Henry D. *Learning from Shōgun: Japanese History and Western Fantasy*. Santa Barbara: University of California Press, 1980.

Smith, Robert. "Preindustrial Urbanization in Japan: A Consideration of Multiple Traditions in a Feudal Society." *Economic Development and Cultural Change*, 9:1, pt. II (1960), 241–57.

———. "Town and City in Premodern Japan." In Edward A. Southall, ed., *Urban Anthropology*. London: Oxford University Press, 1973. 163–210.

Smith, Thomas C. *Nakahara: Family Farming and Population in a Japanese Village, 1717–1830*. Stanford: Stanford University Press, 1977.

Statler, Oliver. *Japanese Inn*. New York: Random House, 1961.

Toby, Ronald P. "Carnival of the Aliens: Korean Embassies in Edo Period Art and Popular Culture." *Monumenta Nipponica* 41:4 (Winter 1986).

———. *State and Diplomacy in Early Modern Japan: Asia in the Development of the Tokugawa Bakufu*. Princeton: Princeton University Press, 1984.

Totman, Conrad. *The Green Archipelago: Forestry in Preindustrial Japan*. Berkeley: University of California Press, 1989.

———. "Tokugawa Peasants: Win, Lose or Draw?" *Monumenta Nipponica* 41:4 (Winter 1986), 457–76.

Tsuji, Tatsuya. "Politics in the Eighteenth Century" (Harold Bolitho, trans.). In John W. Hall and James L. McClain, eds., *Early Modern Japan*, volume 4 in *The Cambridge History of Japan*. Cambridge: Cambridge University Press, 1991. 425–500.

Vaporis, Constantine N. "Post Stations and Assisting Villages." *Monumenta Nipponica* 41:4 (Winter 1986), 377–414.

Varley, H. Paul, with Ivan Morris and Nobuko Morris. *Samurai*. New York: Dell, 1970.

Walthall, Anne. "Peripheries: Rural Culture in Tokugawa Japan." *Monumenta Nipponica* 39:4 (Winter 1984), 371–92.

———. *Social Protest and Popular Culture in Eighteenth Century Japan*. Tucson: University of Arizona Press, 1986.

———. "Village Networks: Sodai and the Sale of Edo Nightsoil." *Monumenta Nipponica* 43:3 (Autumn 1988).

Watanabe, Shoichi. *The Peasant Soul of Japan*. New York: St. Martin's Press, 1980.

Webb, Herschel, and Marleigh G. Ryan. *Research in Japanese Sources: A Guide*. New York: Columbia University Press, 1965.

Wigmore, John H., ed. *Law and Justice in Tokugawa Japan*. Tokyo: Kokusai Bunka Shinkokai, 1969.

Yamamura, Kozo. "Samurai Income and Demographic Change: The Genealogies of Tokugawa Bannermen." In Susan B. Hanley and Arthur P. Wolf, eds., *Family and Population in East Asian History*. Stanford: Stanford University Press, 1985. 62–80.

Yang, Sunny, and Rochelle M. Narasin. *Textile Art of Japan*. New York: Kodansha International, 1989.

Yazaki, Takeo. *Social Change and the City in Japan: From Earliest Times Through the Industrial Revolution*. Translated David L. Swain. New York: Japan Publications, 1968.

Index

Page numbers in *italics* refer to illustrations.

About the Author

LOUIS G. PEREZ is Professor of Japanese History at Illinois State University in Normal, Illinois. He is the author of *The History of Japan* (Greenwood, 1998).

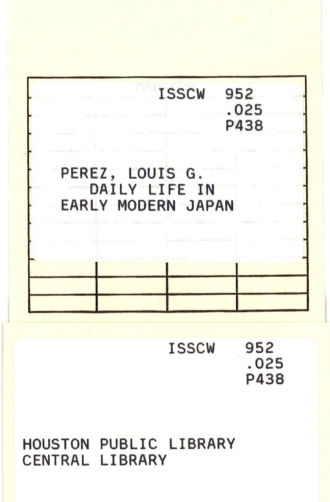